ILLUSTRATED PLAN OF
THE SIX MAIN SECTIONS

Section I
Trees with Needlelike or
Scalelike Leaves.
Plates 1–5. Text p. 32.

Section VI
Palms, Cacti, Yuccas.
Plates 47–48. Text p. 218.

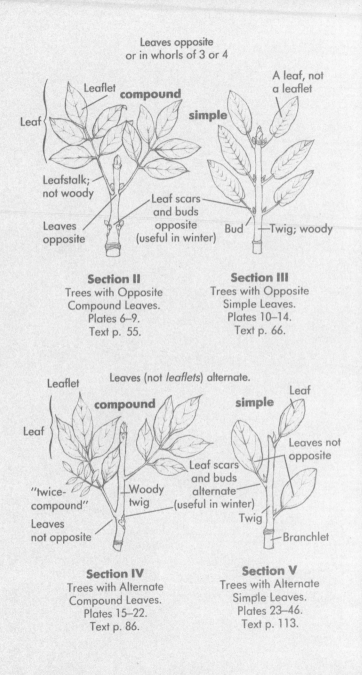

Leaves opposite
or in whorls of 3 or 4

Leaflet **compound**

Leaf

A leaf, not
a leaflet

simple

Leafstalk;
not woody

Leaves
opposite

Leaf scars
and buds
opposite
(useful in winter)

Bud — Twig; woody

Section II
Trees with Opposite
Compound Leaves.
Plates 6–9.
Text p. 55.

Section III
Trees with Opposite
Simple Leaves.
Plates 10–14.
Text p. 66.

Leaves (not *leaflets*) alternate.

Leaflet

compound

Leaf

simple

Leaf

Leaves not
opposite

Leaf scars
and buds
alternate
(useful in winter)

"twice-
compound"

Woody
twig

Leaves
not opposite

Twig

Branchlet

Section IV
Trees with Alternate
Compound Leaves.
Plates 15–22.
Text p. 86.

Section V
Trees with Alternate
Simple Leaves.
Plates 23–46.
Text p. 113.

THE PETERSON FIELD GUIDE SERIES

Edited by Roger Tory Peterson

THE PETERSON FIELD GUIDE SERIES

A Field Guide to
Eastern Trees

Eastern United States and Canada

George A. Petrides

Illustrated by
Janet Wehr

Sponsored by the National Audubon Society,
the National Wildlife Federation,
and the Roger Tory Peterson Institute

HOUGHTON MIFFLIN COMPANY · BOSTON

For information about permission to reproduce selections from this book, write to Permissions, Houghton Mifflin Company, 2 Park Street, Boston, Massachusetts 02108.

Library of Congress Cataloging-in-Publication Data

Petrides, George A.
A field guide to eastern trees.

(The Peterson field guide series; 11)
Rev. ed. of: A field guide to trees and shrubs. 2nd ed. 1972.
Bibliography: p. 253.
Includes index.
1. Trees—United States—Identification. 2. Trees—Canada, Eastern—Identification. 3. Trees—United States—Pictorial works. 4. Trees—Canada, Eastern—Pictorial works. I. Wehr, Janet. II. Petrides, George A. Field guide to trees and shrubs. III. Title.
QK115.P46 1988   582.160974   87-22591

ISBN 0-395-46731-4
ISBN 0-395-46732-2 (pbk.)

Printed in the United States of America

VB   10   9   8   7   6   5

To
Miriam

Editor's Note

This completely new version of Dr. Petrides' *Field Guide* supersedes his previous book by including all states east of the Great Plains down to the Gulf Coast. However, it confines its coverage to trees; the shrubs and woody vines are not included.

A Field Guide to the Birds, the first book in the Peterson Field Guide Series, was published in 1934, and the principle on which it was founded — a schematic treatment pointing out the visual or field differences between species — proved a sound one. Checklist or phylogenetic order was often subordinated to an artificial but more practical arrangement of the figures on the plates, so as to make things easier for the tyro. For example, the chimney swift was placed with the swallows, and ducklike birds such as the coot were placed near the ducks. It was inevitable that Field Guides to botanical subjects should follow. In fact, as far back as 1941 I had planned to do a book on trees and had actually started when I learned that Dr. George Petrides was deep in a very similar project. Upon examining his work I concluded that his version adhered to the basic principles of the Field Guide system even more than mine, so I switched my time budget to wildflowers, offering him bits of supplementary material — tree silhouettes, drawings of fruits and flowers, etc. — that would have gone into my own book on trees. He had based his approach mostly on leaf, twig, and bud characters.

Dr. Petrides, a veteran field naturalist with a record of teaching and research, first in the National Park Service and the U.S. Fish and Wildlife Service and then at Michigan State University, had long felt the need for an approach to plant recognition that his students in ecology and game management would understand. It is well enough to be tutored in basic plant taxonomy, but more often than not the student, even after considerable training, is still confused when confronted by many problems of identification.

The resulting *Field Guide to Trees and Shrubs,* first published in 1958, covered the trees, shrubs, and woody vines that grow wild in the northeastern and north-central United States and in southeastern and south-central Canada. It was in a sense a pictorial key, using obvious similarities and differences of form and structure by which the beginner could quickly run down his tree, shrub, or vine. True, some botanists may have raised their eyebrows because the plants were not in the traditional order of their relationships, but there were many formal botanies so arranged; it would have been pointless to produce another. This innovative Field Guide was an effective shortcut. Actually, the student could also learn the relationships (even if indirectly) because a key in the appendices made things quite clear. The leaf and twig plates were the ingenious and painstaking labor of Dr. Petrides, while the other figures (silhouettes, drawings on the legend pages, etc.) were mine. A much-revised second edition appeared in 1972.

In this completely new version, a total of 455 species of trees are treated. Of these, 132 are confined basically to the state of Florida. If all exotics were included (such as those in suburbia, parks, and botanical gardens) there would be many more. Only those trees of foreign origin that are now widely established and on their own are included.

The new illustrations, artfully painted by Janet Wehr, are less schematic and more representational in treatment than the leaf and twig diagrams in the previous book, but retain the comparative approach and are equally effective in putting across their message.

Do not leave this book at home on the library shelf: take it along on your woodland rambles or on your drives in the countryside. In the ecology-oriented years ahead this handy book will inform you about the green mantle of plants that clothe our "small blue planet," the only home we've got.

ROGER TORY PETERSON

Preface

This Field Guide differs from the earlier *Field Guide to Trees and Shrubs* (Petrides 1958, 1972) in three basic ways: It deals only with trees; it covers a larger geographic area—all of the eastern United States and Canada, rather than just the northeastern and north-central United States and eastern Canada; and it offers detailed and beautiful paintings in full color, supplemented by black-and-white drawings. The identification charts facing the color plates are another new feature, as are the maps showing the geographical range of each species. As in the previous book, trees that look alike are grouped together, both in the text and in the color plates. Characteristics essential for identification are described for trees in both summer and winter condition. Secondary characteristics considered desirable to confirm identification are also noted, together with items of general interest. The guide describes field marks without using technical jargon.

The geographical area treated includes all of eastern Canada and the United States east of the Great Plains. The territory extends westward through the eastern portions of Manitoba, North Dakota, South Dakota, Nebraska, Kansas, Oklahoma, and Texas. Essentially all of the trees growing naturally east of the Black Hills and Rocky Mountains are covered. Most, but not all, of the species found in central and south Texas have been included. The area is limited elsewhere by the coastlines of the Atlantic Ocean and the Gulf of Mexico. Inasmuch as many of the species described occur beyond this circumscribed territory, however, the guide is useful in a broader geographical area.

Within the region described above, all native trees are considered as well as trees of foreign origin that regularly survive and reproduce successfully. The only exceptions are the hawthorns (*Crataegus*), whose many species and hybrids are not always identifiable even by specialists. The guide discusses examples from this group, however. In addition, a few frequently encountered and widely cultivated trees introduced from abroad are included as space allows.

Botanical varieties and forms below the rank of species are not considered unless they differ markedly from the typical species. The discussion encompasses 455 species in 210 genera, including three hawthorns; three varieties of full species also are considered to be sufficiently distinctive from their parent forms to be included and given separate accounts.

The above total includes 132 species that basically occur in our region only in Florida. Most of these trees are found only in the most southern (tropical) portion of the state. Several trees that occur only in Florida have been selected for full color and text treatment. Most, however, are assembled on Plates F-7 through F-46D at the center of the book. Segregation of the Florida-only species makes it possible to simplify the identification of unknown plants both in Florida and farther north.

The species considered are those that Elbert L. Little, Jr., (1979) lists for the area. The scientific names given are those used by Little and approved by the Forest Service Tree and Range Plant Name Committee.

Although Little (1979) is a standard technical reference, not all botanists agree with Little's treatment of some plant groups. It might have been better to adopt the analyses of special groups made by other authorities, but I felt that the danger of confusing the average reader with a battery of synonymous scientific and common names outweighed any benefits.

For the sake of consistency, I have retained the definition of a tree used in Little's *Checklist*. According to the Forest Service authorities, a tree is a woody plant attaining a height of 13 feet or more and having a trunk at least three inches in diameter at breast height (4½ feet).

This book avoids technical botanical terms. It is sometimes claimed that anyone seriously interested in the subject will be willing to learn such terminology. Moreover, certain terms are necessary to prevent unduly long descriptions. Still, there seems to be little point in describing a leaf shape as "cordate," for instance, when a botanical glossary defines the word as meaning merely "heart-shaped." One might as well say "heart-shaped" from the beginning. Similarly, "stoloniferous" means "with runners," "coriaceous" is "leathery," "cuneate" means "wedge-shaped," "ovate" is "egg-shaped," "lanceolate" means "lance-shaped," "denticulate" is "with fine teeth," and so on. Many botanical terms, in short, can be translated easily into plain English with no loss in accuracy. In adopting a simplified terminology for this book, I trust that I have avoided the dangers of oversimplification and loss of accuracy and that I will have promoted interest in plant identification.

Persons wishing to identify unknown plants are often baffled by botanical manuals and sometimes even by books described as popular guides. Several difficulties are commonly encountered. First, the technical language used may be enough to dampen enthusiasm. Second, a "popular" book may not include all species, and the layperson may feel uncertain that the specimen is really the plant indicated in the book. Third, in some books final identification depends on floral characteristics, and the specimen at hand may not be in bloom. Sometimes, too, identification depends on leaf characteristics not visible on specimens in winter. This field guide seeks to avoid such pitfalls by making only limited use of technical terms, by including all trees that grow wild in the area covered, and by stressing characteristics of twigs and leaves that are present the year round.

The reasons for learning about trees vary from the purely recreational to the strictly serious. As I noted in *A Field Guide to Trees and Shrubs,* there is growing concern that people are destroying the environment on which they depend for their prosperity and even for their survival. Many human ills are related to the destruction of plants. Like all other creatures, we depend totally on green plants, which convert inorganic chemicals into organic foods and also help to maintain essential atmospheric gases in a healthful balance.

In any area the presence or absence of certain plant species or their tendencies to increase or decrease may reflect erosion, overexploitation, or pollution in that particular spot. In addition to serving as indicators of environmental quality, trees and shrubs play immensely important aesthetic and monetary roles because of their beauty. Anyone who doubts that ecology and economics are interlinked has only to consult a forester, a soils scientist, a watershed biologist, a wildlife ecologist, a fisheries limnologist, or a hydrologist. Simpler yet, though, he can ask any urban dweller or real estate broker about the positive effect of green space on morale and property values.

A number of people assisted generously at several points in the preparation of this book. John Beaman, curator of the Beal-Darlington Herbarium in the Department of Botany at Michigan State University, provided office space and gave me access to the remarkably complete and thoroughly catalogued collections in his care. (The extensive contributions of John A. Churchill, M.D., and William Gillis to this herbarium deserve special mention.) Robert K. Jansen, now at the University of Connecticut, extended similar courtesies. George W. Parmelee, curator of woody plants at Michigan State University, made available his extensive living collections of labeled specimens. David Johnson and his wife, Nancy Murray Johnson, now at the New York Botanical Garden, were most kind in allowing me to draw upon their extensive knowledge and their photographic files of tropical species. Niles Kevern, chairman, Department of Fisheries and Wildlife, Michigan State University, and his staff allowed me to use office equipment. The curatorial graduate assistant, Martha Case, was most kind and efficient in locating needed specimens. Her predecessors Cheryl Crowder and Lucille McCook were also very helpful. Edward G. Voss of the University of Michigan Herbarium loaned several specimens.

Janet Wehr not only produced the fine illustrations for the book but also assisted in the preparation of the index and frequently helped with other details. Her son, Peter Wehr, made the computer map renditions. Susan Hazard, word processor extraordinaire, coped magnificently with difficult handwritten manuscript copy. Marcia Brubeck did a fine job assisting in the final editing. She revised a number of complex statements in a clear and concise manner. Harry Foster of the Houghton Mifflin Company was most helpful in providing overall editorial guidance.

In my review of tropical, subtropical, and other trees peculiar to Florida, I was greatly aided by Angus Gholson, who maintains the Gholson Herbarium at Chattahoochee. Roger W. Sanders, taxonomist at the Fairchild Tropical Gardens near Miami, generously let me preview his manuscript treatment of the Florida palms in a book now in preparation. Jim Watson, herbarium assistant, also reviewed the materials for Plates 47 and 48 and made a number of useful suggestions. Roger L. Hammer, director of the Castellow Hammock Nature Center at Goulds, generously made me the beneficiary of his detailed knowledge of regional taxonomic field botany.

GEORGE A. PETRIDES

Contents

ILLUSTRATED PLAN OF
THE SIX MAIN SECTIONS
Fig. 1

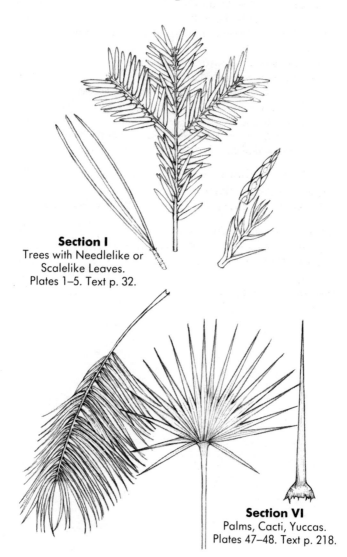

Section I
Trees with Needlelike or
Scalelike Leaves.
Plates 1–5. Text p. 32.

Section VI
Palms, Cacti, Yuccas.
Plates 47–48. Text p. 218.

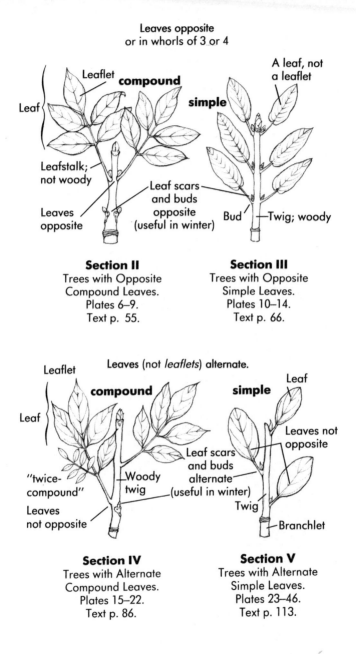

**Leaves opposite
or in whorls of 3 or 4**

Leaflet **compound**

Leaf

A leaf, not
a leaflet

simple

Leafstalk;
not woody

Leaf scars
and buds

Leaves
opposite

Leaf scars
and buds
opposite
(useful in winter)

Bud — Twig; woody

Section II
Trees with Opposite
Compound Leaves.
Plates 6–9.
Text p. 55.

Section III
Trees with Opposite
Simple Leaves.
Plates 10–14.
Text p. 66.

Leaves (not *leaflets*) alternate.

Leaflet

compound

simple

Leaf

Leaf

Leaves not
opposite

"twice-
compound"

Woody
twig

Leaf scars
and buds
alternate
(useful in winter)

Twig

Leaves
not opposite

Branchlet

Section IV
Trees with Alternate
Compound Leaves.
Plates 15–22.
Text p. 86.

Section V
Trees with Alternate
Simple Leaves.
Plates 23–46.
Text p. 113.

A Field Guide to
Eastern Trees

How to Use This Book

Please read this section: People using field guides tend naturally to head straight for the illustrations, either ignoring the introduction and text or simply skimming them. Anyone who seriously wants to identify trees, however, should not overlook this part of the book. The following pages explain the difference between opposite and alternate leaves and between compound and simple leaves. Here, too, are definitions of other terms that will reappear in later sections. Even the word "twig" has an essential specific meaning that may be new to you!

General Organization: The text is divided into six principal sections, beginning with the most easily recognized types of trees:
  I. Trees with needlelike or scalelike leaves
 II. Trees with opposite compound leaves
III. Trees with opposite simple leaves
 IV. Trees with alternate compound leaves
  V. Trees with alternate simple leaves
 VI. Trees with parallel-veined leaves (palms, yuccas, cacti)
Sections II–VI contain the broad-leaved plants.

The six basic leaf types and arrangements are illustrated on pp. xvi–xvii and can be learned in a few minutes. In summer, plants can readily be assigned to one of these sections. In winter, plants without leaves can be placed in the combined opposite-leaved categories (Sections II and III) or in the alternate-leaved categories (Sections IV and V), according to leaf-scar arrangements (see drawings of leaf types and arrangements preceding the text for each section).

Within each principal section, too, trees are grouped, beginning with the most recognizable characteristics (thorns, lobed leaves, toothed leaves, etc.) and ending with species having the fewest obvious distinguishing features. It is a good idea to work from front to back within the book as a whole and within each section.

The identification charts and other keys, which are explained below under "Identifying Unknown Plants," will further help you identify species. Appendix A provides a comprehensive winter key to all non-evergreen species. A summary of family and other relationships of eastern trees appears as Appendix B. The meanings of some terms are summarized in the Glossary. A rule on the back cover permits conversion of inches to millimeters. The

1

References include works cited and other publications of interest. The complete scientific names of trees found only in Florida are listed at the end of the book.

Leaf Types and Patterns

When they are in leaf, all woody plants fall into one of the six major categories described above under General Organization and illustrated in Fig. 1 on pp. xvi–xvii.

Plants whose leaves are obviously not needlelike or scalelike are *broad-leaved plants*. Foresters often call them *hardwoods*, in contrast with the needle-bearing *softwoods*.

A *simple leaf* has only a single blade and is joined by its stalk to a woody *twig*. A distinct leaf scar remains on the twig when the leaf and its leafstalk are plucked.

Compound leaves are divided into three (rarely two) to several dozen *leaflets*. The leaflet of a compound leaf is attached by its stalk to a midrib of the leaf. This midrib is not especially woody and exhibits only an indefinite mark when the leaflet is plucked. The midrib of the compound leaf is attached to the woody twig, and as with the simple leaf, a definite *leaf scar* (see Fig. 2) remains when the leafstalk is removed. In a relatively few species (Pls. 15 and 22), the leaflets of the compound leaf are themselves divided into (sub-)leaflets. Such leaves are *twice-compound* and may involve 4 to 800 or more leaflets.

Both compound and simple leaves may vary in shape, size, texture, and other characteristics, but despite all variations, these two main leaf types are fundamental.

Opposite leaves may be either compound or simple and occur in opposing pairs along the twigs. *Whorled leaves* occur less frequently as three or more leaves arise together. Their leaf scars tend to encircle the twigs at intervals. Plants with whorled leaves have been included in the opposite-leaved category.

Alternate leaves are arranged singly at intervals along the twigs. One should be careful not to misidentify the opposite leaflets of some compound leaves, even of alternate compound leaves, as opposite simple leaves. Furthermore, some alternate-leaved plants bear *spur branches*, on which leaves are densely clustered (see Fig. 3). These can be mistaken for opposite or whorled leaves if one is not careful to select strong-growing specimen twigs for study (see **Identifying Unknown Plants**, p. 11). Leaflets of compound leaves and simple leaves both have essentially the same parts.

Leaf shape within a species normally varies somewhat. This book illustrates and describes typical leaf shapes and the usual range of variation.

LEAF AND TWIG TERMINOLOGY

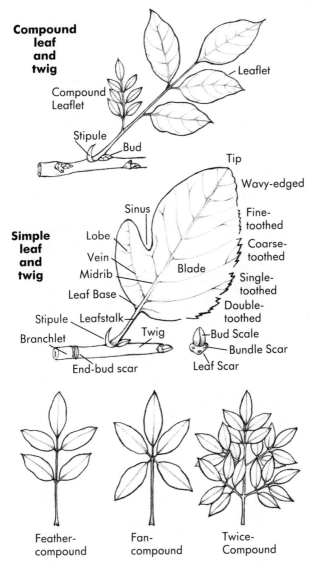

Compound leaf and twig

- Leaflet
- Compound Leaflet
- Stipule
- Bud

Simple leaf and twig

- Tip
- Wavy-edged
- Sinus
- Fine-toothed
- Lobe
- Coarse-toothed
- Vein
- Midrib
- Blade
- Single-toothed
- Leaf Base
- Double-toothed
- Stipule
- Leafstalk
- Branchlet
- Twig
- Bud Scale
- Bundle Scar
- End-bud scar
- Leaf Scar

Feather-compound

Fan-compound

Twice-Compound

Fig. 2A

LEAF SHAPES

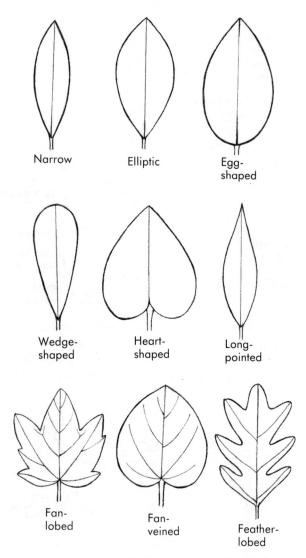

Narrow

Elliptic

Egg-shaped

Wedge-shaped

Heart-shaped

Long-pointed

Fan-lobed

Fan-veined

Feather-lobed

Fig. 2B

Twig and Bud Types

A *twig* is not just any small division of a branch but the end portion—the part that constitutes the newest growth. It is separated from the *branchlet,* which is several recent years' growth, by a series of encircling *end-bud scars.*

In winter, *non-evergreen* broad-leaved plants compose two main groups: (1) those of Sections II and III, with leaf scars arranged on the twigs in opposing pairs, or, much less commonly, in whorls of three or four, and (2) those of Sections IV and V, with leaf scars arranged singly on the twigs in a more or less scattered pattern (see Fig. 3).

It is not always possible to distinguish between the leaf scars of compound and simple leaves, though those of compound leaves are often larger and have more than three bundle scars. Further subdivisions within the opposite- or alternate-leaved groups reflect the number of bundle scars, the type of buds, the type of pith, the presence of milky sap, and other characters. Bud descriptions apply to mature winter buds. The term *chambered pith* is used here to include all types of segmented, transversely divided pith, including pith that is diaphragmed and partitioned. The main characteristics of winter twigs and buds are illustrated in Fig. 3. Unless otherwise specified, bark characteristics are mentioned only with regard to the trunk bark.

I have designated end buds true or false (see Fig. 3) reluctantly, since the distinction is not always evident when specimens are being examined. Some books mention end buds as present or absent rather than as true or false. In this volume, true end buds and clear sap may be considered to be present unless otherwise stated. Central end buds are lacking in several species with opposite buds, as shown on Pl. 7.

Plates

Each plate attempts to show those plants that most resemble each other in leaf and twig characteristics. These plants may or may not be related. Wherever possible, however, related species have been depicted on plates as close to one another in sequence as possible, given the main objective of grouping plants similar in appearance.

The reader will recognize that not all specimens precisely resemble the illustrations, but the pictures do offer the designated critical points of identification. Stipules (see Fig. 2A) have been illustrated only when they are of diagnostic value, since they often drop early.

TWIG AND BUD TERMINOLOGY

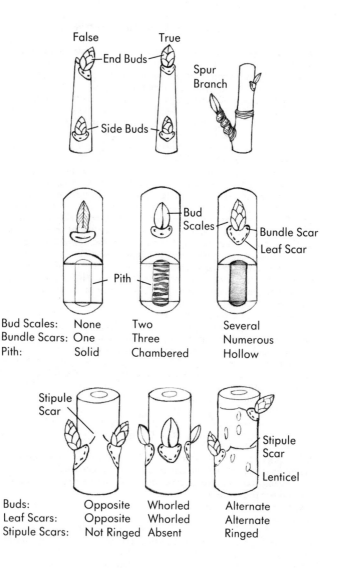

Fig. 3

On any one plate, the leaves of the several species have been drawn to indicate their relative size. There may be differences in scale, however, for plants shown on different plates. Leaf and plant sizes are given in the text. The illustrations of twigs, buds, and other small parts have often been enlarged to make their details more readily evident.

As I noted above, many tropical and semitropical species appear in our area only in Florida. To facilitate tree identifications in both regions, most of these plants are grouped on a series of plates beginning after p. 137.

Identification Charts

Opposite each plate is a matrix-type identification chart. The charts provide a large amount of information in a compact form and offer an improved approach to "keying out" a plant in that they present a series of species characteristics, summarizing the differences between similar species in one place for easy comparison. Trees can rarely be identified by a single field mark, and key features are not always present or may not be readily apparent on the specimen at hand (whether the end buds are false or true, for instance). Thus, having a series of field marks to cross-check can be crucial to correct identification. The plates and appropriate identification charts alone may be enough to identify an unknown tree.

The charts indicate whether a species does (+) or does not (−) possess a particular characteristic or whether it possesses that characteristic in an intermediate or variable (±) form. In a few cases, the chart will indicate (o) that the characteristic cannot apply to a particular species. In general the charts list the features most important for identification first. One should therefore read the plus-or-minus columns from left to right. Additional descriptive notes indicate further distinctive characteristics. The distribution data given in the charts represent merely a general guide to assist in identification; the reader should refer to the more detailed maps in the text.

The scientific names listed in the identification tables lack the authors' names. These appear in the text or, for species occurring only in Florida, in the section immediately preceding the plates of Florida trees.

Botanical Keys

The identification charts offer advantages when a dozen or so species are to be compared. However, in cases where either a very few or a large number of species must be classified, the charts become cumbersome. In such instances, as at the beginning of each section in the text and in Appendix A, traditional botanical keys are employed. The keys to plant identification may seem formidable at first but should be treated rather like a book's table of contents: their function is merely to divide the subject matter, in this case plant species, into subsections, further sub-subsections, and eventually species or groups of species.

For the most part, keys attempt to divide the many species into two groups. Each group in turn is then divided in two. This process is repeated again and again until species or groups of species are named.

In such a key, the person trying to identify a tree chooses first between the two number ones, then between the two number twos, the two number threes, and so on. Using a key is simply a matter of following a trail that forks repeatedly but typically offers only two paths at any single fork. The seeker continues to make choices between the options that bear the same number, making certain at each point that the choice made fits the plant being identified, until an end point is reached.

Species Descriptions

Plant Names: Both common and scientific names are given for each species. Although for many species common names are well established, the same name or a similar one is sometimes also applied to a different, even unrelated species. In our area, for instance, Ironwood is used as the common name for at least seven species in six genera. Species names which include the name of another unrelated group, for example Osage-orange, are either hyphenated or joined together to indicate that they are not true members of the group.

In an effort to assist in standardization, the name preferred by Little (1979) has generally been chosen for use in this book. In a few instances, if a name used in the earlier Field Guide (Petrides 1972) seemed to offer advantages (by being more descriptive, by better indicating plant relationships, or by involving only one or two words), it was retained. In several cases where it seemed best to adopt the name given by Little (1979), I have supplied the name from the earlier Field Guide in parentheses.

The names suggested by Little (1979) proved not to be in common use in southern (tropical) Florida for many species found there. In these cases I have supplied the names employed by local botanists and confirmed either by Everglades National Park authorities (Stevenson 1969) or by Long and Lakela (1971) or Tomlinson (1980).

Scientific names have three essential parts: the name of the *genus* (plural, *genera*), the name of the *species* (plural, *species*), and the name or names, commonly abbreviated, of the botanist(s) who assigned the scientific names. In the case of *Quercus rubra* L., for example, the initial stands for Carolus Linnaeus (also known as Carl von Linné), who is regarded as the father of systematic botany.

Varieties are recognizably distinct subpopulations of a species. In most instances, the distinction is minor. Only three varieties in our area (Pondcypress, Lombardy Poplar, and Cherrybark Oak) are sufficiently distinctive to require separate identification and thus to need separate listings here. In such a case, the varietal name and the name of the authority (or authorities) responsible for it follows the basic scientific name of the species—for example, *Taxodium distichum* var. *nutans* (Ait.) Sweet.

A main purpose of scientific nomenclature is standardization so that botanists anywhere in the world may discuss a plant with the assurance that they are indeed talking about the same species. Scientific nomenclature is an international cataloguing system that also indicates plant relationships within certain limits. Scientific names may change, however, as authorities decide that a species is more closely related to members of a genus different from that to which it was first assigned, that plants once considered to belong to two species should instead be regarded as two varieties of a single species, that a species originally thought to be new has already been named, and so forth.

The rules of botanical nomenclature are much too involved to be explained here. The reader will probably find scientific names of value principally as they make it possible to locate the same species in other reference books.

In the United States and Canada nowadays, scientific names tend to be anglicized when they are spoken, and most pronunciations are acceptable. Anyone who can say "hibiscus" or "hydrangea" is already using scientific names. In speech, the authors' names are usually omitted.

Recognition: This guide limits plant descriptions largely to identification characteristics. A statement of the general growth habits of the species is followed by characteristics of foliage, twigs, and bark. Individual specimens of a species inevitably vary. Where individual differences may cause confusion in identification, their extent has been indicated in the text. I have attempted to describe degrees of hairiness where it was possible to do so, but the exact extent of hairiness in leaves and twigs is sometimes difficult to indicate in words. Nearly all leaves will show some fine hairs if they are examined closely under a hand lens. Plants described in the text or on the plates as being hairy are usually markedly so. On "hairless" plants, hairiness is not conspicuous. A hand lens is useful in ascertaining the abundance of hairlike structures. Descriptions of bark refer to the mature bark of large stems unless otherwise indicated.

Measurements are given for leaf lengths, plant heights, and trunk diameters. Minimum and maximum leaf lengths are generalizations for normal leaves and *include the length of the leafstalk* unless otherwise stated. Sprouts of some species bear abnormally large leaves. The common minimum height and diameter for mature trees are followed by the common maximum for each measurement and, in parentheses, the exceptional maximum. Diameters are for tree trunks at breast height (about 4½ feet above the ground—the forester's diameter at breast height). All these figures are given as only general guides. The several maximum measurements are not usually all evident on a single specimen. The "largest" Jack Pine recorded by the American Forestry Association, for example, is only 27 feet tall, although it is 42 inches in circumference. All measurements are given in feet, inches, and fractions rather than in metric-system units, since English units are more widely familiar in our area.

Flower and fruit data have been supplied only to the extent that, as general identification characteristics, they usefully supplement vegetative characteristics. Further details are provided only for those species not easily recognized by leaf and twig characteristics alone. A tree's fruit clusters, not usually mentioned, are of the same type as the clusters described for the flowers. The extreme dates given for flowering and fruiting may need to be modified by a month or so, depending on locality. Where fruiting dates are lacking, dates for the flowers will indicate at least the earliest possible time when fruits might appear. Fruit colors apply to ripe fruits only. The habitat named indicates the vegetation type in which the species is usually found.

General statements regarding the distinctiveness of certain species' characteristics apply to the geographic area of the book.

Similar species: Critical differences are discussed for species that most closely resemble one another when they are in foliage and when they are leafless.

Distribution: Maps showing the limits of distribution in the eastern areas north of Mexico have been published for most tree species in several volumes of the *Atlas of United States Trees* (Little 1971, 1977, 1978). I have followed these maps in preparing the book. For a few species, however, the range is described verbally, with distributional limits reported from northeast to northwest and southeast to southwest.

Remarks: General observations accompany descriptions of plants that serve as sources of lumber, fuel, medicine, food, drink, poison, fiber, ornament, tannin, and Christmas trees, or are of especial value in soil and wildlife management. References to wildlife are usually limited to game birds and to mammals of chipmunk size or larger. Most such data have been recorded by Van Dersal (1938).

Identifying Unknown Plants

Before attempting to identify unknown plants, one should first learn the general appearance of Poison-ivy, Poison-sumac, and, in southern Florida, Poisonwood (Fig. 4, p. 17). Once their main characteristics are known, these sources of skin irritants can easily be avoided.

It is better to make identifications in the field than to collect specimens for later identification at home. In the wild, additional materials are available, and growth habits are evident. If field identification is impractical, then ample twig specimens, with leaves when they are available, may be gathered and either carried fresh or pressed. *Good specimens are essential for correct identification.* Dwarfed, twisted, or gnarled twigs should be avoided. Abnormally large sucker shoots may not show typical hairiness characteristics, but otherwise strong, quick-growing twigs should be collected for study. On such twigs, the leaves and leaf scars are larger and all details are more evident.

In summer, the first step in identifying an unknown plant is to place it in one of the six main groups, according to leaf type and arrangement (see Fig. 1):

1. Leaves needlelike or scalelike.   **Section I, p. 32.**
1. Leaves broad:
    2. Leaves opposite or whorled:
        3. Leaves compound.   **Section II, p. 55.**
        3. Leaves simple.   **Section III, p. 66.**
    2. Leaves alternate:
        4. Leaves compound.   **Section IV, p. 86.**
        4. Leaves simple.   **Section V, p. 113.**
1. Palms, yuccas, cacti.   **Section VI, p. 218.**

You should turn next to the proper section, scan the plates, and select the species most like the unknown one. It is important to review the facing *identification charts* next and to follow up by checking the *distribution map* and reading the *text description* of the species. You should verify that the specimen and its geographic range and description agree, or else make another attempt to run it down. The text portion on similar species may also help you interpret identification marks.

You may of course prefer to disregard the sectional leaf keys and the identification charts and to rely upon spotting the proper illustration, since the plates themselves are a pictorial key. It is often possible to proceed in this way if the species falls in Sections I through IV or in Section VI. Relatively few plants have need-lelike, compound, opposite, or palm-frond leaves. Unless a Section V specimen with alternate simple leaves has other quite distinctive characteristics, however, you should follow the keys, tables, maps, and so on.

In winter, unless the plant is evergreen, you must either find leaf remains on or under the specimen (and run some risk of picking up part of another tree) or rely on twig and other winter characteristics. If you find dried leaves, you can attempt to proceed as you would in summer. Otherwise you should look for good twig specimens. Both the identification charts and the winter botanical key (Appendix A) should be used.

The most trying time for woody plant identification is usually early spring, when buds have burst but leaves are small and new twigs soft. Some plants may be difficult to identify for a month or so.

Everyone would like to discover a rare specimen. Before you conclude that you have found a species outside its usual range or have unearthed something entirely new to science, however, recheck carefully to verify that you do not have a case of mistaken identity. If it still seems likely that the plant is something unusual, you might collect a specimen (with flowers or fruits, if possible, and always with notes indicating the exact location, date of collection, and your own name and address), carefully press it, dry it, and forward it to the department of botany at your state or provincial university or agricultural college with a request for confirmation of identification.

Equipment

Fortunately, plant identification requires little paraphernalia. Only two items are essential: a field guide or manual and a hand lens. *A good hand lens is as essential to the botanical naturalist as binoculars are to the bird watcher.* The hand lens is especially helpful in ascertaining twig characteristics but is also essential for assessing leaf hairiness, leafstalk glands, etc. Furthermore the lens discloses hidden beauty in small blossoms and in other plant parts. Lenses for general use should magnify $6\times$ to $10\times$. Those manufactured by well-known optical companies are generally worth the slightly higher price usually asked for them. Hand lenses are priced between $8 and $15 and are practically indestructible. Secondhand ones can often be procured cheaply, especially in university towns.

As previously noted, it is *strongly suggested that identification be made in the field,* where additional specimens and supplementary data are available. When you need to collect specimens, however, a large plastic bag will preserve them until they can be pressed. A roll of newspapers held by a strap, or even a large magazine, may also do well as a field carrier if specimens are being carried for early identification, but serious collectors will want to acquire a plant press, available from any biological supply house. Two large firms are Carolina Biological Supply Company, Burlington, North Carolina 27215, and Herbarium Supply Company, P.O. Box 883003, San Francisco, California 94188.

In a press, plants are placed within newspaper pages, which are inserted between blotters and placed between sheets of corrugated cardboard. The entire series is packaged between wooden frames and securely tied by straps. Specimens will dry more quickly in dry weather when the press is mounted outside a moving car. A stream of heated air blown through the press will also hasten drying. Otherwise it will occasionally be necessary to replace newspapers and blotters to permit thorough drying and to prevent molds from invading the collection.

Plant Succession

Every plant species, through evolutionary processes, has become something of a specialist. Each one lives in a certain type of *habitat* and thrives under a particular set of climatic, soil, and water conditions. On a newly available site, local conditions are varied, and seeds or other reproductive parts of several species usually manage to be present. As a result a *plant community* composed of several species becomes established. Once they are entrenched most plants and plant communities alter the site so that it becomes less and less suitable for them with the passage of time. (We are not the only species that fouls its nest!) Increasing fertility due to root decay and leaf fall, for example, may invite competition from species originally unable to become established on the site. Alternatively, increasing shade may prevent seedlings from surviving even though they are adjacent to, or are even surrounded by, their parents. These factors and others bring about *succession* as plant communities and the soils they occupy pass through a series of stages until a stable community of plants and mature soil structure finally develops. This end product—a mature and relatively permanent community—is the *climax* plant association.

Primary plant succession occurs when community development begins and develops from a bare surface or in open water. Primary succession may begin on such areas as cliff faces, rockslides, gravel slopes, road cuts, sand dunes, lava flows, peat deposits, or gully sides or on shallow lake bottoms, in bogs, or on river bars and deltas. In such places *pioneer* communities become established and are eventually succeeded by other plant communities, each of which tends to be more intermediate in its moisture requirements than its predecessor. That is, within the limits set by climate, succeeding communities beginning in a wet environment live on progressively drier sites, while those in a dry environment live on moister sites, with the climax community occurring on neither wet nor dry sites but intermediate, moist ones.

Secondary plant succession occurs when a plant community is entirely or partly killed or removed, exposing a soil that has already advanced to some degree toward maturity. Such plant destruction might be accomplished by fire, trampling, drainage, windthrow, lumbering, cultivation, or other means. The secondary plant community series that follows a change in the original vegetation generally differs from the primary successional series.

Species in developmental stages of plant succession may be geographically more widespread than those of the climax stage. They may even take a part in succession in regions with different climax types. Some species may occupy somewhat different habitats and successional stages in different portions of their ranges, whereas others are restricted to only a portion of a single climax area.

Knowledge of local successional stages is essential in studies of land use, soil conservation, forestry, wildlife management, and outdoor recreation. The amateur botanist will find it an interesting and valuable project to prepare a plant succession chart for his or her locality; see Oosting (1956).

Climax Vegetation Types

From north to south and from east to west in our area, major changes in the character of the climax vegetation are evident. These major units are mostly characterized by distinctive vegetative *life forms* (evergreen trees, deciduous trees, grasses, etc.) and are termed *plant formations*. On the *tundra* of the far North and of the mountaintops of eastern Canada and New England grow sedges, grasses, lichens, herbs, and low and creeping shrubs. The northern evergreen or *boreal forest* that covers most of Canada and part of the northern United States is dominated by White Spruce and Balsam Fir, although American Larch becomes prominent along its northern edge. The *hemlock-hardwood* forest of the Great Lakes area—a formation of mixed conifers and broad-leaved trees—is sometimes also designated the *lake forest*. Its dominant species include Hemlock, Beech, Sugar Maple, Yellow Birch, and White Pine.

Over most of our area is the broad-leaved *deciduous forest*.

Several principal climax associations occur in this formation: (1) Mixed Mesophytic (Beech-Sugar Maple-Tuliptree-White Oak-Red Oak-Hemlock) in southern mountain valleys and some lowlands; (2) Beech-Sugar Maple in moist deep soils; (3) Oak-Hickory or Oak-Pine (and formerly Oak-Chestnut) mostly in drier areas; and (4) Sugar Maple-Basswood in parts of Wisconsin and Minnesota. On the flat coastal plain in the Southeast is a portion of the *southeastern evergreen forest,* principally of Loblolly and Shortleaf pines. In extreme southern Florida, numerous *tropical hardwood* trees occur that have wider distributions in the West Indies and American tropics. No climax forest types which involve these species, however, have been described. *Prairie* formations occur in the western part of our area, with woody species important only in valley bottoms.

Poisonous Plants

Only a few species among wild plants in our area irritate the skin. Especially in tropical southern Florida, there are still other irritating species (see Pl. F-46C). The four below, however, are most widespread. All have compound leaves and small, dry, *white or yellowish* fruits. They should be avoided!

POISON-SUMAC *Toxicodendron vernix*   **Fig. 4**
This shrub or small tree has large leaves consisting of 7–13 pointed leaflets which are *not* toothed. It has small white fruits and occurs mostly in open, *swampy* places. See Fig. 4.

POISON-IVY   **Fig. 4**
Toxicodendron radicans (L.) Kuntze or *Rhus radicans* L.
This plant is not a tree but a small erect shrub or tree-climbing vine frequently encountered in the field. Learn to recognize the three-parted leaves, which are variably toothed but have a pointed end leaflet on a longer stalk than the side ones. The stems of old vines may be densely black-fibrous, while young stems are merely brown-hairless.

POISON-OAK   Not illus.
T. toxicodendron (L.) Britton or *Rhus toxicodendron* L.
This plant is very similar to Poison-ivy but more southern and always erect and has leaves that are mostly blunt-tipped.

FLORIDA POISONWOOD   **Fig. 4, Pl. F-46B**
Metopium toxiferum (L.) Krug & Urban
This species does not occur north of central Florida. Its mostly triangular and leathery evergreen leaves are usually marked with black spots.

Plants Poisonous to Touch

The 2 tree species shown here have alternate feather-compound leaves. Poison-ivy also is illustrated because it too must be shunned and commonly grows as a vine on trees. Though members of the cashew family, all should be avoided![1]

Species and remarks

	Growing to tree size	Only a shrub or vine	Leaflets per leaf	Leaflets toothed	Leaflets wavy-edged	Leaves leathery, evergreen	Twigs stout	Fruit color[2]
Poison-sumac *Toxicodendron vernix* Mostly shrubby. Mostly wet places.	+	−	7–13	−	−	−	+	W
Poison-ivy *Toxicodendron radicans* End leaflet long-stalked. Widespread.	−	+	3	±	±	−	−	W
Florida Poisonwood[1] *Metopium toxiferum* Leaves black-spotted. Bark flaking.	+	−	3–7	−	+	+	+	Y

[1] Other trees of cen. and s. Fla. that produce substances irritating to the skin of some people include the Brazil Peppertree (Pl. F-21A), Lime (p. 120), Cajeput-tree (Pl. F-46A), Mango (Pl. F-46B), and Manchineel (Pl. F-46C). All have alternate leaves; those of Brazil Peppertree and Lime are compound.
[2] W = white, Y = yellowish.

POISON-SUMAC

POISON-IVY

FLORIDA POISONWOOD

Fig. 4

Tree Silhouettes

(by R.T.P.)

An expert bird watcher can often identify a bird by its silhouette alone. Birds are dependable: a grackle always is shaped precisely like a grackle, and one starling invariably resembles another starling. Trees, on the other hand, are not so consistent. The beginner, learning his trees, yearns for a book that will give him shapes and field marks by which he can make snap identifications from a moving car. But it isn't that easy. True, an elm somehow always looks like an elm, but many trees assume a variety of shapes. A young tree might look entirely unlike a grizzled veteran of the same species. And a forest-grown tree, reaching for the light, might be tall, slender, and restricted in its branching compared to a field-grown example where plenty of sun, soil, and moisture have enabled it to develop a maximum crown.

But within limits one can, with a little practice, recognize by shape and manner of growth quite a few of the trees and also some of the shrubs. On the following pages are presented some silhouettes of a selection of trees (and one or two shrubs). Not all examples will look like these, but they are, on the whole, typical. They represent open-grown specimens, not those of crowded woodland situations. If in doubt check the leaf and twig characters in the text.

WHITE PINE
Tall dark trunk; spreading horizontal limbs; delicate spraylike foliage

LOBLOLLY PINE
Tall, clean cinnamon trunk; open crown, drooping lower limbs

RED PINE
Tall, erect trunk; stout right-angle branches, symmetrical crown; long dark green foliage, ascending tips

PITCH PINE
Usually low, irregular, scraggly; many dead branches; coarse foliage in rigid tufts

WHITE SPRUCE

Pyramidal; upper branches
ascending, lower nearly horizontal;
foliage bluish green

RED SPRUCE

Rather open-branched, tips
upcurved; foliage yellowish green

BLACK SPRUCE

Slender; short branches; foliage
bluish green

NORWAY SPRUCE

Usually near houses; pyramidal;
strongly drooping lateral branchlets

BALSAM FIR
Conical; branches ascending; erect cones; flat needles

HEMLOCK
Loose, irregular, feathery; short flat needles

EASTERN REDCEDAR
Conical head (wider with age); short stem

NORTHERN WHITE-CEDAR
Dense conical head clothed almost to base; flat sprays

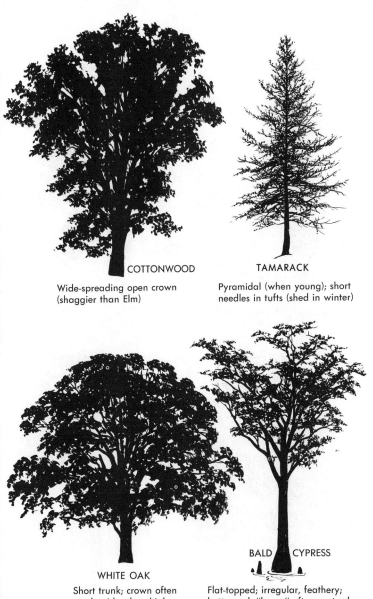

COTTONWOOD

Wide-spreading open crown
(shaggier than Elm)

TAMARACK

Pyramidal (when young); short
needles in tufts (shed in winter)

WHITE OAK

Short trunk; crown often
much wider than high

BALD CYPRESS

Flat-topped; irregular, feathery;
buttressed; "knees" often protrude
from water

LOMBARDY POPLAR

Tall, slender; trunk continuous; many hugging branches

COMMON CATALPA

Round-topped; large heart-shaped leaves; long beanlike pods

SUGAR MAPLE

Short stem; full egg-shaped head

AMERICAN ELM

Vase-shaped; trunk divided into large outspreading limbs

SUGAR MAPLE

Short trunk; many ascending
branches; symmetrical oval head;
dark flaky bark

RED MAPLE

Short trunk; broad oval head
(sometimes broader at top);
gray beechlike upper branches

WHITE ASH

Trunk often divided low down;
oval head: cross-shaped branching;
diamond-ridged bark

TULIP TREE

Upright trunk; branches often
angle upward; erect dry seed cones

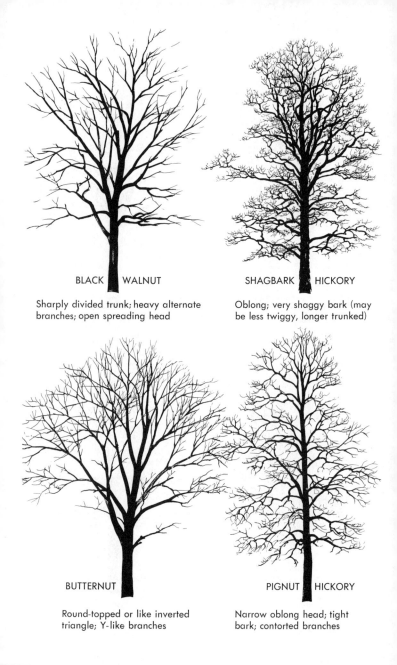

BLACK WALNUT

Sharply divided trunk; heavy alternate branches; open spreading head

SHAGBARK HICKORY

Oblong; very shaggy bark (may be less twiggy, longer trunked)

BUTTERNUT

Round-topped or like inverted triangle; Y-like branches

PIGNUT HICKORY

Narrow oblong head; tight bark; contorted branches

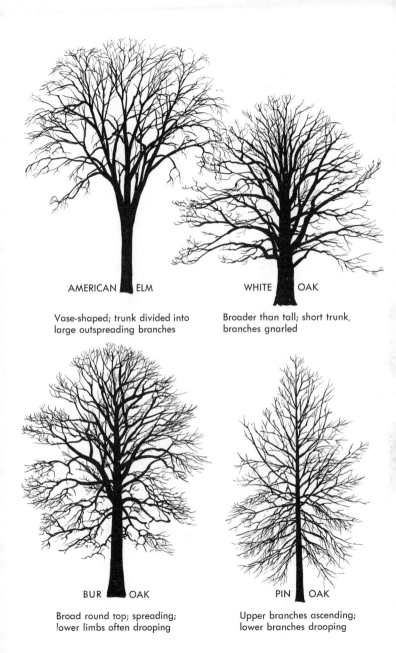

AMERICAN ELM

Vase-shaped; trunk divided into large outspreading branches

WHITE OAK

Broader than tall; short trunk, branches gnarled

BUR OAK

Broad round top; spreading; lower limbs often drooping

PIN OAK

Upper branches ascending; lower branches drooping

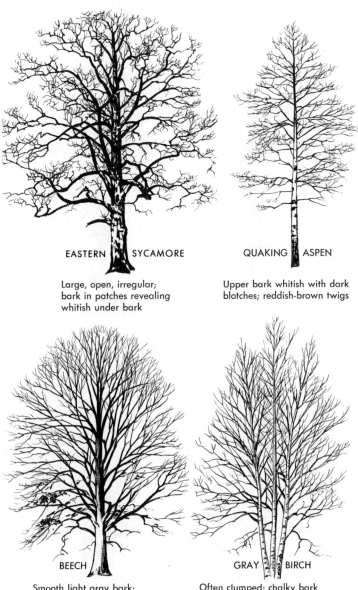

EASTERN SYCAMORE

Large, open, irregular;
bark in patches revealing
whitish under bark

QUAKING ASPEN

Upper bark whitish with dark
blotches; reddish-brown twigs

BEECH

Smooth light gray bark;
dense ovate head; often a few
persistent leaves

GRAY BIRCH

Often clumped; chalky bark
(not peeling) with dark triangular
patches; slender twigs

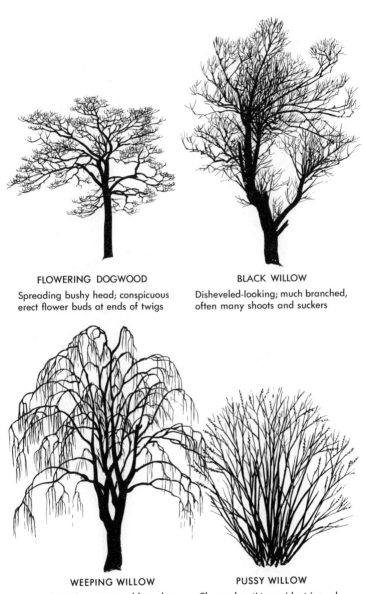

FLOWERING DOGWOOD
Spreading bushy head; conspicuous erect flower buds at ends of twigs

BLACK WILLOW
Disheveled-looking; much branched, often many shoots and suckers

WEEPING WILLOW
Drooping twigs and branches

PUSSY WILLOW
Clumped; catkins evident in early spring

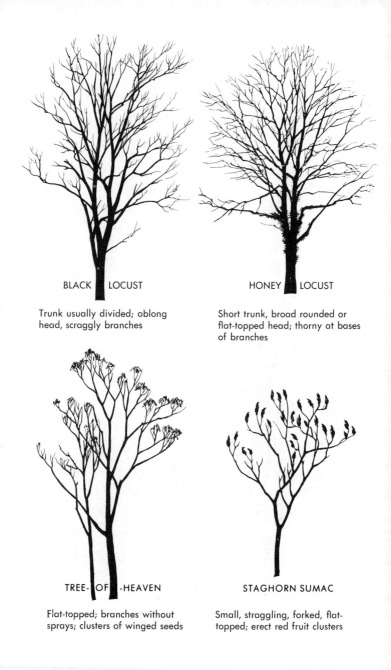

BLACK LOCUST

Trunk usually divided; oblong head, scraggly branches

HONEY LOCUST

Short trunk, broad rounded or flat-topped head; thorny at bases of branches

TREE-OF-HEAVEN

Flat-topped; branches without sprays; clusters of winged seeds

STAGHORN SUMAC

Small, straggling, forked, flat-topped; erect red fruit clusters

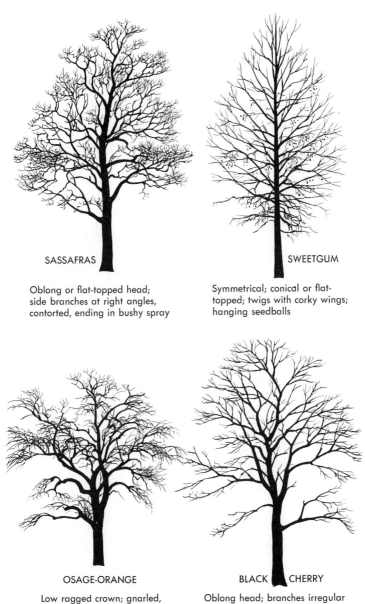

SASSAFRAS

Oblong or flat-topped head;
side branches at right angles,
contorted, ending in bushy spray

SWEETGUM

Symmetrical; conical or flat-
topped; twigs with corky wings;
hanging seedballs

OSAGE-ORANGE

Low ragged crown; gnarled,
thorny; often in hedges

BLACK CHERRY

Oblong head; branches irregular
spreading, often zigzag

I

Trees with Needlelike or Scalelike Leaves, Mostly Evergreen (Plates 1–5)

The cone-bearing trees and a few non-coniferous plants with tiny evergreen leaves compose this well-defined group. The leaves are either long and slender (needlelike) or small and overlapping (scalelike). Though individual needles and needle clusters may drop throughout the year, most conifers are green the year around. The larches and Baldcypress, however, are exceptions. They drop all of their foliage in autumn; their branches remain bare until spring. Conifers are not the only evergreen trees; many broad-leaved trees (such as American Holly) and tropical trees,

Fig. 5. Needlelike or scalelike leaves.

such as palms, also hold green leaves throughout the year, but they are not described in this section.

The fruits of conifers are usually woody cones with seeds developed at the bases of the cone scales. The plates illustrate the mature female cones. Male cones are small pollen-producing organs that are obvious only during the early flowering period. Female cones may take more than one year to mature. If none is present on the tree, old ones can often be found on the ground nearby.

The Yew, Torreya, and junipers (Pls. 4, 5) have fleshy, somewhat berrylike fruits. While these bear little resemblance to the usual cones of members of the pine family, all of them develop from naked ovules. Higher flowering plants have ovules enclosed in ovaries.

Identify unknown plants in this section by looking through Pls. 1–5, or trace the proper plate number by means of the key below:

1. Leaves ¾″–18″ long, needle-shaped:
   2. Needles in groups along the twigs:
      3. Needles many, clumped on short spurs.
         Larches, Pl. 1
      3. Needles bound at the base in bundles:
         4. Needles 3–5 per bundle.   **Pines I, Pl. 1.**
         4. Needles 2 per bundle.   **Pines II, Pl. 2.**
   2. Needles attached singly to twigs:
      5. Needles flat, in flattened sprays.   **Firs, etc., Pl. 4.**
      5. Needles four-sided, not in flattened sprays.
         Spruces, Pl. 3.
1. Leaves small and hugging the twigs, either blunt and scalelike or hollowed and sharp-pointed, or both kinds present.
         White-cedars, junipers, etc., Pl. 5.

Conifers with Needles in Clusters I: Larches and Pines I (Plate 1)

The larches and the baldcypresses (Pl. 4) are our only conifers that *drop their leaves* in autumn. In larches, there are conspicuous *warty "spurs"* on the twigs. In season, numerous needles are clustered at the ends of these spurs. Leaf scars have 1 bundle scar. Larch cones lack prickles and have relatively few scales, thinner than those of pines.

TAMARACK (AMERICAN LARCH)   Pl. 1
Larix laricina (Du Roi) K. Koch.

A medium-sized to large pointed-top tree with many slender needles ¾″–1″ long, on *short spurs*. On longer shoots, needles

are single. Branchlets do *not* droop. Cones ½″–13/16″ long and nearly as wide. Trunk bark dark, flaking off in small scales. Height 40′–80′ (90′); diameter 1′–2′ (3′). Northern wet soils.
Similar species: (1) European Larch has longer needles and cones, drooping branchlets, and bark with large plates. (2) Baldcypresses (Pl. 4) are trees of southern swamps.
Remarks: An important northern timber tree (used for poles, posts, railroad ties). Seeds, needles, or inner bark eaten by ruffed and sharp-tailed grouse, snowshoe hare, red squirrel, porcupine, and deer.

EUROPEAN LARCH   *Larix decidua* Mill.   Not illus.
This European form sometimes spreads from northern plantings. Needles 1″–1½″ long; branchlets may *droop.* Cones 13/16″–1⅜″ in length. Red-brown trunk bark divided into large plates. More of an upland species.

PINES.   The pines are probably the most important timber trees in the world. Growing principally on dry, sandy soils of little value, they yield not only lumber but also turpentine, tar, pitch, and a medicinal oil.
The pines are cone-bearing evergreen trees with slender needles occurring in groups of 2 to 5 along the twigs. The needle groups are bound in bundles at the base. Only the White Pine has 5 needles per cluster. All the remaining species, generally known as yellow pines, have 2 or 3 needles per bundle.
The mature bark of the White, Scotch, Spruce, and Sand pines is dark and furrowed, but that of other pines is usually divided into more or less rectangular plates. Pine branches usually occur in whorls around the trunks; normally the tree is topped by a new whorl each year. Only a few pine species occur in any one state;

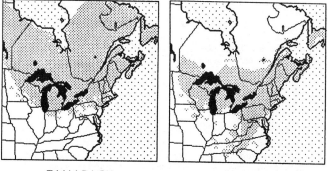

TAMARACK   WHITE PINE

they are more numerous to the south and east. The distribution maps will often assist in identification.

Several western pines produce edible seeds: those of the pinyon pines (*Pinus edulis* and *P. monophylla*) of the Great Basin region are especially delicious. Seeds of many species rank high among the foods of nearly all game birds, rabbits, hares, squirrels, and chipmunks and are also eaten by coyote and black bear. The twigs and needles serve as food for deer, moose, and other browsing animals but mostly when preferred foods are lacking.

WHITE PINE   *Pinus strobus* L.   **Pl. 1**

A tall upland tree with relatively few large limbs in horizontal whorls. Needles 2″–4″ long, slender, flexible, and occurring *5 to the bundle.* Cones slender, tapering, thornless, long-stalked, 3″–10″ long. Bark not scaly, as in most other pines, but dark with deep furrows. A dwarf matted form occurs in windswept northern areas. Height 80′–110′; diameter 2′–3′ (6′).

Similar species: The only native five-needle pine in the eastern U.S. and Canada.

Remarks: One of the most important and tallest timber trees in the Northeast. So extensively lumbered that few virgin trees, which once grew to heights of 200′ to 220′, remain. In some areas reforestation is considerable. Wood light, soft, straight-grained, and generally not as resinous as in other pines; of great value for house construction. Plagued by white pine blister rust, a fungus attacking the inner bark, and white pine weevil, an insect that kills the topmost shoot, deforming the tree and limiting its value. The rust can be controlled by removal of currant and gooseberry shrubs—upon which the fungus spends a portion of its life cycle—from within a quarter mile of the pines.

PITCH PINE   *Pinus rigida* Mill.   **Pl. 1**

A medium-sized tree of the Northeast and Appalachians with needles 3″–6″ long, *3 per cluster.* Needles coarse, stiff, dull, yellow-green. This species and the next are our only pines that produce trunk *sprouts,* especially after fires. Cones stout, 1″–3″ long, often remaining long on the tree; cone scales tipped with thorns up to ⅛″ long. Height 40′–60′ (70′); diameter 1′–2′ (3′). Mainly dry sites. See map, p. 36.

Similar species: When Shortleaf has needles in 3's it may be identified by its slender blue-green needles and weak cone prickles.

POND (SWAMP) PINE   *Pinus serotina* Michx.   **Pl. 1**

Similar to Pitch Pine but more *southern,* with needles more flexible and 4″–8″ long. Trunk *sprouts* are often present. Cones 2″–3″, *nearly round,* opening late and remaining attached, with prickles weak or absent. Crown branches tend to be tangled. A lowland species (see map, p. 36); height to 80′; diameter to 2′.

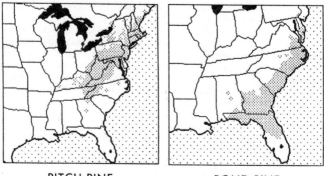

PITCH PINE   POND PINE

Similar species: Shortleaf and Loblolly pines have cones that are less globular. Shortleaf has shorter blue-green foliage, while Loblolly has longer needles. Neither produces sprouts, and both have top branches that are less gnarled than those of Pond Pine. See Pitch Pine.

LOBLOLLY PINE *Pinus taeda* L.   **Pl. 1**
A tall *southern* tree with dull, *light green* needles 6″–9″ long and 3 per cluster. Twigs ¼″ in diameter; end buds brown. Cones more or less cylindrical, 3″–6″ long; many old ones remain on the tree. Cone scales mostly under ½″ wide; when the cone is squeezed, the thorn-tipped scales hurt the hand. Height 80′–100′ (115′); diam-

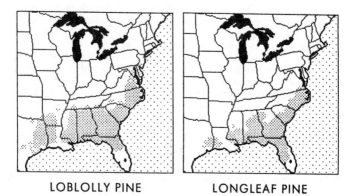

LOBLOLLY PINE   LONGLEAF PINE

eter 1'–2' (5'). Old fields, dry and wet sites; common, Coastal Plain and Piedmont.

Similar species: (1) Pitch Pine has shorter needles and cones. (2) Longleaf Pine has longer needles; longer, less prickly cones; much stouter twigs; and white end buds. (3) Pond Pine has shorter needles and smaller, more ball-shaped and less thorny cones. (4) Shortleaf Pine may have some needles in 3's, but its needles and cones are shorter and cone prickles more slender. (5) Slash Pine typically has two-needle clusters of glossy, dark green foliage, much stouter twigs, and larger cones which do not accumulate on the tree.

Remarks: An important lumber tree. Invades old fields.

LONGLEAF PINE   Pl. 1
Pinus palustris Mill. (*P. australis* Michx. f.)

A beautiful straight *southern* tree with *very long needles* grouped in 3's. Needles dark green, 8″–18″ (mostly more than 11″) long, and clustered toward the ends of twigs, giving a tufted appearance. Twigs *very stout,* diameter ½″ or more, ending in a *large, white-silvery bud.* Cones conical, 6″–10″ long; scales more than ¾″ wide, with thin prickles (less prominent than those of Loblolly Pine). Height 60′–70′ (85′); diameter 1′–2′ (3′6″). Coastal Plain soils.

Similar species: No other pine has such long needles, stout twigs, or white buds. See Slash Pine.

Remarks: The most important turpentine pine and a valuable timber tree in South. Quick-growing and fire-resistant.

Conifers with Needles in Clusters II: Pines II (Plate 2)

The following are two-needle pines, a few of which sometimes also carry three-needle clusters:

JACK PINE   *Pinus banksiana* Lamb.   Pl. 2

A scrubby, small or medium-sized *northern* tree (see map, p. 39); needles *very short,* only 1″–1½″ long. Portions of the twigs and branchlets where needle clusters were recently attached are quite rough. Cones usually curved or *bulging* on one side. 1½″–2½″ long; persistent; scales either thornless or with tiny weak prickles. Height 15′–40′; diameter 9″–15″.

Similar species: No other pine in our area has such short needles or curved cones.

Remarks: Produces poor timber but widespread in some northern areas of dry, infertile soils that would otherwise support no tree growth. Fires cause cones to open and release seeds.

Northern and Appalachian Pines, with Clues for Roadside Identification

Species and remarks	Average needle length (inches)	Average cone length (inches)	Open cones longer than wide [1]	Many old cones on tree	Needles per bundle [2]
Jack Pine *Pinus banksiana* Cones sharply curved. See Pl. 2.	1	2	+	+	2
Virginia Pine *P. virginiana* Needles gray-green, stiff.[3] See Pl. 2.	2	2	±	+	2
Scotch Pine *P. sylvestris* Upper bark orange. See Pl. 2.	2	2	±	−	2
Mountain Pine *P. pungens* Cones heavy, very thorny. See Pl. 2.	2	3	±	+	2
Red Pine *P. resinosa* Needles dark green, flexible. See Pl. 2.	5	2	+	−	2
Pitch Pine *P. rigida* Needles yellow-green, stiff.[4] See Pl. 1.	5	2	±	+	3
(**Austrian Pine**[5] *P. nigra*) Needles dark green, stiff.	5	3	+	−	2
White Pine *P. strobus* Needles blue-green, flexible. See Pl. 1.	4	5	+	−	5

[1] ± = more or less ball-shaped; + = elongated.
[2] Not a "roadside" characteristic but essential if close scrutiny is undertaken.
[3] Branches usually more tangled and trunk more twisted than other pines.
[4] May show trunk sprouts after fire; see also Pond Pine, p. 35.
[5] Mostly planted specimens.

SCOTCH PINE   *Pinus sylvestris* L.   **Pl. 2**
A medium-sized to tall northern tree with needles in 2's and 2″–3″ long. Twigs where old needles have dropped are rather smooth. Cones 1½″, seldom remaining on the tree; scales with a raised, more or less sharp point but actually thornless. Higher trunk and

branches *bright orange color*. Height 60'–90'; diameter 1'–2'.
Similar species: (1) Jack Pine has shorter needles and curved cones. (2) Austrian and Red pines have longer needles and rough twigs. (3) Virginia Pine has tough branches and slender cone prickles. (4) Mountain Pine has coarser needles and heavy, long-thorny cones. None of these species has bright orange upper bark.
Remarks: Imported from Europe and spreads from forest and Christmas tree plantings.

AUSTRIAN PINE   *Pinus nigra* Arnold   Not illus.
Needles *dark green,* stiff, and 3"–6" long. Twigs rough where old needles have fallen. Cones 2"–4", somewhat pointed, and soon dropping; scales with short but stout thorns. Height 50'–100' (165'); diameter 1'–2' (3').
Similar species: Red Pine lacks cone prickles, the needles are somewhat longer, and the trunk bark is usually brighter.
Remarks: Mostly in northern landscaped parks but sometimes spreading from cultivation there.

RED PINE   *Pinus resinosa* Ait.   **Pl. 2**
A tall *northern* tree with 4"–6" *flexible* dark green needles in 2's. Twigs more or less smooth. Cones 1½"–2½" long; scales thornless. Old cones do not accumulate on the tree. Bark plates yellow-red. Height 50'–80' (85'); diameter 1'–2' (3'). Upland sites.
Similar species: (1) Shortleaf Pine is more southern, has somewhat prickly cones. Old cones are retained on the tree. (2) Scotch Pine has shorter light green needles and orange upper bark. (3) Austrian Pine has stiffer needles and thorny, larger cones.
Remarks: A beautiful tree widely used in reforestation. Often called Norway Pine but native only to N. America.

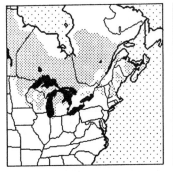

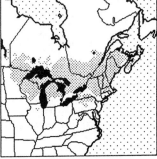

JACK PINE   RED PINE

Southern Pines,
with Clues for Roadside Identification

Species and remarks	Average needle length (inches)	Average cone length (inches)	Open cones longer than wide[1]	Many old cones on tree	Needles per bundle[2]
Sand Pine *Pinus clausa* Sandhills, Fla., and se. Ala. See Pl. 2.	2	2½	±	+	2
Spruce Pine[3] *P. glabra* Bark dark, fine cracks. See Pl. 2.	2	2	+	+	2
Shortleaf Pine *P. echinata* Needles dull, blue-green. See Pl. 2.	4	2	+	+	2–(3)
Pond Pine *P. serotina* Trunk sprouts after fire.[4] See Pl. 1.	6	2	±	+	3
Loblolly Pine *P. taeda* Needles dull, yellow-green. See Pl. 1.	7	4	+	+	3
Slash Pine *P. elliottii* Needles glossy, dark green. See Pl. 2.	8	4	+	−	2–3
Longleaf Pine *P. palustris* Twigs ½″; end buds white. See Pl. 1.	13	8	+	−	3

[1] ± = more or less ball-shaped; + = elongated.
[2] Not a "roadside characteristic" but essential if close scrutiny is undertaken.
[3] Usually scattered in broadleaf forests.
[4] Needles yellow-green, dull. See also Pitch Pine, p. 35.

MOUNTAIN PINE *Pinus pungens* Lamb.   **Pl. 2**
A small to medium-sized tree with 2″–3″ stiff needles in 2's and
rough twigs. Cones 2″–4″ long, *unusually* heavy, woody, opening
late and remaining long on the tree; scales tipped by *long thorns,*
more than ³⁄₁₆″ long. Height to 60′; diameter to 2′. Mainly dry
Appalachian locations.
Similar species: Cones are distinctive, and limited range is
helpful. See under Scotch and Virginia pines.

VIRGINIA (SCRUB) PINE *Pinus virginiana* Mill.   **Pl. 2**
A mostly small or medium-sized tree of the south-central states
with 2"–3" needles in 2's. Unlike our other pines, whose smaller
branches (those about ½" in diameter) snap cleanly, the branches
of this species are tough, fibrous, and quite *difficult* to break.
Twigs rather smooth and yellowish or somewhat purplish. Cones
somewhat egg-shaped, 2"–3", numerous, remaining on tree for
many years; scales tipped by ⅟₁₆"–⅛" thorns. Height 30'–40' (60');
diameter 1'–2' (3'). Poor soils and old fields.
Similar species: (1) Scotch and (2) Mountain pines have needles
of this length, but their ½" branches snap easily. Upper bark of
Scotch Pine is bright orange, and cones are thornless. Mountain
Pine cones have strong, sharp thorns ³⁄₁₆" or longer. Scotch Pine
spreads from plantings mostly north of Virginia Pine range.

SHORTLEAF PINE *Pinus echinata* Mill.   **Pl. 2**
A tall, mostly southern tree with 2 and sometimes also with 3
slender *blue-green* needles per bundle. Needles 3"–5" and flexible.
Twigs rough. Small (½") branches break cleanly. Cones 1½"–3"
long; scales with a straight but weak prickle. Height 90'–100'
(150'); diameter 3'–4'. Old fields and uplands. See map, p. 42.
Similar species: (1) Virginia Pine has shorter, two-needle clusters and branches difficult to break. (2) Pitch Pine has 3 stout,
yellow-green needles per cluster and stout cone scale prickles. (3)
Loblolly Pine is abundant in the range of the Shortleaf but has
longer, lighter green needles in 3's and large cones. (4) Austrian
Pine occurs mostly in plantings and has stiff, dark green needles.
Remarks: An important timber tree, larger and more common
west of the Mississippi River.

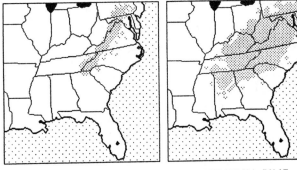

MOUNTAIN PINE   VIRGINIA PINE

SPRUCE PINE   *Pinus glabra* Walt.   **Pl. 2**

Scattered in southern hardwood (broad-leaved) forests, this mostly small to medium-sized and uncommon pine has no outstanding field marks. Needles slender and 2″–4″ long; twigs smooth; cones 1″–2″, with old ones remaining on the tree and prickles tiny or lacking. Trunk bark dark and ridged. Height 80′–100′ (120′); diameter 1′–2′ (3′). Fertile soils.

Similar species: (1) Virginia and (2) Mountain pines are more northern. The branches of Virginia Pine are more fibrous and difficult to break and mature cones of Mountain Pine are rather massive. In Florida and se. Alabama, (3) Sand Pine is almost always confined to poor soils and has stoutly spiny and usually longer cones.

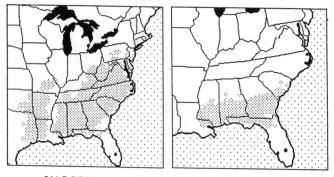

SHORTLEAF PINE   SPRUCE PINE

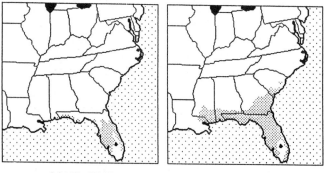

SAND PINE   SLASH PINE

SAND PINE   **Pl. 2**
Pinus clausa (Chapm. ex Engelm.) Vasey ex Sarg.
Occurring in cen. to ne. Florida and again in nw. Florida and se.
Alabama, this small to medium-sized pine has cones with short
but *stout* prickles. Needles are 2″–4″ long; twigs smooth; the 2″–3″
cones persist on the tree. Height 15′–20′ (25′); diameter to 1′. On
poor sandy soils.
Similar species: See Spruce Pine.
Remarks: Capable of rapid recolonization after fires.

SLASH PINE   *Pinus elliottii* Engelm.   **Pl. 2**
Resembles Loblolly in southern distribution but needles are
broader, more rigid, and glossy *dark green* and tend to be longer.
Both two- and three-needle clusters may be present. The twigs are
¼″–½″ in diameter, with end buds rusty silver. Cones are 3″–6″,
the old ones *not* accumulating on the tree. The cone scales are
½″–¾″ wide and tipped with small but stout and prickly thorns.
Cone stalks, ¾″–1″ long, may remain attached to the tree when
cones fall. Height 80′–115′; diameter 1′–3′. Moist to dry soils.
Similar species: (1) Loblolly Pine has dull pale green needles in
3's and smaller, more slender cones which tend to remain on the
tree. (2) Longleaf Pine has more tufted clumps of longer needles
in 3's, stouter twigs, white end buds, and larger cones with slight
prickles.

Not Pines but Resembling Them

AUSTRALIAN-PINE (HORSETAIL CASUARINA)   **Fig. 6**
Casuarina equisetifolia L. ex J. R. & G. Forst.
Drooping "needles" are up to 1′ long and attached *singly*. Each
"needle" comprises a series of *jointed,* fine-grooved green sections,
which are technically twigs; the true leaves form whorls of 6–8
tiny gray scales fringing each joint. The 1″ fruits are brown and
conelike but ball-shaped. Height 60′–90′ (100′); diameter 10″–15″
(18″). Seashores and other sandy soils.
Similar species: No native tree has jointed "needles."
Remarks: The casuarinas, or beefwoods, represent a large group
of tropical species. Unlike the pines, the casuarinas are true
flowering plants. The blossoms are minute. The needles resemble
those of the herbaceous horsetails *(Equisetum)*. Australian-pine
is used in windbreaks and hedges. Though it has value in erosion
control, this fast-growing species has become naturalized and is
becoming a weed in s. Florida.

Fig. 6.
Australian-pine.

BRAZILIAN BEEFWOOD   *C. cristata* Miq.   Not illus.
This casuarina has also been introduced into tropical Florida. It
may be distinguished by having 12–16 scale leaves per joint-
whorl.

Conifers with Mostly Four-sided Needles: Spruces (Plate 3)

Spruces are ornamental, sharply steeple-shaped evergreen trees
of cold climates whose needlelike leaves are somewhat four-
angled, short, stiff, and sharp. They tend to grow all around the
twigs. When these needles are removed, the twigs and branchlets
remain rough from the persistent needle bases. Like firs and
yews, spruce branchlets are tipped with twigs arranged in the
shape of Christian crosses. Spruce cones are brown and woody
when mature. Unlike the firs, they are not erect and do not fall
apart on the tree. Their scales are thin, not heavy or thorny as in
the pines. The bark is rough and dark.
    Spruces grow north to the limit of trees; forests thin down to
dwarf specimens extending far into the tundra. To the south, one
species persists on mountaintops as far south as Georgia.
    Spruces are often used as Christmas trees, but their needles fall
quickly upon drying. The wood is soft, light, resinous, and
straight-grained. It provides a principal source of pulp for paper
and is valuable for sounding boards in pianos and for construction
work, interior finishing, and boatbuilding. Tannin and "bur-
gundy pitch," used in varnishes and medicinal compounds, come
from the bark of certain species. In Europe some spruces are
tapped for turpentine, and in times of food shortage the inner bark
has been ground and added to flour. Spruce beer is reportedly

made from the fermented leaves and twigs of Red or Black spruces after being boiled with honey. Several spruces are of value in landscaping.

BLACK SPRUCE *Picea mariana* (Mill.) BSP.   **Pl. 3**
Twigs and buds *hairy.* Needles *short,* mostly ¼″–⁷⁄₁₆″ long, and green (sometimes blue-green with a white powder). Cones only ¾″–1¼″ long, somewhat gray-brown, with scale edges rather ragged. Cones usually remain on tree for several years. Low, matlike forms are known from northern mountains, especially where exposed to severe winds and cold. Height 25′–30′; diameter 1′–2′. Bogs and wet soils.
Similar species: (1) Red and (2) White spruces have longer needles and cones and occur mostly on uplands. White Spruce has hairless twigs.

RED SPRUCE *Picea rubens* Sarg.   **Pl. 3**
Twigs and buds typically *hairy;* needles *dark or yellow-green,* ½″–⅝″ long and often curved upward. Cones 1¼″–1⅝″ long, more or less reddish brown, with scale edges *smooth.* They fall soon after maturity. Height 60′–70′ (75′); diameter 1′–2′ (3′). Well-drained soils.
Similar species: Black Spruce has shorter needles and cones; it occurs on moist sites.

WHITE SPRUCE *Picea glauca* (Moench) Voss   **Pl. 3**
Twigs and buds *hairless;* needles *blue-green,* ⅜″–¾″ long. Branch-lets do *not* droop. Cones 1″–2″ long, dropping soon after they mature; scales flexible. In Far North and on high mountains, a low, matlike form occurs in exposed locations. Height 50′–60′; diameter 1′–2′. Uplands. See map, p. 46.
Similar species: Black Spruce has shorter needles and hairy twigs and occurs more abundantly in swamps.

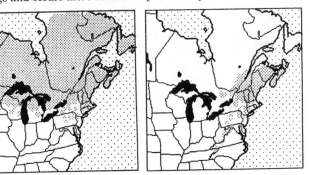

BLACK SPRUCE   RED SPRUCE

NORWAY SPRUCE   *Picea abies* (L.) Karst   **Pl. 3**
Twigs *hairless* or nearly so. Needles *dark green,* mostly ½"–1"
long. The twigs and *branchlets hang downward.* Cones 4"–6" *long,*
falling soon after they mature; scales stiff. Height 60'–90'; diameter 1'–3'. European; occasionally spreads from plantings on
uplands.
Similar species: The only spruce with drooping twigs/branchlets
and the only one in our area with large cones.

Conifers with Flat Needles (Plate 4)

Mostly unrelated cone-bearing species that are alike in having
flat needles.

BALSAM FIR   *Abies balsamea* (L.) Mill.   **Pl. 4**
A steeple-shaped evergreen tree with needles ⅜"–1½" long and
whitened beneath. Needles occur mostly in flattened sprays. Each
needle has a *broad circular base.* Twigs rather *smooth,* with
round, flat scars after needles are removed. Cones 1"–3" long,
upright and fleshy, purplish to green, *no bracts visible between
scales.* The cones fall apart upon ripening, leaving erect, slender
central cores. The plant may grow as a low matlike shrub at
timberline. Bark rather smooth, with resin blisters. Height
40'–60' (75'); diameter 1'–2' (3'). Moist woods.
Similar species: When present, the upright cones are distinctive
characteristics of firs. See also Fraser Fir. Hemlocks have stalked
needles and rough twigs.
Remarks: A good Christmas tree that holds its needles. Soft,
perishable wood of less value than spruce as lumber or pulp.

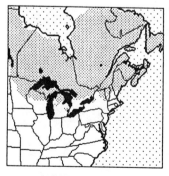

WHITE SPRUCE

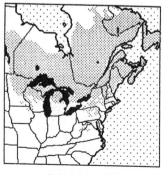

BALSAM FIR

Canada balsam obtained from bark blisters, a gum used by woodsmen as a wound plaster and waterproof cement; sold in stores as a confection before the advent of chicle chewing gum. Formerly used in cementing lenses and in mounting specimens on microscope slides. Fire-by-friction sets are often made of this wood; resinous fir knots were once used as torches. Seeds eaten by ruffed, spruce, and sharp-tailed grouse; twigs browsed by snowshoe hare, white-tailed deer, and moose; bark gnawed by porcupine.

FRASER FIR   *Abies fraseri* (Pursh) Poir.   **Pl. 4**
Differs from Balsam Fir in distribution and cone scale structure. Cones adorned with bracts whose three-parted tips *project obviously* from between the scales. Foliage occurs less frequently in flattened sprays. Appalachians, mostly above 4000' altitude.

EASTERN HEMLOCK   *Tsuga canadensis* (L.) Carr.   **Pl. 4**
Frequently a more round-topped tree than the firs or spruces. Twigs and branchlets, more flexible than in those groups; top shoot bends with the wind. *Needles* 5/16"–9/16" long, *whitened* beneath, attached to the twigs *by slender stalks*. Twigs *rough* when leaves removed. Cones only 5/8"–1" long, brown, few-scaled, pendent. A matlike form occurs in exposed places in n. New England and e. Canada. Bark dark and rough. Height 60'–70' (100'); diameter 2'–3' (6'). Mature forests and wooded ravines.
Similar species: (1) Firs have circular needle bases, smooth twigs. (2) See Carolina Hemlock.
Remarks: The delicate silvery foliage and small, pendent, perfectly formed brown cones of the hemlock make this one of our most beautiful forest trees. It makes a poor Christmas tree because its leaves fall upon drying. Formerly spared the ax

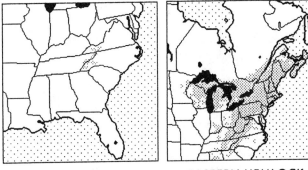

FRASER FIR   EASTERN HEMLOCK

because of the poor quality of its wood and the stonelike hardness of the knots, which will chip steel blades. Even so, however, the increased value of timber has doomed most virgin stands. Lumber is taken for pulp but is, or at least was, particularly useful for railroad ties, since it holds spikes exceptionally well. Bark rich in tannin; a tea was once made from leaves and twigs by woodsmen and Indians. As fuel the wood throws sparks. Seeds and needles eaten by ruffed and sharp-tailed grouse and red squirrel, twigs browsed by deer, snowshoe hare, and cottontail rabbit.

CAROLINA HEMLOCK   *Tsuga caroliniana* Engelm.   **Pl. 4**
Like Eastern Hemlock but with needles ⅝"–¾" long and cones ¾"–1⅜" long. Occurs in mountains from w. Virginia to w. South Carolina, n. Georgia, and e. Tennessee.

BALDCYPRESS   *Taxodium distichum* (L.) Richard.   **Pl. 4**
A handsome *non*-evergreen tall tree of *southern swamps*. Needles ¼"–⅞" long, green on both sides, mostly flat, but sometimes somewhat three-sided; arranged along slender greenish twigs. Needles and most twigs *fall in winter,* leaving branchlets roughened by small, few-scaled buds. Leaf scars lacking; areas similar to leaf scars present but without bundle scars. Bark brown, rather smooth but fibrous. Trunk base often deeply ridged. In deep water, *peculiar root growths* called "cypress knees" grow upward to the surface. Cones *ball-shaped,* about 1" in diameter, with thick scales. Height 80'–120' (140'); diameter 3'–4' (20'). Swamps and streambanks.
Similar species: Larches, our only other non-evergreen conifers, are northern, with needles in clusters and thin cone scales.
Remarks: Once seen, a mature stand of this majestic relative of

CAROLINA HEMLOCK

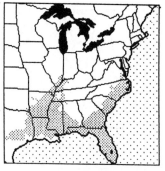

BALDCYPRESS

the Redwood is not soon forgotten. A valuable lumber tree used for construction work, railroad ties, posts, shingles. Wood is soft, light, straight-grained, and very durable and does not warp easily. Only distantly related to true cypresses, such as the famed Monterey Cypress of California. Seeds eaten by cranes and some songbirds. Grows on uplands if planted. The *evergreen* Montezuma Baldcypress (*T. mucronatum* Ten.) of Mexico barely enters Texas in the lower Rio Grande Valley.

PONDCYPRESS   Pl. 4
T. distichum var. *nutans* (Ait.) Sweet

A distinctive form of the Baldcypress with three-sided, *sharp,* needle-shaped leaves *pressed against* the twigs. Growth habits and habitat of the Pondcypress are identical with those of the parent species. The general appearance of the appressed and often drooping foliage, however, is much different from the fernlike sprays of the typical form. Some botanists regard the Pondcypress as a distinct species.

FLORIDA YEW   *Taxus floridana* Nutt. ex. Chapm.   Pl. 4

A rare evergreen shrub or small tree with needles ¾″–1″ long, pointed, *green on both sides.* Needles stalked, stalks following down twig for a distance below needle. Crushed foliage with a mild odor. Twigs *smooth.* On female plants, fruits juicy, red, *berrylike,* about ½″ in diameter; single brown seeds visible from beneath. Height to 25′. Local along the Apalachicola River and near Bristol, Liberty County, nw. Florida.

Similar species: Florida Torreya is also rare and occurs in the same area. Its pointed needles are more stiff and decidedly sharp to the touch, its crushed foliage has a stronger and more pungent odor, and its fruits are larger and green.

Remarks: Fruits possibly *poisonous.*

FLORIDA YEW

FLORIDA TORREYA

FLORIDA TORREYA   *Torreya taxifolia* Arn.   **Pl. 4**
Sometimes called Stinking-cedar, this rare species is a relative of
the Florida Yew and occurs with it in the vicinity of the Apalachicola River and also in adjacent Decatur County, sw. Georgia
(see map, p. 49). The crushed foliage yields a foul odor. See Florida
Yew.

Conifers with Scalelike or Three-sided Hollow Leaves (Plate 5)

Most of these related species differ from all other cone-bearing
trees and possess very small, peculiarly flattened leaves that form
scaly coverings for at least some twigs. *Juniperus* fruits, though
technically similar to cones, are berrylike.

The white-cedars possess only scalelike, flattened needles; the
junipers (especially the redcedars) may bear either scaly or
hollowed and whitened three-sided needles, or both. All needles of
Pondcypress and occasionally some leaves of the Baldcypress (see
Pl. 4) are three-sided rather than flat (see previous group), but
they are not whitened.

The three-sided type of leaf is only approximately triangular in
cross section. It is easily recognized, however, by the concave,
whitish inside surface. The needles may occur in pairs or 3's but
unlike pine needles are never bound at the base in bundles.

It may be necessary to use a hand lens to determine how the
scaly leaves are arranged, but usually more readily determined
characteristics are available. Seedlings may be impossible to
identify. The fruiting structures are quite diverse.

Although several of these species are popularly known as
cedars, only members of the Old World genus *Cedrus,* including
the cedars of Lebanon, N. Africa, and the Himalayas, are true
cedars. They may be seen in this country only where they have
been planted for decorative purposes. True cedars have larchlike
clusters of needles that remain evergreen.

NORTHERN WHITE-CEDAR (ARBOR VITAE)   **Pl. 5**
Thuja occidentalis L.
A medium-sized tree with leaves nearly all scalelike and ¹⁄₁₆″–⅛″
long. They occur in 4 rows around the twigs but are flattened from
the sides. Central leaves show tiny glands. Twigs and leaves occur
in *flattened sprays* that are typically aligned vertically. Heartwood light-colored. Cones slender, more or less bell-shaped, about
½″ long. A prostrate, carpetlike form occurs in Quebec. Bark is
fibrous with numerous cross-thatched ridges. Height 40′–50′
(125′); diameter 2′–3′ (5′). Swamps and limestone soils.
Similar species: (1) Atlantic White-cedar has different range,

less flattened leaves and leaf sprays, globular cones. (2) See French Tamarisk (Fig. 7).

Remarks: An earlier, widely used name is Arbor Vitae, a latinized French name meaning "tree of life." The tree was so named after it cured the men of Jacques Cartier's Canadian expedition of a disease, probably scurvy. As a result of the incident, this became the first tree to be imported from America into Europe. Over 50 varieties are now in cultivation. It was used by the native Americans and is known also as Canoe-wood. Thin slabs of the wood were prepared by pounding the ends of short logs until they separated along the annual rings. Wood is soft, light-colored, and durable. It is used for shingles and fire-by-friction sets. Outer bark supplies tinder. Cedar swamps provide favorite winter quarters and food for deer. Moose, snowshoe hares, and cottontail rabbits also eat the twigs and foliage; red squirrels and many songbirds consume the seeds.

ATLANTIC WHITE-CEDAR   Pl. 5
Chamaecyparis thyoides (L.) B.S.P.

Similar to Northern White-cedar but with the scalelike leaves *narrower* and less distinct. Leaves *less flattened* on the twigs, and foliage sprays not flattened. Cones fleshy, *globular,* $\frac{3}{16}''-\frac{1}{4}''$ in diameter. Height 40'–60'; diameter 1'–2' (3'). Swamps near coast.

Similar species: See (1) Northern White-cedar and (2) French Tamarisk (Fig. 7).

Remarks: Both the lumber and the crushed foliage are aromatic. Wood is soft, durable, very light. The lumber, used in shipbuilding and construction work and as shingles, is of such value that large logs buried in prehistoric times have been mined in New Jersey bogs. Organ pipes used to be made of this resonant wood. White-cedar charcoal was used in making gunpowder during the Amer-

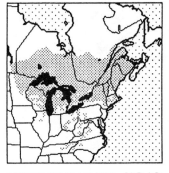

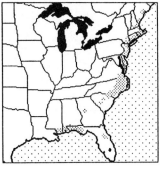

NORTHERN WHITE-CEDAR   ATLANTIC WHITE-CEDAR

ican Revolution. A number of horticultural varieties of this tree and its oriental relatives are used in landscaping because of their beauty and their resistance to insects and disease. Like Northern White-cedar, this species is sometimes known as Arbor Vitae. It is browsed by deer.

COMMON (DWARF) JUNIPER   Pl. 5
Juniperus communis L.

A widespread northern tree, more commonly a shrub, with sharp, hollowed, three-sided needles that occur in *whorls of 3, whitened above* and ¼″–⅞″ long. Twigs, or at least branchlets, are *three-sided*. Fruits are berries, rather hard, blue-black, ball-shaped, and with a white powder. Height 1′–4′ (35′); diameter 1″–6″ (1′). Pastures and infertile soils.

Similar species: Our only tree with needles in 3's and strongly whitened. Pondcypress is southern and aquatic (see Plate 4). French Tamarisk (Fig. 7) is taller, with flowers and fruit capsules.

Remarks: Oil from leaves and wood is used in perfumery, and the aromatic foliage is burned as an incense in India. The plant supplies food for ruffed and sharp-tailed grouse, bobwhite, European partridge, pheasant, white-tailed deer, moose, and smaller birds and mammals. Grows also throughout Europe and all of northern Asia.

ASHE JUNIPER   *Juniperus ashei* Spreng.   Pl. 5

A round-topped shrub or tree of *south-central* distribution. The tiny leaves are nearly *all* scalelike and tightly *pressed* against the twigs. Height to 40′. Fruits blue-black and usually 1 seed per fruit, though there may be 2–3, each more than ³⁄₁₆″ long. Ozarks area to w. Texas. Limestone soils.

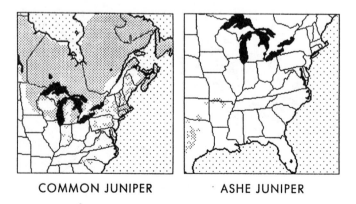

COMMON JUNIPER   ASHE JUNIPER

EASTERN REDCEDAR   *Juniperus virginiana* L.   **Pl. 5**

A medium-sized tree, usually with both scalelike and longer, sharply three-sided, needlelike leaves. Leaves ⅟₁₆″–¼″, entirely green, in pairs along *four-sided twigs* and branchlets. Heartwood reddish. Fruits more or less *globular,* hard whitish to blackish green berries about ¼″ in diameter, with 1–2 seeds, each ⅛″–³⁄₁₆″ long. Bark dry, shreddy, not ridged. Rarely (in severely windswept locations) shrubby and creeping. Height 40′–50′ (62′); diameter 1′–2′ (4′). Old fields and dry soils.

Similar species: (1) Ashe Juniper seldom has needlelike leaves and barely enters our area. (2) French Tamarisk (Fig. 7) has tiny, alternate needles, colorful small flowers, and capsular fruits. (3) See Southern Redcedar.

Remarks: Birds pass the seeds through their digestive tracts undamaged, dropping them particularly along fences. The Redcedar acts as alternate host to apple rust. During half its life cycle, this fungus spots apples and their leaves; during the other half, it forms ball-shaped brown galls on Redcedar twigs. After heavy rains these galls extrude numerous hanging brown gelatinous threads. Do not confuse galls with Redcedar fruits, which are hard but berrylike.

Heartwood is aromatic and of rose-brown color. It is light, strong, durable, and widely used for cedar chests, cabinets, lead pencils, fuel, and fence posts. The outer bark, when stripped, dried, and rubbed between the hands, provides excellent tinder and is used in flint-and-steel and sunglass fire sets. A volatile oil derived from juniper leaves is used in perfumes, and a flavoring may be derived from the berries. The dried berries are used as a cooking spice. In the wild the fruits are consumed by well over 50 species of birds, including bobwhite, sharp-tailed grouse, pheasant, and mourning dove, and also by opossum.

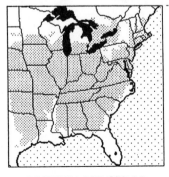

EASTERN REDCEDAR   SOUTHERN REDCEDAR

SOUTHERN REDCEDAR   *J. silicicola* (Small) Bailey
Like the Eastern Redcedar but with twigs more slender (about
1/32″) and drooping. Fruits are only 1/8″–3/16″ in diameter. Moist
sites in the South. See map, p. 53.

Needle-bearing Evergreen Trees Without Cones

In addition to the cone-bearers, a few flowering plants also have
scalelike leaves. French Tamarisk is the only such tree species in
our area. It has colorful blossoms and is becoming widely established. (See also Australian-pine and Brazilian Beefwood, p. 44).

FRENCH TAMARISK   *Tamarix gallica* L.   **Fig. 7**
An importation from southern Europe, this tree is becoming
established widely. Often called Salt-cedar. Pale green leaves less
than 1/16″ long, *scalelike,* on long, slender, often drooping twigs.
Numerous slender spikes of pink, or sometimes whitish, flowers
usually present from May to Sept. Fruits small dry capsules.
Roadsides and thickets; Massachusetts, Indiana, and Kansas to
Florida, s. Texas, and s. California.

Fig. 7. French Tamarisk.

II

Broad-leaved Trees with Opposite Compound Leaves (Plates 6–9)

Only a few plants bear leaves of this type. Their identification is therefore comparatively simple when foliage is present. In s. Florida, the several tropical species with opposite compound leaves are evergreen.

In winter in more northern areas, unless dead leaves are attached to the twigs, there is no indication of whether a plant once bore compound or simple leaves. This section must then be considered in conjunction with the next, whose twigs also bear opposite (or occasionally whorled) leaf scars and buds. The twigs of a leafless unknown plant with opposite leaf scars may be compared with the illustrations in Sections II and III, or see Appendix A (winter key).

Some alternate-leaved plants bear stubby, scarred, leaf-crowded spur branches. Care should be taken that their leaves and leaf scars are not assumed to be opposite or whorled because of this crowding. None of the plants in our area with true opposite or whorled leaf scars ever develops spur branches. Twigs with uncrowded leaves or leaf scars should be selected for identification.

Fig. 8. Opposite compound leaves.

1. Leaves fan-compound, the leaflets arranged like the spokes of a wheel.   **Buckeyes, etc., Pl. 6.**
1. Leaves feather-compound:
    2. Leaflets 3:
        3. Not evergreen, northern.   **Bladdernut, Pl. 7.**
        3. Evergreen trees of Florida. **Torchwoods, Pl. F-7.**
    2. Leaflets 5–11:
        4. Evergreen trees of s. Florida.

            Miscellaneous, Pl. F-7.
        4. Not evergreen:
            5. Fruits fleshy; flower/fruit in upright, flat-topped clusters.   **Elderberry, Pl. 7.**
            5. Fruits dry, winged; flower/fruit clusters drooping, not flat-topped.   **Ashes I and II and Ashleaf Maple, Pls. 8, 9.**

Trees with Opposite Fan-compound Leaves: Buckeyes and Chastetree (Plate 6)

Buckeyes (and the Chastetree, which is usually shrubby) are our only trees with opposite compound leaves whose leaflets are arranged like the spokes of a wheel. Buckeyes have toothed leaflets; Chastetree has smooth-edged foliage. In winter, a combination of characteristics will identify the buckeye group: leaf scars have 3 or more bundle scars, twigs and end buds are large, and side buds have 4 or more pairs of scales. Chastetree twigs are usually four-angled.

If flowers or fruits are present, they can be of considerable help in identifying buckeyes. The stamens (threadlike filaments tipped by pollen-bearing anthers) are shorter than the petals in some species and longer in others. In this group, too, the calyx (the circle of sepals immediately exterior to the petals) is colored like the petals and tubular. The calyx tube is short ($\frac{1}{4}''$–$\frac{3}{8}''$) in most species but longer ($\frac{3}{8}''$–$1''$) in the Red Buckeye. The flowers are in large showy upright spikes at twig ends, and the fruits have three-parted husks that contain 1–3 large shiny brown nuts. Chastetree flower spikes are erect but shorter, and the fruits are small and fleshy.

The native Ohio and Sweet buckeyes may be large and important trees in forests west of the Appalachian Mountains. There they are sometimes dominant with White Oak in the few areas of virgin timber remaining. Hybrids are known. An imported relative, the Horsechestnut, common in shade-tree plantings, occasionally escapes to grow wild.

Seeds, young twigs, and leaves of all buckeyes are sometimes toxic to livestock. Crushed fruits and branches have been used to kill fish for food, but this practice is now illegal.

HORSECHESTNUT   *Aesculus hippocastanum* L.   **Pl. 6**
  A large imported tree with 7–9 wedge-shaped leaflets. End buds more than ½″ long, very *sticky*. Broken twigs have no decidedly disagreeable odor. Trunk bark somewhat scaly. Leaves 4″–15″. Height 60′–75′ (80′); diameter 1′–2′ (3′). Flowers white, clusters 6″–12″, stamens long, May. Fruits with *strongly thorny husks,* Sept.–Oct. European, rarely spreading from northern plantings.
  Similar species: The only buckeye with sticky end buds and strongly thorny fruit husks. The true chestnuts (Plate 32) have large brown nuts but are unrelated and are otherwise dissimilar.

YELLOW (SWEET) BUCKEYE   **Pl. 6**
  Aesculus octandra Marsh.
  Similar to Horsechestnut but usually with 5 (4–7) leaflets and *non-sticky* buds. End buds large, with bud scales not ridged. Broken twigs without foul odor. Trunk bark fairly smooth or broken with large plates. Leaves 4″–15″. Height to 90′; diameter to 3′. Flowers yellow, clusters 4″–7″, stamens short, May–June. Fruits with *smooth husks,* Sept.–Oct. Mature woods.
  Similar species: Ohio Buckeye has ridged end-bud scales and foul-smelling broken twigs.
  Remarks: Fruits, unlike those of other buckeyes, are sometimes eaten by cattle and hogs. They are also said to make an excellent paste when powdered and mixed with water. Wood is light and tough.

OHIO BUCKEYE   *Aesculus glabra* Willd.   **Pl. 6**
  A smaller tree than Yellow Buckeye and with prominently *ridged* scales on end buds, which are more than ½″ long. Twigs emit a *foul*

YELLOW BUCKEYE   OHIO BUCKEYE

odor when broken. Trunk bark scaly. Leaves 4″–15″. Height to 40′; diameter to 2′. Flowers yellow, clusters 4″–6″, stamens long, April–May. Fruit husks with *weak thorns,* fruits Sept.–Oct. Moist forests.

Similar species: (1) Yellow Buckeye has scales of end buds not ridged. (2) Painted Buckeye has fruit husks without prickles.

BOTTLEBRUSH BUCKEYE *Aesculus parviflora* Walt. **Pl. 6**
Rarely growing to tree size, this buckeye has a restricted native range, 5–7 leaflets, and striking blooms. Mature end buds not ridged and *less than* ½″ long. The many-flowered cylindrical stalks of white blossoms are *up to 20″* long, with stamens ½″–1½″ in length and longer than the petals. Fruit husks smooth. Local in Alabama and sw. Georgia.
Similar species: No other buckeye has such long flower spikes.
Remarks: Twigs and fruits said to be poisonous. An attractive species cultivated even in the northern U.S.

RED BUCKEYE *Aesculus pavia* L. **Pl. 6**
A shrub or small tree with 5 leaflets that are narrow to elliptic and hairless when mature. Mature flowers and buds are about ½″ long. Bud scales *ridged.* Flowers bright *red* and long-tubular, stamens about equal to petals in length. Clusters 4″–8″. Fruits not prickly. The Particolored Buckeye (*A. discolor* Pursh.) is now considered part of this species. Coastal Plain woods.

PAINTED (DWARF) BUCKEYE **Pl. 6**
Aesculus sylvatica Bartr.
A thicket-forming shrub or small tree of southern areas. Leaves 4″–15″ long, with 5 leaflets. End buds *less than* ½″ long and *not* keeled. Flowers yellow, cream-colored, or pink, clusters 4″–6″,

BOTTLEBRUSH BUCKEYE   RED BUCKEYE

stamens short. Fruits *not prickly*. Mostly Coastal Plain and Piedmont plateau bottom lands.

CHASTETREE   *Vitex agnus-castus* L.   Not illus.
A small tree but usually shrubby, with opposite fan-compound leaves whose leaflets are long-stalked, long-pointed, and *not toothed*. They are dark green above, gray beneath, and *spicy-scented* when crushed. The twigs also have a spicy odor when rubbed; they are gray-hairy, often four-angled, and with more than 1 bud above each leaf scar. Bundle scar single. The flowers are small, *bluish*, and fragrant, occurring in 2″–4″ erect spikes at the twig ends. The ⅛″ fleshy fruits contain a single seed.
Similar species: Buckeyes are not spicy-scented and have toothed leaves, rounded twigs, and larger flowers and fruits.
Remarks: Native to s. Europe and Asia but spreading from plantings over much of the Coastal Plain, especially in the southern states.

Small Trees with Opposite Compound Leaves: Bladdernut and Elderberry (Plate 7)

Bladdernut and Common Elderberry are *non-evergreen* small trees which occur widely in the eastern United States. Winter twigs lack central end buds. In Florida see Pl. F-7.

BLADDERNUT   *Staphylea trifolia* L.   **Pl. 7**
A shrub or small tree whose leaves have 3 (rarely 5) fine-toothed, elliptic leaflets. Twigs *slender* with few small wartlike lenticels or

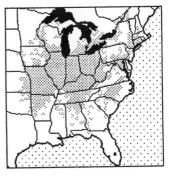

PAINTED BUCKEYE   BLADDERNUT

none. Pith white, *narrow.* Buds brown, with 2–4 scales, small. Leaf scars small, without connecting lines between. Bundle scars 4–7. Bark of older branches greenish or gray *streaked* with white. Leaves 2″–6″. Height 5′–15′ (25′); diameter 1″–2″ (6″). Flowers whitish, clustered at twig ends, drooping, April–June. Fruits inflated papery capsules. 1″–2″, Aug.–Oct.

Similar species: No other woody species has such fruits. Ashleaf Maple (Pl. 9) may have some three-parted leaves, but normally leaves with 5–11 leaflets are also present.

COMMON ELDERBERRY *Sambucus canadensis* L. Pl. 7

A shrub or small tree with large leaves composed of 5–11 coarse-toothed, elliptic leaflets. Twigs *stout* with *large white pith.* Small wartlike lenticels common. Leaf scars large, with connecting lines between; 5–7 bundle scars. Buds small, green or brown. Bark brownish. Leaves 4″–11″. Height 3′–20′; diameter ¾″–3″ (10″). Flowers small, white, in dense terminal *flat-topped* clusters, June–July. Fruits small (mostly less than ³⁄₁₆″ in diameter), juicy, *purple-black,* rarely bright red, yellow, or orange, Aug.–Oct.

Similar species: The pithy twigs and lack of central end buds will separate it from the ashes. In s. Florida, Yellow-elder (Pl. F-7) has more slender twigs and distinctive flowers and fruits.

Remarks: All parts of plants are reported to yield hydrocyanic acid. Regardless, fruits are used in making jam, jelly, wine, pies. Ripe fruits are eaten by 43 species of birds, including pheasant, mourning dove, and wild turkey.

FLORIDA-ONLY TREES Pl. F-7

Four other small-tree species with opposite compound leaves are *evergreen* and are not found north of Collier, Dade, and Monroe counties in tropical s. Florida.

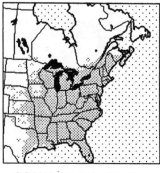

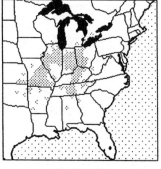

COMMON ELDERBERRY   BLUE ASH

Trees with Opposite Feather-compound Leaves: Ashes and Ashleaf Maple (Plates 8 and 9)

Over most of our area, the ashes and the Ashleaf Maple, or Box-elder, are the only native trees with opposite feather-compound leaves. All are tall trees. Only in southern Florida could several distinctively marked evergreen tropical species (see Pl. F-7) possibly be confused with the Carolina Ash, the only ash to occur so far south.

Young trees may be distinguished from shrubs with similar leaves by the presence of true end buds. In winter, ashes have moderately stout, mostly gray twigs; central end buds present (but not exceptionally large); and opposing leaf scars that do not meet. Leaf scars are large and shield-shaped, with 4 or more bundle scars; buds have a somewhat granular surface texture. Ashleaf Maple has green or purplish, smooth, hairless, often white-powdered twigs whose opposite leaf scars meet at raised points.

Identification of ash species is never simple except in the case of a few well-marked forms. If the winged fruits, which look like the blades of canoe paddles, are present, they can be quite useful evidence. Except as noted (Pls. 8–9), the leaflets may be variably toothed or not. Though the leaflets are found most frequently as illustrated, slight variations are common. The flowers are small, dark, and densely clustered in leaf angles. They are without petals.

The ashes yield quality lumber for furniture, tool handles, baseball bats, baskets, and many special purposes. The twigs serve as deer food; the flowers provide pollen for bees. Native Americans once made a dark bitter sugar from the sap.

Ashes I (Plate 8)

BLUE ASH *Fraxinus quadrangulata* Michx.   **Pl. 8**
A tree of high ground with vigorous twigs often *square* in cross section. Twigs grayish and hairless, with *long lines* leading from leaf scars. Leaflets 7–11, green beneath, stalked, and *always* toothed. Upper edges of leaf scars only shallowly or occasionally deeply concave. Trunk bark whitish and somewhat scaly. Leaves 8″–12″. Height 60′–70′ (115′); diameter 2′–3′ (3½′). Flowers April–May. Fruits with seeds that are not plump; wings extending to the base; and *broad, squared tips;* June–Oct.
Similar species: Where twigs are not sharply angled, the long

lines along them are distinctive. Few other opposite-leaved trees have four-lined or squarish twigs. (1) Burningbush (Pl. 12) has four-lined twigs, but they are green, and bundle scars are single. (2) The winter twigs of Chastetree (p. 59) are four-lined but slender.

Remarks: Inner bark yields a blue dye.

WHITE ASH   *Fraxinus americana* L.   **Pl. 8**
An upland tree with twigs that have the brown side buds usually set in deep U- *or* V-*shaped notches* in upper edges of leaf scars. Twigs round and either hairless or velvety. Leaflets 5–9, toothed or not, stalked (sometimes short-stalked), usually *white* or pale beneath and either toothed or not. Trunk bark rather dark and tight, with rigid interwoven pattern of shallow ridges and furrows. Leaves 8″–12″. Height 70′–80′ (100′); diameter 2′–3′ (7′). Flowers April–June. Fruits *narrow,* not winged to the base, seeds raised above the flat wing, Oct.–Nov.

Similar species: When present, the deeply notched leaf scars are a good field mark among ashes with hairless twigs. Unfortunately, there is some variation in depth of notch in this and other species. Doubtful cases must be identified by fruits.

Remarks: The most valuable and largest native ash, providing hard, strong, durable timber for furniture, interior decorating, agricultural implements, tool handles, oars, tennis rackets, musical instruments, baseball bats, snowshoes, and skis. As a campfire fuel, it ranks with oak and hickory. Biltmore Ash was formerly separated as a variety with velvety-hairy twigs.

BLACK ASH   *Fraxinus nigra* Marsh.   **Pl. 8**
A tree of swamps and bottomlands whose leaflets are *not stalked.* The 7–11 leaflets are *always* toothed. Twigs round, hairless,

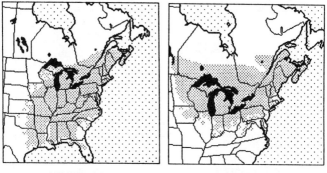

WHITE ASH   BLACK ASH

rather dull. Leaf scars not deeply notched. Buds *very dark,* nearly black. Trunk bark generally rather tight and furrowed but may be somewhat scaly. Leaves 12″–16″. Height 40′–80′; diameter 1′–2′. Flowers April–May. Fruits *blunt at both ends,* winged to the base, seeds not plump, June–Sept.

Similar species: Both (1) White and (2) Green ashes may have short-stalked leaflets, but they lack the dark buds and blunt fruits of this species.

Remarks: Known also as Hoop or Basket Ash. Short logs or planks when hammered repeatedly on the ends split along the annual growth rings into thin sheets that can be cut into strips for weaving pack baskets, chair seats, barrel hoops, etc. Knotty burls of the trunk are made into veneers and furniture.

GREEN (RED) ASH   *Fraxinus pennsylvanica* Marsh.   **Pl. 8**
A lowland tree whose leaflets are stalked (sometimes short-stalked) and slightly winged. Leaflets 5–9, green on both sides, toothed or not. Twigs hairless or velvety; buds *brownish.* Trunk bark tight and closely furrowed. Leaves 10″–12″. Height 60′–70′ (85′); diameter 2′–3′ (4′). Flowers April–May. Fruits wedge-shaped, not winged to the base, seeds plump, Sept.–Oct.

Similar species: See Black Ash.

Remarks: Green Ash was formerly classified as a hairless variety of Red Ash. Now the two have been combined.

Ashes II and Ashleaf Maple (Plate 9)

PUMPKIN ASH   *Fraxinus profunda* (Bush) Bush   **Pl. 9**
A small to large tree of swamps and bottomlands, mostly with

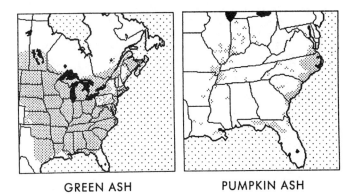

GREEN ASH   PUMPKIN ASH

velvety-hairy twigs. The leaves are *large, shiny above,* and sometimes leathery. The 7–9 *long-pointed* leaflets are *not toothed* but are sometimes wavy-edged; they vary from red-brown hairy to nearly hairless beneath. Trunk bark is tight (with shallow furrows) to somewhat scaly. Trunk base usually *swollen* on wet sites. Leaves 4″–18″. Height to 125′. Flowers April–May. Fruits *long,* 1½″–3″, not winged to the base, seeds plump but not extending to midlength of the fruit. Sept.–Oct.

Similar species: Carolina Ash is strictly southern, and its leaves are neither leathery nor rusty-hairy and are more likely to be toothed.

CAROLINA (WATER) ASH   Pl. 9
Fraxinus caroliniana Mill.

A small tree of *southern swamps* with leaflets mostly toothed and twigs usually hairless but sometimes *velvety-hairy.* Leaflets may nevertheless be hairy or hairless. Trunk bark tight and somewhat scaly. Trunk base usually *swollen* when growing in water. Leaves 7″–12″. Height to 35′; diameter 10″–12″. Flowers April–May. Fruits to 2″; broad-winged to the narrow base, seeds not plump.

Similar species: See Pumpkin Ash.

ASHLEAF MAPLE (BOX-ELDER)   *Acer negundo* L.   Pl. 9
A medium-sized tree of moist, fertile soils, with *hairless,* green or purplish, glossy, frequently white-powdered twigs. Leaflets 3–5 (uncommonly 7) with few coarse *teeth* or none. End leaflets often three-pointed and somewhat *lobed.* Narrow leaf scars *meet in raised points* on opposite sides of twigs. Bundle scars 3 (or 5); buds white-hairy. Trunk bark furrowed. Leaves 4″–10″. Height 50′–75′; diameter 2′–4′. Flowers in hanging clusters, April–May. Fruits paired "keys," Sept.–Oct.

CAROLINA ASH

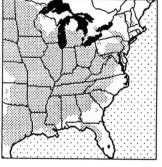

ASHLEAF MAPLE

Similar species: Only ashlike tree with leaf scars meeting in raised points. (1) When only 3 leaflets are present, the foliage often resembles that of Poison-ivy (see Fig. 4), whose leaves are alternate. (2) Other maples (Pl. 11) have simple leaves and dissimilar winter characteristics.

Remarks: The name Box-elder, widely used, fails to indicate proper taxonomic relationships. Soft white wood is used for boxes, etc. Syrup can be made from the sap. Squirrels and songbirds eat the seeds.

III

Broad-leaved Trees with Opposite Simple Leaves (Plates 10–14)

Though the trees with opposite simple leaves are more numerous than those of Section II, they are still so few as to be rather easily identified. In winter, plants with opposite leaf scars may be members of either Section II or Section III, and the illustrations for both sections must be reviewed (see also Appendix A). Care should be taken that the leaves or leaf scars on the stubby, scar-crowded spur branches (see Fig. 3) of some alternate-leaved plants are not interpreted as opposite or whorled.

When opposite simple leaves are present, the plants bearing them may be identified as follows:

1. Leaves large (5″–18″ long), heart-shaped.
   Princess-tree and Catalpas, Pl. 10.
1. Leaves smaller, not heart-shaped:
   2. Leaves with 3–5 lobes. **Maples, Pl. 11.**
   2. Leaves not lobed:
      3. Leaf edges fine-toothed. **Buckthorn, etc., Pl. 12.**
      3. Leaf edges not toothed:
         4. Leaves leathery, evergreen.
            Viburnums, etc., Pl. 13.
         4. Leaves not leathery. **Dogwoods, etc., Pl. 14.**

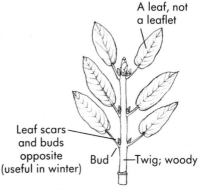

A leaf, not a leaflet

Leaf scars and buds opposite (useful in winter)

Bud

Twig; woody

Fig. 9. Opposite simple leaves.

Trees with Opposite or Whorled, Heart-shaped Leaves: Princess-tree and Catalpas (Plate 10)

The Princess-tree and Catalpas are the only trees in our range that have opposite or whorled heart-shaped leaves. In winter they are differentiated from other species with opposite leaf scars by their stout twigs and *elliptical* series of tiny bundle scars within each circular leaf scar. The twigs lack central end buds.

PRINCESS-TREE (PAULOWNIA) Pl. 10

Paulownia tomentosa (Thunb.) Sieb. & Zucc. ex Steud.
A medium-sized oriental tree with *large, paired heart-shaped* leaves, *chambered* or hollow pith, and clusters of *persistent* large nutlike fruits or husks. Naturalized in the South. Leaves velvety-hairy beneath, usually short-pointed and *not whorled.* Sometimes only with shallowly heart-shaped bases and frequently with 1 or more large teeth. Twigs stout, leaf scars circular, bundle scars numerous. Buds sometimes more than 1 above each leaf scar. Trunk bark rough, with interlaced smooth, often *shiny* areas. Leaves 6″–13″. Height 30′–60′; diameter 1′–2′. Flowers about 2″, *purplish* with yellow stripes inside, in large terminal clusters, April–May; buffy spikes of next year's flowers present after autumn. Fruits 1¼″–1¾″, somewhat *pecanlike woody capsules* containing many small, winged seeds; husks present all winter.
Similar species: Catalpas have solid white pith, sometimes whorled leaves, and long slender fruit capsules.

NORTHERN CATALPA (CATAWBA-TREE) Pl. 10

Catalpa speciosa Warder ex Engelm.
Similar to Princess-tree but with *solid* whitish pith and slender *cigar-shaped* fruits. Leaves paired or in whorls of 3, *long-pointed* and sometimes hairy beneath, with an unpleasant odor when crushed. Trunk bark scaly. Leaves 6″–13″. Height 50′–70′ (120′); diameter 2′–4′ (5′). Flowers *many,* in twig-end clusters, each 2½″–3″ across, white with *few* yellow and purple spots, May––June. Fruits slender pods *less than* ⅟₁₆″ thick and 10″–24″ long, containing many small seeds, Sept.–winter. Wet woods.
Similar species: (1) Princess-tree has chambered or hollow pith. (2) Southern Catalpa has short-pointed leaves and smaller flowers and fruits.
Remarks: Once planted for fence posts, but its rapid growth may be counteracted by insect, storm, and frost damage. Often highly productive of "catawba worms" for fish bait. Native to Mississippi Valley. See map, p. 68.

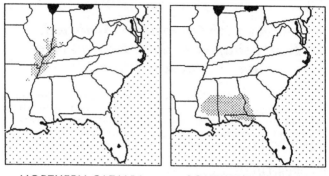

NORTHERN CATALPA   SOUTHERN CATALPA

SOUTHERN (COMMON) CATALPA   **Pl. 10**
Catalpa bignonioides Walt.
Resembles Northern Catalpa but smaller and with somewhat
short-pointed, non-odorous leaves. Height 40′–50′; diameter
1′–4′. Flowers *few* per cluster, each *1″–2″* across, with *numerous*
purple spots, May–July. Fruits 8″–15″ long and *more than* 7/16″
thick.
Remarks: Native to southeastern states but widely planted.

Trees with Opposite, Lobed Leaves: Maples (Plate 11)

Maples are our only trees with opposite, lobed leaves. Some
shrubby viburnums, however, also bear opposite, fan-lobed, ma-
plelike leaves. One of these, Cranberry Viburnum (American
Cranberry-bush, *Viburnum trilobum* Marsh.), is reported to attain small-tree size only rarely and only in Michigan. It is not
given full treatment here, but the three-lobed leaves are hairy
beneath and carry tiny dome-shaped leafstalk *glands* near the
leaf base (use lens). Unlike maples, Cranberry Viburnum has
fleshy red fruits with a single flat seed.
　A related species, Ashleaf Maple, bears opposite compound
leaves and is pictured with the ashes (Pl. 9). Maple flowers are
mostly small and greenish. The dry, double, winged fruits, known
as "keys," are eaten by many birds and by squirrels.
　The native maples are of great value for shade, ornament, and
lumber. Some species yield the delicious maple syrup and maple
sugar sold commercially. Porcupines sometimes eat the inner
bark of maples, and the twigs are a staple food of the cottontail
rabbit, snowshoe hare, white-tailed deer, and moose.

STRIPED MAPLE (MOOSEWOOD)   Pl. 11
Acer pensylvanicum L.

A small, slender, mostly northern tree with *green* bark vertically marked with thin *white stripes.* Leaves *three-lobed,* sometimes with 2 additional small lobes near base, lobes somewhat long-pointed. Foliage double-toothed, hairless, green on both sides, paler beneath. Twigs hairless, mostly greenish. Buds stalked, with *only 2* scales. Leaves 2″–10″. Height 5′–15′ (35′); diameter 1″–2″ (9″). Flowers at *twig ends* in long *hanging* clusters, May–June. Fruits ¾″–1″, June–Sept.

Similar species: Mountain Maple has darker, unstriped bark, hairy twigs, and erect flower clusters.

MOUNTAIN MAPLE   *Acer spicatum* Lam.   Pl. 11

Also a small, mostly northern tree but with bark dark or somewhat greenish and *not* white-striped. Leaves three- to five-lobed, coarsely toothed, hairless or slightly hairy beneath. Twigs *velvety-hairy,* mostly greenish. Buds stalked, with 2 scales. Leaves 2″–10″. Height mostly under 20′. Flowers in long *upright* twig-end clusters. May–Aug. Fruits ½″–¾″, July–Oct.

Similar species: See Striped Maple.

RED MAPLE   *Acer rubrum* L.   Pl. 11

A medium-sized tree with *smooth gray* young bark, at least on the upper trunk (almost white in some localities), and broken darker older bark. Leaves three- to five-lobed, *whitened* and hairless or hairy beneath. Notches (sinuses) between leaf lobes relatively *shallow;* base of terminal leaf lobe *wide.* Twigs and buds *reddish,* the latter blunt and several-scaled. Extra buds may be present above some side buds. Broken twigs do *not* have unpleasant odor. Leaves 2″–8″. Height 20′–40′ (100′); diameter 1′–2′ (4′). Flowers

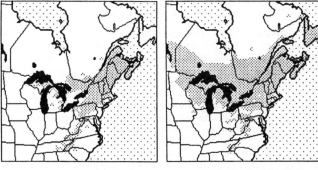

STRIPED MAPLE   MOUNTAIN MAPLE

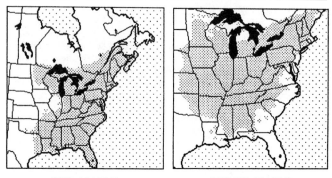

RED MAPLE   SILVER MAPLE

red, rarely yellow, in short clusters along the twigs, March–May. Fruits ½″–1″, reddish, May–July.
Similar species: Though variable, distinguished from (1) Silver Maple by shallow leaf notches, wide base of end leaf lobe, non-odorous twigs, and smoother trunk bark. (2) Sugar Maples that have whitened leaf undersides can be recognized by slender, pointed brown buds.
Remarks: Wood sometimes used for furniture.

SILVER MAPLE *Acer saccharinum* L.   **Pl. 11**
A tall tree with grayish older bark that tends to *flake,* leaving brown spots. Leaves *deeply five-lobed,* with base of terminal leaf lobe *narrowed.* Foliage *whitened,* sometimes hairy beneath. Twigs, buds, and flowers/fruit located as in Red Maple, but broken twigs have *unpleasant odor.* Leaves 2″–10″. Height 40′–60′ (120′); diameter 1′–3′ (5′). Flowers greenish or reddish, short-clustered, Feb.–May. Fruits 1½″–3″, greenish or reddish, April–June.
Similar species: See Red Maple.
Remarks: Sap sweet but less sugary than that of Sugar Maple.

SUGAR MAPLE *Acer saccharum* Marsh.   **Pl. 11**
A large tree with dark brown trunk bark marked with rough vertical grooves and ridges. Leaves mostly *five-lobed,* with moderately deep notches between lobes. Foliage *pale green* and usually hairless *beneath,* occasionally somewhat whitened. Leaf edges firm, *not* drooping. Leafstalk bases not much enlarged; stipules absent or small and not covering buds. Buds slender, sharp-pointed, brown. Side buds occur singly. Twigs glossy and reddish brown. Leaves 2″–10″. Height 40′–60′ (80′); diameter 1′–2′ (3′). Flowers yellowish, in clusters along twigs and at twig ends, April–June. Fruits 1″–1¼″, June–Sept.
Similar species: (1) Black Maple has shallowly lobed leaves with

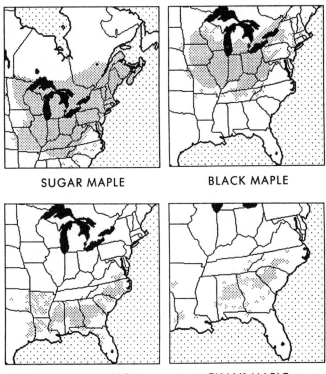

SUGAR MAPLE   BLACK MAPLE

FLORIDA MAPLE   CHALK MAPLE

drooping edges, larger stipules and leafstalk bases, and dull orange-tinged twigs. (2) Florida Maple has whitish gray bark, smaller, mostly three-lobed leaves, and whitened leaf undersides. **Remarks:** One of our most valuable hardwood trees. Neither sap nor wood is differentiated commercially from those of Black Maple; both species supply maple syrup as well as birdseye, curly, tiger, blister, and plain lumber. Wood much used for furniture. Declining vigor of Sugar Maples in some areas is attributed to acid rain.

BLACK MAPLE *Acer nigrum* Michx. f.   **Pl. 11**
Similar to Sugar Maple but with darker older bark and mostly *shallowly lobed* leaves that are darker green and more hairy. Leaf edges tend to *droop*. Leafstalks enlarged at the base and tending to enclose buds. Twigs duller, somewhat orange-brown.

FLORIDA MAPLE   *Acer barbatum* Michx.   **Pl. 11**
  Much like Sugar Maple but with smooth *light gray* bark on young
  trunk resembling that of Red Maple or Beech. Leaves small,
  whitened beneath, and mostly three-lobed. The lobes especially
  the central one, *narrowed* at the base. Leaves 2″–5″. Height
  20′–60′; diameter 1′–2′. Bottomlands and slopes of Coastal Plain
  and Piedmont. See map, p. 71.

CHALK MAPLE   *Acer leucoderme* Small.   **Pl. 11**
  Also related to Sugar Maple and with small leaves and light-
  colored bark like the Florida Maple. The leaves are *green* beneath,
  however, and the leaf lobes are *blunt* and *not narrowed* at the
  base. Height to 40′. Widespread in South but uncommon; bottomlands. See map, p. 71.

Trees with Opposite, Simple, Fine-toothed Leaves (Plate 12)

Surprisingly few woody plants have unlobed, simple, opposite,
toothed leaves. The maples (Pl. 11) have toothed opposite leaves,
but these are also deeply lobed.

COMMON BUCKTHORN   *Rhamnus cathartica* L.   **Pl. 12**
  A European shrub or tree with twigs ending in *sharp spines.*
  Leaves elliptical, hairless, fine-toothed. Leaf veins *depressed* from
  upper surface; main veins *sweep toward* leaf tip. A few leaves may
  be alternate rather than opposite. Twigs dark and unlined, buds
  with several scales and spur branches common. Bundle scars 3,
  occasionally fused and single. Inner bark *yellow.* Leaves 1½″–2″.
  Height to 16′ (26′). Flowers small, greenish, clustered at leaf
  angles and on spurs. May–June. Fruits dark and berrylike.
  Hedgerows and thickets, Nova Scotia and N. Dakota to N. Carolina and Kansas.
  Similar species: The combination of thorn-tipped twigs and
  yellow inner bark is distinctive. The only other thorny tree with
  opposite leaves is the silver-scaly Silver Buffaloberry (Pl. 14). The
  pattern of leaf veins is similar to that of dogwoods (Pl. 14), but
  buckthorn leaves are toothed.

SWAMP FORESTIERA   **Pl. 12**
  Forestiera acuminata (Michx.) Poir.
  An occasionally thorny shrub or small tree. Buds small, straw-
  colored, and *globular,* often more than 1 above each leaf scar.
  Leaves *long-pointed at both ends,* fine-toothed, usually attached
  in 2 planes but often clustered. Twigs hairless or slightly hairy,
  sometimes with small spur branches; buds globose, often multi-
  ple; bundle scars single. Leaves 1½″–3″. Height to 12′ (25′). Flow-

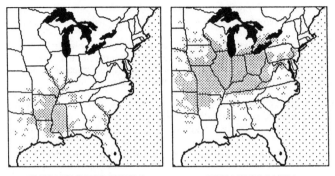

SWAMP FORESTIERA   BURNINGBUSH

ers small, along the twigs, March–May. Fruits small, fleshy, May–Oct. Coastal Plain swamps and riverbanks.
Similar species: Leaf shape of this species unique among shrubs with opposite toothed leaves. When it is thorny, it is the only prickly species with opposite leaves. (1) The only other plant with globose buds and single bundle scars is Buttonbush (Pl. 14), which has leaves often whorled, leaf scars connected by lines, and buds single above leaf scars. (2) See Common Buckthorn.
Remarks: Fruits eaten by wood ducks, mallards, other waterfowl.

BURNINGBUSH *Euonymus atropurpureus* Jacq.   **Pl. 12**
A shrub or small tree with *green, four-lined* twigs. Leaves egg-shaped or elliptic, short-pointed, fine-toothed, somewhat hairy beneath. Twigs nearly round, buds scaly, bundle scar single, leaf scars not connected by lines. Leaves 2″–6″. Height 6′–12′ (25′). Flowers purple, clustered in leaf angles, June–July. Fruits *reddish,* beneath *purplish woody* bracts, Aug.–Nov. Damp woods.
Similar species: Other opposite-leaved species with four-lined twigs have compound leaves: (1) Chastetree (p. 59) has spicy-scented twigs and fan-compound foliage. (2) Blue Ash (Pl. 8) has feather-compound leaves, gray twigs, and 4 or more bundle scars.
Remarks: Fruits reported to be poisonous to children. Recorded as eaten by only a few birds.

VIBURNUMS   **Pls. 12, 13**
Though widespread and common in the eastern U.S., viburnums are difficult to identify as a group. Few of the common names ordinarily include the word "viburnum," and no all-inclusive vegetative characteristics define the group. Most are shrubs. All viburnums, however, have small fleshy fruits containing single flat seeds. Usually the flowers are small and white. They and the

fruits occur in mostly flat-topped clusters 3″–5″ across and growing at the twig tips. Bundle scars are 3. Unlike dogwoods, the leaf scars are *not* raised.

The viburnums that grow to tree size have buds with only 2 scales and leaves with either fine teeth or none. The 3 species on Pl. 12 have foliage that is always toothed. The 2 species on Pl. 13 have somewhat leathery leaves with no teeth.

RUSTY BLACKHAW *Viburnum rufidulum* Raf.   **Pl. 12**
A southern shrub or small tree with short, somewhat flexible side twigs. Leaves elliptic to egg-shaped, blunt or somewhat pointed (but not long-pointed), sharply fine-toothed, and *shiny-surfaced.* Leaf undersides (at least midribs), leafstalks, buds, and sometimes twigs, *densely red-hairy.* Leafstalks *winged.* Foliage may become somewhat leathery. Buds short. Leaf scars narrow. Trunk bark dark, divided into many small, squarish blocks. Leaves 1″–4″. Height 6′–18′ (40′); diameter 2″–10″ (18″). Flowers April–May. Fruits blackish, Sept.–Oct. Woods and thickets.
Similar species: (1) Smooth Blackhaw has leaves and buds not

Viburnums

Leaves with fine teeth or none; white flowers and dark fleshy fruits in flat-topped clusters 2½″–5″ across; leaf scars narrow, with 3 bundle scars; buds with 2 scales. Species and remarks	Distribution	Leaves with fine teeth	Leaf length (inches)	Leaves shiny above	Leaves long-pointed	Leaf bases wedge-shaped	Side twigs short, stiff
Smooth Blackhaw *Viburnum prunifolium* Buds brown, short. See Pl. 12.	N	+	1–3	−	−	−	+
Nannyberry *V. lentago* Scales cover flower buds. See Pl. 12.	N	+	2–5	−	+	−	−
Rusty Blackhaw *V. rufidulum* Leaves/buds red-hairy. See Pl. 12.	S	+	1–4	+	−	±	±
Small-leaf Viburnum[1] *V. obovatum* Leaves short-stalked, blunt, dotted.[2] See Pl. 13.	S	−	1–2	+	−	+	+
Possumhaw Viburnum[1] *V. nudum* Scales partly cover flower buds. See Pl. 13.	S	−	3–5	+	−	±	−

[1] Occasionally leaves may bear some teeth.
[2] Use lens.

hairy; Nannyberry has long-pointed leaves and large flower buds. In trunk bark, (2) Flowering Dogwood (Pl. 14), (3) Persimmon, and (4) Sourgum (Pl. 44) are similar.
Remarks: Fruits eaten by foxes, bobwhites, and several songbirds. Some people also like them.

SMOOTH BLACKHAW   *Viburnum prunifolium* L.   **Pl. 12**
More northern than Rusty Blackhaw; this species has *dull,* nearly hairless leaves and brown buds that are powder-covered or somewhat brown-hairy. Leafstalks *not winged* or with very narrow wings. Twigs mostly stiff and short; buds short-pointed. Leaves 1″–3″. Height 6′–15′ (30′); diameter 2″–6″ (10″). Woods and old fields.

NANNYBERRY   *Viburnum lentago* L.   **Pl. 12**
A northern shrub or small tree with sharply fine-toothed and

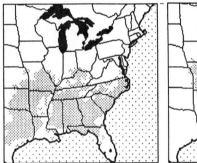

RUSTY BLACKHAW

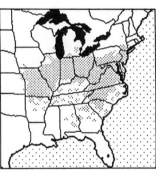

SMOOTH BLACKHAW

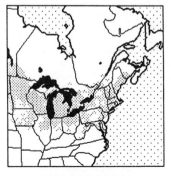

NANNYBERRY

short- to rather *long-pointed* leaves. Leaves hairless or nearly so and somewhat egg-shaped to narrowly elliptic. Leafstalks winged. Twigs long and flexible. The brown or gray buds are long, slender, and have rough-granular scales. They are of 2 sizes, the larger flower buds being *completely covered* by the 2 scales. Twigs rough-granular and side twigs flexible. Leaves 2″–5″. Height 9′–18′ (30′); diameter 1″–3″ (10″). Flowers, May–June. Fruits blue-black, Aug.–Sept. Woods.

Similar species: The only tree viburnum whose leaves and buds are regularly long and slender. Possumhaw Viburnum (Pl. 13) has the large flower buds *not* completely covered by scales.

BASKET WILLOW   *Salix purpurea* L.   **Pl. 39**
Many or even most leaves may be opposite. See Pl. 39 and p. 185.

Trees with Opposite Simple Leaves, Not Toothed and Mostly Leathery (Plate 13)

Trees with opposite, *leathery evergreen* leaves are few north of Florida, and those few typically range on the southern Coastal Plain. Among these, Possumhaw Viburnum extends north on the Coastal Plain to s. Connecticut and has leaves that are not always leathery, especially in northern areas. Yet this species is reviewed here as being in association with the viburnums on Pl. 12. The 2 viburnums on this plate may carry some leaves that are wavy-edged or have only a few teeth. In Florida, see also Pls. F-13A and F-13B. The mangroves are restricted to s. Florida except for the Black Mangrove, whose range extends locally around the Gulf of Mexico.

SMALL-LEAF VIBURNUM   **Pl. 13**
Viburnum obovatum Walt.
A common evergreen shrub or small tree of the southeastern states. Leaves *1″–2½″* long, *short-stalked, wedge-based,* widest and sometimes slightly toothed near the *blunt* tip. Twigs mostly short and stiff, sometimes with spur branches; buds *two-scaled,* brown, and very small. Leaves 1″–2″. Flowers small, white, in flat-topped *end* clusters, March–April; fruits fleshy, black, about ¼″, Sept.–Oct. Wet sites.

Similar species: Florida Forestiera has 4 or more bud scales, only 1 bundle scar, and slender fruits growing in the leaf angles.

POSSUMHAW VIBURNUM   *Viburnum nudum* L.   **Pl. 13**
A small Coastal Plain tree whose principal range is in the South. Leaves are glossy and somewhat leathery (but non-evergreen). They are pointed, often wavy-edged, but rarely fine-toothed.

Twigs long and flexible, glossy or fine-grooved, and with slender brown leaf buds. Flower buds larger, only partly covered by the 2 scales. The single slender end bud usually leans to 1 side. Leaves 3″–5″. Height to 20′. Flowers small, white, May–July. Fruits fleshy, blue, July–Oct. or later. Bottomland forests.

Similar species: (1) Devilwood has evergreen leaves, short blunt buds, and leaf scars with a single bundle scar. (2) See also Pl. 14. (3) Possumhaw Holly (p. 186) is an alternate-leaved plant.

DEVILWOOD *Osmanthus americanus* (L.) Gray   **Pl. 13**
Leaves evergreen, shiny, thick, narrow, green or pale beneath, and with edges rolled under. Twigs hairless, stout, *whitish;* buds *small,* sometimes one above the other. Bundle scar 1. Leaves

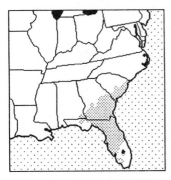

SMALL-LEAF VIBURNUM

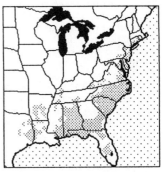

POSSUMHAW VIBURNUM

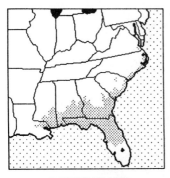

DEVILWOOD

FLORIDA FORESTIERA

2″–6″. Height to 50′. Flowers small, white, fragrant clusters in leaf angles. April–May. Fruits blue, fleshy, one-seeded, about ⅜″ long, June. Bottomlands and swamps.
Similar species: (1) The foliage somewhat resembles that of Mountain Laurel (Pl. 46), whose wider leaves are occasionally opposite. (2) Possumhaw Viburnum has non-evergreen leaves, longer buds, 3 bundle scars, and flat seeds.

FLORIDA FORESTIERA   Pl. 13
Forestiera segregata (Jacq.) Krug & Urban
A southern shrub or small tree of coastal Georgia and Florida with small leathery leaves and tiny buds. Bud scales are 4 or more and buds sometimes above each other. Bundle scars 1. Leaves 1″–2½″. Height to 15′. The small flowers lack petals; clusters are produced in the leaf angles of the branchlets. Spring. Fruits small, fleshy, *slender, black,* and one-seeded. Leaves 1″–2½″. Height to 15′. Swamps. See map, p. 77.
Similar species: (1) Swamp Forestiera (Pl. 12) has toothed leaves. (2) See Small-leaf Viburnum.
Remarks: Like Devilwood, forestieras are members of the olive family.

RED MANGROVE   *Rhizophora mangle* L.   Pl. 13
All mangroves grow in the vicinity of salt water, standing in shallows along tropical and subtropical coasts and inlets. This s. Florida species usually occurs in the deeper shallows and is marked by *arching prop roots* (see Fig. 10). Leaves more or less blunt-tipped and wedge-based, clustered near the twig tips, green beneath, and sometimes with *black dots.* End buds enclosed by a pair of slender stipules 1″–3″ long. These fall as the leaves grow, leaving scars that *encircle* the twigs. Bud scales 2; bundle scars 3. Wood reddish brown, heavy. Leaves 2″–6″. Height to 80′. Flowers

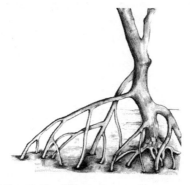

Fig. 10. Red Mangrove with prop roots.

pale yellow, in leaf angles, all year. Fruits 1″–1½″, leathery, brown, germinating and growing much longer even before dropping from the parent tree.
Similar species: (1) Black and (2) White mangroves have erect breather roots and grow in more shallow water. White Mangrove has rounded leaf bases and bears leafstalk glands.

BLACK MANGROVE *Avicennia germinans* (L.) L.   **Pl. 13**
Ranges widely along Florida coasts and also west to s. Louisiana and s. Texas. Occupies shallower embayments than the last species and lives also in brackish and fresh waters near the coast. The numerous *erect breather roots* (see Fig. 11) are a useful first field mark. The thick, blunt-tipped and wedge-based leaves are *whitish hairy* beneath and often display salt grains on the surface. The leaves arise from squarish *ringed* twigs; leaf scars bear a *single* bundle scar. Bud scales 2. Wood dark brown to black. Leaves 2″–6″. Height to 65′. Flowers white, fragrant, at twig ends, May–July or over a longer period in tropical countries. Fruits 1″, yellow-green, irregularly egg-shaped but pointed, splitting, germinating while on the tree, Sept.–Oct. or later.
Similar species: See Red and White mangroves.
Remarks: As on other mangroves, the root systems slow water movements and cause sand, silt, and debris to become deposited, thus extending the shoreline seaward. Bees produce an excellent honey from the blossoms.

Fig. 11. Black Mangrove with breather roots.

WHITE MANGROVE   Not illus.
Laguncularia racemosa (L.) Gaertn. f.
Resembles the Black Mangrove in having erect breather roots,
but these are fewer, wider, and more often branched than in that
species. The 2″–3″ leaves, approximately the same color on both
sides, are marked by *paired leafstalk glands*. Twigs *not* ringed and
buds *without* scales. Wood yellow-brown, heavy. Height to 65′.
Flowers white, fragrant, in loose clusters, at twig ends, April–
June. Fruits fleshy, reddish, ¾," germinating on the tree,
Aug.–Sept. S. Florida coasts.
Similar species: White Mangrove grows landward of (1) Red and
(2) Black mangroves. It often occurs onshore with (3) Buttonwood,
a related but alternate-leaved plant (Pl. F-46A) with leafstalk
glands not as prominent as those of the White Mangrove.
Remarks: Distributed in tropical America and Africa.

CAMPHOR-TREE   Pl. 46
Cinnamomum camphora (L.) J. S. Presl.
Some leaves may be opposite. Glands on leaf veins beneath.

FLORIDA-ONLY TREES   Pls. F-13A and F-13B
There are 13 species with opposite, mostly leathery, non-toothed
leaves, plus Red and White mangroves (above), that do not occur
north of *peninsular* Florida. Most extend throughout s. Florida.
See Pl. F-13A.
    Fourteen species do not occur north of the 3 southernmost
(tropical) counties of Collier, Dade, and Monroe. Five of these
trees have been observed only on the Florida Keys, south of the
mainland. See Pl. F-13B.

Trees with Opposite Simple Leaves, Neither Toothed nor Leathery (Plate 14)

The remaining trees with opposite simple leaves without teeth
have thin and membranous leaves as in most plants. Of the
several dogwood species in the eastern United States, 3 reach tree
size. Only the Flowering Dogwood has large blossoms; the other
2 species have small flowers in clusters at the twig ends. All
dogwoods, however, have leaf veins which tend to *follow* the outer
edge of the leaf. Dogwoods have 2 bud scales and 3 bundle scars
per leaf scar. In contrast to viburnums, the leaf scars on dogwood
twigs are *raised*. Possumhaw Viburnum (Pl. 13 and p. 76), with
leaves usually leathery, may sometimes have thin, nonleathery
foliage like the plants shown on this plate. See also Basket
Willow, p. 185 and Pl. 39.

ROUGHLEAF DOGWOOD   Pl. 14
Cornus drummondii C. A. Meyer

A midwestern shrub or, in the South, a medium-sized tree. Leaves *sandpapery above, woolly beneath,* egg-shaped or elliptic with 3–5 pairs of veins. Twigs *red-brown* or brownish; branchlets brown or gray. Buds slender, somewhat hairy, pointed. Pith *brown,* rarely white. Leaves 2″–5″. Height 1′–15′ (50′); diameter 2″–8″ (10″). Flowers small, whitish, in round-topped clusters, May–June. Fruits white, ³⁄₁₆″–¼″, Aug.–Oct.

Similar species: No other dogwood has sandpapery leaves. Both the (1) Flowering and (2) Stiff dogwoods have white pith.

Remarks: Fruits eaten by many songbirds and by prairie chicken, sharp-tailed and ruffed grouse, bobwhite, wild turkey, pheasant.

FLOWERING DOGWOOD   *Cornus florida* L.   Pl. 14

A small to medium-sized tree with hidden side buds and *stalked* flower buds. Leaves hairless or nearly so, elliptic to egg- or wedge-shaped, *5–6 pairs* of veins. Twigs and branchlets sometimes green, *mostly dark purple,* often swollen from insect attacks. Flower buds globular, *stalked.* Pith white. Trunk bark dark, *deeply checkered* like an alligator hide. Leaves 2″–5″. Height 10′–40′; diameter 12″–18″. Flowers small, clustered, each cluster with 4 (rarely 6–8) *large white or, seldom, pink bracts* (not true petals). March–June. Fruits *red* or rarely yellow. Aug.–Nov.

Similar species: The only dogwood with showy white bracts, hidden side buds, and stalked flower buds. Checkered bark less corky than similar bark of (1) blackhaw viburnums (Pl. 12), (2) Persimmon, and (3) Sourgum (Pl. 44).

Remarks: Powdered bark is reported to have been made into a

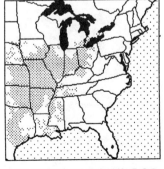

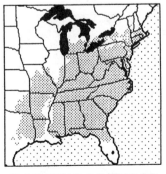

ROUGHLEAF DOGWOOD   FLOWERING DOGWOOD

toothpaste, a black ink (when mixed with iron sulphate), and a quinine substitute. Bark of the roots yields a scarlet dye. Shuttles, bobbins, tool handles, mallets, and the heads of golf clubs are manufactured from the hard, close-grained wood. Humans find the bitter red fruits inedible, but with twigs, they are important foods for numerous song and game birds, skunks, deer, rabbits, and squirrels.

STIFF DOGWOOD   Not illus.
Cornus stricta Lam. (*C. foemina* Mill.)
A stiff-branched shrub or small tree with leaves green on both sides, slightly paler beneath, somewhat long-tipped, 4–5 pairs of veins. Twigs and branchlets *reddish* or brown; pith white. End bud often absent, leaving *paired lateral buds* at the twig end and resulting in forked branching. Leaves 2″–5″. Height to 15′. Flowers small, whitish, in somewhat *round-topped clusters,* May–June. Fruits *blue.* Aug.–Oct. Wet places.

BUTTONBUSH *Cephalanthus occidentalis* L.   Pl. 14
An *aquatic* shrub with leaves over 2½″ long, often occurring in 3's and 4's, elliptic and short-pointed. Leafstalks often red. Side buds embedded in bark. Twigs round, hairless, not ringed, with single bundle scar. Leaves 3″–6″. Height 3′–8′ (18′). Flowers small, white, tubular, densely clustered in *ball-like heads* at twig ends. May–Aug. Fruits small, dry, Sept.–Dec. or later.
Similar species: Pinckneya occurs only in the South. It has larger leaves, ringed twigs, and bell-shaped flowers.
Remarks: Honey plant. Wilted leaves may poison stock.

PINCKNEYA *Pinckneya pubens* Michx.   Fig. 12
An uncommon small tree of the se. Coastal Plain. Leaves *large* (3″–8″), sometimes in 3's or 4's, hairy, and tapering at both ends.

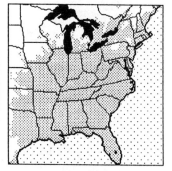

STIFF DOGWOOD   BUTTONBUSH

Fig. 12

The twigs are round, hairless or slightly hairy, and *ringed*. Buds have centrally ridged scales and sometimes occur one above the other. Leaf scars are raised, with 1 bundle scar. Pith is white. Height to 25′. Large, pinkish, petal-like sepals form *conspicuous, bell-shaped blossom clusters* at the twig ends, May. Fruits dry, 1″, or two-parted capsules, Aug.–Sept. Damp soils.

Remarks: As a relative of *Chincona,* the plant that produces quinine, this species was once thought to be a useful substitute and gained the alternate names of Fevertree and Georgia-bark.

FRINGETREE   *Chionanthus virginicus* L.   **Pl. 14**
A shrub or small tree with leaves moderately large, non-evergreen, non-aromatic, and hairless or nearly so, narrowly egg-shaped to elliptic. Twigs moderately stout, more than ¹⁄₁₆″ thick, slightly hairy or hairless. Buds scaly, bundle scar 1. Leaves 3″–8″. Height 8′–18′ (35′); diameter 1″–4″ (8″). Flowers white, in

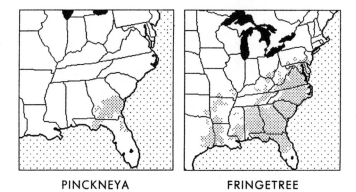

PINCKNEYA   FRINGETREE

drooping clusters from side buds, petals very slender, May–June.
Fruits purple, ball-shaped, fleshy, Sept.–Oct. Floodplains.
Similar species: (1) The privets have twigs less than $\frac{1}{16}$" thick.
(2) Viburnums (Pls. 12, 13) have only 2 bud scales. (3) Ashes (Pls.
8, 9) have larger leaf scars and more bundle scars.
Remarks: The showy flower clusters give rise to the alternate
common name of Old-Man's-Beard.

CALIFORNIA PRIVET   Pl. 14
Ligustrum ovalifolium Hassk.
A Japanese shrub or small tree planted widely and escaping from
cultivation in the southeastern states. Leaves firm, shiny, sometimes evergreen, slightly less than $2\frac{1}{2}$" long, elliptic, and hairless. Leafstalks *less than* $\frac{1}{4}$" long. Twigs slender ($\frac{1}{16}$" or less thick)
and *hairless*. The buds have 8–12 or more *long-pointed* scales.
Leaf scars are much raised and contain only a single bundle scar.
Leaves 1"–$2\frac{1}{4}$". Height to 15'. Flowers small, white, in cone-
shaped clusters at twig ends, June–July. Fruits small, black
berries, Sept.–Oct. or longer.
Similar species: (1) The next 2 privets have either fewer and less
pointed bud scales or hairy twigs. (2) In winter, Fringetree has
stouter twigs.

JAPANESE PRIVET   *Ligustrum japonicum* Thumb.   Not illus.
Similar to the California Privet in having hairless twigs, but the
leafstalks are *more than* $\frac{1}{4}$" long and the buds are tighter, darker,
and have *fewer* pointed (but *not long-pointed*) scales. The leaves
are sometimes longer, 2"–4". This oriental species is planted in the
Southeast and has become naturalized in some localities.

CHINESE PRIVET   *Ligustrum sinense* Lour.   Not illus.
Similar to the California Privet but with twigs fine-hairy. Widely
escaped in the southeastern region.

SILVER BUFFALOBERRY   Pl. 14
Shepherdia argentea (Pursh) Nutt.
A *western* shrub or small tree with twigs and somewhat leathery,
wedge-shaped leaves covered with *silver scales*. Small leaves may
be present at bases of leafstalks. Twigs often thorn-tipped. Buds
two-scaled, with narrowed bases. Leaves $1\frac{1}{2}$"–$2\frac{1}{2}$". Height to 15'.
Flowers small, greenish yellow, bell-shaped, along the twigs.
April–June. Fruits bright red, berrylike, July–Sept. Streambanks.
Similar species: The only opposite-leaved plant with all-silver
scales. (1) Russian-olive (p. 177) also has all-silver scales but has
narrow alternate leaves. It is widely planted on the prairies as a
windbreak and in the East for ornament. (2) The opposite-leaved
Canada Buffaloberry [*S. canadensis* (L.) Nutt.] and (3) the

alternate-leaved American Silverberry (*Elaeagnus commutata* Bernh.) have brown and silver scales, but both are shrubs.
Remarks: Fruits, sometimes known as soapberries (but see p. 108), contain a bitter substance that foams in water.

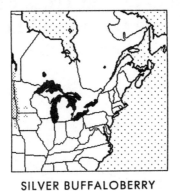

SILVER BUFFALOBERRY

IV

Broad-leaved Trees with Alternate Compound Leaves (Plates 15–22)

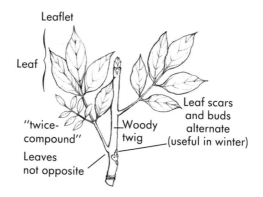

Fig. 13. Alternate compound leaves.

Relatively few trees have compound leaves. Those with opposite leaves were presented in Section II (Pls. 6–9). The rest are in this section. In winter, the alternate leaf scars may sometimes indicate by their large size the former presence of compound leaves. Where there is doubt, however, the twigs of a leafless unknown plant with alternate leaf scars will have to be compared with the illustrations of *both* Sections IV and V or will have to be identified by means of the Winter Key in Appendix A. **Warning:** Poison-ivy, Poison-sumac, and several tropical trees, including Florida Poisonwood (see Fig. 4) have leaves of this type. Do not handle them. Be careful of unknown plants of this type.

1. Plants thorny:
>   **2.** Specimens growing north of Florida. **Locust, etc., Pl. 15.**
>   **2.** Specimens found growing in Florida. **See Pls. 15, F-15.**

1. Plants without thorns:
>   **3.** Leaves only once-compound:
>>   **4.** Leaflets toothed (though in Tree-of-heaven with only 1 basal pair of glandular teeth):
>>>   **5.** Buds easily visible (somewhat hidden in Tree-of-heaven):
>>>>   **6.** Leaflets mostly 11–14 (rarely 7–9):
>>>>>   **7.** Buds white-woolly, brown-woolly, or red-gummy.   **Walnuts, etc., Pl. 16.**
>>>>>   **7.** Buds yellow, yellow-brown, or brown-hairy.   **Hickories I, Pl. 17.**
>>>>   **6.** Leaflets 5–9:
>>>>>   **8.** End buds more than ½″ long; twigs stout.   **Hickories II, Pl. 18.**
>>>>>   **8.** End buds less than ½″ long; twigs slender.   **Hickories III, Pl. 19.**
>>>   **5.** Buds nearly hidden beneath the leafstalk bases.   **Sumacs, Pl. 20.**
>>   **4.** Leaflets not toothed (sometimes wavy-edged):
>>>   **9.** Bundle scars more than 5.   **Sumacs, Pl. 20.**
>>>   **9.** Bundle scars 1–5:
>>>>   **10.** Leaves thin, deciduous.   **Hoptree, etc., Pl. 21.**
>>>>   **10.** Leaves leathery, evergreen.   **Florida species, Pls. F-21A and B.**
>   **3.** Leaves twice- or thrice-compound (leaflets as well as leaves divided into leaflets):
>>   **11.** Trees of cen. and s. Florida.   **Lebbek, etc., Pls. 22, F-22.**
>>   **11.** Trees of the Midwest and South.   **Chinaberry, etc., Pl. 22.**

Thorny Trees with Alternate Feather-compound Leaves (Plate 15)

The following few species are the only thorny trees with compound leaves, whether alternate or opposite. Most of these species (the bean-producing legumes and the Trifoliate Orange) have smooth-edged or fine-toothed leaflets whose leafstalks never bear thorns. The prickly-ashes have more coarsely toothed leaflets and often thorny leafstalks. The upright thorny plants with alternate simple leaves appear on Pls. 23–24. For the few opposite-leaved thorny trees, see Pls. 12 and 14. In Florida see also Pl. F-15.

HONEY LOCUST *Gleditsia triacanthos* L.   **Pl. 15**
A tall tree with *feather-compound* leaves, often some *twice-compound* leaves. Bark dark, somewhat scaly, in the wild uncultivated form. Numerous stout *branched thorns,* each *several inches* long, are usually present; a thornless cultivated variety is becoming widely planted. Leaves divided into numerous narrow leaflets, which may be slightly toothed. The leaflets, in turn, are frequently subdivided. Hairless buds, hidden by the leafstalk bases in summer, are surrounded by leaf scars when twigs are leafless. They may be supplemented by smaller buds located just above them. End buds false. Twigs stout; bundle scars 3. Leaves 6″–15″. Height 70′–80′ (140′); diameter 2′–3′ (6′). Flowers small, greenish, clustered May–July. Fruits *8″–18″,* flattened twisted pods with sweet pulp between numerous oval seeds, Sept.–Feb.
Similar species: (1) Only Water Locust has equally long thorns. (2) Black Locust has small paired thorns.
Remarks: Honey Locust, believed originally to have been restricted to Mississippi Valley, is now common eastward. The long thorns have been used by woodsmen for pins, spear points, and animal traps. Heavy, durable wood used for railroad ties, fence posts, and agricultural implements. Unlike most legumes, the tree does not harbor root bacteria capable of fixing nitrogen. Fruits eaten by cattle, deer, rabbits, squirrels, and bobwhite.

WATER LOCUST *Gleditsia aquatica* Marsh.   **fruit, Pl. 15**
Similar to Honey Locust but smaller, with leaflets somewhat shorter, thorns mostly *unbranched,* and fruit pods *1″–2″,* pulpless,

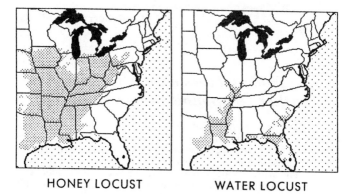

HONEY LOCUST   WATER LOCUST

containing only 1–3 seeds. Coastal Plain and Mississippi flood-plain swamps.
Similar species: A hybrid Water/Honey Locust is reported from the lower Mississippi Valley.

TRIFOLIATE ORANGE   *Poncirus trifoliata* (L.) Raf.   **Fig. 14**

A shrub or small tree imported from the Orient and often planted as a hedge in the South. Easily identified by stiff *green* twigs that bear many stout *green* thorns. Leaves divided into 3 small, blunt, wavy-edged leaflets. Crushed leaves aromatic and leafstalks *winged.* Buds bright red, ball-like; leaf scars very small, with 1 scarcely visible bundle scar; end buds false. Small citrus fruits are bitter. Height rarely to 20'. Flowers white, April–May. Fruits Sept.–Oct. Thickets.

SOUTHEASTERN CORALBEAN   **Fig. 14**

Erythrina herbacea L.

A shrub in most of the southeastern U.S., this species attains tree size in s. Florida. The leaves are three-parted, with the leaflets rather triangular or *nearly three-lobed,* long-pointed, and smooth-edged. The midrib may be prickly beneath. The stout green twigs often bear curved thorns. Bundle scars indefinite. Bark smooth to ridged, gray, with some thorns. Leaves 6"–8". Flowers red, tubular, in showy upright clusters, April–June. Fruits are slim, *beaded* pods, 3"–6" long, containing poisonous *red* seeds.

NORTHERN PRICKLY-ASH   **Pl. 15**

Zanthoxylum americanum Mill.

A shrub or small tree, often thicket-forming, with *paired prickles* flanking leaf scars and buds. Leaves once-compound, with 5–11

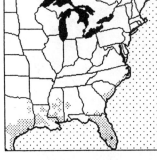

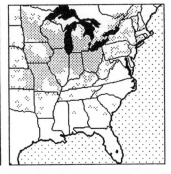

SOUTHEASTERN
CORALBEAN

NORTHERN PRICKLY-ASH

egg-shaped, hairless leaflets that are quite finely toothed, and often with *prickly* leafstalks. Foliage has *lemonlike odor* when crushed and is *hairy* when young. Buds small, blunt, *red-hairy,* located above leaf scars. Bundle scars 3. True end buds present. Specimens without prickles are encountered rarely. Leaves 3″–10″. Height 4′–10′ (25′). Flowers small, greenish, clustered, April–May. Fruits small, dry, reddish brown, one- to two-seeded (not bean-type) pods, Aug.–Oct.

Similar species: (1) Among once-compound thorny trees with many leaflets, the locusts have hidden buds, leafstalks that are not prickly, and beanpod fruits. (2) See Southern Prickly-ash.

Remarks: A member of the citrus family. Leaves, fruits, or bark were once chewed to cure toothache. Known as Toothache-tree in some places. The genus is also spelled *Xanthoxylum.*

SOUTHERN PRICKLY-ASH   leaf, Pl. 15
Zanthoxylum clava-herculis L.

This southern shrub or tree is similar to but larger than the northern species. Has a peculiar smooth gray trunk bark decorated with scattered *large corky knobs,* often prickle-tipped. Leaflets toothed, somewhat curved and *asymmetrical.* Buds small, blunt, dark, *hairless.* Leaves 8″–16″. Height 10′–20′ (50′); diameter 4″–8″ (18″). Poor Coastal Plain soils.

Remarks: This species and *Aralia spinosa,* also in this group, are both known alternatively as Hercules-club.

BLACK LOCUST   Pl. 15
Robinia pseudoacacia L.

A medium-sized tree with *once-compound* leaves. Leaflets 6–20, blunt, egg-shaped. Strong ½″–1″ *paired thorns* flank nearly circular leaf scars. *Hidden* white-hairy buds burst through leaf scars

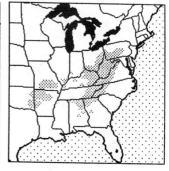

SOUTHERN PRICKLY-ASH   BLACK LOCUST

upon enlargement. Tiny additional buds may be present above the leaf scars. Twigs moderately stout, hairless; bundle scars 3. End buds false. Bark on old trunks dark, deeply ridged, and cross-hatched. Leaves 6″–12″. Height 70′–80′ (100′); diameter 2′–3′ (6′). Flowers medium-sized, *white*, clustered, fragrant, May–June. Fruits 2″–6″ long, flat pods, Sept.–April.

Similar species: Among other once-compound species, other *Robinia* locusts have bristly, glandular, or hairy twigs and mostly hidden buds. (1) Prickly-ashes are smaller trees and have exposed buds, toothed leaflets, and usually thorny leafstalks. (2) Honey and Water locusts have large unpaired thorns. (3) Southeastern Coralbean has only 3 leaflets.

Remarks: Black Locusts are often planted for fence posts. Wood strong, hard, and durable in the soil. Young shoots and bark sometimes poisonous to livestock, but seeds eaten by bobwhite, pheasant, mourning dove, cottontail rabbit, snowshoe hare, and deer.

CLAMMY LOCUST   *Robinia viscosa* Vent.   **twig, Pl. 15**
A shrub or small tree; leaves similar to those of Black Locust. Thorns paired, *weak*, usually no more than ¼″ long; twigs covered with *sticky glands*. Bark smooth, light brown, marked with short horizontal streaks. Leaves 6″–12″. Height 5′–20′ (40′); diameter 1″–3″ (6″). Flowers *pink*, not fragrant, May. Fruits sticky pods, 2″–3″, Aug.–Sept. Mountain woods.

KELSEY LOCUST   *Robinia kelseyi* Hutch.   Not illus.
Localized in the mountains of western N. Carolina, this shrub or small tree resembles the other Robinias, but the leaflets are *narrow* and pointed, the leaves and twigs are *hairless,* and the 2″–3″ fruit pods are *sticky-hairy*. Leaves 4″–6″ with 9–16 leaflets. Flowers *pink*, spring. Woods.

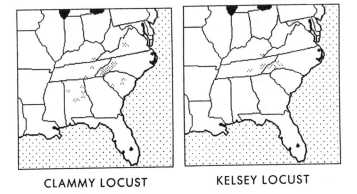

CLAMMY LOCUST   KELSEY LOCUST

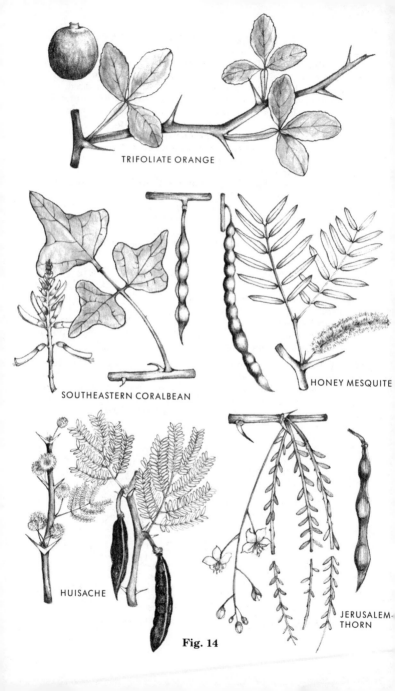

TRIFOLIATE ORANGE

SOUTHEASTERN CORALBEAN

HONEY MESQUITE

HUISACHE

JERUSALEM-THORN

Fig. 14

HONEY MESQUITE   *Prosopis glandulosa* Torr.   **Fig. 14**

A thorny *southwestern* shrub or small tree whose drooping, twice-compound leaves have 4–10 major portions (pinnae), each bearing 12–20 *narrow 1″–2″* leaflets. Usually single (less commonly paired) 1″–2″ spines and short knobby *spurs* occur at the leafstalk bases. Occasionally thornless. Leaves 6″–8″. Height to 30′. Flowers small, greenish yellow, in elongate spikes. May–Sept. Fruits 4″–10″ beans, somewhat beaded and flattened.

Similar species: (1) Huisache has tiny leaflets, thorns invariably paired, ball-shaped flower clusters, and shorter fruit pods. (2) Jerusalem-thorn has long, slender, grasslike leaves with early-falling, tiny (less than ¼″ long) leaflets. Grasslands and pastures.

Remarks: A plant of western rangelands whose seeds are spread by livestock and white-tailed deer and possibly also by javelinas, raccoons, and other wildlife. Foliage is consumed by hoofed animals; fruits and seeds are eaten by numerous mammals and birds. Mesquite beans have been pounded into a nutritious flour by native Americans and others; reported also to have been fermented and made into a beverage. A gum exuded from the branches is said to have been chewed as candy and used to mend pottery.

HUISACHE   *Acacia farnesiana* (L.) Willd.   **Fig. 14**

This shrub or small tree has finely divided twice-compound foliage. There are 4–8 pairs of side pinnae, each of which is subdivided into *numerous* ¼″-long *leaflets*. A pair of 1″–3″ thorns occurs at the leafstalk bases. Buds small; end buds false. Bundle scars single. Leaves 2″–4″. Height to 30′. Flowers in fragrant, ball-shaped, yellow, long-stalked clusters. Fruits stout, brownish pods, 2″–3″ long.

Similar species: Silktree (Pl. 22) is thornless and has larger leaves and leaflets and pink flowers.

Remarks: Southwestern in its original distribution but now becoming widespread in the Gulf states. Cultivated in Europe for perfume. Sap has been used as a glue. Pronounced weesatch-ay.

JERUSALEM-THORN   *Parkinsonia aculeata* L.   **Fig. 14**

Thorny green-barked shrub or small tree whose 40–60 tiny (⅛″–³⁄₁₆″) leaflets drop early, leaving 2–4 evergreen *grasslike* midribs, 10″–15″ long, on the plant to represent the primary leaflets of the twice-compound leaf. One or more thorns occur at the leafstalk bases, one usually being larger (to 1″). The green and drooping twigs tend to have fine lengthwise grooves. Bundle scars 3. Flowers yellow, pealike, spring and summer. Fruits 2″–4″ bean pods. Dry soils, Gulf states. Also called Paloverde, though this name is better reserved for species of *Cercidium,* a group of western desert plants.

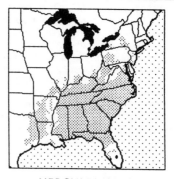

HERCULES-CLUB

HERCULES-CLUB　*Aralia spinosa* L.　　　　　　　　**Pl. 15**
A *very spiny* shrub or small tree with *very large twice- or even thrice-compound* leaves. Trunk and twigs stout, with numerous coarse prickles. Leaflets toothed, pointed; leafstalks thorny. Long, narrow leaf scars have about 20 bundle scars. End buds may be false. Leaves 2′–4′. Height 5′–15′ (35′); diameter 1″–4″ (9″). Flowers white, in flat-topped clusters, July–Sept. Fruits black, fleshy, one-seeded, Aug.–Nov.
Similar species: Prickly stout stems and V-shaped leaf scars with numerous bundle scars are distinctive at all seasons.
Remarks: This species is sometimes called Devil's Walking-stick. The name "Hercules-club" is also an alternate name for the Southern Prickly-ash (p. 90).

FLORIDA-ONLY TREES　　　　　　　　　　　**Pl. F-15**
Seven species of thorny trees with compound leaves occur only in s. and cen. Florida.

Walnuts and Similar Trees (Plate 16)

These are trees with alternate, feather-compound leaves. The leaflets are numerous and toothed, although the Tree-of-heaven often has only one pair of gland-bearing teeth at the leaflet bases.

BLACK WALNUT　*Juglans nigra* L.　　　　　　　　**Pl. 16**
A tall tree whose large leaves have 7–17 narrow, toothed leaflets slightly hairy beneath. Often the end leaflet is *lacking*. Crushed leaves are spicy-scented. Twigs hairless, stout; pith light brown and chambered by woody partitions (pith of branchlets usually

better developed than that of twigs). Buds *whitish woolly;* leaf scars large, *without hairy fringe;* bundle scars in 3 groups. True end buds present. Bark dark and deeply grooved; ridges not shiny. Leaves 12″–24″. Height 70′–100′ (150′); diameter 2′–4′ (6′). Flowers catkins, April–June. Fruits *large spherical nuts* with husks of 1 piece, Oct.–Nov. Fertile soils.

Similar species: (1) Black Walnut and (2) Butternut are the only plants with compound leaves that have chambered pith. Butternut has hairy ridge above leaf scar, darker pith, end leaflet present, bark shiny-ridged, fruits oblong and four-lined.

Remarks: One of the most valuable and beautiful native trees. Heavy, strong, durable heartwood easily worked, in great demand for veneers, cabinetmaking, interior finishing, and gunstocks. Large trees have been almost exterminated in some regions. Bark is used in tanning; yellow-brown dye can be made from nut husks. Nuts eaten by humans, squirrels, and mice; twigs by deer. The bruised nut husks were once used to kill fish for food, but this practice is now illegal. Tomatoes, apples, and other species may not survive near large walnut trees.

BUTTERNUT   *Juglans cinerea* L.   **Pl. 16**

Similar to Black Walnut but with prominent *hairy fringe* above leaf scar. Pith dark brown; end leaflet normally *present.* The wider bark ridges are smooth-topped, making a *shiny,* interlaced gray network superimposed upon the black fissures. Number of leaflets 7–17. Twigs and leafstalk bases somewhat hairy. Height 40′–80′ (100′); diameter 1′–2′ (3′). Fruits are somewhat *oblong and sticky;* nuts with one-piece, *four-lined* husks. Oct.–Nov.

Remarks: Also known as White Walnut; wood lighter in color than that of its more valuable relative. Lumber is light, soft, and weak but easily worked and polished; darkens upon exposure to

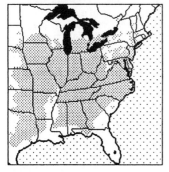 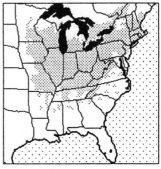

BLACK WALNUT   BUTTERNUT

air. Though not an important timber species, it is used for interiors, cabinetwork, furniture, and instrument cases. The early colonists are reported to have prepared a yellow-brown stain by boiling the soft, half-ripe fruits. They also pickled the boiled nuts and made a dark stain from the husks and inner bark to dye uniforms. Indians are said to have boiled the nuts to obtain oil for use as butter. The nutmeats were then collected and dried. In spring, sap was boiled down to make syrup. The crushed fruits were once also used to poison fish. Bark yields useful drugs. Nuts are eaten by many wild animals.

TREE-OF-HEAVEN (AILANTHUS) Pl. 16
Ailanthus altissima (Mill.) Swingle

A fast-growing, small to large tree with very large leaves having 11–41 leaflets. Leaflets *not toothed* except for pair of *gland-tipped teeth near bases*. Twigs hairless, yellow-brown, stout, with continuous yellowish pith. Buds small, brown-woolly; end buds false. Leaf scars *very large*, somewhat triangular, with numerous bundle scars. Bark gray-brown, smooth, or with narrow light-colored grooves. Leaves 12″–24″ or more. Height 80′–100′; diameter 1′–2′. Flowers small, yellowish, clustered, male blossoms with foul odor, June–July. Fruits in large clusters, dry, narrow, one-seeded, winged, Sept.–winter.

Similar species: No other tree has such gland-tipped leaflet lobes. In winter, stout twigs, false end buds, large leaf scars, and numerous bundle scars are distinctive. The Coffeetree (Pl. 22) has large leaf scars but fewer bundle scars. It has twice-compound leaves and salmon-colored pith.

Remarks: An oriental species; has become a weed here. Imported by way of England, where it was first planted in 1751. Most rapidly growing woody plant in our area. Will thrive under extremely adverse conditions, growing as much as 8′ in a year. Annual sprouts 12′ long not uncommon where a tree has been cut down. Since it is adapted to disturbed sites, even a crack between bricks in an alleyway may provide a seedbed for this plant. Immune to dust and smoke and useful in polluted cities where other plants will not grow. It may grow to a large size. The soft wood has limited lumber and fuel values. The common name, supposed to be of Asiatic or Australian origin, refers to the tree's height.

AMERICAN MOUNTAIN-ASH Pl. 16
Sorbus americana Marsh.

A shrub or small tree. Compound leaves have 11–17 long, narrow, toothed, *long-pointed* leaflets; leaflets *more than 3 times as long as broad*. Leaves and twigs hairless. Buds *reddish, sticky, and hairless;* leaf scars narrow, with 3 or 5 bundle scars. End buds true. Spur branches may be present; bark rather smooth and

gray-brown. Leaves 6″–9″. Height to 40′; diameter to 12″. Flowers small, about ¼″, clustered, May–June. Fruits *small,* about ¼″, *orange-red, clustered,* Aug.–March. Woods and openings.
Similar species: (1) Showy Mountain-ash has wider leaflets, flowers, and fruits. (2) European Mountain-ash has hairy leaves and woolly buds.
Remarks: One of the most ornamental northern trees. Colorful, fleshy fruits often remain on tree late in winter. Eaten by many birds and mammals, including ruffed and sharp-tailed grouse, ptarmigan, fisher, and marten. Deer and moose browse twigs.

SHOWY MOUNTAIN-ASH   Leaflet and fruit, Pl. 16
Sorbus decora (Sarg.) Schneid.
Like American Mountain-ash but leaflets *less than 3 times* as long as broad and somewhat whitened beneath. Flowers about ⅜″ across and *fruits red, more than* ⁵⁄₁₆″. Woods and rocky places.
Remarks: Also known as the Northern Mountain-ash.

EUROPEAN MOUNTAIN-ASH   Leaflet and fruit, Pl. 16
Sorbus aucuparia L.
Widely cultivated in northern states and Canada and established in the wild. Resembles previous 2 species except that leaflets are somewhat *hairy;* buds *white-woolly* and not sticky. Leaflets short-pointed or blunt. Flowers and fruits resemble those of Showy Mountain-ash.

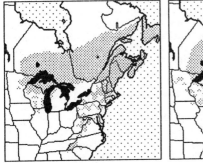

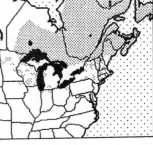

AMERICAN
MOUNTAIN-ASH

SHOWY
MOUNTAIN-ASH

Hickories I–III (Plates 17–19)

The hickories are trees with feather-compound leaves whose leaflets are toothed and mostly long-pointed. Twigs are stout and tough yet flexible, pith continuous. Buds and leaf scars are conspicuous. End buds are true, bundle scars numerous. The male flowers are in prominent catkins, occurring in spring. Husks of hickory nuts characteristically break into 4 rather separate parts upon ripening; those of walnuts and many other nut-bearing species remain whole.

Most non-thorny plants with alternate compound leaves have false end buds. Among those that resemble the hickories in having true end buds, Black Walnut and Butternut (Pl. 16) have chambered piths, and the mountain-ashes (Pl. 16) have narrow leaf scars.

Fruits of several hickories, especially Pecan and Shagbark, are edible and have commercial value. They usually fall in September and October. Nuts of most species are eaten by domestic swine, squirrels, opossums, wild turkey, and occasionally ducks. Twigs are browsed by rabbits and deer. Crushed green nut husks were formerly used to poison fish for food, but this practice is now illegal.

Hickory wood is strong, heavy, tough, and elastic, but is subject to insect attacks and decays on contact with moisture. It is of value in the manufacture of skis, tool handles, agricultural implements, wagons, gunstocks, chair backs, and baskets and was once important as best American wood for barrel hoops. As fuel it is excellent, producing great heat and high-grade charcoal.

The hickories may be divided into 3 groups: *pecans,* with paired and usually yellow bud scales and four-ridged nuts; *shagbarks,* with large end buds (more than ½″ long), stout twigs (more than ⅛″ in diameter), thick nut husks (more than ⅛″ thick, and, for 2 species, mature trunk bark that peels in strips; and *pignuts,* with small end buds, slender twigs, thin nut husks, and tight bark.

Hickories I: Pecans (Plate 17)

PECAN *Carya illinoenis* (Wang.) K. Koch   **Pl. 17**
A tall tree with 9–17 leaflets per leaf. End buds ⅜″–⅝″ long, with 2–3 *pairs* of non-overlapping *yellow-hairy* bud scales. Twigs hairless; bark closely ridged, *not peeling.* Nuts edible; considerably longer than wide. Husks *thin,* ridged along 4 joint lines. Bark medium dark, with numerous vertical ridges. Leaves 12″–20″. Height 100′–120′ (160′); diameter 3′–4′ (6′). Floodplains.
Similar species: Three other hickories have bud scales in pairs

with edges meeting: (1) Water Hickory has brownish buds with yellowish glands that soon fall off; (2) Bitternut has permanently yellow hairless bud scales and 7–9 leaflets; (3) Nutmeg Hickory has yellow-hairy buds, 5–9 leaflets, and thick nut husks.

Remarks: About 100 varieties of this tallest hickory are cultivated in the Southeast for their delicious nuts. Fruits of orchard trees have thinner husks than those of wild specimens. Although originally a species of Mississippi River bottoms, it will grow in sheltered places on uplands as far north as Massachusetts. Fruits rarely mature in North, where pecans are mostly planted for ornament. In South, opossums, wild turkeys, and squirrels feed on nuts.

BITTERNUT HICKORY   Pl. 17
Carya cordiformis (Wang.) K. Koch

A medium-sized to tall tree. Leaflets 5–11, somewhat hairy beneath. Buds *bright yellow-powdery,* with scales in *pairs,* not overlapping. End buds more than ½″ long, sometimes more than 2 scales exposed. Twigs *slender,* mostly hairless. Bark *tight* with network of fine smooth ridges. Nuts cylindrical, smooth, and bitter; husks *thin,* ridged toward outer end and not splitting. Hybrids with Pecan and Shagbark Hickory sometimes occur. Leaves 6″–12″. Height 50′–60′ (100′); diameter 18″–24″ (36″). Woods.

Similar species: See Pecan.

WATER HICKORY (BITTER PECAN)   Pl. 17
Carya aquatica (Michx. f.) Nutt.

Similar to Pecan but more southern and smaller. Buds *red-brown* with yellowish gland spots that soon disappear. Bark in long, loose, *shaggy* strips. Nuts bitter, egg- or *ball-shaped.* Husks

PECAN

BITTERNUT HICKORY

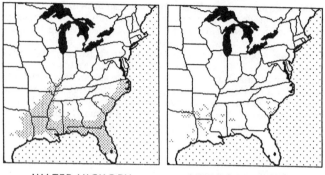

WATER HICKORY   NUTMEG HICKORY

wrinkled, not splitting to base. Leaves 8″–18″. Height 50′–70′ (100′); diameter 12″–24″ (30″). Coastal Plain rivers and swamps.

NUTMEG HICKORY   Pl. 17
Carya myristiciformis (Michx. f.) Nutt.
A rare tree of scattered southern swamps, with 5–9 leaflets, often *shiny* beneath. Buds brown- to yellow-hairy or granular. Trunk bark smooth to scaly. Leaves 6″–15″. Height to 110′; diameter 2′. Nut husk ⅛″ thick, smooth, *splitting* to the base; kernel edible. Bottomlands.
Similar species: See Pecan.

Hickories II: Shagbarks (Plate 18)

SHAGBARK HICKORY   *Carya ovata* (Mill.) K. Koch   Pl. 18
A tall tree with leaves with 5–7 (usually 5) hairless leaflets. When present, dense tufts of hair on leaflet *teeth* (use lens) are field marks. Buds covered by many overlapping scales; end buds *more than* ½″ long. Twigs *stout, red-brown,* slightly hairy to shiny. Bark light-colored, *very shaggy,* in long, loose strips. Nuts *egg-shaped,* 1⅜″–3″, edible, four-angled, not ridged. Nut husk yellowish, thick, splitting to base. Leaves 8″–14″. Height 60′–90′ (120′); diameter 2′–3′ (4′). Dry woods.
Similar species: This is the only one of the shagbark group with so few leaflets; the 3 other hickories with 5–7 leaflets are in the pignut group (Pl. 19), and all have small end buds and tight bark. On this plate (1) Shellbark Hickory has 7–9 leaflets that are soft-hairy beneath, light tan or orange twigs, and shaggy mature bark. (2) Mockernut Hickory also has 7–9 leaflets, but its woolly twigs and foliage, early-falling outer bud scales, and tight trunk bark distinguish it.

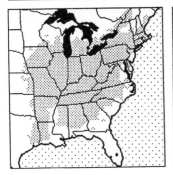

SHAGBARK HICKORY

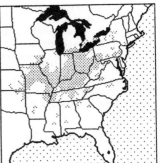

SHELLBARK HICKORY

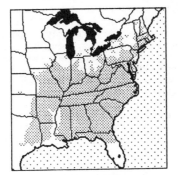

MOCKERNUT HICKORY

SHELLBARK HICKORY
Pl. 18

Carya laciniosa (Michx. f.) Loud.

A tall tree. Leaflets *7–9*, hairless, or short-hairy beneath. Buds have overlapping scales; end buds ½"–1", somewhat hairy, *darker outer scales present*. Twigs *stout, orange-brown, hairless* or slightly hairy. Bark *very shaggy,* loosening in *long strips*. Nuts egg-shaped 1⅛"–2⅜", edible, angled but not ridged. Husks thick, splitting to base. Leaves 15"–22". Height 80'–100' (120'); diameter 3'–4'. Rich soils.

Similar species: See Shagbark Hickory.

MOCKERNUT HICKORY
Pl. 18

Carya tomentosa (Poir.) Nutt.

A medium-sized to tall tree with *7–9* leaflets; leaf undersides and twigs *matted-woolly*. Hairs curly and clustered. Leaves *extra-*

fragrant when crushed, pale or orange-brown beneath. Buds have overlapping scales. End buds ⅝″–1″; *outer scales fall* in autumn. Twigs stout. Bark *tight* and deeply furrowed. Nuts ball- to egg-shaped, edible, with thick husk *not* splitting to base. Bark tight with network of smooth ridges. Leaves 8″–15″. Height 50′–80′ (100′); diameter 18″–24″ (36″). Hills and dry soils.
Similar species: Three hickories have end buds more than ½″ long. This is the only one with tight bark, end buds dropping the outer scales in autumn, and matted-woolly twigs and foliage.

Hickories III: Pignuts (Plate 19)

SAND (PALE) HICKORY   **Pl. 19**
Carya pallida (Ashe) Eng. & Graebn.
The only hickory with 7–9 leaflets and *small* (less than ¼″ long) end buds. Leaflets usually 7 and silvery beneath. Buds usually yellowish. Leafstalks usually long-hairy. Twigs slender, fine-hairy or not. Trunk pale to dark gray, smooth to furrowed, sometimes shaggy. Fruit husks very *thin,* yellow-powdery, ridged, typically split to the base. Nuts sweet. Height 40′–50′ (110′); diameter 18″–20″. Southeastern forests.
Similar species: The very small end buds tend to be distinctive. See Pignut Hickory.

PIGNUT HICKORY   *Carya glabra* (Mill.) Sweet   **Pl. 19**
A tall tree with leaves of 5 (less commonly 7) hairless leaflets. Buds have overlapping scales; end bud ⅜″–½″, silky-hairy after outer scales drop in autumn. Twigs *slender* (to ⅛″ thick), red-brown, and hairless. Bark dark, *tight,* and smooth-ridged. Nuts egg-shaped, ⅝″–1⅜″, hard-shelled, sometimes sweet. Nut husks

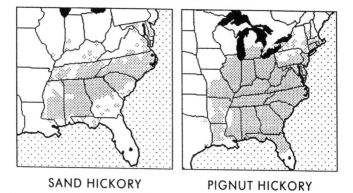

SAND HICKORY   PIGNUT HICKORY

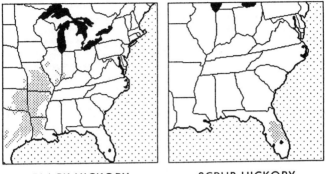

BLACK HICKORY   SCRUB HICKORY

thin, brown, usually *not* splitting to the base. Leaves 6″–12″. Height 80′–90′ (120′); diameter 2′–3′ (4′). Dry woods.
Similar species: (1) Also with 5–7 leaflets, Shagbark has loose bark, large end buds and end leaflets; (2) Sand Hickory has end buds less than ¼″ long. Two others may have tight bark and overlapping bud scales: (3) Mockernut has large end buds, hairy twigs, and 7–9 woolly leaflets; (4) Black Hickory, with 5–7 leaflets, has rusty-hairy twigs and leaves.

BLACK HICKORY *Carya texana* Buckl.   **Pl. 19**
Like Pignut Hickory, a large, close-barked, small-budded tree with 5–7 leaflets, usually 7. Twigs, buds, and leaf undersides are *rusty-hairy*. The outer bud scales fall early. Fruits ball- to egg-shaped, to 2″. Nut edible, husk yellow-scaly. Does not range into Florida (see Scrub Hickory). Dry woods.

SCRUB HICKORY *Carya floridana* Sarg.   **Pl. 19**
Like Black Hickory but known only as an uncommon species in the sand-pine scrub country of cen. Florida. The twigs are rusty-hairy but the outer bud scales *do not* fall early. Leaflets 5–7, usually 5. Height to 80′; diameter to 1½′. Fruit to 1½″.
Similar species: Pignut Hickory is not rusty-hairy, and its outer bud scales fall early.

Sumacs and Relatives (Plate 20)

Warning: Two poisonous species occur among the non-thorny plants with alternate compound leaves. See under Poison-sumac and Florida Poisonwood in this group and also Pl. F-21A.

Plants of fields and forest openings, the sumacs and their relatives vary by species, only some of which have toothed leaves. *Rhus* sumacs are red-fruited, with upright, cone-shaped clusters of small, dry, hairy fruits present much of the year. They provide an apparently little-relished but available food supply for wildlife. Twigs are stout with large brown pith. These sumacs have hairy side buds, in summer mostly hidden by the leafstalk bases and in winter nearly surrounded by the leaf scars. End buds are false and sap in summer is often milky. Bundle scars are numerous. The flowers are small, greenish, and clustered. The fruits of Poison-sumac and Florida Poisonwood are smooth and whitish or yellow-orange; the irritating sap is not milky.

WINGED SUMAC *Rhus copallina* L.   **Pl. 20**
A shrub or, especially in South, sometimes a small tree. Leaves large, divided into 11–23 narrow, *smooth-edged, shiny, short-pointed* leaflets, each about ¾″ wide; the midrib bordered by thin *"wings."* Twigs and leafstalks *velvety,* round, and marked with obvious raised dots. Buds hairy, partly surrounded by U-shaped leaf scars. Trunk is dark and smooth, with numerous raised cross-streaks (lenticels). Leaves 6″–14″. Height 4′–10′ (30′); diameter 1″–3″ (10″). Flowers small, yellow-green, July–Sept. Fruits red, short-hairy.
Similar species: (1) In Texas and Oklahoma, see Prairie Sumac. (2) In Florida, see Wingleaf Soapberry (Pl. 21).
Remarks: Bark and leaves can be used in tanning leather. Twigs cropped by deer; seeds eaten by ruffed and sharp-tailed grouse, bobwhite, ring-necked pheasant, and many songbirds.

PRAIRIE SUMAC *Rhus lanceolata* (Gray) Britton **leaf, Pl. 20**
A western plant similar to and often considered a variety of Winged Sumac. The leaflets and midrib wings are quite *narrow*— leaflets less than ½″ wide and *long-pointed.* Leaves 5″–10″. Thickets, s. Oklahoma and e. Texas to New Mexico.
Similar species: (1) Western Soapberry (Pl. 21) lacks winged midribs; (2) Wingleaf Soapberry (Pl. 21) occurs in the U.S. only in Florida and se. Georgia. The soapberries have larger yellow, fleshy, single-seeded fruits.
Remarks: Fruits eaten by prairie chickens and other birds.

STAGHORN SUMAC *Rhus typhina* L.   **Pl. 20**
A shrub or small tree with *very hairy* twigs and leafstalks. Leaves large, made up of 11–31 *toothed* leaflets. Twigs round, no obvious dots. Sap milky in summer at fresh cuts. Buds hairy, surrounded by U-shaped leaf scars. Bark dark and smooth, with numerous raised cross-streaks. Leaves 12″–24″. Height 4′–15′ (50′); diameter 2″–4″ (15″). Flowers June–July. Fruits red, long-hairy.
Similar species: (1) Lack of winged midribs and twig dots

differentiates this species from Winged Sumac. (2) Hybridization with Smooth Sumac sometimes occurs, and intermediate characteristics result.

Remarks: Aptly named, branches bear a marked resemblance to the antlers of a deer "in velvet." Staghorn Sumac is cultivated in Europe and the West. Bark and leaves rich in tannin; it is reported that a black ink can be made by boiling leaves and fruit. The long-haired fruits have been found in stomachs of many songbirds, ruffed and sharp-tailed grouse, bobwhite, pheasant, mourning dove, and skunk. Twigs cropped by moose, white-tailed deer, and cottontail rabbit.

SMOOTH SUMAC *Rhus glabra* L.   **Pl. 20**

Much like Staghorn Sumac but with twigs and leafstalks *hairless.* Twigs somewhat flat-sided. Fruits red, short-hairy.

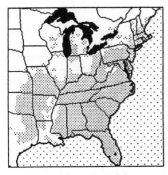

WINGED SUMAC

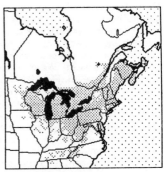

STAGHORN SUMAC

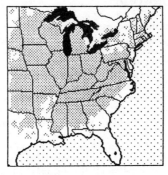

SMOOTH SUMAC

POISON-SUMAC
Fig. 4, p. 17

Toxicodendron vernix (L.) Kuntze

Danger: Do not touch or burn any part of this plant. All parts contain a watery, dangerous skin irritant. Shrub or small tree with large leaves composed of 7–13 pointed leaflets *not toothed.* Twigs and buds round, *hairless;* leaf scars crescent- or shield-shaped, do *not* surround buds. End bud true. Bark smooth and dark with numerous narrow cross-streaks often tending to encircle trunk. Sap clear, quickly turning black, and poisonous. Leaves 6″–12″. Height 6′–20′ (30′); diameter 3″–8″ (10″). Flowers May–July. Fruits *white,* Aug.–spring. Widespread but local.

Similar species: Over most of our area the only tree or shrub with *hairless* buds and twigs and *once-compound* leaves that are *not toothed.* Its open, *swampy* habitat is a clue. Most similar are (1) Yellowwood, with blunt-tipped leaflets and (2) Western Soapberry, with greater height and only 3 bundle scars (see Pl. 21).

Remarks: Though more virulent than Poison-ivy, this species is generally uncommon; largely confined to moist soils. Contact with the plant (or with smoke from burning it) usually results in itching and other symptoms within a few hours. Washing the exposed parts of the body with a thick lather of soap is of value soon after exposure. Water alone, unless in large amounts, may only spread the oil. Mild irritations may be treated with astringent lotions, but cases involving the eyes or genitals and widespread irritations of other parts of the body should be treated promptly by a physician. The merits of taking injections for the prevention of sumac poisoning are a matter for medical opinion. Common names such as Poison-elder or Poison-dogwood usually refer to Poison-sumac. Fruits eaten by numerous birds, including bobwhite, pheasant, and ruffed grouse. Twigs browsed by cottontail rabbit. Foliage may turn yellow or red in autumn.

FLORIDA POISONWOOD
Fig. 4; Pl. F-21A

Metopium toxiferum (L.) Krug & Urban

Danger: Poisonous. Do not touch or burn. Like Poison-sumac, the sap of this species is caustic, and all parts should be avoided. A shrub or small tree of cen. and s. Florida with *mostly triangular, leathery, evergreen* leaves. The 3–7 alternate, smooth- or wavy-edged leaflets may be pointed or blunt, and squarish based or not. The clear sap turns *black* and may mark the foliage and outer bark. The latter is thin, brown, and *flaky* and shows the *orange* underbark. Leaves 6″–10″. Height to 40′. Flowers yellowish green. Fruits yellow-orange, ½″ long, fleshy, shiny, one-seeded.

Similar species: See Pl. F-21A.

Remarks: Common within its tropical range south and east of Lake Okeechobee in s. Florida. An attractive plant but one whose undesirable characteristics should be learned. Contact with it should be avoided!

Trees with Alternate, Once-compound Leaves, Not Toothed (Plate 21)

Except for some sumacs (Pl. 20), only 17 species in our area have leaves of this type. Thirteen of these occur only in Florida (see Pls. F-21A, F-21B), and 2 others are mainly west of the Mississippi River. Only the first 2 beyond occur widely in the eastern U.S., and they are common only locally. The twigs are generally hairless. Buds may be more than 1 above each leaf scar. End buds are false.

HOPTREE   *Ptelea trifoliata* L.   **Pl. 21**
An upright shrub or small tree with *three-parted leaves* that are usually hairless but may be hairy beneath. Leaflets usually without teeth; the end leaflet *short-stalked.* Crushed leaves may emit a musky odor. Twigs brownish and round; buds hairy and hidden in summer by leafstalks; leaf scars U-shaped; bundle scars 3. Trunk bark rather smooth, light-colored, shallowly grooved. On Lake Michigan sand dunes, a variety has velvety twigs and leaves. Leaves 4″–10″. Height 10′–20′ (25′); diameter 2″–10″ (16″). Flowers greenish, small, clustered, May–July. Fruits flat, circular, papery, two-seeded, Sept.–spring. Fertile woods.
Similar species: Small specimens are often mistaken for Poison-ivy (see Fig. 4), but the end leaflet of that irritating shrub or vine is long-stalked.

YELLOWWOOD   **Pl. 21**
Cladrastis kentukea (Dum.-Cours.) Rudd
A medium-sized tree with 7–11 *smooth-edged* and sometimes silky leaflets, each 2″–4″ long, arranged alternately along the

HOPTREE   YELLOWWOOD

midrib. Buds hairy, brownish, often several above each other, mostly hidden beneath hollow leafstalk bases or, in winter, surrounded by U-shaped leaf scars. Twigs brownish, stout; bundle scars 5. Bark smooth, gray; wood *yellow*. Leaves 5"–8". Height to 60'; diameter to 3'. Flowers white, clustered, May–June. Fruits pealike pods, Sept.–Oct. Rich soils.

Similar species: The only other thornless species with alternate once-compound toothless leaves of more than 3 leaflets are: (1) Poison-sumac (see Fig. 4), which is usually shrubbier and has more or less visible buds; (2) Winged Sumac (Pl. 20), with winged midribs and velvety twigs; and (3) Western Soapberry, with an even number of narrow leaflets, visible buds, and 3 bundle scars. (4) In winter, Beech (Pl. 32) has similar bark but long, slim, and hairless buds.

WINGLEAF SOAPBERRY   *Sapindus saponaria* L.   **Pl. 21**
Principally a tree of s. Florida, but reported north to coastal Georgia. Leaves feather-compound, with 6–12 pointed and usually opposite leaflets, each leaflet *3"–5"* long, hairless to velvety beneath. Generally the end leaflet is lacking. Midribs are typically *winged* (though a non-winged form has been described as *S. marginatus* Wildl.). Twigs hairless, buds small, smooth, globular, with 2 visible scales. Bundle scars 3. Bark gray to reddish, scaly. Leaves 6"–9". Height to 50'. Flowers small, white, in loose 6"–10" end clusters, November. Fruits in spring; *yellow,* smooth, half-inch, rounded, single-seeded, **poisonous.**

Similar species: See Brazilian Peppertree (Pl. F-21A).

Remarks: According to Little (1979), this species and Hopbush (Pl. F-46B) are the only trees native both to Hawaii and the continental U.S. Wingleaf Soapberry also occurs on other Pacific islands and southward to Argentina. In water, the fruits produce a soapy lather that is **poisonous** when taken internally. Seeds may be made into buttons, beads, etc.

WESTERN SOAPBERRY   **Pl. 21**
Sapindus drummondii Hook. & Arn.
Typically a tree of the Great Plains, this tree has leaves with *8–18 narrow, sharply pointed, somewhat leathery* leaflets that are not toothed. Leaflets usually opposite and end leaflets lacking. Buds usually hairy, small. Bark light gray, scaly. Pulp of clustered fruits forms lather in water and is reportedly **poisonous.** Flowers white, clustered, May–June. Fruits ball-shaped, white, Sept.–Oct. or longer. Leaves 4"–15". Height 20'–50' (75'); diameter 10"–18" (24"). Bottomlands.

TEXAS SOPHORA   *Sophora affinis* Torr. & Gray   **Pl. 21**
Barely penetrates Louisiana, Arkansas, and Oklahoma from its main range in cen. and e. Texas. The leaves are 6"–10" long and

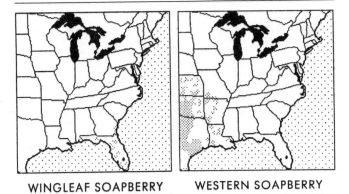

WINGLEAF SOAPBERRY   WESTERN SOAPBERRY

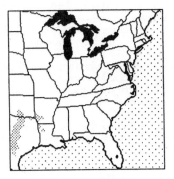

TEXAS SOPHORA

divided into 13–15 or more 1″, nearly hairless, pointed or some-what blunt leaflets. Twigs thornless and green to brown; buds woolly; bundle scars 3. Buds *surrounded* by the leafstalk base and leaf scars. Bark red-brown, scaly. Leaves 6″–10″. Flowers white, ½″ long, pealike, in 3″–5″ clusters, April–June. Fruits black, 2″–3″ long, non-splitting pods, beaded, summer. Height 18′–20′; diameter 8″–10″. Limestone soils.

FLORIDA-ONLY TREES   **Pls. F-21A, F-21B**
Thirteen other trees, mostly with evergreen alternate compound leaves that are not toothed, occur only in tropical Florida.

Thornless Trees with Twice-compound Leaves (Plate 22)

These, plus the several prickly species on Pl. 15, are the only trees in our area with foliage of this type. (In Florida, see also Pl. F-22.) In these plants, not only are the leaves divided into leaflets, but the leaflets are further divided. The leaves are large, the twigs hairless, and the end buds false. Except for Chinaberry, these species are all legumes and produce characteristic beanlike or pealike fruit pods.

CHINABERRY   *Melia azedarach* L.   **Pl. 22**
An oriental tree, widely planted in dooryards in the South, which often escapes to the wild. Leaves with *toothed,* 1″–3″, pointed leaflets. Twigs *stout.* Buds small, nearly spherical, fuzzy, not sunken as in Coffeetree. Leaf scars *large,* somewhat three-lobed, with 3 groups of scattered bundle scars. Pith white. Leaves 8″–16″. Height to 40′. Flowers purplish with an unpleasant odor, clustered, May–June. Fruits usually present; *yellowish, ball-like,* internally **poisonous.**
Remarks: Fruits have been used to make flea powder. They are known, too, to have paralyzed livestock and birds. Their bad taste may account for the relatively few cases of human poisoning. The bark has been used to stun fish.

COFFEETREE   *Gymnocladus dioica* (L.) K. Koch   **Pl. 22**
A tall tree with *very large* leaves. Leaflets 1″–3″, *very numerous, pointed, not toothed.* Twigs very stout, somewhat whitened; leaf

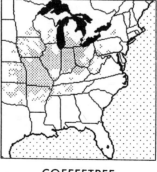

COFFEETREE

scars large, shield-shaped, 3–5 bundle scars. Buds silky, sunk in bark, often one above the other. Pith pinkish. Bark dark and scaly. Leaves 17″–36″. Height 40′–60′ (100′); diameter 1′–2′ (3′). Flowers whitish, clustered, May–June. Fruits 2″–10″ brown pods, Sept.–winter.

Similar species: In our area, the only other thornless trees with twice-compound leaves are (1) Chinaberry, with toothed leaflets; (2) Lebbek, with blunt leaflets; and (3) Silktree, with foliage like that of Sensitive Fern. In winter the sunken lateral buds of Coffeetree are distinctive among species with large alternate-leaf scars.

Remarks: As a shade tree, often planted in city parks along eastern seaboard; sometimes escapes. Native mostly west of Appalachians. One of few members of pea family which do not grow bacterial root nodules capable of fixing nitrogen. Seeds were roasted and used as coffee in some areas during Civil War. Indians are supposed to have roasted seeds, eating them as nuts. Pulp between seeds is nevertheless reported to be poisonous; cattle become sick when leaves or fruits drop into their drinking water. Reddish wood is strong and coarse but takes a good polish. Useful in cabinetwork and for fence posts and railroad ties.

LEBBEK   *Albizia lebbeck* (L.) Benth.   Pl. 22

A deciduous tropical tree of s. Florida and the Keys. It has 6″–16″ leaves and 2–4 pairs of major leaflets. The many subleaflets are ¾″–1¾″ long, opposite, smooth-edged, and *rounded* at both ends. Twigs slender; leaf scars small. Leaves 8″–14″. Height to 50′. Flowers whitish yellow, in round clusters, with numerous 1″–1½″ threadlike (pollen-bearing) stamens protruding. Fruits 5″–8″ dry pods *more than 1″* wide and containing loose seeds when ripe.

Similar species: The only other twice-compound species with blunt leaflets are found only on the Florida Keys and have smaller leaflets (see Pl. F-22).

Remarks: The impolite alternate common name, Woman's Tongue, is said to refer to the rattle of loose seeds in wind-blown fruit pods. A native of tropical Asia naturalized in s. Florida and other tropical areas. The wood is of high quality and is used for furniture, veneer, and paneling.

SILKTREE (ALBIZIA)   Pl. 22
Albizia julibrissin Durazzini

A small tree with feathery *fernlike foliage.* There are 6–16 pairs of major leaflets and numerous tiny, pointed leaflets less than ½″ long. On being handled, leaflets *close like pages of a book.* Twigs hairless, slender, leaf scars small, with 3 bundle scars. Buds few-scaled, small, blunt, not sunk in bark, sometimes occur one above the other. Pith whitish. Bark smooth, light brownish. Leaves 5″–8″. Height 20′–40′; diameter 6″–12″. Flowers powder-pufflike, pink, June–Aug. Fruits beanlike pods. 2″–3″.

Similar species: Other trees with such feathery foliage occur only in lower Florida (see Pl. F-22).
Remarks: Native to S. Asia but widely planted and naturalized in the eastern U.S.

FLORIDA-ONLY TREES   Pl. F-22
Trees of this type that are distributed only in peninsular Florida and the Keys include the Lebbek (above) and 3 other species.

V

Broad-leaved Trees with Alternate Simple Leaves (Plates 23–46)

Over half of our trees fall in this category. Because a number of species therefore resemble one another in having alternate simple leaves, the separation of the group into subdivisions facilitates identification. The outline below, which indicates the major characteristics used in subdividing the group, may be used as a general guide to identification. A winter key to leafless plants with alternate leaf scars appears in Appendix A.

Major Subdivisions of Broad-leaved Plants with Alternate Simple Leaves

1.   Trees with thorns.   **See Pls. 23–24.**
1.   Trees without thorns:
    2.   Leaves fan-lobed or fan-veined.   **See Pls. 25–27.**
    2.   Leaves feather-lobed or feather-veined:
        3.   End buds clustered, fruits acorns.
                        Oaks. See Pls. 28–31.
        3.   End buds not clustered or, if so, then fruits not acorns:
           4.   Leaves toothed.   **See Pls. 32–43.**
           4.   Leaves not toothed.   **See Pls. 44–46.**

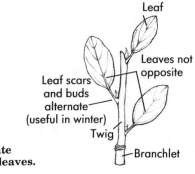

Fig. 15. Alternate simple leaves.

Thorny Trees with Alternate Toothed Leaves (Plate 23)

In addition to the species below, Common Buckthorn (Pl. 12) has spine-tipped twigs and may bear some alternate leaves. Sour Orange (Pl. 24) may occasionally be somewhat thorny.

HAWTHORNS   *Crataegus* species   **Pl. 23**
These plants, distinctive though they are as a group, are virtually indistinguishable as species except by the few botanists who have given the genus special study. Frequent hybridization complicated by great individual variation confounds accurate identification. Even the specialists vary greatly in their decisions regarding the validity of many forms. The number of species of *Crataegus* in the U.S. has been variously determined as more than 1,000 and as less than 100. In this volume, therefore, no attempt is made to differentiate between the many species. The drawings serve only to indicate major leaf types as an aid to identification of the genus. Thornless hawthorns are occasionally encountered.

In general, the hawthorns are a widespread group of very dense shrubs or small trees with long thorns and smooth or scaly bark. Bundle scars are 3. Buds are nearly spherical, end buds true. Spur branches are usually present. Hawthorn spines are *long and slender,* without buds or leaves. They may occur on twigs as well as on older wood.

The fruits are small, yellow to red, and applelike. They often remain on the plants all winter, providing food for numerous birds and mammals, including bobwhite, ring-necked pheasant, ruffed and sharp-tailed grouse, gray fox, cottontail rabbit, and white-tailed deer. Apparently because of their density, hawthorns are much used for nesting by many songbirds. They are important honey plants but are pests in pastures. They were formerly widely used for fences in England. Many varieties are used in landscaping. The name "haw" comes from the same root as "hedge."

The hawthorns illustrated are the **Dotted Hawthorn** (*C. punctata* Jacq.), the **Downy Hawthorn** (*C. mollis* Schede), and the **Cockspur Hawthorn** (*C. crus-galli* L.).
Similar species: (1) Some crabapples and plums may have long thorns, but some or all thorns usually carry buds or leaves on them. Plums have false end buds. (2) Possumhaw Holly (Pl. 40) is not a hawthorn. It is not thorny and has only 1 bundle scar. (3) Possumhaw Viburnum (Pl. 13), with opposite leaves and no thorns, is also not a hawthorn.

NATIVE CRABAPPLES *Malus* species   **Pl. 23**

Crabapples have no glands on leafstalks, sharp leaf teeth, scaly non-striped bark, true end buds, 3 bundle scars, and several-seeded fruits. In crabapples and plums, the thorns occur only on the older wood (not on the twigs) and usually bear buds or leaves. Some hawthorns have thorns, leaves, and fruits resembling those of apples, but their thorns never bear buds or leaves and may also occur on the twigs. Spur branches occur in all 3 groups.

Some apple species are more regularly thorny than others. The following three are the only apples native to our area. The domesticated apple and pear (Pl. 43) introduced from the Old World do escape to grow wild but are not likely to be thorny. Since they could be sharp-twigged, however, their text discussions (p. 203) should also be reviewed in identifying members of the group. Hybrids between species are frequent and usually have intermediate characteristics. Botanists may use either *Malus* or *Pyrus* (and sometimes *Sorbus*) as the name for the genus.

AMERICAN CRABAPPLE *Malus coronaria* L.   **Pl. 23**

A thicket-forming shrub or small tree of north-central states with hairless twigs and leaves. Leaves have *round or heart-shaped bases*. Those on vigorous shoots are deeply toothed to somewhat lobed. Though usually heart-shaped to triangular, foliage may be narrowly long-pointed. Buds sharp-pointed. Bark gray, rough, cracked vertically. Leaves 1″–5″. Height 15′–30′; diameter 6″–14″. Flowers pink or white, highly fragrant, March–May. Fruits yellow-green, 1¼″–2″, bitter, Sept.–Nov. Woods borders.

Similar species: (1) Narrowleaf Crabapple is more southern and has leaves more elliptic and wedge-based. (2) Prairie Crabapple is woolly.

Remarks: Widely planted for ornament. Fruits used in preserves

AMERICAN CRABAPPLE   NARROWLEAF CRABAPPLE

and vinegar. Trunks used as stock on which to graft less hardy cultivated apples.

NARROWLEAF CRABAPPLE   Pl. 23
Malus angustifolia Ait.
More southern than American Crabapple, with elliptic leaves, leaf bases more *wedge-shaped* and tapering, and leaf tips often more blunt. Leaves tend to be evergreen in some areas, but even where they are not, dead leaves can often be found and will assist in winter identification. Twigs hairy or not. Fruits less than 1″ and bitter but used for preserves and cider. Southern woods and thickets. See map, p. 115.

PRAIRIE CRABAPPLE   Not illus.
Malus ioensis (Wood) Bailey
Midwestern. Similar to American Crabapple, but twigs and leaf undersurfaces densely woolly. Flowers April–May. Fruits bitter but make delicious jelly; eaten by many wildlife species. Thickets and open places.

WILD PLUMS   *Prunus* species   Pls. 23, 37
Though the cherries, also in the genus *Prunus,* are never spiny, the plums are variously thorny or not. Allegheny Plum (p. 174), for example, sometimes has spine-tipped twigs. For cherries and such usually thornless plums, see Pls. 36 and 37.

Some thorns of plums may be simple spikes, but most are short, stiff, bud-bearing spur branches with sharpened tips. Thorns are generally present on branchlets and absent from twigs. As on other species of *Prunus,* leafstalks of most plums (usually lacking in American Plum) bear small paired glands. The distinctive "almond" odor of broken twigs is less prominent in plums than in cherries. Bundle scars 3. Bark often marked with horizontal linelike lenticels. Unlike the end buds on cherries, those on wild plums are mostly regarded as *false,* though their status is not always easily determined. Wild plum fruits are small and ball-shaped, with single large seeds.

The American Plum (Pl. 23) is the only regularly thorny plum that usually lacks leafstalk glands. The several other plums are not easy to identify as to species. Those that regularly bear thorns, however, may usually be separated by the following key. Also see species accounts.

1.   Twigs velvety or woolly:
    2.   Leaf teeth sharp; fruits yellow-red.   **American Plum.**
    2.   Leaf teeth rounded; fruits blue-black.   **Bullace Plum.**
1.   Twigs hairless or nearly so; fruits yellow or red:
    3.   Leaf teeth sharp; buds red-brown, about ⅛″ long; fruits ¾″–1″.   **American Plum.**

3. Leaf teeth rounded:
   4. Leaves broad, length no more than twice width; buds gray to black, about ³/₁₆″; fruits 1–1¼″.
      Canada Plum.
   4. Leaves narrow, length more than twice width; buds reddish, about ⅛″; fruits ½″.   **Chickasaw Plum.**

AMERICAN PLUM   *Prunus americana* Marsh.   **Pl. 23**
A shrub or small tree with *shaggy bark*. Leaves dull, bases heart- to wedge-shaped, hairless or nearly so, somewhat long-pointed, *sharply* and often doubly toothed. Usually *no glands* on leafstalks or leaf teeth. Twigs hairy or hairless and reddish brown. Buds *red-brown*, mostly about ⅛″, *narrow*. Leaves 1″–5″. Height 15′–30′ (35′); diameter 5″–10″ (14″). Flowers about 1″ across, white, 3–5 in clusters, April–June. Fruits red or yellow, ¾″–1″, seed somewhat flattened, Aug.–Oct. Thickets.
Similar species: This is the only thorny plum that has sharp leaf teeth and usually lacks glands on leafstalks.
Remarks: Several hundred varieties have been named. Some are cultivated.

BULLACE PLUM   *Prunus institia* L.   Not illus.
Similar to American Plum but with *hairy* twigs and leaf under- sides and with smaller leaves. Leaves 1½″–3″. Flowers mostly in pairs, white, 1″ across. Height to 20′. Fruits blue to black. Eurasian; occasionally spreading from cultivation.
Remarks: Little (1979) regards this only as a variety—*P. domestica* var. *institia* (L.) Fiori & Paoletti—of the Garden Plum (Pl. 37).

CANADA PLUM   *Prunus nigra* Ait.   Not illus.
Similar to American Plum, but leaf teeth *rounded* and *glands*

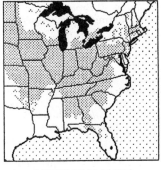

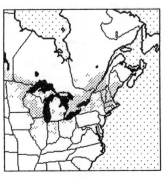

AMERICAN PLUM   CANADA PLUM

usually present on leafstalks. Twigs hairless. Buds *gray* or blackish, about ³⁄₁₆″. Leaves 1″–5″. Height 6′–20′ (25′); diameter 4″–10″ (12″). Flowers white to pink, April–June. Fruits yellow to reddish, 1″–1¼″, slightly elongate, Aug.–Oct. Thickets.

CHICKASAW PLUM   *Prunus angustifolia* Marsh.   **Pl. 23**
A southern shrub or small tree with *shiny,* hairless, narrow leaves with very fine, gland-tipped, *rounded* teeth. Leafstalks bear small glands. Twigs *hairless, reddish;* buds about as long as wide; leaf scars raised. Leaves 1″–3″. Height to 20′; diameter to 10″. Flowers white, clustered, March–April. Fruits red to yellow, ½″, seeds nearly spherical, July–Aug. Thickets.

JUJUBE   *Ziziphus jujuba* Mill.   Not illus.
Shrub or small tree with ¼″–¾″ *paired* thorns at the leafstalk bases. Leaves egg-shaped and pointed, with *3 main veins* meeting at the leaf base. Twigs hairy, usually green; bundle scar 1; spur branches present. Leaves 1″–2½″. Height to 50′. Flowers tiny, greenish, March–May. Fruits red-brown at maturity, edible, July–November. Thickets.
Remarks: Native of s. Asia and se. Europe, escaped in Gulf states. Not a plum. Sugared fruits are tasty; also known as Chinese Date.

Thorny Trees with Alternate Leaves, Not Toothed (Plate 24)

Trees in this category are essentially southern in distribution. Only Osage-orange has been transplanted and naturalized in some northern areas. All species have single, mostly strong, thorns and spur branches. Sap is *milky* in all Bumelias and the Osage-orange. Five of these plants, including 3 *Citrus* species, occur mainly in Florida.

GUM (WOOLLY) BUMELIA   **Pl. 24**
Bumelia lanuginosa (Michx.) Pers.
A shrub or small tree with sharp thorns at the leaf bases and some twig ends. Leaves wedge-shaped or parallel-sided, tips *blunt* and *rusty-* or *gray-hairy* beneath, mostly clustered near twig tips. Spur branches present. Twigs and buds *woolly.* Buds ball-like. Bundle scars 3. Leaves 1″–4″. Height to 50′. Flowers, small, white, bell-shaped, clustered in leaf angles, June–July. Fruits small, black, cherrylike.
Similar species: See other bumelias and Osage-orange. A clear gum can be collected from freshly cut wood or at trunk wounds.

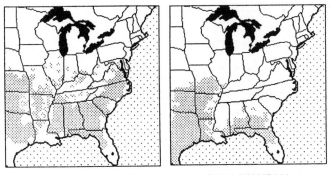

CHICKASAW PLUM   GUM BUMELIA

TOUGH BUMELIA *Bumelia tenax* (L.) Willd.   Not illus.
A small tree of the Atlantic Coastal Plain. Similar to Gum
Bumelia, but the sometimes evergreen leaves are *yellow- or
white-silky* beneath. Branches are difficult to break. Leaves 1″–3″.
Height to 30′.

BUCKTHORN BUMELIA   Pl. 24
Bumelia lycioides (L.) Pers.
Similar to Gum Bumelia but with narrow to elliptic, egg-shaped,
or even parallel-sided leaves that are *pointed and hairless* to
slightly silky beneath. Twigs and buds also hairless to slightly
silky. Leaved 3″–6″. Height to 30′. Moist soils.

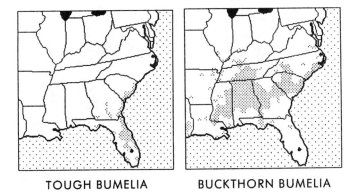

TOUGH BUMELIA   BUCKTHORN BUMELIA

Remarks: Buckthorn Bumelia should not be confused with buckthorns of the genus *Rhamnus* (Pls. 12 and 43).

SAFFRON-PLUM BUMELIA   Not illus.
Bumelia celastrina H. B. K.

Mainly Caribbean in distribution with *small, blunt, hairless,* evergreen, leathery leaves and 1″ thorns. Leaves 1″–2″. Height to 20′. Flowers late summer to early winter. Fruits black, sweet, edible, autumn or later. Florida and s. Texas, mainly coastal ridges.

OSAGE-ORANGE   *Maclura pomifera* (Raf.) Schneid.   Pl. 24

A medium-sized tree. Leaves egg-shaped, somewhat *long-pointed, not toothed.* Strong, unbranched thorns at each leaf scar. Sap *milky* (**caution:** sap causes a rash in some people). Wood *yellow.* Buds nearly ball-shaped; end ones false. Bundle scars 1–5. Bark orange-brown, furrowed, tight, fibrous. Leaves 1″–8″. Height 50′–60′; diameter 18″–36″. Flowers May–June. Fruits green, *totally wrinkled, grapefruit-sized,* Oct. Thickets.

Similar species: Osage-orange and the bumelias are our only thorny plants with milky sap. This species differs from the bumelias in leaf shape and in having shorter, more rounded spur branches.

Remarks: Once native in n. Texas, se. Oklahoma, and nearby Arkansas, home of the Osage Indians, this species was widely planted for living fences before invention of barbed wire. It is now widely distributed in our area. Because of its use in making bows, French name *bois d'arc* (colloquially Bodarc, Bodock) is still heard. Bark yields tannin; boiled wood chips yield yellow dye.

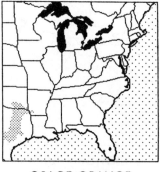

OSAGE-ORANGE

Fig. 16. Key Lime

TALLOWWOOD   *Ximenia americana* L.   **Pl. 24**
   A shrub or twisted small tree of peninsular Florida and world
   tropics. The small, leathery evergreen leaves are variously sharp,
   blunt, or notched at the tip and usually have a tiny *bristle tip* and
   wedge base. Stout straight thorns and spur branches are present.
   Bundle scars 1. Wood yellow. Leaves 1"–3". Height to 20'. Flowers
   yellowish, clustered, in leaf angles, April–May or later. Fruits
   yellow, plumlike, edible, oily, nearly all year.
   Remarks: Often parasitic on the roots of other trees. Fragrant
   and fine-grained wood takes a fine polish. Bark useful in tanning.

FLORIDA-ONLY TREES
   In addition to Saffron-plum Bumelia and Tallowwood (above),
   which also do not occur in our area except in Florida, 3 commercially important citrus species of Asiatic origin have escaped from
   cultivation to grow also in the wild. They are evergreen with
   leathery or near-leathery leaves; their fruits have the structure of
   the familiar oranges, lemons, and grapefruits of commerce. Their
   gland-dotted leaves are *aromatic* when crushed, and the twigs are
   green. Trees are also marked by leafstalks with widened, or
   winged, edges. See identification chart, Pl. 24, for Lime (Key
   Lime) [*Citrus aurantifolia* (Christmann in L.) Swingle], Sour
   Orange (*C. aurantium* L.), and Sweet Orange (*C. sinensis*
   Osbeck), which is reported also from Georgia.

Trees with Alternate, Fan-lobed Leaves
(Plate 25)

These are the only thornless, alternate-leaved trees with fan-
lobed leaves. The mulberries and Sassafras have leaves that may
be either lobed or not. White Poplar (Pl. 27) has white-woolly
leaves that are rarely somewhat lobed. The fan-lobed leaves of
maples (Pl. 11) are opposite, not alternate.

TULIPTREE   *Liriodendron tulipifera* L.   **Pl. 25**
   A tall, straight tree with unique *notched-tip, four-pointed*
   hairless leaves. Pairs of large leafy stipules attach to twigs and
   enclose buds. Twigs hairless, with *completely encircling lines*
   (stipule scars) at leaf scars. Pith *chambered*. Only 2 bud scales
   cover each end bud; side buds small or indistinct. Crushed buds
   and leaves *spicy-aromatic;* bundle scars more than 3. Bark light
   gray, *often whitened* in grooves and in patches on younger bark.
   Leaves 6"–10". Height 50'–100' (190'); diameter 2'–6' (10'). Flowers large, *tuliplike,* orange and green, May–June. Fruits slim,
   winged, whitish, 1"–2", clustered upright in conelike structure
   about 3" long, Sept.–Nov., or longer; often central stalks of cones
   remain throughout winter and are evident on higher limbs.

Similar species: None; distinctive at all seasons.

Remarks: Tallest and in many ways handsomest eastern forest tree. Second only to Sycamore in trunk diameter. Wood straight-grained, fine, soft, resistant to splitting, and easily worked. Used for furniture, interiors, shingles, boats, implements, boxes, toys, pulp, and fuel. Indians made trunks into dugout canoes. Seeds eaten by squirrels and songbirds. Though widely known as Yellow Poplar and Tulip Poplar, this relative of magnolias (Pl. 45) is not closely related to true poplars (Pl. 27).

SASSAFRAS *Sassafras albidum* (Nutt.) Nees **Pl. 25**

A medium-sized to large tree. Leaves not toothed, lobed or not, in *3 patterns* (3 "fingers," a "thumb-and-mitten" outline, or smooth egg shape), usually all present. Leaves hairless to velvety-hairy beneath. Twigs *green,* often *branched,* sometimes hairy. Only 1

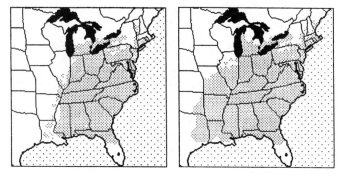

TULIPTREE   SASSAFRAS

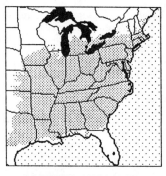

EASTERN SYCAMORE

bundle scar per leaf scar; true end buds present. Crushed leaves, twigs, and bark *spicy-fragrant.* Mature bark *red-brown* and furrowed. Leaves 2″–9″. Height 10′–50′ (90′); diameter 2″–12″ (6′). Flowers greenish yellow, April–June. Fruits blue, fleshy, one-seeded, Aug.–Oct.

Similar species: Green forked twigs, peculiar leaf outlines, and aromatic odor distinctive.

Remarks: The durable coarse lumber was once used for barrels, buckets, posts, small boats, dugout canoes, and fuel. A pleasant tea may be made by boiling pieces of the outer bark of roots. Sassafras oil used in some soaps; a bark extract can be used to dye wool orange. Fruits eaten by songbirds, bobwhite, wild turkey, and black bear. Twigs browsed by marsh and cottontail rabbits and by white-tailed deer.

EASTERN SYCAMORE   *Platanus occidentalis* L.   **Pl. 25**

A very large lowland tree with distinctive mottled brown bark that flakes off in jigsaw-puzzlelike pieces, exposing *yellowish and whitish underbark.* Leaves nearly hairless, *three- or five-lobed,* edged with *large* teeth. Leafstalk bases hollow, covering buds; leaf scars *surround* buds. Single saucerlike, leafy, toothed stipule clasps and encircles twig at points of leaf attachment; stipule scars *ring* winter twigs. Buds covered by a *single* scale; end buds false. Bundle scars many. Leaves 6″–10″. Height 50′–130′ (175′); diameter 3′–8′ (14′). Flowers small, in *globose* heads, April–June. Fruits small and hairy, in tight, brown, long-stalked hanging *balls,* ¾″–1½″ in diameter, Oct., often through winter.

Similar species: Old World sycamores, often planted in our cities, are called Plane-trees. They usually have 2 (London Plane, *P. acerifolia* Willd.) or more (Oriental Plane, *P. orientalis* L.) fruit balls per stalk rather than 1 and have more yellowish underbark.

Remarks: Tuliptree may occasionally be taller, but Sycamore is generally conceded to be the most massive tree of eastern U.S. Attains greatest size in Ohio and Mississippi river basins but, unlike sequoias, redwoods, and bristlecone pines of California, is old at 500–600 years. Hard coarse-grained wood used for boxes, barrels, butchers' blocks, cabinetwork, and furniture. Indians used trunks for dugouts. One such canoe reported to have been 65′ long and to have weighed 9000 pounds. Twigs eaten by deer and muskrats. Cavities sought for nests and shelter by wood duck, opossum, and raccoon.

CHINESE PARASOLTREE   Not illus.
Firmiana simplex (L.) W. F. Wight

An oriental tree of the chocolate family, planted throughout the southern states and locally growing wild. Large, long-stalked leaves are sycamorelike, 3–5 lobed, with narrow sinuses and *without teeth.* Bark rather smooth and *gray-green;* twigs green and *not* ringed. Buds hairy, with 2–3 scales. Bundle scar single or indistinct. Bark smooth, gray-green. Height to 35'. Leaves 6"–12". Flowers small, in greenish yellow clusters mostly at twig ends. Fruits leathery capsules 2"–4", opening into 5 leaflike sections. Dark fluid released when capsule opens. Thickets and woods.

SWEETGUM *Liquidambar styraciflua* L. **Pl. 25**
A tall tree with *star-shaped,* toothed, hairless leaves. Leaves may be *five-* or *seven-lobed;* pleasantly fragrant when crushed. Twigs not ringed; branchlets often *corky-winged.* Stubby spur branches densely covered by leaf scars or crowded leaves. Bud scales numerous, glossy and hairy-fringed; bundle scars 3; pith continuous. Mature bark grayish, regularly grooved. Leaves 5"–8". Height 50'–120' (140'); diameter 3'–4' (5'). Flowers in spherical heads, April–May. Fruits in brown, dry, somewhat *prickly, long-stemmed, hanging balls,* Sept.–Nov. or longer.
Similar species: None in summer. In winter the twigs of some elms (Pl. 33) and Bur Oak (Pl. 29) may have corky wings. Elms have false end buds, and their bud scales often have dark borders without a hairy fringe. Bur Oak has clustered end buds.
Remarks: Both common and scientific names allude to the sap that exudes from wounds. Hardened clumps of this gum are chewed by some people. Sweetgum veneer takes a high polish and is widely used for furniture. Lumber also used for interiors, woodenware, boats, toys, boxes, and fuel. Fruits often painted and used to decorate Christmas trees. Seeds eaten by songbirds, bobwhite, wild turkey, chipmunks, and gray squirrel.

MULBERRIES **Pl. 25**
These plants have toothed leaves that are either lobed or not.

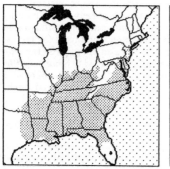
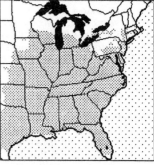

SWEETGUM   RED MULBERRY

Usually, when the tree is in leaf, both lobed and unlobed foliage is present at the same time. Unlobed leaves are generally heart-shaped. Sap of twigs and leafstalks *milky* (sap not always evident in winter twigs), with 3–5 main veins meeting near the ends of the leafstalks. End buds false. Number of bundle scars per leaf scar is more than 3, varying by species.

PAPER-MULBERRY   Pl. 25
Broussonetia papyrifera (L.) Vent.

A medium-sized Asiatic tree with *sandpaper-textured* leaves and twigs. Leaves fine-toothed, varying from unlobed and heart-shaped to deeply and intricately *lobed*. Leaves "sandpapery" above and velvety below, with *uneven* bases. Twigs *rough-hairy;* buds with only 2–3 visible scales. Bundle scars more than 3 per leaf scar. Pith blocked by a *woody partition* near each bud. Bark a *yellow-brown* smooth network of fine ridges. Leaves 4″–11″. Height to 50′; diameter to 4′. Flowers April–May. Fruits red, fleshy, barely edible, Sept. Fencerows.

Similar species: North of Florida, no other plant has such rough leaves and twigs. In Florida, see (1) Geiger-tree (p. 204), (2) Florida Trema, etc. (Pl. 26).

Remarks: In this and the next several species, the fibrous inner bark, especially of roots, can be twisted into improvised ropes and cords. Inner bark once was used as paper.

WHITE MULBERRY   *Morus alba* L.   Pl. 25

A Chinese tree whose toothed leaves are hairless and *not sand-papery.* Leaf bases often uneven, sometimes heart-shaped at the base. Foliage often lobed. Twigs *hairless* or slightly hairy. Buds *red-brown,* with 5–6 visible scales *lacking* darker scale borders. Bundle scars more than 3 per leaf scar. Pith continuous. Trunk bark *yellow-brown.* Leaves 3″–10″. Height 30′–60′ (80′); diameter 1′–3′ (4′). Flowers April–June. Fruits *whitish,* rather tasteless, June–July. Thickets.

Similar species: Red Mulberry is quite similar in winter but may be separated by its greenish brown buds and red-brown bark.

Remarks: Introduced by the British before the Revolution in an unsuccessful attempt to establish a silkworm industry. Now widespread.

RED MULBERRY   *Morus rubra* L.   Pl. 25

The only native mulberry and widespread in our area. Similar to White Mulberry, but leaves *"sandpapery"* above and hairy beneath, bases *even;* buds *greenish brown,* mostly *with* darker scale borders; bark *red-brown.* Fruits red-black, blackberrylike, tasty. Lowlands.

Remarks: Fruits eaten by squirrels and numerous song and game birds as well as by humans.

BLACK MULBERRY *Morus nigra* L.   Not illus.
Of Asiatic origin but a longtime resident especially in the south-eastern states. Leaves often unlobed but with deeply heart-shaped bases. Otherwise like Red Mulberry.

FLORIDA-ONLY TREES
Two species with alternate, fan-lobed leaves occur as trees only in tropical Florida: Papaya (*Carica papaya* L.) and Castorbean (*Ricinus communis* L.).

Trees with Alternate, Fan-veined and Triangular or Heart-shaped Leaves (Plate 26)

These trees have more or less triangular leaves with 3–5 main veins meeting at the leaf base. Leaf bases are either heart-shaped or uneven. End buds are false. See also mulberries (Pl. 25), Strawberry-tree (Pl. 32), and Camphor-tree (Pl. 46).

FLORIDA TREMA *Trema micrantha* (L.) Blume   **Pl. 26**
Found only in Florida from Palm Beach and Hendry counties southward, this *evergreen* species has toothed, long-pointed, short-stalked leaves *rough-hairy* above. Twigs mostly *hairy;* buds tiny, spur branches present. Leaves 2″–5″. Height to 80′, usually smaller. Flowers *greenish,* inconspicuous, all year. Fruits small, one-seeded, orange-yellow. Pioneer species, open sites.

WEST INDIES TREMA   Not illus.
Trema lamarckiana (Roem. & Schult.) Blume
Similar to the Florida Trema but smaller and with *short-pointed* leaves only ½″–1″ long. Twigs densely hairy. Flowers *white;* fruits pink. Miami area and Upper Keys.

REDBUD *Cercis canadensis* L.   **Pl. 26**
A small tree with *showy reddish* springtime flowers that appear before the leaves. Leaves smoothly *heart-shaped,* hairless or slightly hairy beneath. Twigs hairless. Buds dark, mostly more than 1 per leaf scar, covered by a number of scales; flower buds stalked. Bundle scars 3 per leaf scar. Most leaf scars *fringed* with hairs at top, with 2 or sometimes 3 lines descending from them on twigs. Bark dark with fine grooves. Leaves 2″–6″. Height 20′–40′ (50′); diameter 10″–12″. Flowers *red-purple* (rarely white), in showy clusters, March–May. Fruits dry pods, July–Aug. or longer.
Similar species: Leaves distinctive. In winter, combination of 3

bundle scars, raised and fringed leaf scars, buds with many scales, and false end buds differentiates it from other species.

Remarks: Blossoms, not buds, reddish. Flowers sometimes eaten in salads; red roots yield a dye. Wood of commercial value in some areas. Though a member of the pea family, Redbud is exceptional in *not* growing nitrogen-fixing root nodules. Only bobwhite and a few songbirds are known to eat the seeds.

NORTHERN (AMERICAN) HACKBERRY   Pl. 26
Celtis occidentalis L.

A small to large tree with *long-pointed,* coarse-toothed leaves; bases mostly *uneven.* Typically, foliage is *rough-hairy* above and hairless beneath. Twigs hairless; *pith usually chambered* throughout, sometimes only near the leaf scars. Side buds triangular; bud scales 4–5, hairy. Bundle scars 3 (rarely more). Bark basically light gray, rather smooth, but becoming covered with *dark warty knobs* and ridges. Leaves 3″–5″. Height 20′–70′ (100′); diameter 1′–3′ (4′). Flowers greenish, April–May. Fruits spherical, $5/16″–7/16″$, one-seeded, becoming *wrinkled* when dry, Oct.–Nov., or longer. Mostly floodplains.

Similar species: All 3 hackberries are highly variable and furthermore may hybridize. (1) Sourgum (Pl. 44) and (2) Tupelo (Pl. 43) are similar in having chambered winter twigs but have true end buds and fleshy fruits.

Remarks: Wood similar to ash; of commercial value. Fruits ("sugarberries") eaten by numerous birds, including bobwhite, lesser prairie chicken, sharp-tailed grouse, pheasant, and wild turkey. W. H. Wagner, Jr., an authority on *Celtis,* described (1974) some of the identification marks for the 3 species and suggested the preferred common names given here.

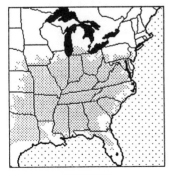

REDBUD

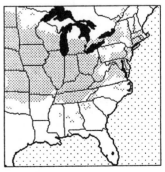

NORTHERN HACKBERRY

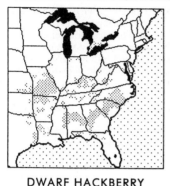
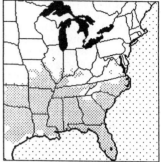

DWARF HACKBERRY   SOUTHERN HACKBERRY

DWARF (UPLAND) HACKBERRY   Pl. 26
Celtis tenuifolia Nutt.
Similar to the previous species but smaller and *upland*. Leaves
either toothed or not, short-pointed, with *few side veins* and larger
spaces (areoles) between them. Foliage may be sandpapery or not.
Leaves 2″–3″. Height to 25′. Fruits *smooth* upon drying, ³⁄₁₆″–⁵⁄₁₆″,
Sept.–Oct. Dry sites.

SOUTHERN (LOWLAND) HACKBERRY   Pl. 26
Celtis laevigata Willd.
Like Northern Hackberry, but leaves mostly not toothed and
often with very long-pointed tips. Leaves 2″–4″. Fruits *smooth*
upon drying, ³⁄₁₆″–⁵⁄₁₆″, Oct.–Nov. Mostly southern Coastal Plain
bottomlands.

SEA HIBISCUS   *Hibiscus tiliaceus* L.   Pl. 26
An evergreen shrub or small tree native to Asia, reportedly
escaped to the wild along Florida coasts. Leaves 5″–10″, heart-
shaped, 9–11 main leaf veins, *teeth absent* or few, slightly *hairy* to
velvety beneath, with one or several lengthened dark *glands* on
the bases of main leaf veins beneath. Twigs ringed by narrow
stipule scars. Height to 20′. Flowers large, showy, yellow to red.
Fruits dry capsule *splitting* into 5 valves.
Similar species: (1) Named after the basswoods *(Tilia);* the
foliage is similar but lacks teeth. (2) See Portiatree.
Remarks: The fibrous bark can be twisted into cord to make fish
nets, mats, and rope. Highly ornamental and a honey plant.

PORTIATREE   Not illus.
Thespesia populnea Soland. ex Correa
Similar to Sea Hibiscus in appearance, distribution, and habitat.

The leaves, however, are *hairless,* with only 5–7 main veins and *vein glands lacking.* Leaves 5″–10″. Height to 50′. Flowers yellow, with purple spreading from the petal bases. Fruits dry capsules, nearly spherical, *not splitting* to the base.

BASSWOODS   *Tilia* species   **Pl. 26**

The basswoods, or lindens, make up a small but complex group of trees. As a genus, characterized by more or less *heart-shaped, fine-toothed* leaves with *uneven* bases. Buds green to bright red and with only 2–3 visible bud scales; end buds false. Bundle scars more than 3 per leaf scar. Pith continuous and round in cross section; sap clear. Bark dark and shallowly grooved when mature but often smooth grayish on the upper parts. Leaves 3″–10″. Height 50′–80′ (125′); diameter 2′–3′ (4′). Flowers yellow, fra-

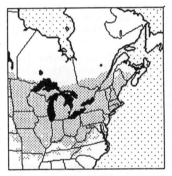

AMERICAN BASSWOOD
Tilia americana L.

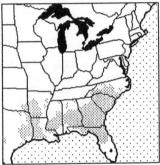

CAROLINA BASSWOOD
Tilia caroliniana Mill.

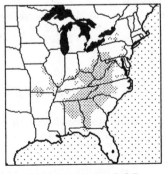

WHITE BASSWOOD
Tilia heterophylla Vent.

grant, June–Aug. Fruits small nutlets clustered beneath large leafy wings that act as spinning parachutes upon ripening, Aug.–Oct. Mostly in moist fertile soils.

The basswoods (species of *Tilia*) are difficult to separate. The following key provides a tentative basis for identification, but see also the identification chart facing Pl. 26. In addition to our 3 native species, European and Asiatic imports occasionally escape from cultivation.

1. Grown leaves hairless:
   2. Leafstalks and flower stalks hairless. Northern states and Canada. **American Basswood, Pl. 26.**
   2. Leafstalks and flower stalks hairy. Coastal Plain, southern. **Carolina Basswood.**
1. Grown leaves hairy beneath:
   3. Leaf undersides green, hairs loose. **Carolina Basswood.**
   3. Leaf undersides white-velvety. Mainly in Appalachians. **White Basswood.**

Similar species: In winter, the Chestnut (Pl. 32) sometimes has more than 3 bundle scars per leaf scar and 2–3 bud scales per bud. Nowadays it rarely reaches tree size. The buds are brown, and the pith is irregular rather than round in cross section. It typically occurs on dry sites rather than moist ones.

Remarks: As with the mulberries, elms, and some other species, the inner bark of basswoods, especially of roots, is tough and fibrous and can be twisted into cords, mats, and lines. Buds and fruits eaten by ruffed grouse, prairie chickens, bobwhite, squirrels, and chipmunks; twigs eaten by deer and cottontails. Lumber is used in commerce. Important honey plants.

FLORIDA-ONLY TREES   Pl. 26

Among the species on Pl. 26, Florida Trema and Sea Hibiscus may range into the Caribbean and/or other tropical regions. They occur in the eastern U.S. only in Florida.

Poplars and Tallowtree (Plate 27)

The poplars, aspens, and cottonwoods are all members of the genus *Populus*. The leaves are mostly toothed and somewhat triangular, with 3–5 main veins meeting near the leaf base. The leafstalks of all poplars are unusually long. In some species the leafstalks are flattened so that the leaves flutter even in a slight breeze.

Poplar buds are unique among plants with 3 bundle scars in that the lowermost bud scale is directly above the leaf scar. End buds are true and may have more scales than side buds. The bark of most species is distinctively smooth and greenish white when young and dark-furrowed when older. The twigs are often sharply angled (somewhat ridged). Fruits of poplars are in long, clustered, caterpillarlike catkins, which often release "cottony" seeds. The sexes are separate. Male plants of White Poplar and Balm-of-Gilead (see Balsam Poplar) are unknown in our area.

Distributed widely in the Northern Hemisphere, trees of the poplar group may form extensive forests on barren, burned, or cleared areas. Rapid-growing, short-lived species, they are of most value for paper pulp, though some of the soft lumber is used in construction work and in the manufacture of boxes and woodenware. Some kinds are of value as ornamentals and windbreaks. Seeds, buds, and twigs are important foods of numerous birds and mammals, including ruffed, spruce, and sharp-tailed grouse, prairie chicken, white-tailed deer, moose, beaver, porcupine, snowshoe hare, cottontail rabbit, and black bear.

Tallowtree resembles aspens, though they are not related.

QUAKING ASPEN   *Populus tremuloides* Michx.   **Pl. 27**
A medium-sized tree; leaves with *flattened* leafstalks and edged with 20–40 pairs of *fine teeth*. Twigs hairless and dark brown; end buds shiny, ¼"–⅜". Mature bark mostly *smooth, chalk white to yellow-green*. Leaves 2"–6", appearing earlier in spring than leaves of Bigtooth Aspen. Height 20'–50' (75'); diameter 1'–2' (3').
Similar species: (1) Bigtooth Aspen has fewer and larger leaf teeth, hairy buds, and more yellowish bark. (2) Lombardy Poplar (and its parent form, Black Poplar) has dark bark, yellow twigs,

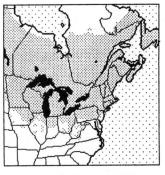

QUAKING ASPEN

and more heart-shaped or triangular leaves. (3) See also Eastern Cottonwood. (4) Tallowtree has smooth-edged leaves and milky sap.

TALLOWTREE *Sapium sebiferum* (L.) Roxb.   **Fig. 17**
Resembling Quaking Aspen but unrelated. Of Chinese origin, planted and spread widely in the South. Leaves pointed at *both* ends and *not toothed* but may be wavy-edged. Leafstalks *not* flattened and with a pair of *glands* at the leaf base. Sap is *milky* and **poisonous** if rubbed in the eyes or taken internally. Twigs *green,* visible bud scales 3; bundle scars 3, indistinct. Leaves 2″–6″. Height to 30′. Flowers small, yellow-green, 2″–4″ clusters at twig ends, spring. Fruits ½″ waxy capsules that split to expose 3 white seeds that cling to a central stalk.
Similar species: Aspens have toothed, square-based leaves and clear sap. Their mature twigs are not green.
Remarks: Introduced from the Orient so that waxy fruits could be used in making soap and candles. Also called Popcorn-tree, from the white seeds, and Milktree, from the milky sap. Foliage red in autumn.

BIGTOOTH ASPEN *Populus grandidentata* Michx.   **Pl. 27**
A small to medium-sized tree with 5–15 pairs of *large* leaf teeth and flattened leafstalks. Leaves white-woolly beneath when young. Twigs hairless or slightly gray-silky; end buds more than ⅜″ long, decidedly *gray-hairy.* Bark mostly *smooth yellow-green.* Leaves 2″–6″. Height 30′–40′ (80′); diameter 1′–2′.
Similar species: (1) Quaking Aspen is similar in general aspect but has fine-toothed leaves, hairless buds, and often more whitish mature bark; its leaves appear earlier in the spring. (2) See Tallowtree.

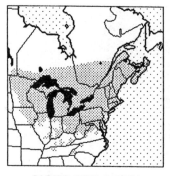

BIGTOOTH ASPEN

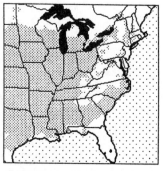

EASTERN COTTONWOOD

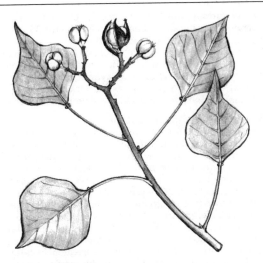

Fig. 17. Tallowtree.

EASTERN (COMMON) COTTONWOOD   Pl. 27
Populus deltoides Bart. ex Marsh
A tall tree with *coarse-toothed* leaves that have 2–3 small but
obvious *glands* (use lens) at upper end of *flattened* leafstalks.
Twigs usually hairless, *yellowish,* sometimes four-angled on vigorous shoots. End buds ⅝″–1″, quite *gummy* and with 6–7 scales.
They are *not* spicy-fragrant when crushed. Side buds usually hug
twig. Bark smooth, yellow-green when young but on mature trees
dark and ridged. Leaves 2″–8″. Height 40′–80′ (100′); diameter
1′–2′ (3½′). Bottomlands.
Similar species: Of the poplars with flattened leafstalks, only
this species has glands on the stalks. (1) Lombardy Poplar trees
have columnar growth form. (2) Balsam Poplar is more northern
and has large gummy end buds with fewer scales; when crushed,
they have a firlike fragrance. (3) Quaking Aspen has fine-toothed
foliage and brown twigs. (4) Tallowtree has leafstalk glands but
nonflattened leafstalks, leaves not toothed, greenish twigs, and
milky sap.

LOMBARDY POPLAR   Pl. 27
Populus nigra var. *italica* Muenchh.
An imported tall, thin, *steeplelike* tree much used to border
gardens and for windbreaks. Leaves *fine-toothed;* flattened leafstalks *lack* glands. Twigs hairless, *yellowish;* end buds less than

⅜″ long, not gummy; side buds not usually pressed against twigs. Bark furrowed, rather dark. Leaves 2″–8″. Height 30′–70′ (100′); diameter 1′–2′ (3′). Escape from plantings.

Similar species: (1) Typical Black Poplar (*P. nigra* L.) may occur locally; lacks peculiar thin spirelike shape but has same leaf, twig, and bud characteristics as this variety. In *P. nigra* form, it is unlike (2) Quaking Aspen in having dark bark, yellow twigs, and much more sharply triangular or even heart-shaped leaves.

BALSAM POPLAR *Populus balsamifera* L. **Pl. 27**

A northern tree with *fine-toothed, narrowly heart-shaped* leaves and *rounded* (or occasionally slightly flattened) leafstalks. Leaves usually hairless but may be slightly hairy on veins beneath. May have 2 small glands at leaf base. Twigs dark brown and hairless. End buds *more than ⅝″ long, gummy,* and *spicy-fragrant* when crushed; 5 bud scales. Side buds have 2 visible scales. Mature bark dark and grooved; gray-green and smooth on younger parts. Leaves 6″–10″. Height 30′–80′ (100′); diameter 1′–3′ (6′).

Similar species: See (1) Eastern and (2) Swamp cottonwoods.

Remarks: This species along with a sterile form, possibly a hybrid with another *Populus* species, is frequently called Balm-of-Gilead. Sterile plants spread mainly by sprouts and may have leaf undersides, leafstalks, and twigs somewhat *hairy*.

SWAMP COTTONWOOD *Populus heterophylla* L. **Pl. 27**

Mainly a southern tree with *fine-toothed* and *broadly heart-shaped* leaves with *rounded* leafstalks. Leaves and dark brown twigs *white-woolly* or hairless; end buds ⅜″–⅝″, hairless or white-hairy toward base and *somewhat gummy*. Bark dark and deeply ridged. Leaves 6″–10″. Height 40′–60′ (90′); diameter 1′–2′ (3′).

Similar species: Only poplar with gummy end buds less than ⅝″ long. See Balsam Poplar.

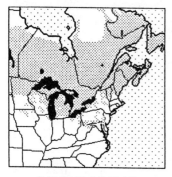

BALSAM POPLAR   SWAMP COTTONWOOD

WHITE POPLAR *Populus alba* L.   **Pl. 27**
European but widely naturalized, especially in the North. A tall tree with *white-woolly* leaves, twigs, and buds. Leaves somewhat leathery, with a few large blunt teeth or lobes. Leafstalks flattened. Bark smooth and whitish above, often thick and dark at base. Spreads by means of sucker shoots. Leaves 2″–6″. Height 60′–80′ (100′); diameter 2′–3′ (4′). Thickets.

Similar species: No other tree is as silvery white in all aspects. (1) Bigtooth Aspen leaves may be white-woolly, but they are many-toothed and with flattened leafstalks.

Oaks I–IV (Plates 28–31)

The oaks are usually tall trees and have great and diversified values. Group identification points are: true end buds clustered at tips of twigs, more than 3 bundle scars per leaf scar, and acorn fruits. Only a very few other plants have clustered end buds— principally Corkwood (Pl. 45) and the Fire or Pin Cherry (Pl. 36)—and they lack the other characteristics. Male flowers appear in May and early June as slender drooping clusters of long catkins. Female blossoms are inconspicuous. Acorns begin development shortly thereafter, becoming green at first and finally brown.

The genus *Quercus* is generally divided into 2 sections: the red (or black) oaks and the white oaks. Red oaks differ from white in that the (1) leaves or their lobes or teeth have hairlike bristle tips, (2) broken brown acorn shells (not the cups) have hairy inner surfaces, and (3) acorns require 2 years to mature, so that both tiny first-year and larger second-year acorns are usually present on the twigs and branchlets, respectively, of mature trees in summer. White oaks have leaves that lack bristle tips and have hairless inner acorn shells and acorns that mature in 1 year, growing on the twigs. Acorns of red oaks are yellow, bitter, and usually inedible; those of some white oaks are white, relatively sweet, and often edible. The bark of many red oaks is dark in color; that of white oaks is mostly light. Within the white oak group, however, the chestnut oaks are a distinctive subdivision. They have wavy-edged or toothed leaves, mostly bitter and inedible acorns, and often dark, frequently deeply ridged barks. The 34 tree-sized species of the eastern U.S. include 13 white and 21 red oaks.

To provide for more simple identification, the oaks are here divided into groups primarily according to whether the leaves are lobed, wavy-edged, or neither. Though variable, most oaks can be identified in season by their leaf shapes alone, as shown on the plates. Exceptions are the Scarlet-Pin Oak group and hybrids

Text continues on p. 138.

Oaks in Winter

All oaks have clustered end buds and produce acorns. Distributions given are the areas where each species is most common; see maps in text for full ranges.

Species and remarks	End buds over ¼"	End buds sharp	End buds hairy[1]	End buds angled[2]	Twigs hairy	Acorn cup shape[3]	White (W) or Red (R) Oak	Major distribution[4]	Plate number
Blackjack Oak (p. 144) Twigs angled, dull; bark blocky.	+	+	+	+	+	B	R	E	28
Black Oak (p. 142) Twigs angled, shiny; bark ridged.	+	+	+	+	−	B	R	E	28
Turkey Oak (p. 143) Southern Coastal Plain. End buds thin, ¼–½".	+	+	+	−	−	B	R	S	
Shumard Oak (p. 141) Southern lowlands.	+	+	−	+	−	S	R	S	
Chestnut Oak (p. 149) Trunk dark; deep furrows. Uplands.	+	+	−	−	−	B	W	A	30
Basket Oak (p. 149) Trunk light, flaky. Southern lowlands.	+	+	−	−	−	B	W	S	30
English Oak (p. 147) Acorn stalks 1"–3" long.	+	−	−	±	−	B	W	w	29
Southern Red Oak (p. 142) See text for Cherrybark Oak.	±	+	+	−	+	S	R	S	28
Bluejack Oak (p. 151) Trunk blocky, dark or gray. Southeast.	±	+	+	−	±	S	R	S	31
Scarlet Oak (p. 139) Buds white-tipped. Appalachians.	±	±	+	−	−	B	R	A	28
Northern Red Oak (p. 141) Trunk dark; shiny ridges.	±	±	−	−	−	S	R	E	28
Water Oak (p. 150) Buds often white-tipped. Southern Coastal Plain.	−	+	+	+	−	S	R	S	31
Nuttall Oak (p. 140) Acorn cups stalked. Southern Mississippi Valley.	−	+	+	−	−	B	R	S	
Shingle Oak (p. 150) Acorn cups not stalked. North-central.	−	+	+	−	−	B	R	M	31
Willow Oak (p. 152) Southern uplands. Not evergreen.	−	+	−	+	−	S	R	S	31
Laurel Oak (p. 152) Southern lowlands. Often evergreen.	−	+	−	+	±	S	R	S	31
Arkansas Oak (p. 150) Scattered; nw. Fla. to sw. Ariz.	−	+	−	−	+	S	R	S	31

Species and remarks	End buds over 1/4"	End buds sharp	End buds hairy[1]	End buds angled[2]	Twigs hairy	Acorn cup shape[3]	White (W) or Red (R) Oak	Major distribution[4]	Plate number
Pin Oak (p. 139) Lowlands. Low branches slope down.	−	+	−	−	−	S	R	M	
Jack Oak (p. 140) Northern uplands. Cups taper. Trunk dark.	−	+	−	−	−	B	R	M	
Chinkapin Oak (p. 149) Uplands. Trunk gray. Midwest.	−	+	−	−	−	B	W	M	30
Durand Oak (p. 147) Buds globular. Southern.	−	−	+	−	−	S	W	S	30
Oglethorpe Oak (p. 152) Stone Mt., Ga., and nearby.	−	±	−	−	−	B	W	S	31
Bur Oak (p. 147) Slender stipules among end buds.	−	−	+	−	±	U	W	M	29
Post Oak (p. 145) Small trees. Dry soils. South.	−	−	+	−	+	B	W	S	29
Bear Oak (p. 144) W.Va. to s. New England. South.	−	−	−	−	+	B	R	A	28
Chapman Oak (p. 147) S.C. to Fla.	−	−	−	−	±	B	W	C	30
Overcup Oak (p. 146) Buds chestnut brown. South.	−	−	−	−	−	U	W	S	29
Swamp Oak (p. 149) Acorn stalks 1"–3". North-central.	−	−	−	−	−	B	W	N	30
White Oak (p. 145) Buds red-brown. Widespread.	−	−	−	−	−	B	W	E	29
Georgia Oak (p. 144) Scattered; S.C., n. Ga., n. Ala.	−	−	−	−	−	S	R	S	
Myrtle Oak (p. 152) Evergreen; acorn stalks short. Southeast.	−	+	−	−	±	S	R	S	31
Virginia Live Oak (p. 152) Evergreen; acorn stalks ¾"–1". South.	−	−	−	−	±	B	W	S	31

[1] Use lens.

[2] In cross section.

[3] B = bowl-shaped, deep; S = saucer-shaped, shallow; U = unique (see text).

[4] A = Appalachians, C = Coastal Plain, E = East, M = Midwest, N = North, S = South, w = widespread.

Plates

PLATE 1

Conifers with Needles in Clusters: Larches and Pines I

Larches (*Larix*):
Needles numerous at ends
of warty spur branches;
dropping in autumn,
leaving tree bare.
Pines (*Pinus*): Needles
2–5 in bundles, evergreen.
Five- and three-leaved
pines on this plate;
two-leaved on following
plate. Also see charts,
pp. 38 and 40.

Species and remarks

	Geographic distribution[1]	Needles per cluster[2]	Needle length (inches)	Trunk sprouts after fire	Many old cones on tree	Cones more than 3" long	Cones longer than wide[3]	Cone prickle type[4]	Text page
Tamarack *Larix laricina* Trunk dark, scaly.	N	M	¾–1	–	–	–	±	o	33
(**European Larch** *L. decidua*) Trunk bark yellowish plates.	N	M	1–1½	–	–	–	+	o	34
White Pine *Pinus strobus* Branches in parallel whorls.	N/M	5	2–4	–	–	+	+	o	35
Pitch Pine *P. rigida* Needles stout, yellow-green.	N/M	3	3–6	+	+	–	±	s	35
Pond Pine *P. serotina* Needles slender, yellow-green.	S	3	4–8	+	+	–	±	t/o	35
(**Shortleaf Pine** *P. echinata*)[5] Needles slender, blue-green. See Pl. 2.	M/S	2(3)	3–5	–	+	–	+	t	36
Loblolly Pine *P. taeda* Needles dull, light green.	S	3	6–9	–	+	+	+	s	36
(**Slash Pine** *P. elliottii*)[5] Needles glossy, dark green. See Pl. 2.	S	2–3	5–11	–	–	+	+	t	43
Longleaf Pine *P. palustris* Twigs ½" thick, end buds white.	S	3	8–18	–	–	+	+	t	37

Note: In peninsular Fla., for tree called Australian-pine, see Pl. 2 and p. 44.
[1] N = northern, M = middle states, S = southern.
[2] M = many.
[3] Cone shape: ± = more or less ball-shaped.
[4] Cone prickles: o = lacking, s = stout, t = thin.
[5] Two- and three-needle clusters usually present; see Pl. 2.

TAMARACK

WHITE PINE

PITCH PINE

POND PINE

LOBLOLLY PINE

LONGLEAF PINE

PLATE 2

Conifers with Needles in Clusters: Pines II

These pines typically have 2 needles per bundle.[1] Five- and three-leaved pines on preceding plate. Also see charts pp. 38, 40. None of these species sprouts after fires.

Species and remarks	Geographic distribution[2]	Needle length (inches)	Twigs rough near needles[3]	Many old cones on tree	Cones more than 3" long	Cones longer than wide[4]	Cone prickle type[5]	Text page
Jack Pine *Pinus banksiana* Cones sharply curved.	N	1–1½	+	+	−	+	t/o	37
Scotch Pine *Pinus sylvestris* Upper branches bright orange.	N	2–3	−	−	−	±	o	38
(Austrian Pine *Pinus nigra*) Escapes cultivation; see text.	N	3–6	+	−	±	+	s	39
Red Pine *Pinus resinosa* Needles glossy, dark green.	N	4–6	±	−	−	+	o	39
Mountain Pine *Pinus pungens* Cones heavy, thorny.	M	2–3	+	+	±	±	s	40
Virginia Pine *Pinus virginiana* ½" branches fibrous, tough to break.	M	2–3	−	+	−	±	t	41
Shortleaf Pine *Pinus echinata*[1] ½" branches snap cleanly.	M/S	3–5	+	+	−	+	t	41
Spruce Pine *Pinus glabra*[6] Scattered in broadleaf forests.	S	2–4	−	+	−	+	t/o	42
Sand Pine *Pinus clausa* Fla./se. Ala. only.	S	2–4	−	+	−	±	s	43
Slash Pine *Pinus elliottii*[1] Needles glossy, dark green.	S	5–11	+	−	+	+	s	43
(Australian-pine *Casuarina equisetifolia*[7]) "Needles" jointed. Fla.	S	10–12	o	±	−	±	o	43

[1]Three-needle clusters may also be present in Shortleaf and Slash pines.
[2]N = northern, M = middle states, S = southern.
[3]On portions of the twig immediately adjacent to the needles; "smooth" twigs are reasonably smooth.
[4]Cone shape: ± = more or less ball-shaped.
[5]Cone prickles: o = lacking, s = stout, t = thin.
[6]Spruce Pine; not a spruce species.
[7]Not a pine; see text, p. 43 and Fig. 6, p. 44.

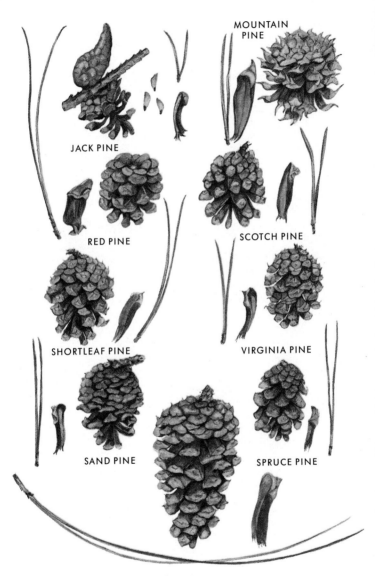

MOUNTAIN PINE

JACK PINE

RED PINE

SCOTCH PINE

SHORTLEAF PINE

VIRGINIA PINE

SAND PINE

SPRUCE PINE

SLASH PINE

PLATE 3

Conifers with
Mostly Four-sided Needles:
Spruces

Evergreen trees with
needles square in cross
section, stiff, sharp,
attached singly. Twigs
rough when needles
removed. Cones are
pendent; brown, woody.
Mostly northern.

Species and remarks

	Twigs hairy[1]	Needle length (inches)	Branchlets drooping	Grows on boggy sites	Cone length (inches)	Text page
Black Spruce *Picea mariana* Old cones remain. Canada, n. U.S.	+	1/4–7/16	–	+	3/4–1 1/4	45
Red Spruce *Picea rubens* E. Canada to Smokies.	+	1/2–5/8	–	–	1 1/4–1 5/8	45
White Spruce *Picea glauca* Canada and northern U.S.	–	3/8–3/4	–	–	1–2	45
Norway Spruce *Picea abies* European; mostly planted.	–	1/2–1	+	–	4–6	45

[1]Remove needles and use hand lens.

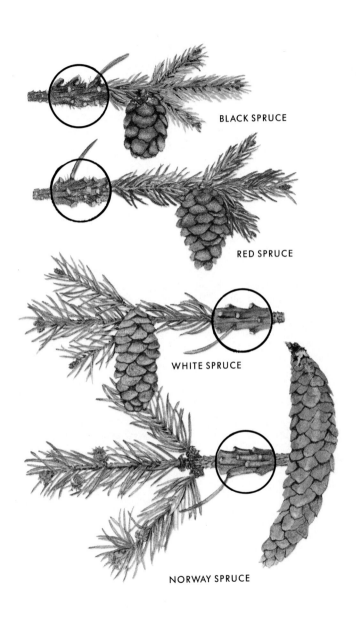

BLACK SPRUCE

RED SPRUCE

WHITE SPRUCE

NORWAY SPRUCE

PLATE 4

Conifers with Flat Needles

Evergreen[1] trees with needles flat and attached singly; needles and twigs arranged in flat sprays.

Species and remarks

	Needles with slender stalks	Needles white-striped beneath	Needles sharp-pointed	Twigs rough	Major distribution[2]	Text page
Balsam Fir *Abies balsamea* Bracts hidden by cone scales.	−	+	−	−	N	46
Fraser Fir *Abies fraseri* Bract tips visible between cone scales.	−	+	−	−	A	47
Eastern Hemlock *Tsuga canadensis* Needles to 9/16″.	+	+	−	+	N	47
Carolina Hemlock *Tsuga caroliniana* Needles more than 10/16″.	+	+	−	+	A	48
Baldcypress *Taxodium distichum*[1] Southern swamps. Foliage fernlike.	+	−	+	+	S	48
Florida Yew *Taxus floridana* Fruits red, berrylike.	+	−	+	−	F	49
Florida Torreya *Torreya taxifolia* Fruits green/purple, olive-like.	−	−	+	−	F	50

[1] Baldcypress leaves (and most twigs) drop in winter and are not evergreen; branchlets rough; leaf scars lacking. **Pondcypress** (*T. distichum* var. *nutans*) needles three-sided, pressing close to drooping twigs rather than lying in flat sprays; not evergreen.

[2] N = northern states and Appalachian Mts.; A = Appalachians, mainly in the w. Carolinas (Smoky Mts.); S = South; F = nw. Fla. and sw. Ga. Rare.

BALSAM FIR

FRASER FIR

EASTERN HEMLOCK

CAROLINA HEMLOCK

PONDCYPRESS

FLORIDA YEW

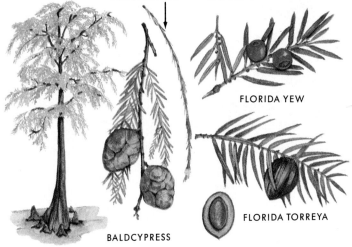

BALDCYPRESS

FLORIDA TORREYA

PLATE 5

Conifers with Scalelike or
Three-sided Hollow Leaves

Evergreen trees with leaves in pairs or whorls
and often of two types, either or both of which
may be present. See also Pondcypress (Pl. 4)
and French Tamarisk (Fig. 7), with pointed
leaves.

Species and remarks

	Tiny scalelike leaves present	Pointed, sharp leaves present	Leaf sprays flattened	Major distribution[1]	Text page
Northern White-cedar *Thuja occidentalis* Cones slim, dry; ½" long.	+	–	+	N	50
Atlantic White-cedar *Chamaecyparis thyoides* Fruits round, fleshy, ¼" diameter.	+	–	+	C	51
Common Juniper[2] *Juniperus communis* Old fields, dry soils.	–	+	–	N	52
Ashe Juniper[3] *J. ashei* Small round-topped tree. Ozarks, etc.	+	–	–	O	52
Eastern Redcedar[4] *J. virginiana* Pointed tree; dry sites. Fruits ¼".	±	±	–	w	53
(**Southern Redcedar**[4] *J. silicicola*) Similar to Eastern Redcedar; wet sites. Fruits ³⁄₁₆".	±	±	–	SC	54

[1] N = North, C = Coastal Plain, O = Ozarks region, S = South, w = widespread.

[2] Needles in whorls of 3, 1 side white.

[3] The only species in this group with scalelike leaves that are not gland-dotted.

[4] Both scalelike and longer, sharp-pointed leaves may be present; either type may occur alone. Scalelike leaves less than 1.5mm (¹⁄₁₆") in Eastern Redcedar and more than 2mm (¹⁄₁₂") in Southern Redcedar. Eastern Redcedar is widespread but occurs on Coastal Plain only from Va. northward.

NORTHERN WHITE-CEDAR

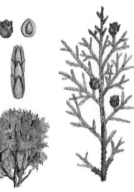

ATLANTIC WHITE-CEDAR

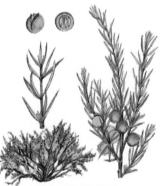

COMMON JUNIPER

ASHE JUNIPER

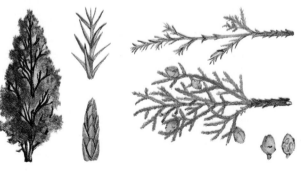

EASTERN REDCEDAR

PLATE 6

Trees with Opposite Fan-compound Leaves: Buckeyes and Chastetree

The only trees with opposite compound leaves whose leaflets are arranged like the spokes of a wheel. Buckeyes have toothed leaflets and large, mostly thick-husked nuts.

Species and remarks

Species and remarks	Trees growing to large size	Leaflets per leaf	End buds more than ½" long	Bud scales keeled[1]	Trunk bark scaly[2]	Flower cluster length (inches)	Flower color[3]	Stamens longer than petals[4]	Fruit husks prickly[4]	Major distribution[5]	Text page
Horsechestnut *Aesculus hippocastanum* European, planted; buds gummy.	+	7–9	+	–	+	6–12	W	+	+	w	57
Yellow Buckeye A. *octandra* Broken twigs with sweet odor.	+	5	+	–	±	4–7	Y	–	–	A	57
Ohio Buckeye A. *glabra* Broken twigs with foul odor.	+	5	+	+	+	4–6	Y	+	+	M	57
Bottlebrush Buckeye A. *parviflora* Native Ga. and Ala.; planted elsewhere.	–	5–7	–	–	–	8–20	W	+	–	S	58
Red Buckeye A. *pavia* Calyx long-tubular (½" or more).[6]	–	5	±	+	–	4–8	R	–	–	S	58
Painted Buckeye A. *sylvatica* Flowers often particolored.	–	5	–	–	–	4–6	Y/R	–	–	P	58
(Chastetree *Vitex agnus-castus)* Leaflets not toothed; twigs four-angled.[7]	–	5	–	–	–	2–4	B	+	–	C	59

[1] With a central ridge; use lens.
[2] Rather than smooth.
[3] B = pale blue, R = dark red, Y = yellowish, W = white.
[4] Stamens are slender filaments ending in pollen-bearing anthers.
[5] A = Appalachians, C = Coastal Plain, M = Midwest, P = Piedmont plateau, S = South, w = widespread.
[6] Calyx = circle of sepals (here fused and colored like the petals) surrounding the base of the petals.
[7] Crushed foliage and twigs spicy.

BOTTLEBRUSH BUCKEYE

HORSECHESTNUT

RED
BUCKEYE

PAINTED
BUCKEYE

YELLOW BUCKEYE

OHIO BUCKEYE

PLATE 7

Small Trees with
Opposite Compound Leaves:
Bladdernut and Elderberry

Leaves three-parted or feather-compound.
Leaflets pointed, flowers white. Central
end bud lacking. Both species are
distributed widely. In Fla., see also
Pl. F-7.

Species and remarks	Leaflets per leaf	Leaflets toothed	End leaflet present	Twigs stout[1]	Fruit color[2]	Text page
Bladdernut *Staphylea trifolia* Fruits inflated, balloonlike.	3–5	+	+	–	D	59
Common Elderberry *Sambucus canadensis* Flat-topped flower/berry clusters.	5–11	+	+	+	P	60

[1] Also leaf scars large and connected by lines.
[2] D = dry, brownish; P = purplish.

BLADDERNUT

COMMON ELDERBERRY

PLATE 8
Trees with Opposite Feather-compound Leaves: Ashes I

Twigs fine-hairy or smooth. Fruits dry, one-seeded, single-winged. None occurs primarily in southern swamps.

Species and remarks

Species and remarks	Leaflets per leaf	Leaflets toothed	Twigs hairy	Seeds plump[1]	Fruits winged to base	Trunk[2]	Habitat[3]	Major distribution[4]	Text page
Blue Ash *Fraxinus quadrangulata* Twigs four-lined or square in cross section.	7–11	+	–	–	+	S	U	C	61
White Ash[5] *F. americana* Leaf scars deeply notched.	5–9	±	±	+	–	F	U	w	62
Black Ash *F. nigra* No leaflet stalks. Buds blackish.[6]	7–11	+	–	–	+	F/S	L	N	62
Green Ash[7] *F. pennsylvanica* Leaflet stalks slightly winged.	7–9	±	±	+	–	F	L	w	63

[1] Seeds raised above the flat wing.
[2] F = furrowed, S = scaly.
[3] Habitat: L = lowland, U = upland.
[4] C = North-central states, N = northern U.S. and s. Canada, w = widespread.
[5] Including the velvety-twigged form sometimes called Biltmore Ash.
[6] Brown in other species.
[7] Red and Green ashes (once separated) have been combined as 1 species.

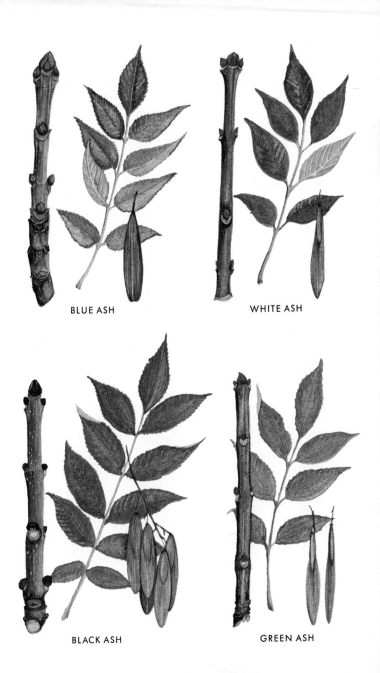

BLUE ASH

WHITE ASH

BLACK ASH

GREEN ASH

PLATE 9

Trees with Opposite Feather-compound Leaves: Ashes II and Ashleaf Maple

Twigs hairy or not.
Fruits winged.

Species and remarks

Species and remarks	Leaflets per leaf	Leaflets toothed	Twigs hairy	Seeds plump[1]	Fruits winged to base	Mostly southern swamps[2]	Trunk[3]	Major distribution[4]	Text page
Pumpkin Ash *Fraxinus profunda* Twigs and leafstalks velvety.	7–9	−	+	+	−[5]	+	F/S	S	63
Carolina Ash *F. caroliniana* Twigs and leafstalks hairless.	5–7	+	+	−	+[6]	+	S	S	64
Ashleaf Maple (Box-elder) *Acer negundo* Twigs green or purplish, hairless.	3–5	+	−	+	−[7]	−	F	w	64

[1] Raised above the flat wing.
[2] Trunk bases of swamp trees often swollen.
[3] F = furrowed, S = scaly.
[4] S = southern, w = widespread.
[5] Seeds not extending to midlength of fruit.
[6] Seeds extending beyond midlength of fruit; fruits often three-winged.
[7] Fruits are double maple "keys" rather than single-winged ash fruits.

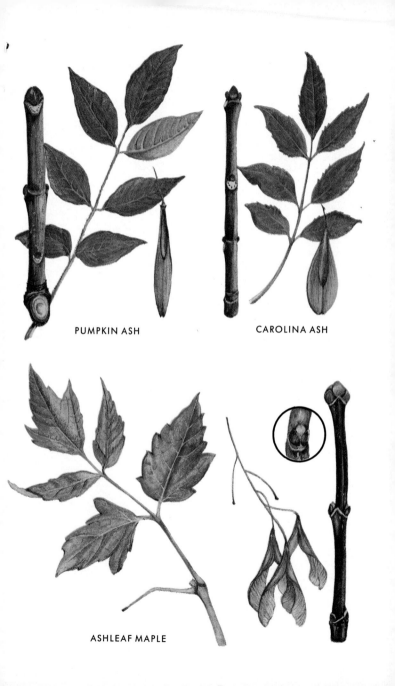

PUMPKIN ASH

CAROLINA ASH

ASHLEAF MAPLE

PLATE 10

Trees with Opposite or Whorled Heart-shaped Leaves: Princess-tree and Catalpas

Trees with large, opposite or whorled heart-shaped leaves. Twigs stout; central end buds lacking; leaf scars large and circular, bundle scars in ellipse. Flowers showy; fruits woody, hollow, many-seeded. Widespread from distribution centers.

Species and remarks	Leaves per node	Leaves long-pointed	Buds per leaf scar	Pith[1]	Flowers[2]	Fruits[3]	Major distribution[4]	Text page
Princess-tree *Paulownia tomentosa* Trunk with shiny ridges.	2	–	1 +	C	PC	P	S	67
Northern Catalpa *Catalpa speciosa* Trunk bark scaly; blossoms 2½" across.	2–3	+	1	S	WO[5]	C	C	67
Southern Catalpa *Catalpa bignonioides* Trunk bark scaly; blossoms 1"–2" across.	2–3	–	1	S	WC	C	S	68

[1] C = chambered or hollow; S = solid, white.
[2] P = purple; W = white; C = in crowded clusters; O = in open clusters.
[3] C = cigar-shaped, 8"–18" long; P = pecan-shaped, 1½" long.
[4] C = north-central states, S = South.
[5] Illustrated.

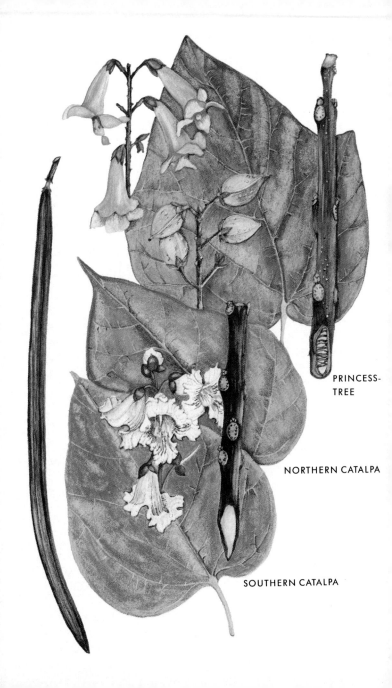

PRINCESS-
TREE

NORTHERN CATALPA

SOUTHERN CATALPA

PLATE 11

Trees with Opposite, Lobed Leaves:
Maples

Our only trees with opposite,
three- to five-lobed leaves.[1]

Species and remarks

	Number of leaf lobes	Leaves whitened beneath	Leaves mostly less than 4" long[2]	Buds with only 2 scales[3]	Extra buds often clustered	Fruit length (inches)[4]	Trunk bark whitish	Major distribution[5]	Text page
Striped Maple *Acer pensylvanicum* Bark green; thin white stripes.	3	–	–	+	–	¾–1	–	N	69
Mountain Maple *A. spicatum* Bark brown; twigs velvety-hairy.	3	–	–	+	–	½–¾	–	N	69
Red Maple *A. rubrum* Leaves with shallow divisions.	3(–5)	+	–	–	+	½–1	±	w	69
Silver Maple *A. saccharinum* Leaves with deep divisions.	5	+	–	–	+	1½–3	–	w	70
Sugar Maple *A. saccharum* Leaf edges firm, sharply toothed.	5	–	–	–	–	¾–1¼	–	N	70
Black Maple *A. nigrum* Leaf edges droop; more wavy.	5	–	–	–	–	¾–1¼	–	N	71
Florida Maple *A. barbatum*[6] Leaf lobes narrowed at base.	3(–5)	+	+	–	–	½–¾	+	S	72
Chalk Maple *A. leucoderme*[6] Leaf lobes blunted at tips.	3(–5)	–	+	–	–	¾–1¼	+	S	72

[1] Cranberry Viburnum (*Viburnum trilobum*), a shrub, has three-lobed maple-like leaves, but these are hairy beneath and have leafstalk glands.
[2] Including leafstalk.
[3] Also fruits in narrow clusters at the twig ends; in other species fruit clusters arise from points along the twig.
[4] A fruit is half of the winged pair of "keys."
[5] N = North, S = South, w = widespread.
[6] Low southern trees with small, few-toothed leaves.

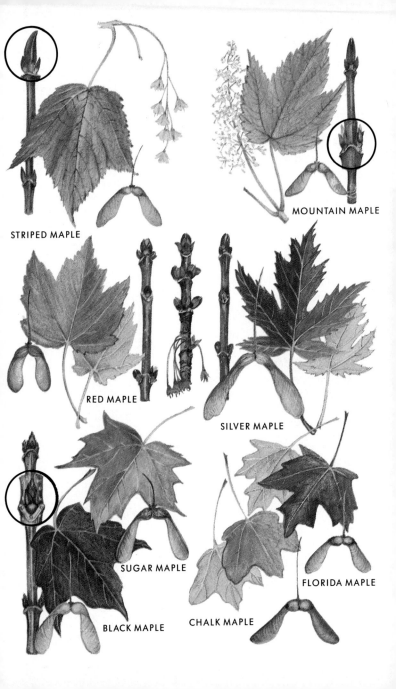

STRIPED MAPLE

MOUNTAIN MAPLE

RED MAPLE

SILVER MAPLE

SUGAR MAPLE

BLACK MAPLE

CHALK MAPLE

FLORIDA MAPLE

PLATE 12

Trees with Opposite, Simple, Fine-toothed Leaves

Species and remarks	Twig tips spiny	Leaves long-pointed	Leafstalks often winged	Leaves shiny above	Buds with only 2 scales	Bundle scars per leaf scar	Major distribution[1]	Text page
Common Buckthorn *Rhamnus cathartica* Inner bark yellow.	+	–	–	–	–	3	w	72
Swamp Forestiera *Forestiera acuminata* Buds globular, often double.	±	+	–	–	–	1	S	72
Burningbush *Euonymus atropurpureus* Twigs green, four-lined.	–	–	–	–	–	1	M	73
Rusty Blackhaw *Viburnum rufidulum* Buds and midrib red-hairy.	–	–	+	+	+	3	S	74
Smooth Blackhaw *V. prunifolium* Buds brown, shorter, not hairy.	–	–	–	–	+	3	M	75
Nannyberry *V. lentago* Buds very long, slender, brown or gray.	–	+	+	–	+	3	N	75
(Basket Willow *Salix purpurea*) Some leaves alternate; see Pl. 39.	–	–	–	–	–	3	N	76

[1] M = midlatitudes, N = North, S = South, w = widespread.

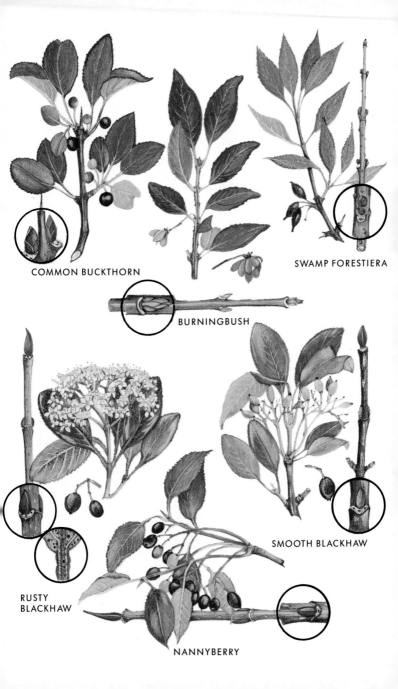

COMMON BUCKTHORN

SWAMP FORESTIERA

BURNINGBUSH

RUSTY
BLACKHAW

SMOOTH BLACKHAW

NANNYBERRY

PLATE 13

Trees with Opposite, Simple, Mostly Leathery Leaves, Not Toothed

Species of the southern Coastal Plain and seacoasts. Most have evergreen leaves with edges rolled under. See also Pl. 14. In Fla., see also Pls. F-13A and F-13B.

Species and remarks	Leaves leathery, evergreen	Leaves blunt	Leaves wedge-based	Leafstalks with glands	Leaf length (inches)	Twigs ringed	Bud scales per bud	Bundle scars	Seacoasts only	Mature fruit color[1]	Text page
Small-leaf Viburnum *Viburnum obovatum*[2] Leaves short-stalked, fine-dotted.[3]	±	+	+	−	1–2	−	2	3	−	BK	76
Possumhaw Viburnum *V. nudum*[2] Buds long, slender; see Pl. 14.	−	−	±	−	3–5	−	2	3	−	BU	76
Devilwood *Osmanthus americanus* Buds small, twigs whitish.	+	−	+	−	2–6	−	2	1	−	BU	77
Florida Forestiera *Forestiera segregata* Flowers in leaf angles.	±	+	+	−	1–2	−	4+	1	±	BK	78
Red Mangrove *Rhizophora mangle*[4] Deep shallows; arching prop roots; see Fig. 10.	+	±	±	−	2–6	+	2	3	+	BR	78
Black Mangrove *Avicennia germinans* Tidal shallows; breather roots erect; see Fig. 11.	+	+	+	−	2–6	+	2	1	+	G	79
(White Mangrove *Laguncularia racemosa*)[4] Shorelines; erect breather roots few.	+	+	−	+	2–3	−	0	1	+	R	80
(Camphor-tree *Cinnamomum camphora*) Crushed leaves with camphor odor; see Pl. 46.	+	−	±	−	3–7	−	0	2	−	D	80

Note: Leaf length includes stalk. Names in parentheses are of similar trees not illustrated here; see text.

[1] BK = black, BR = brown, BU = blue, D = dark, G = green, R = red.
[2] Two species have leaves that are fine-toothed, at least in part.
[3] Use lens.
[4] Fla. only.

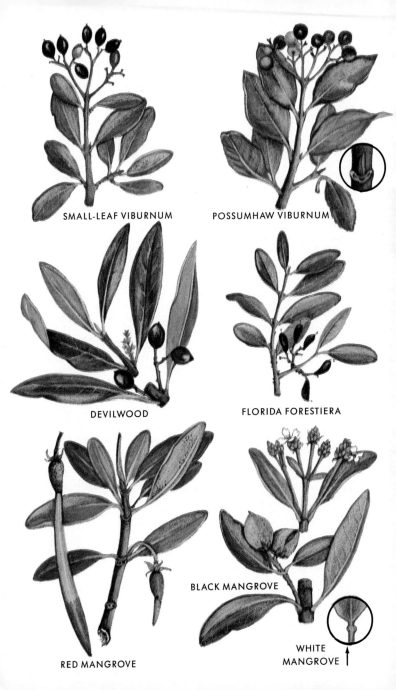

SMALL-LEAF VIBURNUM

POSSUMHAW VIBURNUM

DEVILWOOD

FLORIDA FORESTIERA

RED MANGROVE

BLACK MANGROVE

WHITE MANGROVE

PLATE 14

Trees with Opposite Simple Leaves, Neither Toothed nor Leathery

In the South, Crapemyrtle (Pl. 44) also may have some opposite leaves.

Species and remarks	Veins follow leaf edges	Leaves often in 3's, 4's	Leaves more than 2½" long	Bud scales, more than 2	Bundle scars	Aquatic habitat	Major distribution[1]	Text page
Roughleaf Dogwood *Cornus drummondii* Pith brown; twigs red-brown.	+	−	±	−	3	−	E	81
Flowering Dogwood *Cornus florida* Pith white; twigs purple.	+	−	+	−	3	−	E	81
(**Stiff Dogwood** *Cornus stricta*) End buds in pairs; pith white.	+	−	±	−	3	±	S	82
(**Possumhaw Viburnum** *Viburnum nudum*)[2] End buds single, slender.	−	−	+	−	3	−	S	76
Buttonbush *Cephalanthus occidentalis* Flowers/fruits ball-shaped.	−	+	+	±[3]	1	+	E	82
(**Pinckneya** *Pinckneya pubens*) Leaves large; twigs ringed. See Fig. 12.	−	+	+	±	1	±	S	82
Fringetree *Chionanthus virginicus* Bud scales with central ridges.	−	−	+	+	1	−	S	83
California Privet *Ligustrum ovalifolium* Twigs hairless; buds many-scaled.	−	−	−	+	1	−	S	84
(**Japanese Privet** *Ligustrum japonicum*) Twigs hairless; buds few-scaled.	−	−	−	+	1	−	S	84
(**Chinese Privet** *Ligustrum sinense*) Twigs fine-hairy.	−	−	−	+	1	−	S	84
Silver Buffaloberry *Shepherdia argentea* Leaves and twigs silver-scaly.[4]	−	−	−	−	1	−	W	84

Note: Leaf length includes stalk. Names in parentheses indicate that the trees are not shown here but are similar; see text.

[1] E = East, widespread; S = South; W = West.

[2] See Pl. 13 and text.

[3] Buds often embedded in bark; bud scales indistinct; flowers/fruits replace central end bud.

[4] Side twigs often spine-tipped.

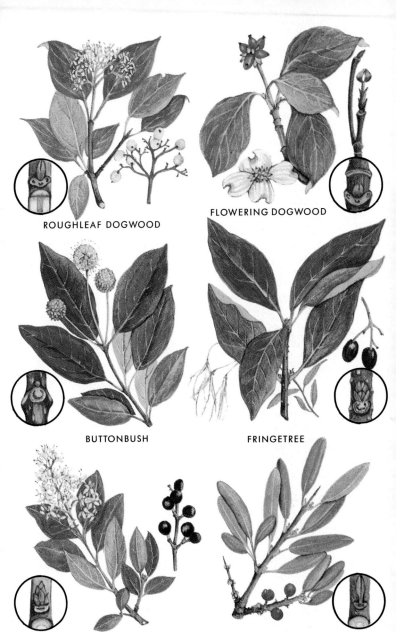

ROUGHLEAF DOGWOOD

FLOWERING DOGWOOD

BUTTONBUSH

FRINGETREE

CALIFORNIA PRIVET

SILVER BUFFALOBERRY

PLATE 15

Thorny Trees with Alternate Feather-compound Leaves

There are several other thorny trees with compound leaves; see also pp. 89, 91, and 93. See drawings in text (Fig. 14, p. 92); in Fla. see Pl. F-15.

Species and remarks	Thorns paired	Leaves twice-compound	Leaflets toothed	Crushed leaves aromatic	Bundle scars	Flower color[1]	Bean pods (inches)[2]	Major distribution[3]	Text page
Honey Locust *Gleditsia triacanthos*[4] Uplands. Thorns 2″–10″, branched.	–	±	±	–	3	W	8–18	M	88
Water Locust *G. aquatica* Lowlands. Thorns 3″±, mostly unbranched.	–	±	±	–	3	G	1–2	C	88
Northern Prickly-ash *Zanthoxylum americanum* Trunk not knobby; buds red-hairy.	+	–	+	+	3	G	–	N	89
(Southern Prickly-ash *Z. clava-herculis*[5]) Trunk with thorny knobs; buds dark, hairless.	±	–	+	+	3	G	–	S	90
Black Locust *Robinia pseudoacacia* Twigs/pods hairless; buds hidden.	+	–	–	–	3	W	2–6	w	90
Clammy Locust *R. viscosa* Twigs and pods sticky-hairy.	+	–	–	–	3	P	2–3	A	90
Hercules-club *Aralia spinosa*[5] Leaves 2′–4′ long; trunk thorns.	–	+	+	–	20+	W	–	S	94

Note: Leaf length includes stalk.
[1] G = greenish, P = pink, R = red, W = white, Y = yellow.
[2] Minus means species not in the bean family.
[3] A = Appalachians; C = Coastal Plain; M = Midwest; N = North; S = South; T = Tex., etc.; w = widespread.
[4] A thornless variety widely planted.
[5] Both of these species are known as Hercules-club. *A. spinosa* is also called Devil's Walking-stick.

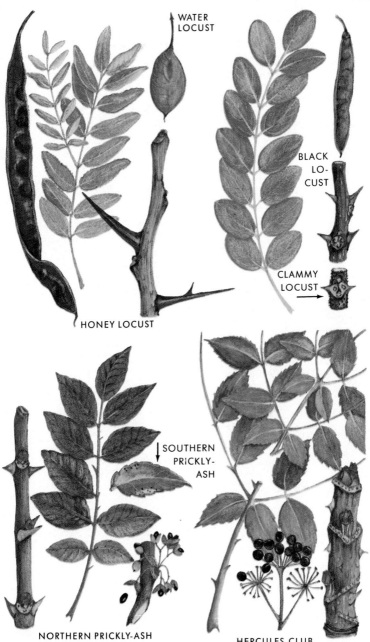

WATER
LOCUST

BLACK
LO-
CUST

CLAMMY
LOCUST →

HONEY LOCUST

↓ SOUTHERN
PRICKLY-ASH

NORTHERN PRICKLY-ASH   HERCULES-CLUB

PLATE 16
Walnuts and Similar Trees

Leaves alternate and feather-compound, with 7–14 toothed or glandular leaflets. Most are plants of Canada, the northern states, and the high Appalachians. Walnuts and Tree-of-heaven are widespread in distribution.

Species and remarks	Leaves toothed, no glands	Mature pith chambered	Leaf scars narrow	Bundle scars	Bud type[1]	End buds true	Fruit type[2]	Fruit length (inches)	Text page
Black Walnut *Juglans nigra* Upper edge of leaf scar not hairy.	+	+	−	3	WW	+	BN	2	94
Butternut *J. cinerea* Upper edge of leaf scar hairy.	+	+	−	3	WW	+	ON	2	95
Tree-of-heaven *Ailanthus altissima* Basal leaf glands. Widespread weed tree.	−	−	−	9 ±	BW	−	WS	1½	96
American Mountain-ash *Sorbus americana* Leaflets narrow, long-pointed.	+	−	+	3–5	RG	+	OB	¼	96
Showy Mountain-ash *Sorbus decora* Leaflets broad, short-pointed.	+	−	+	3–5	RG	+	RB	⅜	97
European Mountain-ash *Sorbus aucuparia* Leaflets small, hairy.	+	−	+	3–5	WW	+	RB	⅜	97

[1] BW = brown-woolly; RG = red-gummy; WW = white-woolly.
[2] BN = ball-shaped nut; ON = oblong nut; OB = orange, berrylike; RB = red, berrylike; WS = dry winged seed.

IV

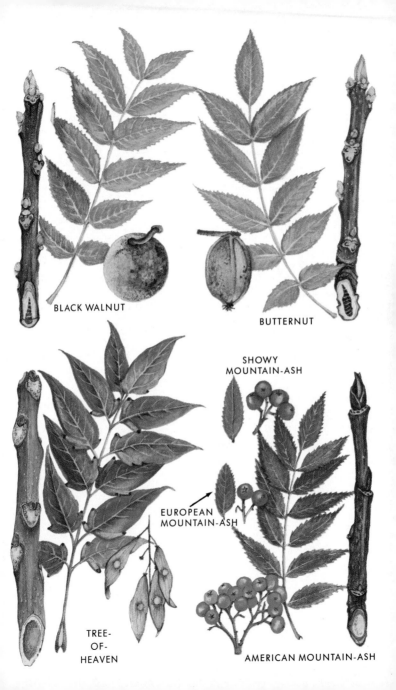

BLACK WALNUT

BUTTERNUT

SHOWY MOUNTAIN-ASH

EUROPEAN MOUNTAIN-ASH

TREE-OF-HEAVEN

AMERICAN MOUNTAIN-ASH

PLATE 17

Hickories I: Pecans

Trees with alternate, toothed, feather-compound leaves. Husks of nuts four-parted. These species have somewhat hairy twigs and buds with paired and mostly yellow scales.

Species and remarks

	Leaflets per leaf	End buds more than ½" long	Outer bud scales fall early[1]	Mature bark shaggy	Major distribution[2]	Text page
Pecan *Carya illinoensis* Buds yellow, hairy.	9–17	–	–	–	M	98
Bitternut Hickory *C. cordiformis* Buds yellow, hairless.	5–11	+	–	–	w	99
Water Hickory *C. aquatica* Buds brown with yellow glands.	9–17	–	–	+	S	99
Nutmeg Hickory *C. myristiciformis* Buds yellow- and brown-hairy.	5–9	–	–	–	S	100

[1] Buds look quite smooth after scales drop.
[2] M = Midwest, S = South, w = widespread.

PECAN

BITTERNUT HICKORY

WATER HICKORY

NUTMEG HICKORY

PLATE 18

Hickories II: Shagbarks

Trees with alternate, toothed, feather-compound leaves. Husks of nuts four-parted. These species have large end buds more than ½″ long and with scales overlapping, twigs and nut husks (not shells) both more than ⅛″ thick.

Species and remarks

	Leaflets per leaf	Leaflets hairy	Outer bud scales fall early[1]	Twigs hairy	Mature bark shaggy	Major distribution[2]	Text page
Shagbark Hickory *Carya ovata* Twigs red-brown.	5–7	–	–	±	+	N	100
Shellbark Hickory *C. laciniosa* Twigs pale orange.	7–9	±	–	±	+	C	101
Mockernut Hickory *C. tomentosa* Twigs red-brown; woolly.	7–9	+	+	+	–	S	101

[1] Buds look quite smooth after scales drop in autumn.
[2] C = central, N = northern and central states, S = southern (but north to s. New England).

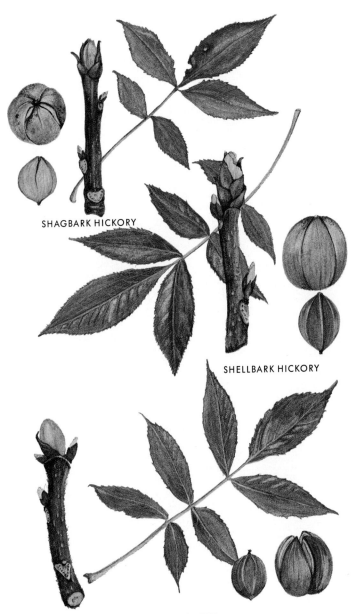

SHAGBARK HICKORY

SHELLBARK HICKORY

MOCKERNUT HICKORY

PLATE 19

Hickories III: Pignuts

Trees with alternate, toothed, feather-compound leaves. Husks of nuts four-parted. These species have end buds less than ½" long with scales overlapping, slender twigs, and thin nut husks.

Species and remarks

Species and remarks	Leaflets per leaf	Outer bud scales fall early[1]	Twigs hairy	Mature bark shaggy	Major distribution[2]	Text page
Sand Hickory *Carya pallida* End buds less than ¼" long, yellowish.	7–(9)	−	±	±	M	102
Pignut Hickory *C. glabra* End buds ⅜"–½" long; silky.	5–(7)	+	−	−	w	102
Black Hickory *C. texana* Buds rusty-hairy. Not in Fla.	(5)–7	+	+	−	O	103
Scrub Hickory *C. floridana* Buds rusty-hairy. Cen. Fla.	5–(7)	−	+	−	F	103

[1] Buds look quite smooth after scales drop in autumn.
[2] F = Fla. only, M = midlatitude states, O = Ozark region, w = widespread.

IV

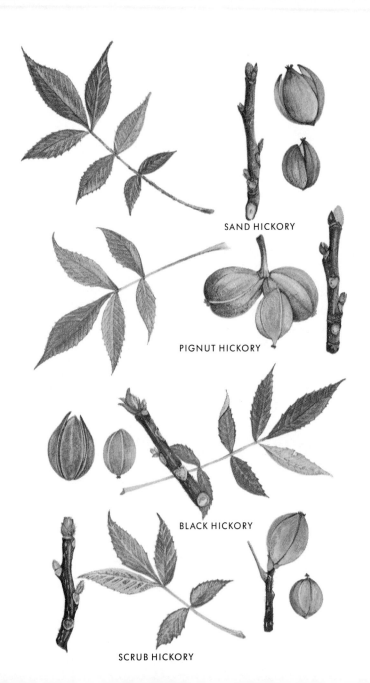

SAND HICKORY

PIGNUT HICKORY

BLACK HICKORY

SCRUB HICKORY

PLATE 20

Sumacs and Relatives

Leaves alternate, feather-compound with 7–31 leaflets, toothed or not. Four red-fruited *Rhus* species have leaf scars U-shaped enclosing buds, buds hairy and mostly hidden when leaves present. Fruits red-hairy in dense, upright clusters. Two somewhat similar and related **poisonous**[1] species with 3–7 leaflets are also compared here (see Fig. 4, p. 17).[2]

Species and remarks	Midrib winged	Leaflets toothed	Leaves leathery, evergreen	Twigs densely hairy	Twigs flat-sided	Fruit type[3]	Major distribution[4]	Text page
Winged Sumac *Rhus copallina* Leaflets ¾″ wide, short-pointed.	+	–	–	+	–	R	w	104
Prairie Sumac *R. lanceolata* Leaflets less than ½″ wide.	+	–	–	+	–	R	T	104
Staghorn Sumac *R. typhina*	–	+	–	+	–	R	N	104
Smooth Sumac *R. glabra*	–	+	–	–	+	R	w	105
(**Poison-sumac** *Toxicodendron vernix*[1]) See Fig. 4.	–	–	–	–	–	W	w	106
(**Florida Poisonwood** *Metopium toxiferum*[1]) Leaves triangular; black spots.	–	–	+	–	–	Y	F	106

[1] Two species contain chemicals that irritate the skin and eyes (see p. 106).
[2] All on this plate are members of the cashew family.
[3] R = red-hairy in dense upright clusters; W = white, small, smooth, spherical; Y = yellow-orange, ½″ long, smooth, oval.
[4] F = Fla. only; N = northern states and nearby Canada; T = Texas or nearby (see p. 104); w = widespread. All species occur mainly in old fields and forest openings.

IV

WINGED SUMAC

PRAIRIE SUMAC

STAGHORN SUMAC

SMOOTH SUMAC

PLATE 21

Trees with Alternate Once-compound Leaves, Not Toothed

Twigs hairless; buds often several at a leaf scar; end buds false. Flowers white or greenish white. See also Pl. 20 and thornless form of Honey Locust, Pl. 15. In Fla., see Pls. F-21A and F-21B.

Species and remarks	Leaflets per leaf	Leaf scars U-shaped[1]	Buds hairy	Bundle scars	Fruit type[2]	Major distribution[3]	Text page
Hoptree *Ptelea trifoliata* Buds silvery.	3	+	+	3	C	w	107
Yellowwood *Cladrastis kentukea* Leaflets alternate; wood yellow.	5–11	+	+	5	P	M	107
Wingleaf Soapberry *Sapindus saponaria* Midrib usually winged.	6–12	−	−	3	B	F	108
Western Soapberry *Sapindus drummondii* Midrib not winged.	7–19	−	±	3	B	O	108
Texas Sophora *Sophora affinis* Fruits "beaded."	13–15	±	+	3	P	T	108

[1] Buds mostly hidden when leaves present.
[2] C = circular, papery; P = peapod; B = berrylike.
[3] F = Fla. and se. Ga.; M = Midwestern states; O = Ozark region; T = Tex., etc.; w = widespread.

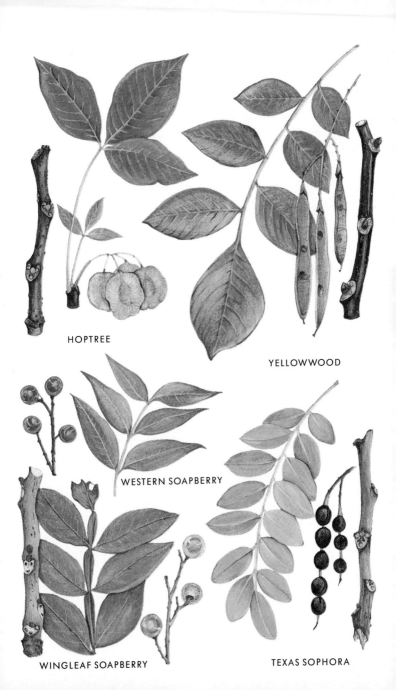

HOPTREE

YELLOWWOOD

WESTERN SOAPBERRY

WINGLEAF SOAPBERRY

TEXAS SOPHORA

PLATE 22

Thornless Trees with Twice-compound Leaves

Mostly southern species with leaves large, twigs hairless, and end buds false. See also thornless form of Honey Locust, Pl. 15. In Fla., see also Pl. F-22.

Species and remarks

Species and remarks	Leaflets toothed	Leaves more than 12" long	Leaflets more than ¾" long	Leaf tips blunt	Pairs of major leaflets	Twigs stout[1]	Flower color[2]	Major distribution[3]	Text page
Chinaberry *Melia azedarach* Buds fuzzy, not sunken.	+	+	+	−	4–6	+	L	S	110
Coffeetree *Gymnocladus dioica* Buds silky, sunk in bark.	−	+	+	−	5–9	+	W	M	110
Lebbek *Albizia lebbeck* Pods more than 1″ wide, seeds 8–10.	−	±	+	+	2–4	−	Y	F	111
Silktree *Albizia julibrissin* Pods slender, more than 15 seeds.	−	−	−	−	9–12	−	P	S	111

[1] Also leaf scars large, buds hairy, and trunk dark and rough.
[2] L = lavender, P = pink, W = white, Y = yellow.
[3] F = s. Fla. including Keys, M = midwestern states and s. Ontario; S = southern states.

IV

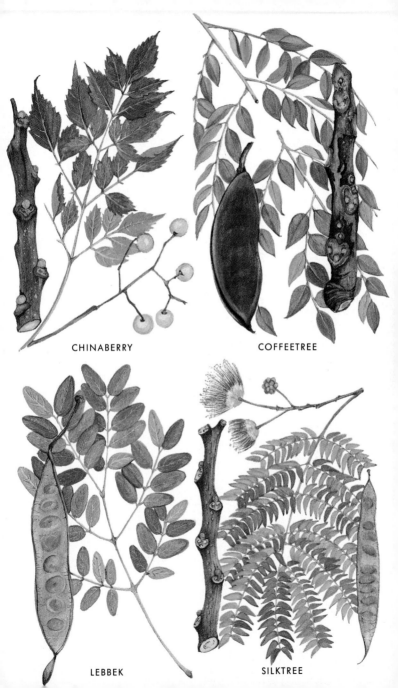

CHINABERRY

COFFEETREE

LEBBEK

SILKTREE

PLATE 23

Thorny Trees with Alternate, Toothed Leaves

Long slender spines in hawthorns; spine-tipped short branches in crabapples and plums; thorns paired in Jujube. Spur branches present. Bundle scars 3 (1 in Jujube). Flowers white to pink. In Fla., see also Lime (Fig. 16, p. 120) and Governor's-plum (Pl. F-46C). For thornless relatives see Pls. 37 and 43.

Species and remarks	Bark with horizontal lines[1]	Broken twigs with sour odor[2]	Leafstalks with glands	Leaf teeth sharp	Leaf bases wedge-shaped	Twigs hairy	Major distribution[3]	Text page
Hawthorns[4] *Crataegus* species Spines long, without buds.	−	−	−	+	±	−	w	114
American Crabapple *Malus coronaria* Fruits 1¼″–2″. North-central.	−	−	−	+	−	−	M	115
Narrowleaf Crabapple *Malus angustifolia* Fruits less than 1″. Southeast.	−	−	−	+	+	±	S	116
(**Prairie Crabapple** *Malus ioensis*) Twigs, leaves woolly. Midwest.	−	−	−	+	−	+	M	116
American Plum *Prunus americana* Buds red-brown, ⅛″.	+	+	−	+	±	±	M	117
(**Bullace Plum** *Prunus institia*) See Garden Plum, Pl. 37.	+	+	+	−	±	+	N	117
(**Canada Plum** *Prunus nigra*) Buds gray-black, ³⁄₁₆″.	+	+	+	−	±	−	N	117
Chickasaw Plum *Prunus angustifolia* Leaf scars raised; twigs reddish.	+	+	+	−	+	−	S	118
(**Jujube** *Ziziphus jujuba*) Thorns paired; leaves fan-veined.	−	−	−	−	−	+	S	118

Note: Names in parentheses indicate that the trees are not shown here but are similar; see text.

[1] These species also have false end buds and fruits with single seeds.

[2] The sour (almond) odor is weak in plums. It is difficult to describe but once learned is helpful in identifying cherries and (sometimes) plums.

[3] M = Midwest, N = North, S = South, w = widespread.

[4] A complex and difficult group whose species are poorly defined; see p. 114.

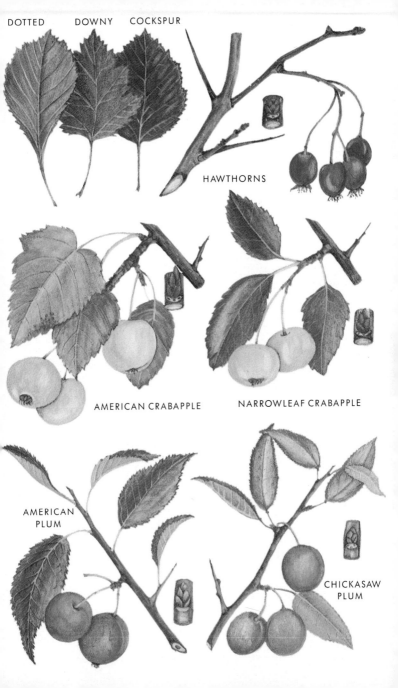

DOTTED DOWNY COCKSPUR

HAWTHORNS

AMERICAN CRABAPPLE

NARROWLEAF CRABAPPLE

AMERICAN
PLUM

CHICKASAW
PLUM

PLATE 24

Thorny Trees with Alternate Leaves, Not Toothed

Thorns single. Spur branches with clustered leaves often present. Southern species.

Species and remarks	Sap milky[1]	Leaves wedge-based	Leaves blunt-tipped	Leaves velvety-hairy	Leafstalks winged[2]	Bundle scars per leaf scar	Flowers[3]	Fruits[4]	Fla. only,[5] evergreen	Text page
Gum (Woolly) Bumelia *Bumelia lanuginosa* Leaves red- or gray-woolly.	+	+	+	+	−	3	C	B	−	118
(Tough Bumelia *Bumelia tenax*) Leaves yellow- or white-silky.[6]	+	+	+	+	−	3	C	B	−	119
Buckthorn Bumelia *Bumelia lycioides* Leaves 3″–6″ long.	+	+	−	−	−	3	C	G	−	119
(Saffron-plum Bumelia *Bumelia celastrina*) Leaves 1″–2″. Cen. & s. Fla., s. Tex.	+	+	+	−	−	3	C	B	C	120
Osage-orange *Maclura pomifera* Leaves long-pointed.	+	−	−	−	−	1–5	B	GW	−	120
Tallowwood *Ximenia americana* Parasitic on tree roots.	−	±	±	−	−	1	C	YP	S	121
(Lime or Key Lime *Citrus aurantifolia*)[7] Fruit pulp green. See Fig. 16.	−	−	−	−	N	1	S	GO	S	121
(Sour Orange *Citrus aurantium*)[7] Fruit sweet, core hollow; thorns few.	−	−	−	−	B	1	S	YO	C	121
(Sweet Orange *Citrus sinensis*)[7] Fruit acidic, core solid.	−	−	−	−	N	1	S	YO	G	121

[1] Try broken leafstalks or twigs.

[2] Leaves evergreen, gland-dotted (use lens), aromatic when crushed, leafstalks winged, twigs green; B = wings ½″ broad, N = wings narrow.

[3] B = ball-shaped, green; C = clustered, white; S = single or paired, white.

[4] B = berrylike, black; G = green; GO = green, orangelike; GW = green, coarse, much wrinkled; YO = yellow or green, orangelike; YP = yellow, plumlike.

[5] Fla. only = species not found in other states (but G = also Ga.); C = cen. Fla. and southward; S = southern three counties and/or Keys.

[6] Russian-olive (p. 177), seldom growing wild in the East, has silver-scaled leaves and twigs and is sometimes spiny.

[7] Asian origin, cultivated, escaped to wild; leaves may be wavy-edged.

GUM BUMELIA

BUCKTHORN BUMELIA

OSAGE-ORANGE

TALLOWWOOD

PLATE 25
Trees with Alternate Fan-lobed Leaves

Some or all leaves lobed.[1]
Even unlobed leaves have 3–5 main veins meeting near their bases. Leaf bases mostly heart-shaped or broad. See also Chinese Parasoltree (p. 123), Papaya, and Castorbean (p. 126); the latter two occur as trees only in tropical Florida. See also White Poplar, Pl. 27.
Species and remarks

Species and remarks	Leaf lobes per leaf[1]	Sap milky[2]	Leaves toothed	Leaves sandpapery	Leaf undersides[3]	Leaf bases uneven	Crushed leaves/buds spicy	Twigs ringed[4]	Bud scales per bud	Major distribution[5]	Text page
Tuliptree *Liriodendron tulipifera* Leaves notched; pith chambered.	4	–	–	–	N	–	+	+	2	E	121
Sassafras *Sassafras albidum* Twigs green, forked.	1–3	–	–	–	N/V	–	+	–	4	E	122
Eastern Sycamore *Platanus occidentalis* Leafstalks cover buds; trunk flaking.	3–5	–	+	–	N	–	–	+	1	E	123
Sweetgum *Liquidambar styraciflua* Branchlets often corky-winged.	5	–	+	–	N	–	+	–	5–6	S	124
Paper-mulberry *Broussonetia papyrifera* Twigs rough-hairy.[6]	1–5	+	+	+	V	+	–	–	2–3	w	125
White Mulberry *Morus alba* Buds reddish, scales not dark-edged.	1–5	+	+	–	N	±	–	–	5–6	w	125
Red Mulberry *M. rubra*[7] Buds greenish; scales dark-edged.	1–3	+	+	+	H	–	–	–	5–6	E	125

[1] In Sassafras, Parasoltree, and mulberries, some (rarely all) leaves not lobed.
[2] Try breaking leafstalks or twigs.
[3] H = hairy, N = not hairy, V = velvety.
[4] Stipule scars encircle twigs beneath each bud.
[5] E = widespread, eastern U.S.; F = tree-sized only in Fla.; N = North, principally northeastern states; S = South; w = widespread.
[6] Pith blocked by a thin woody partition near each bud (cut twig lengthwise).
[7] Black Mulberry (M. *nigra*, p. 126) has deeply heart-shaped leaf bases.

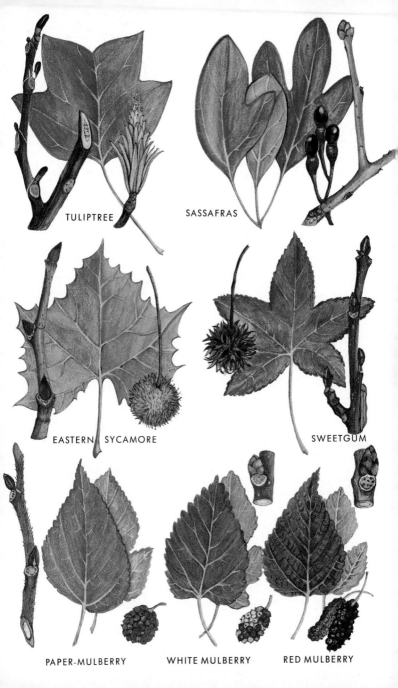

TULIPTREE

SASSAFRAS

EASTERN SYCAMORE

SWEETGUM

PAPER-MULBERRY

WHITE MULBERRY

RED MULBERRY

PLATE 26
Trees with Alternate Fan-veined and Triangular or Heart-shaped Leaves

Leaves mostly heart-shaped or triangular with 3–5 main veins meeting at their bases. Leaf bases heartshaped or uneven. End buds false. Two species are evergreen and occur only in Fla.; also see West Indies Trema (p. 126) and Portiatree (p. 128). See also Pl. 27, basswoods (p. 130), and Camphor-tree (p. 216).

Species and remarks	Leaf length (inches)	Leaves toothed	Leaf-tip shape[1]	Leaves sandpapery above	Leaves hairy beneath	Visible bud scales[2]	Bundle scars[2]	Inner bark fibrous	Pith chambered	Major distribution[3]	Text page
Florida Trema *Trema micrantha* Flowers greenish; fruits orange.	2–5	+	L	+	+	E^2	E^2	–	–	F	126
Redbud *Cercis canadensis* Leaf scars hairy-fringed at top.	2–6	–	S	–	–	5–6	3	–	–	w	126
Northern Hackberry *Celtis occidentalis* Dry fruits much wrinkled.	3–5	+	L	±	–	4–5	3	–	+	N	127
Dwarf Hackberry *Celtis tenuifolia* Dry fruits smooth; leaf veins few.	2–3	±	S	±	–	4–5	3	–	+	S	128
Southern Hackberry *Celtis laevigata* Dry fruits smooth.	2–4	–	L	±	–	4–5	3	–	+	S	128
Sea Hibiscus *Hibiscus tiliaceus* 9–11 main veins, glands on veins.[4]	5–10	–	S/L	–	+	E^2	E^2	+	–	F	128
American Basswood *Tilia americana* Inner bark fibrous.	5–10	+	S	–	–	2–3	3+	+	–	N	130

Note: Leaf length includes stalk.

[1] L = long-pointed, S = short-pointed.

[2] Counts of visible bud scales and bundle scars are unnecessary in evergreen (E) Fla.-only species.

[3] A = Appalachians, F = Fla. only, N = North, S = South, w = widespread.

[4] Lengthened glands on veins on underside of leaf, at leaf base.

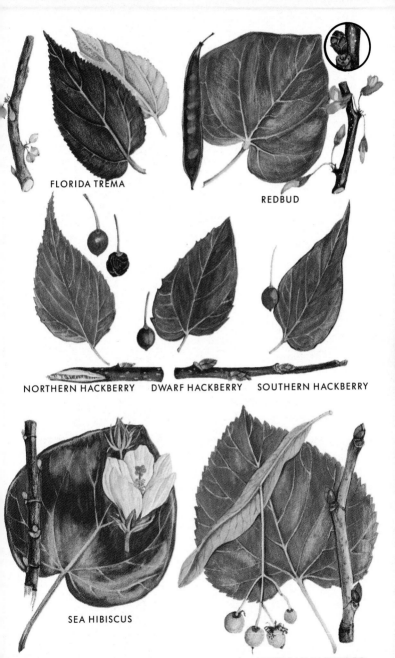

FLORIDA TREMA

REDBUD

NORTHERN HACKBERRY   DWARF HACKBERRY   SOUTHERN HACKBERRY

SEA HIBISCUS

AMERICAN BASSWOOD

PLATE 27

Poplars and Tallowtree

Poplars with triangular toothed leaves, mostly with 3–5 main veins meeting near the leaf base. Leafstalks quite long. Lowermost bud scale exactly above the leaf scar. Flowers and fruits in catkins. Bundle scars 3. Young bark often smooth, greenish white. Tallowtree foliage aspenlike but without leaf teeth.

Species and remarks	Leafstalks flattened[1]	Leaf bases with glands	Leaf length in inches[2]	Leaf teeth large, coarse	Twigs yellowish[3]	Bud characteristics[4]	Major distribution[5]	Text page
Quaking Aspen *Populus tremuloides* Buds to ⅜″ long, shiny. Leaves rounded.	+	–	2–6	–	–	–	N	131
(**Tallowtree** *Sapium sebiferum*) Twigs green, sap milky[6] ; see Fig. 17, p. 133.	–	+	2–6	o	–	–	S	132
Bigtooth Aspen *P. grandidentata* Buds more than ⅜″ long, dull.	+	–	2–6	+	–	H	N	132
Eastern Cottonwood *P. deltoides* Branches large; tree spreading.	+	+	2–8	+	+	–	N	133
Lombardy Poplar *P. nigra* var. *italica* Branches slender; tree column-shaped.	+	–	2–8	–	+	–	w	133
Balsam Poplar *P. balsamifera* Leaves narrowly heart-shaped.	–	±	6–10	–	–	S	N	134
Swamp Cottonwood *P. heterophylla* Leaves broadly heart-shaped.	–	–	6–10	–	–	G	S	134
White Poplar *P. alba* Leaves and twigs white-woolly.	–	–	2–6	–	–	H	w	135

[1] At least at the leaf base.
[2] As always, including leafstalk.
[3] Not dark brown or red-brown (green in Tallowtree).
[4] Especially end buds may be: G = gummy, H =hairy, S = spicy-scented; a minus sign means "none of the above."
[5] N = North, S = South, w = widespread.
[6] Milky sap poisonous internally and to eyes; fruits white ("Popcorn-tree").

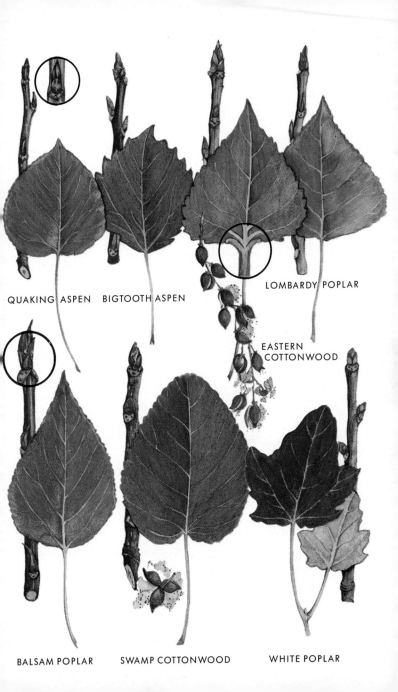

QUAKING ASPEN   BIGTOOTH ASPEN

LOMBARDY POPLAR

EASTERN
COTTONWOOD

BALSAM POPLAR   SWAMP COTTONWOOD   WHITE POPLAR

PLATE 28
Oaks I: Leaves Feather-lobed, with Bristle Tips

End buds clustered; bundle scars more than 3. All species on this plate are "red oaks": leaves bristly, two-year acorn development, inside of acorn shell (not cup) hairy. Trunks dark. In winter see also chart, pp. 136–137. See also pp. 139–144.

Species and remarks	Leaf sinus depth[1]	Leaves thick/leathery	Leaves glossy above	Leaves hairy beneath[2]	End buds more than 1/4" long	End buds sharp	End buds hairy	End buds angled	Twigs hairy	Acorn cup shape[3]	Major distribution[4]	Text page
Scarlet Oak *Quercus coccinea* Buds often white-tipped.	D	–	+	–	±	±	+	–	–	B	A	139
(**Pin Oak** *Quercus palustris*) Low branches slope down.	D	–	+	–	–	+	–	–	–	S	N	139
(**Jack Oak** *Quercus ellipsoidalis*) Northern; acorn cup conical.	D	–	+	–	–	+	–	–	–	B	N	140
(**Nuttall Oak** *Quercus nuttallii*) Southern Mis. R. valley.	D	–	+	–	–	+	+	–	–	B	S	140
(**Shumard Oak** *Quercus shumardii*) Widespread, esp. in South.	D	–	+	–	+	+	–	+	–	S	S	141
Northern Red Oak *Q. rubra* Trunk dark with shiny ridges.	M	–	–	–	±	±	–	–	–	S	w	141
Black Oak *Q. velutina* Twigs angled; trunk dark.	M	+	+	–	+	+	+	+	–	B	w	142
Southern Red Oak *Q. falcata* 3 main leaf lobes, base rounded.	D	±	+	+	±	+	+	–	+	S	S	142
Bear Oak *Q. ilicifolia* Leaves small. Northeastern.	M	–	–	+	–	–	–	–	+		E	144
Blackjack Oak *Q. marilandica* Twigs angled; bark dark, blocky.	S	+	+	+	+	+	+	+	+	B	S	144

[1] D = deep, M = medium, S = shallow.
[2] Plus tufted vein angles.
[3] B = bowl, S = saucer.
[4] A = Appalachians, E = Northeast, M = Midwest, N = North, S = South, w = widespread.

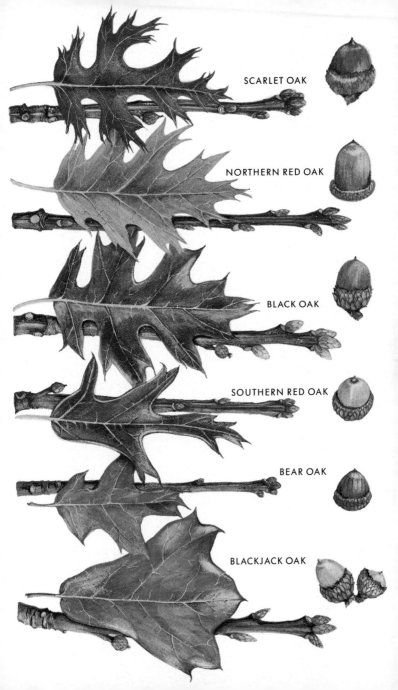

SCARLET OAK

NORTHERN RED OAK

BLACK OAK

SOUTHERN RED OAK

BEAR OAK

BLACKJACK OAK

PLATE 29

Oaks II: Leaves Feather-lobed, without Bristle Tips

End buds clustered; bundle scars more than 3. Part of the "white oak group": These oaks lack bristle tips on the leaves and have acorns which mature in 1 summer and hairless inner acorn-shell (not cup) surfaces (see Pl. 28). Other white oaks are on Pls. 30 and 31. In winter, also see chart, pp. 136–137.

Species and remarks	Depth of leaf sinus[1]	Leaves thick, leathery	Leaves whitened beneath	Leaves hairy beneath[2]	End buds more than 1/4" long	End buds sharp	End buds hairy	End buds angled	Twigs hairy	Acorn cup shape[3]	Major distribution[4]	Text page
White Oak *Quercus alba* Leaves with 7–11 lobes.	M	–	+	–	–	–	–	–	–	B	E	145
Post Oak *Q. stellata* Leaves resemble a cross.	D	+	–	+	–	–	+	–	+	B	S	145
Overcup Oak *Q. lyrata* Cup nearly encloses nut.	M	–	+	+	–	–	–	–	–	U	S	146
Bur Oak *Q. macrocarpa* Slender stipules among end buds.[5]	D	±	+	+	–	–	+	–	±	U	M	147
English Oak *Q. robur* Leaves small; acorn stalks 1"–3" long.	M	–	–	–	+	–	–	±	–	B	P	147

[1] D = deep, M = medium.
[2] In addition to tufts in vein angles.
[3] B = bowl shape; U = unique (see plate).
[4] E = East, M = Midwest, P = spreading from plantings in North, S = South.
[5] Corky wings often present on some branchlets.

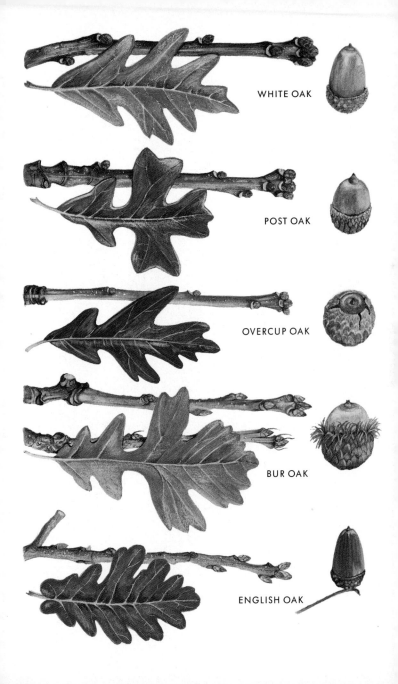

WHITE OAK

POST OAK

OVERCUP OAK

BUR OAK

ENGLISH OAK

PLATE 30

Oaks III: Leaves Wavy-edged or Toothed

Recognized as oaks by clustered end buds and acorns. None has bristle-tipped leaves; all are in the "white oak group" (see Pl. 28). Only Durand Oak may have hairy twigs; none of these species has hairy or angled end buds. Trunk bark light gray (except Chestnut Oak). (Specimens of species on Pl. 31 may have some wavy-edged or toothed leaves.) In winter also see chart, pp. 136–137.

Species and remarks	Leaf edges[1]	Leaves thick, leathery	Leaves whitened beneath	Leaves hairy beneath	End buds more than 1/4″ long	End buds sharp	Acorn cup more than 1″ across	Acorn cup shape[2]	Moist-soil habitat	Major distribution[3]	Text page
Durand Oak *Quercus durandii* — Variable foliage; buds rounded.	L/W	+	+	–	–	–	–	S	±	S	147
Chapman Oak *Q. chapmanii* — Leaf tips often notched.	W	+	–	–	–	–	–	B	–	SE	147
Chinkapin Oak *Q. muehlenbergii* — Sharp teeth, 8–13 pairs. Uplands.	S	–	–	±	–	+	–	B	–	M	149
Basket Oak *Q. michauxii* — Blunt teeth, 7–16 pairs. Lowlands.	R	–	±	+	+	+	+	B	+	S	149
Swamp Oak *Q. bicolor* — Acorn stalks 1″–3″ long; 4–6 pairs teeth.	R	–	+	–	–	–	±	B	+	M	149
Chestnut Oak *Q. prinus* — Teeth 7–16 pairs; trunk dark, ridged.	R/W	±	–	±	+	+	–	B	–	A	149

[1] L = lobed, R = teeth rounded, S = teeth sharp, W = wavy.
[2] B = bowl-shaped, deep; S = saucerlike, shallow.
[3] A = Appalachians, M = Midwest, S = South, SE = Southeast.

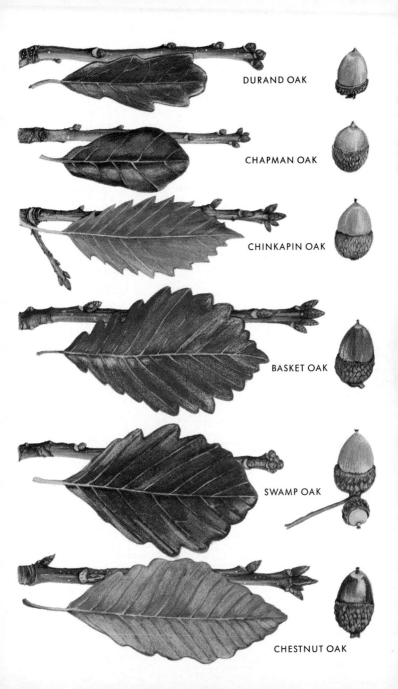

DURAND OAK

CHAPMAN OAK

CHINKAPIN OAK

BASKET OAK

SWAMP OAK

CHESTNUT OAK

PLATE 31
Oaks IV: Leaves Typically Smooth-edged

Clustered end buds and acorns identify these mostly southern trees as oaks. The two white oak species have leaves which lack terminal bristle tips.[1] End buds small, mostly less than 3/16″ long (see Bluejack Oak). See also Pl. 30. In winter, also see chart, pp. 136–137.

Species and remarks	Leaves thick, leathery	Leaves glossy above	Leaves hairy beneath	End buds sharp	End buds hairy	End buds angled	Twigs hairy	Acorn cup shape[2]	Red (R)/White (W) oak[3]	Text page
Arkansas Oak *Quercus arkansana* Leaves wide.	−	−	−	+	−	−	+	S	R	150
Water Oak *Q. nigra* Leaves wide near tip.	−	−	−	+	+	+	−	S	R	150
Shingle Oak *Q. imbricaria* Leaves 4″–10″ long. North-central.	−	+	+	+	+	−	−	B	R	150
Bluejack Oak *Q. incana* End buds 3/16″–5/16″ long; leaves white beneath. Southern.	+	+	+	+	+	−	±	S	R	151
Oglethorpe Oak *Q. oglethorpensis* W. S.C., ne. Ga. Leaves yellow beneath. A white oak.[3]	−	−	+	±	−	−	−	B	W	152
Willow Oak *Q. phellos* Leaves narrow, dull beneath.	−	+	±	+	−	+	−	S	R	152
Laurel Oak *Q. laurifolia* Leaves wider, shiny (±) beneath.	±	+	−	+	−	+	±	S	R	152
Myrtle Oak *Q. myrtifolia* Leaves 1″–2″ long; acorn stalks short.	+	+	−	+	−	−	±	S	R	152
Virginia Live Oak *Q. virginiana* Leaves 2″–4″ long; acorn stalks 3/4″–1″ long. A white oak.[3]	+	+	±	−	−	−	−	B	W	152

Note: Leaf length includes stalk.

[1] Leaves may be other than smooth-edged on specimens of several of these species. Bristle tips may be absent, too, from some leathery-leaved members of the red oak group.

[2] B = bowl-shaped, deep; S = saucerlike, shallow.

[3] Major oak categories (see charts accompanying Pls. 29, 30).

V

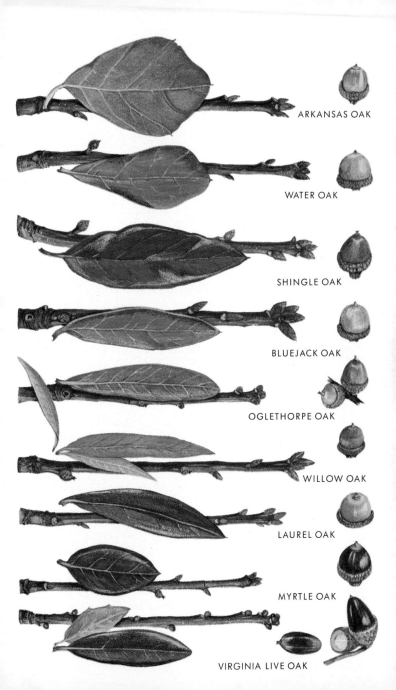

ARKANSAS OAK

WATER OAK

SHINGLE OAK

BLUEJACK OAK

OGLETHORPE OAK

WILLOW OAK

LAUREL OAK

MYRTLE OAK

VIRGINIA LIVE OAK

PLATE 32

Trees with Alternate, Coarse-edged Leaves

Trees with large, sharp leaf-teeth or deeply wavy-edged leaves. Bundle scars usually 3; sometimes more in Chestnut. Species and remarks	Leaf length (inches)	Leaves long, 3–4 times width	Leaves sharply toothed	Leaf bases uneven	Leaves hairy beneath	Twigs hairy	Buds hairy	End buds false	Major distribution [1]	Text page
Chestnut *Castanea dentata* Large specimens now rare.	5–8	+	+	−	−	−	−	+	A	154
Ozark Chinkapin *C. ozarkensis* Leaves white-downy beneath.	5–8	+	+	−	+	±	±	+	O	155
Allegheny Chinkapin *C. pumila* Leaves white-woolly beneath.	3–5	±	+	−	+	+	+	+	S	155
Florida Chinkapin *C. alnifolia* Leaves beechlike.	2–4	±	+	−	−	−	±	+	S	155
Beech *Fagus grandifolia* Buds long, slender; bark smooth gray.	3–6	−	+	−	−	±	−	−	w	155
Common Witch-hazel *Hamamelis virginiana* Buds without scales, stalked.	3–6	−	−	+	±	±	+	−	w	157
Groundsel-tree *Baccharis halimifolia* Twigs ridged; top leaves not toothed.	1–3	−	±	−	−	−	−	+	C	157
Strawberry-tree [2] *Muntingia calabura* Main leaf veins 3. Cen. and s. Fla.	2–4	−	+	+	+	+	+	+	F	158

[1] A = Appalachians, F = Fla., O = Ozarks, C = Coastal Plain, S = southeastern states, w = widespread.
[2] Leaf outline is similar to that of elms (Pl. 33).

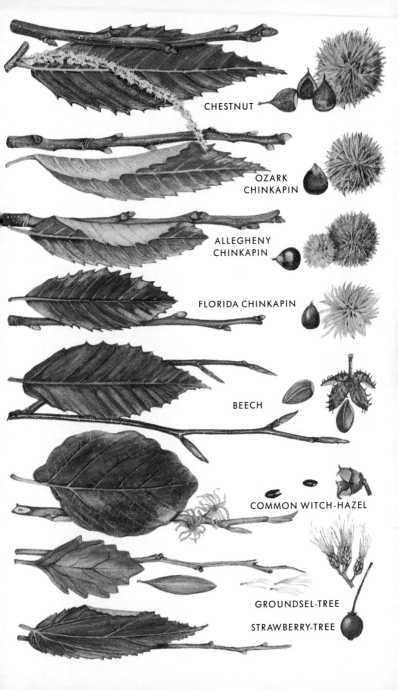

CHESTNUT

OZARK CHINKAPIN

ALLEGHENY CHINKAPIN

FLORIDA CHINKAPIN

BEECH

COMMON WITCH-HAZEL

GROUNDSEL-TREE

STRAWBERRY-TREE

PLATE 33

Elms and Water-elm

Trees mostly with double-toothed[1] and uneven-based leaves. Buds many-scaled, the scales in 2 regular rows; end buds false. Bundle scars 3. Inner bark tough, fibrous. In Florida, see Strawberry-tree (Pl. 32).

Species and remarks

	Leaf length (inches), including stalk	Leaves sandpapery above	Branchlet "wings" common[2]	Twigs hairy	Bud scales dark-edged	Fruits more than 3/8" long	Fruit tip deeply notched[3]	Fruit hairiness pattern[4]	Fruiting season[5]	Major distribution[6]	Text page
American Elm *Ulmus americana* Disease has killed many.	4–6	+	–	–	+	±	+	–	S	w	158
Slippery Elm *U. rubra* Buds red-hairy.	4–8	+	–	+	–	+	–	*	S	w	159
Winged Elm *U. alata* Leafstalks less than ¼" long; "wings" wide.	1–2	–	+	–	+	–	+	±	S	S	159
Rock Elm *U. thomasii* Leafstalks more than ¼" long; low branches droop.	2–4	–	+	+	+	+	–	–	S	N	161
Cedar Elm *U. crassifolia* Corky "wings" not prominent.	1–2	+	+	–	–	±	+	+	F	M	161
(**September Elm** *U. serotina*) South-Midwest; uncommon.	2–4	–	+	–	–	±	+	–	F	C	161
(**Siberian Elm** *U. pumila*)[1] Buds dark and blunt; fruits circular.	1–3	–	–	–	–	+	+	o	S	W	161
Water-elm *Planera aquatica*[1] Fruits fleshy, without wings.	2–4	+	–	–	–	–	o	o	S	S	161

[1] Siberian Elm and Water-elm have single-toothed leaves.
[2] But not always present.
[3] Deep (+), slight (−), and none (o).
[4] All surfaces hairy (+), centers only (*), edges only (−), not hairy (o).
[5] S = spring, March–May; F = fall, Sept.–Oct.
[6] C = central states, M = lower Mississippi Valley, N = north-central states, S = South, W = West, w = widespread.

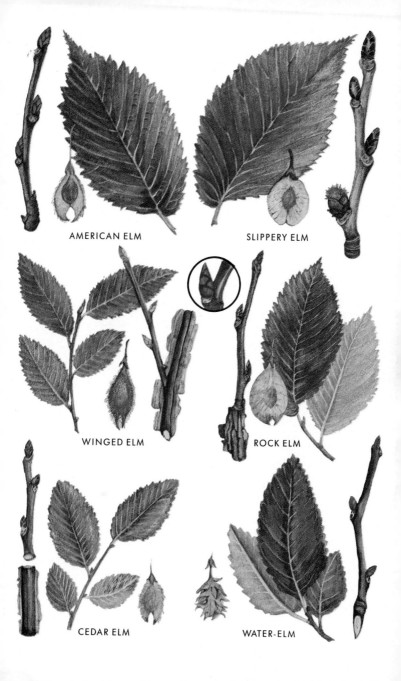

AMERICAN ELM

SLIPPERY ELM

WINGED ELM

ROCK ELM

CEDAR ELM

WATER-ELM

PLATE 34

Birches

Leaves double-toothed, even-based. Bark with many narrow cross-stripes. Buds with 2–3 scales. Bundle scars 3. Fruiting catkins on short spur branches.

Species and remarks	Trunk bark color[1]	Trunk bark peeling	Leaves long-pointed	Wintergreen odor[2]	Twigs rough-warty	Buds hairy	Buds sharp	Fruit catkins erect[3]	Major distribution[4]	Text page
Paper Birch *Betula papyrifera* — Trunk chevrons[5] few.	W	+	–	–	–	–	–	–	N	163
Gray Birch *B. populifolia* — Trunk chevrons[5] large, black.	W	–	+	–	–	–	–	–	E	163
Sweet Birch *B. lenta* — Broken twigs sharply aromatic.[2]	D	–	–	+	–	–	+	+	A	164
Yellow Birch *B. alleghaniensis* — Broken-twig aroma reduced.[2]	Y	+	–	+	–	+	–	+	N	164
River Birch *B. nigra* — Fruits develop over winter.	O	+	–	–	+	±	–	+	S	165
(Virginia Birch *B. uber*) — Smyth Co., sw. Va.; rare.	D	–	–	+	–				S	166

Note: Virginia Birch is not shown but is included here in parentheses because it is very similar to Sweet (Black) Birch and may be a variety of that species.
[1] D = dark, O = orange, W = white, Y = yellowish or silver-gray.
[2] Broken twigs yield a wintergreen or peppermint odor and taste.
[3] Fruiting catkins either (+) short-stalked and rather upright or (−) long-stalked and pendent.
[4] A = Appalachians, E = New England and Maritime Provinces, N = North, S = South.
[5] Chevron-shaped (shallow inverted Vs) dark trunk markings at bases of branches.

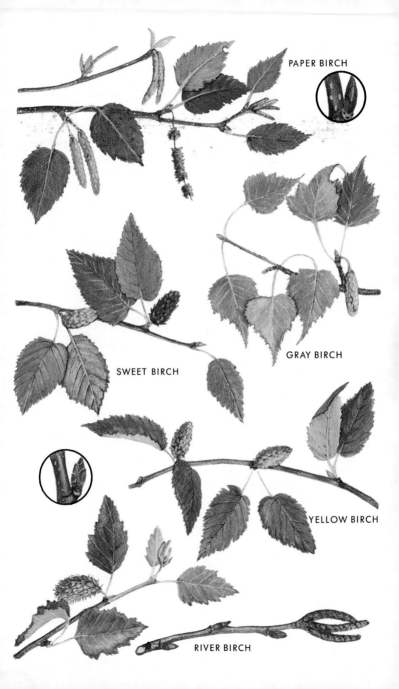

PAPER BIRCH

SWEET BIRCH

GRAY BIRCH

YELLOW BIRCH

RIVER BIRCH

PLATE 35

Other Trees with Mostly Double-toothed Leaves and/or Small, Woody "Cones"

Leaves broad, 2″–5″ long (including stalks), bases even. Twigs variably hairy or hairless. Bundle scars 3. Flowers/fruits in catkins. Alder cones are distinctive.

Species and remarks	Buds stalked, reddish, blunt[1]	Bud scales per bud	Leaves double-toothed	Leaf base U- or V-shaped	Trunk bark[2]	Fruit type[3]	Site[4]	Major distribution[5]	Text page
Ironwood *Carpinus caroliniana* Trunk "sinewy"; leaf veins not forked; buds angled.	–	10+	+	U	G	N	M	E	167
Hornbeam *Ostrya virginiana* Some side veins forked.	–	6–8	+	U	B	S	M	E	167
Smooth Alder *Alnus serrulata* Few white trunk speckles; cones erect.	+	2–3	±	V	D	C	W	E	168
Speckled Alder *Alnus rugosa* Trunk speckles many; cones droop.	+	2–3	+	U	D	C	W	N	169
European Alder *Alnus glutinosa* Leaves blunt; twigs gummy.	+	2–3	+	U	D	C	W	N	169
Seaside Alder *Alnus maritima* Leaves pointed; bud scales separated.	+	2–3	–	V	D	C	W	—[6]	169

[1] And end buds true.

[2] B = brown, rough, shreddy; D = dark, smoothish, with short white, horizontal stripes; G = gray, smooth, "muscular."

[3] C = small, woody, pine-cone-like catkins; N = tiny nuts attached to three-pointed leafy bracts; S = clustered sacs containing flat nuts.

[4] W = wet, M = moist.

[5] E = East, widespread; N = northern states and Canada.

[6] Eastern Md., Del., and again in Okla.

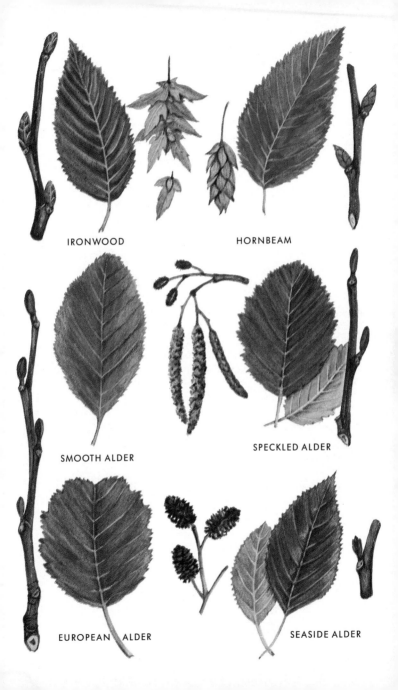

IRONWOOD   HORNBEAM

SMOOTH ALDER   SPECKLED ALDER

EUROPEAN ALDER   SEASIDE ALDER

PLATE 36

Cherries and Peach

Plants mostly with single-toothed[1] leaves and leaf-stalks bearing glands (use lens). Trunk bark with narrow cross-stripes. Broken twigs with characteristic sour odor. End buds true. Bundle scars 3. Flowers white; fruits fleshy, with a large mostly globular seed.

Species and remarks

	Leaves narrow[2]	Leaf teeth sharp	Buds more than 1/4" long	Bud scales pointed	Spur branches present[3]	Flowers/fruits in slender clusters	Fruit with persistent calyx[4]	Fruit color[5]	Major distribution[6]	Text page
Chokecherry *Prunus virginiana* Midrib bare.	−	+	+	−	−	+	−	P	N	170
Black Cherry *Prunus serotina* Midrib often hairy-fringed beneath.	+	−	−	+	−	+	+	P	E	171
(European Bird Cherry *Prunus padus*) Fruits bitter; seeds grooved.	±	+	−	+	−	+	−	B	N	172
Peach *Prunus persica* Buds/fruits velvety; seeds pitted.	+	+	+	−	+	−	−	Y	w	172
Fire Cherry *Prunus pensylvanica* Leaves/buds crowded at twig tips.[7]	+	+	−	+	+	−	−	R	N	172
Sweet Cherry *Prunus avium* Spurs leafless; 10–14 pairs of veins.	−	±	+	±	+	−	+	R/B	w	173
Sour Cherry *Prunus cerasus* Spurs leafy; 6–8 pairs of veins.[8]	−	−	+	±	+	−	+	R	w	173
(Mahaleb Cherry *Prunus mahaleb*) Leaves aromatic, rounded; twigs hairy.	−	−	−	+	+	−	−	B	N	173

Note: The 2 cherries in parentheses are similar to others in this group; see text.
[1] Sweet and sour cherries have double-toothed leaves.
[2] Narrow leaves (including leafstalks) are four or more times as long as broad.
[3] Spur branches are short with crowded leaf scars and grow from older growth (not twigs); see illustration, p. 6.
[4] The calyx is the circle of sepals located just beneath the flower petals and, usually dried, at the base of the cherry fruit.
[5] B = black, P = purple, R = red, Y = yellow.
[6] E = East, widespread; N = North; w = widespread from plantings.
[7] Not just on spur branches.
[8] Also central main trunk lacking.

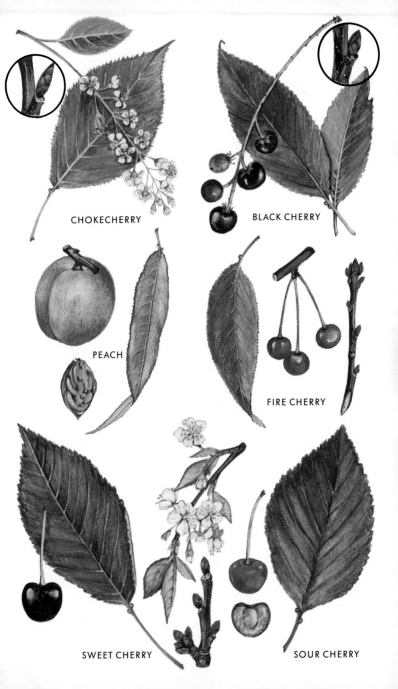

CHOKECHERRY

BLACK CHERRY

PEACH

FIRE CHERRY

SWEET CHERRY

SOUR CHERRY

PLATE 37

Thornless Plums

Leaves toothed and usually with leafstalk or leaf-base glands; end buds false. Bundle scars 3. Fruiting spurs present on branchlets (except in Hortulan Plum). Flowers white, mostly in rounded or flat-topped clusters. Fruits fleshy, single-seeded, stone mostly flattened and with opposite lengthwise ridges. Broken twigs often with weak sour odor. Plants sometimes with thorns. See also thorny plums on Pl. 23.

Species[1] and remarks	Leaf teeth sharp	Leafstalk glands present[2]	Twigs hairy	Fruit color[3]	Seeds pointed both ends	Text page
Allegheny Plum *Prunus alleghaniensis* Mountains. Leaves long-pointed.	+	±	+	P	+	174
Flatwoods Plum *Prunus umbellata* Coastal Plain. Leaves short-pointed.	+	±	+	B	+	174
Mexican Plum *Prunus mexicana* Leaves double-toothed, base broad. Mississippi Valley.	+	+	−	P	−	174
Hortulan Plum *Prunus hortulana* Spurs lacking; fruits on twigs. Upper Midwest.	−	+	−	R/Y	+	175
Wildgoose Plum *Prunus munsoniana* Spurs not lacking; fruits on spurs. Midwest.	−	+	−	R/Y	−	176
Garden Plum *Prunus domestica* Perhaps a variety of Bullace Plum (p. 117).	−	+	−	P	−	176

[1] Some Florida species also called plums are unrelated; see Pls. F-46A, F-46B, F-46C.

[2] On upper leafstalk or nearby leaf base, use lens.

[3] B = black, P = purple, R = red, Y = yellow.

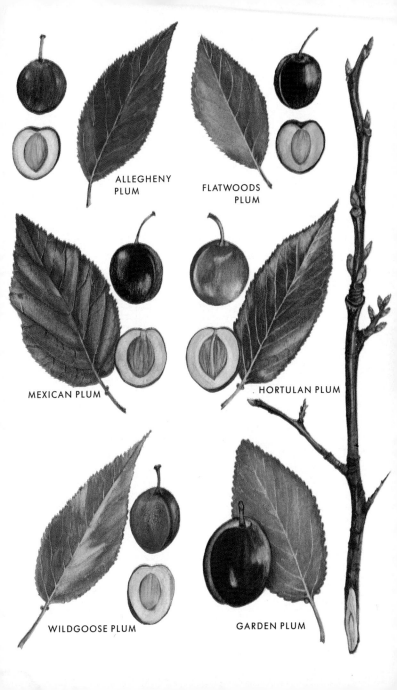

ALLEGHENY
PLUM

FLATWOODS
PLUM

MEXICAN PLUM

HORTULAN PLUM

WILDGOOSE PLUM

GARDEN PLUM

PLATE 38

Willows I: Leaves Very Narrow to Medium in Width

Catkin-bearing trees with a single hoodlike bud scale. Bundle scars 3; end buds false. Leaves mostly slender and usually toothed. See also Russian-olive (p. 177). For winter identification, see text chart, p. 178.

Species and remarks	Leaf width[1]	Leaves toothed	Leaves long-pointed	Leaves whitened beneath	Leaves hairy at least beneath	Leafstalk glands present[2]	Leaf teeth mainly above middle	Twigs brittle-based[3]	Stipules usually present[4]	Leaf bases mostly U- or V-shaped	Major distribution[5]	Text page
Black Willow *Salix nigra* — Leafstalks less than 5/16″ long.	N	+	+	−	−	−	±	+	+	V	E	179
Meadow Willow[6] *S. petiolaris* — Leafstalks ¼″–½″ long.	N	+	+	+	−	−	−	−	−	V	N	180
Sandbar Willow *S. exigua* — Leafstalks nearly lacking.	N	±	−	±	±	−	+	−	−	V	N	180
Osier Willow *S. viminalis* — Leaves dense white beneath.	N	−	±	+	+	−	−	−	±	V	N	181
Weeping Willow *S. babylonica* — Twigs long, hang vertically.	I	+	+	+	±	+	−	+	−	V	w	181
Coastal Plain Willow *S. caroliniana* — Twigs do not hang.	I	+	+	+	−	−	−	+	±	U	S	181
Crack Willow *S. fragilis* — Buds somewhat sticky.	I	+	+	−	−	+	−	+	−	V	w	182
White Willow *S. alba* — Leaves white-hairy.	I	+	±	+	+	±	−	−	−	V	w	182
Silky Willow[6] *S. sericea* — Leaves mostly silky beneath.	I	+	−	+	+	−	−	+	+	V	N	182
Ontario (Satiny) Willow *S. pellita* — Leaves often leathery.	I	−	−	+	+	−	−	−	−	V	N	183

[1] N = narrow, 8–15 times longer than width; I = intermediate, 5–7 times longer than width.
[2] At apex of stalk near leaf base.
[3] Twigs easily detached at the base "with a flick of the finger or by high winds" (Gordon 1960).
[4] Stipules often tiny but sometimes large, conspicuous, paired leafy structures at each side of buds or leafstalk bases, dropping early and lacking in some species.
[5] E = eastern states, N = North, S = South, w = widespread.
[6] Young leaves become black upon drying.

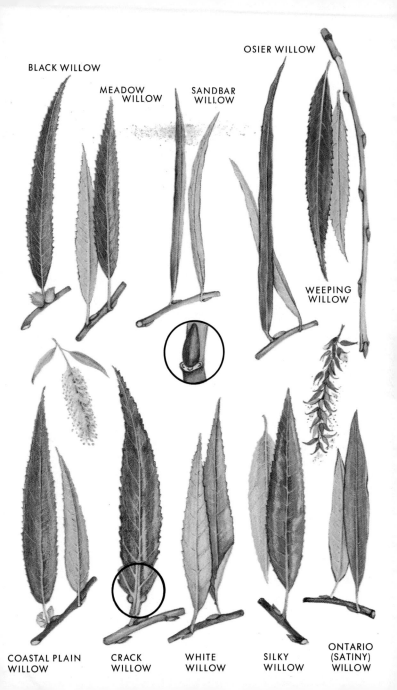

BLACK WILLOW

MEADOW WILLOW

SANDBAR WILLOW

OSIER WILLOW

WEEPING WILLOW

COASTAL PLAIN WILLOW

CRACK WILLOW

WHITE WILLOW

SILKY WILLOW

ONTARIO (SATINY) WILLOW

PLATE 39

Willows II: Leaves Relatively Wide

Catkin-bearing trees with a single hoodlike bud scale. The leaves of these willows are somewhat wider than those of the preceding plate.[1] Bundle scars 3; end buds false. Mostly northern species. See also Russian-olive (p. 177). For winter identification, see text identification chart, p. 178.

Species and remarks	Leaves toothed	Leaves long-pointed	Leaves whitened beneath	Leaves hairy at least beneath	Leafstalk glands present[2]	Leaf teeth mainly above middle	Twigs brittle-based[3]	Stipules usually present[4]	Leaf bases mostly U- or V-shaped	Text page
Shining Willow *Salix lucida* Leaves shiny; twigs dark.	+	+	−	−	+	−	+	+	U	183
Peachleaf Willow *S. amygdaloides* Leaves dull; twigs light.	+	+	+	−	−	−	−	−	U	183
Pussy Willow *S. discolor* Leafstalks more than ½″ long.	+	−	+	−	−	+	−	+	V	184
Broadleaf Willow[5] *S. glaucophylloides* Leaf bases often heart-shaped.	+	−	+	−	−	−	−	+	U	184
Bebb Willow *S. bebbiana* Leafstalks less than ⅜″ long.	±	−	±	+	−	−	−	−	V	184
Basket Willow *S. purpurea* Leaves nearly opposite; see chart opposite Pl. 12.	±	−	+	−	−	+	−	−	U	185
Balsam Willow *S. pyrifolia* Crushed leaves spicy.	+	−	+	±	−	−	−	−	U	185
Florida Willow *S. floridana* Local; s. Ga. to cen. Fla. only.	+	−	+	+	−	−	+	−	U	185

[1] N = narrow, 8–15 times longer than wide; I = intermediate, 5–7 times longer than wide.

[2] At apex of stalk, near leaf base.

[3] Twigs easily detached at base "with a flick of the finger or by high winds" (Gordon 1960).

[4] Stipules often tiny but sometimes large, conspicuous, paired leafy structures at each side of buds or leafstalk bases, dropping early or lacking in some species.

[5] Young leaves become black upon drying.

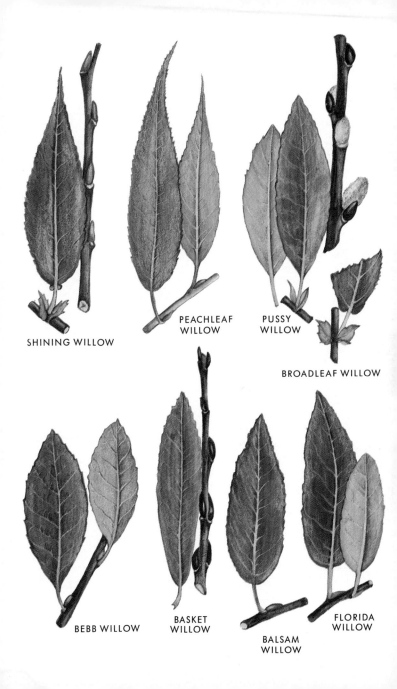

SHINING WILLOW

PEACHLEAF
WILLOW

PUSSY
WILLOW

BROADLEAF WILLOW

BEBB WILLOW

BASKET
WILLOW

BALSAM
WILLOW

FLORIDA
WILLOW

PLATE 40
Deciduous Hollies

As a group, hollies lack obvious distinctive vegetative characteristics. Paired tiny dark stipules are theoretically present at leaf bases but more often at twig bases. They drop early. Spur branches are usually numerous on the older wood. The thin, toothed, mostly pointed leaves are alternate along fast-grown twigs and clustered on spurs. Small greenish flowers or fruits are often crowded among the leaves. Twigs are hairless, two or more buds may be present at a leaf scar, bundle scars are single, and end buds are true. Species on this plate have red or orange fruits. Evergreen hollies are shown on Pl. 41.

Species and remarks	Leaf edges scalloped[1]	Leaf bases narrowly V-shaped	Leaves hairy beneath	Leaves fine-toothed	Buds pointed	Flower/fruit stalks more than ½" long	Seeds ridged[2]	Wet sites	Major distribution[3]	Text page
Possumhaw Holly *Ilex decidua* Side twigs stiff;[4] leaf tips blunt.	+	+	–	–	+	–	+	+	S	186
Largeleaf Holly *Ilex montana* Leaves 4"–6½" long (including stalks), largest of group.	–	±	–	+	+	–	+	–	A	187
Common Winterberry Holly *Ilex verticillata* Leaves dull above.	–	+	+	–	–	–	–	+	E	187
Smooth Winterberry Holly *Ilex laevigata* Leaves shiny above.	–	+	–	+	–	–	–	+	C	187
Carolina Holly *Ilex ambigua*	–	±	±	–	+	–	+	–	S	188
Georgia Holly *Ilex longipes*	–	+	–	+	–	+	+	+	S	188
(**Juneberry Holly** *Ilex amelanchier*) Rare. See text.	–	–	+	+	+	±	+	+	S	188

[1] Larger wavy teeth alternate with small sharp teeth.
[2] On curved surfaces.
[3] A = Appalachians; E = eastern U.S.; C = mostly Coastal Plain, Maine to S.C.; S = South.
[4] Not spur branches; also buds often one above another.

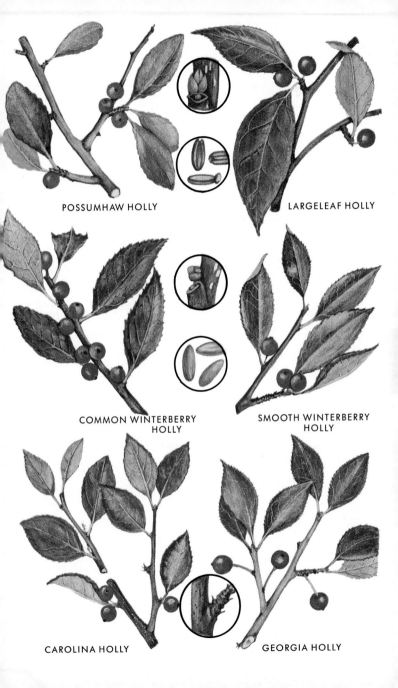

POSSUMHAW HOLLY

LARGELEAF HOLLY

COMMON WINTERBERRY HOLLY

SMOOTH WINTERBERRY HOLLY

CAROLINA HOLLY

GEORGIA HOLLY

PLATE 41

Evergreen Hollies

Except for the American Holly, the holly group is difficult to identify (details on Pl. 40). The species on this plate have leathery leaves, usually with edges rolled under. They occur principally on the Coastal Plain in the southeastern states.

Species and remarks

Species and remarks	Leaves small, less than 1½" long (including stalk)	Leaf bases V-shaped	Leaf edges spiny or wavy	Leaf teeth mainly above middle	Fruits red or black	Seeds ridged[1]	Text page
Yaupon Holly *Ilex vomitoria* Leaf tips blunt.	+	±	+	−	R	+	189
Myrtle Holly *I. myrtifolia* Side twigs stiff.	+	+	−	+	R	+	190
Dahoon Holly *I. cassine* Twigs hairy or not.	−	+	−	+	R	+	190
Tall Gallberry Holly *I. coriacea* Leaves black-dotted beneath (use lens).	−	+	−	+	B	−	190
American Holly *I. opaca* Only native holly with thorny leaves.	−	−	+	−	R	+	191
Tawnyberry Holly *I. krugiana* Mainland—Dade Co., Fla. Usually no leaf teeth. Leaves dry black.	−	−	+	−	B	−	191

[1] On curved surface; see illustrations on Pl. 40.

YAUPON HOLLY

MYRTLE HOLLY

DAHOON HOLLY

TALL GALLBERRY HOLLY

AMERICAN HOLLY

TAWNYBERRY HOLLY

PLATE 42

Miscellaneous Trees with Alternate, Toothed Leaves

These species lack the characteristics of other trees with alternate toothed leaves (Pls. 32–39). Except for Sourwood, this group has true end buds. Only Loblolly-bay has thick, leathery leaves. See also minor juneberries (pp. 193, 194) and Little Silverbell (p. 197).

Species and remarks	Buds slim, pink, black-tipped	Pith chambered	Flower/fruit clusters long, slender	Flowers showy, more than 2" wide	Leafstalks winged	Buds hairy	Bundle scars per leaf scar	Major distribution[1]	Text page
Downy Juneberry *Amelanchier arborea* Leaf teeth 14–30/inch, medium-pointed.	+	−	−	−	−	−	3	E	192
Roundleaf Juneberry *A. sanguinea* Leaf teeth 6–12/inch, to leaf base.	+	−	−	−	−	−	3	N	193
Mountain Pepperbush *Clethra acuminata* End buds larger than side buds, hairy; fruits three-parted.	−	−	+	−	−	+	1	M	194
Sourwood *Oxydendrum arboreum* End buds false, small, hairless; fruits five-parted.	−	−	+	−	−	−	1	E	195
Carolina Silverbell *Halesia carolina* Fruits broadly four-winged; buds sharp.	−	+	−	−	−	−	1	S	195
Two-wing Silverbell *Halesia diptera* Fruits broadly two-winged.	−	+	−	−	−	−	1	P	197
Loblolly-bay *Gordonia lasianthus*[2] Leaf bases narrowly V-shaped.	−	−	−	+	±	+	1	P	197
Virginia Stewartia *Stewartia malachodendron* Leaf bases U-shaped; trunk mottled.	−	−	−	+	+	+	1	M	197
Mountain Stewartia *Stewartia ovata* Leaf bases U-shaped; trunk smooth.	−	−	−	+	+	+	1	P	198

[1] E = East, widespread, M = mountains, southern; N = northern states, etc.; C = Coastal Plain, southern; S = South, widespread.
[2] See *Franklinia* text, p. 197; extinct in wild.

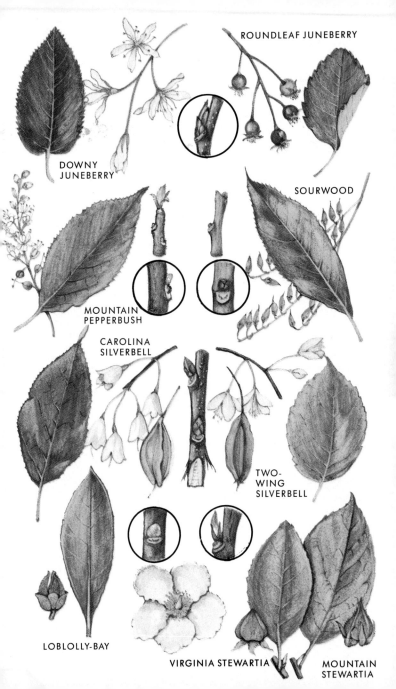

ROUNDLEAF JUNEBERRY

DOWNY
JUNEBERRY

SOURWOOD

MOUNTAIN
PEPPERBUSH

CAROLINA
SILVERBELL

TWO-
WING
SILVERBELL

LOBLOLLY-BAY

VIRGINIA STEWARTIA

MOUNTAIN
STEWARTIA

PLATE 43

Miscellaneous Trees with Alternate Leaves, Sometimes Toothed

See text for other distinctive features of these species. Also see European Buckthorn and American Snowbell (p. 201), Ogeechee Tupelo (p. 202), Geiger-tree (p. 204), Groundsel-tree (p. 157 and Pl. 32), and Sparkleberry (p. 212 and Pl. 46).

Species	Leaves/twigs resin-dotted,[1] aromatic	Male plants with catkins[2]	Buds without scales	Pith chambered	Spur branches usually present	Leaves evergreen, leathery[3]	Leaves hairy beneath	Twigs hairy	Bundle scars per leaf scar	Major distribution[4]	Text page
Southern Bayberry *Myrica cerifera*	+	+	−	−	−	+	−	±	3	S	199
Evergreen Bayberry *M. heterophylla*	+	+	−	−	−	+	−	+	3	S	199
Northern Bayberry *M. pensylvanica*	+	+	−	−	−	−	−	+	3	N	199
Carolina Buckthorn *Rhamnus caroliniana*	−	−	+	−	−	−	±	+	3	S	201
Bigleaf Snowbell *Styrax grandifolius*	−	−	+	−	−	−	+	+	1	S	201
Sweetleaf *Symplocos tinctoria*	−	−	−	+	−	±	±	−	1	S	201
Water Tupelo *Nyssa aquatica*	−	−	−	+	−	−	±	−	3	S	202
Domestic Apple *Malus sylvestris*	−	−	−	−	+	−	+	+	3	w	202
Domestic Pear *Pyrus communis*	−	−	−	−	+	−	−	−	3	w	203
Carolina Laurelcherry *Prunus caroliniana*	−	−	−	−	−	+	−	−	3	S	203

Note: Leaf length includes stalk.
[1] Use lens. Crushed leaves spicy scented.
[2] Catkins are crowded flower spikes. Mature female plants with small, whitish wax-covered nutlets.
[3] See also Pl. 46.
[4] C = Coastal Plain, N = Northeast, S = South, w = widespread.

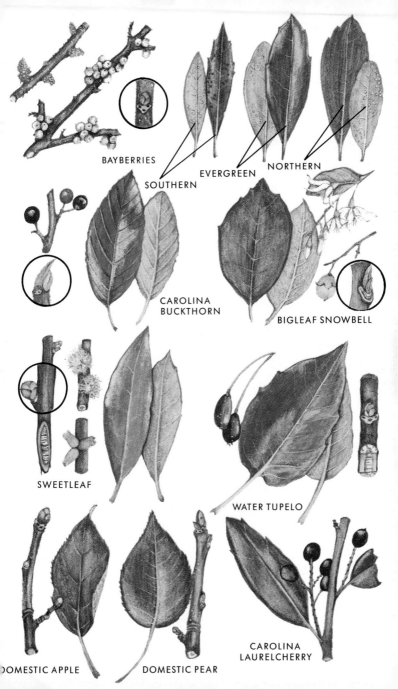

BAYBERRIES

SOUTHERN   EVERGREEN   NORTHERN

CAROLINA
BUCKTHORN

BIGLEAF SNOWBELL

SWEETLEAF

WATER TUPELO

DOMESTIC APPLE   DOMESTIC PEAR

CAROLINA
LAURELCHERRY

PLATE 44

Trees with Leaves Neither Toothed nor Evergreen

These species plus those of Pl. 43, when leaf teeth are lacking, and the magnolias (Pl. 45) compose a rather small group of trees with foliage of this type. The leaves of Persimmon and Sourgum are sometimes somewhat leathery but never evergreen. Except for Persimmon, all on this plate have true end buds.

Species and remarks	Leaves mostly more than 6″ long	Leaf tips blunt	Twigs hairy	Pith partitioned	Bundle scars per leaf scar	Bud scales per bud	Major distribution[1]	Text page
Common Pawpaw *Asimina triloba* Buds hairy, no scales; flowers more than 1″ across.	+	−	−	±	3	0	M	205
(**Smallflower Pawpaw** *A. parviflora*) As above but blossoms less than 1″ across.	±	−	−	±	3	0	S	205
American Smoketree *Cotinus obovatus* Rare. Leaves blunt, fruits feathery.	−	+	−	−	3	2–4	M	205
Alternate-leaf Dogwood *Cornus alternifolia* Veins follow leaf edges.	−	−	−	−	3	2	N	206
Corkwood *Leitneria floridana* End buds large, clustered.	−	−	+	−	3	3+	S	206
Common Persimmon *Diospyros virginiana* Bark deeply checkered; buds blackish.	−	−	±	±	1	2	S	207
Sourgum *Nyssa sylvatica* Bark deeply checkered; buds brown.	−	−	−	+	3	3	S	207
Crapemyrtle *Lagerstroemia indica* Some leaves opposite; flowers showy.	−	±	−	−	1	2	S	208
Elliottia *Elliottia racemosa* Rare; Ga. only. Fruits dry; end clusters.	−	−	−	−	1	2–3	S	208

[1] M = midlatitudes; N = North, S = South.

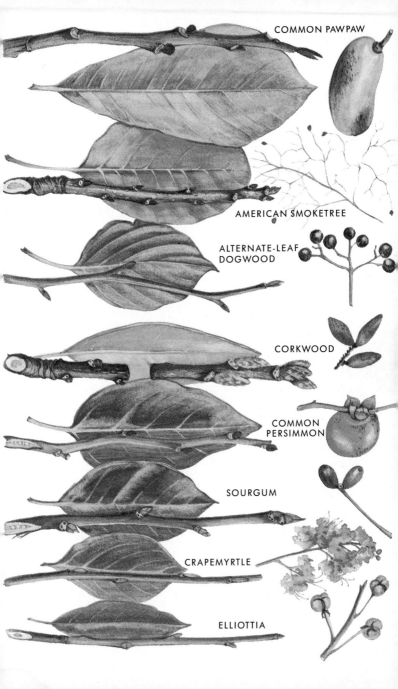

COMMON PAWPAW

AMERICAN SMOKETREE

ALTERNATE-LEAF
DOGWOOD

CORKWOOD

COMMON
PERSIMMON

SOURGUM

CRAPEMYRTLE

ELLIOTTIA

PLATE 45

Magnolias

Leaves not toothed. Twigs ringed; buds with a single bud scale; bundle scars many. Flowers large and white (green in Cucumber Magnolia); fruit "cones" woody with fleshy seeds. See also Pyramid Magnolia (p. 211); in Fla. see also Ashe Magnolia (p. 212) and Pls. F-46A–D.

Species and remarks	Leaf length (inches), including stalk	Leaf base shape[1]	Leaves crowded near twig tips[2]	Leaf underside hairy[3]	Leaf underside and bud color[4]	Twigs stout	End bud color[4]	Pith chambered	Cone shape[5]	Major distribution[6]	Text page
Southern Magnolia *Magnolia grandiflora* Leaves leathery, evergreen.	6–8	U	–	+	B	+	B	+	E	S	209
Sweetbay Magnolia *M. virginiana* Crushed leaves/buds spicy.[7]	4–6	V	–	+	W	–	G	+	E	S	209
Cucumber Magnolia *M. acuminata* Leaf scars U-shaped.[8]	4–10	U	–	±	G	–	W	–	C	A	211
Umbrella Magnolia *M. tripetala* Flower odor unpleasant.	10–24	V	+	–	G	+	P	–	C	A	211
Earleaf Magnolia *M. fraseri* Leafstalks more than 3″ long.	8–12	E	+	–	G	+	P	±	C	A	211
Bigleaf Magnolia *M. macrophylla* Southeast, north of Fla.	20–30	E	+	+	W	+	W	–	E	A	211

[1] E = ear-lobed, U = U-shaped, V = V-shaped.
[2] And at twig swellings; also end buds more than 1″ long.
[3] Buds and twigs also hairy (twigs hairless in Cucumber Magnolia).
[4] B = brown, G = pale green, P = purplish, W = white- or silvery-hairy.
[5] C = candle-shaped (upper right corner of plate), E = egglike (center left of plate).
[6] S = South, A = Appalachians.
[7] Leaves may be evergreen and somewhat leathery in South.
[8] Leaf scars not crescent-shaped or circular, as in other magnolias.

SOUTHERN MAGNOLIA

SWEETBAY MAGNOLIA

CUCUMBER MAGNOLIA

UMBRELLA MAGNOLIA

EARLEAF MAGNOLIA

BIGLEAF MAGNOLIA

PLATE 46
Trees with Leathery Evergreen Leaves, Mostly Not Toothed

Except for the rhododendrons and Mountain Laurel, these species are mainly restricted to the South. See text for other distinctive features of these species. See also Pls. 31, 41–43, and 45. In Florida, see also Pls. F-46A–D.

Species	Leaf length in inches, including stalk	Flower clusters finger-shaped	Leafstalks short or lacking	Crushed leaves odorous	Leaf edges rolled under	Leaves clustered near twig tips	Leaf tips rounded	Some leaves wavy or toothed	Fruits[1]	Southernmost Fla.[2]	Major distribution[3]	Text page
Sparkleberry *Vaccinium arboreum*	1–2	–	±	–	–	–	±	+	F	C	S	212
Tree Lyonia *Lyonia ferruginea*	1–3	–	–	–	+	–	±	+	C	N	C	212
Buckwheat-tree *Cliftonia monophylla*	1–2	+	+	–	±	±	–	–	L	N	S	212
Cyrilla *Cyrilla racemiflora*	2–4	+	+	–	±	±	±	–	L	C	S	213
Odorless Bayberry *Myrica inodora*	2–4	+	±	–	+	–	±	–	W	N	G	215
Mountain Laurel *Kalmia latifolia*	2–5	–	–	–	±	±	±	–	C	N	A	215
Florida Anise-tree *Illicium floridanum*	3–6	–	–	+	–	+	–	±	S	N	G	215
Redbay *Persea borbonia*	3–8	–	–	+	+	–	±	–	F	S	S	215
Catawba Rhododendron *Rhododendron catawbiense*[4]	3–9	–	–	–	+	±	–	–	C	–	A	216
Great Rhododendron *Rhododendron maximum*[4]	3–11	–	–	–	+	±	–	–	C	–	A	216
Camphor-tree *Cinnamomum camphora*	2–6	–	–	+	–	–	–	±	F	S	S	216

[1] C = capsules dry; F = fleshy, black or blue; L = long fingerlike clusters of tiny dry fruits; S = star-shaped with many points; W = waxy spheres, small.
[2] Southernmost distribution in Fla. (see also Pls. F-46A–D); C = central counties, N = northern (northwestern, except Mountain Laurel), S = southern; minus sign means "absent from Florida."
[3] A = Appalachians, G = Gulf Coastal Plain, C = southeastern Coastal Plain, S = southeastern states.
[4] Spring flower clusters large and showy. Compare width of leaf base.

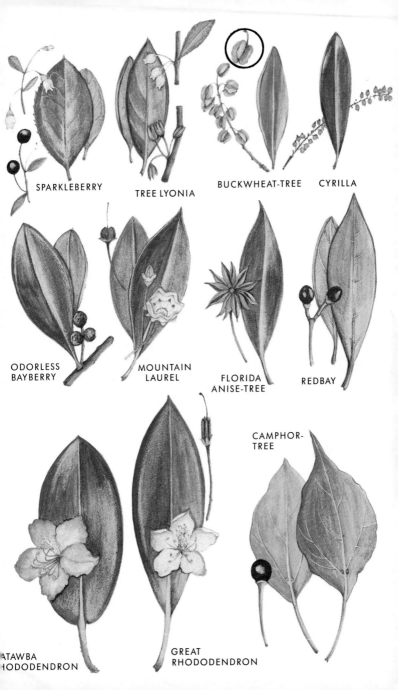

SPARKLEBERRY

TREE LYONIA

BUCKWHEAT-TREE

CYRILLA

ODORLESS BAYBERRY

MOUNTAIN LAUREL

FLORIDA ANISE-TREE

REDBAY

CAMPHOR-TREE

CATAWBA RHODODENDRON

GREAT RHODODENDRON

PLATE 47

Fan-leaved Palms

Evergreen leaves 1'–4' in diameter and fan-shaped; segments with parallel veins. Trunks single, unbranched.[1] Southern plants.

Species and remarks

	Leafstalk penetrates leaf blade	Trunks several, clumped[1]	Old leafstalks cover trunk	Fiber matting covers trunk[2]	Leafstalks thorny	Leafstalk bases forked[3]	Flower color[4]	Fruit color[4]	Occurs in s. Fla. only[5]	Text page
Cabbage Palm *Sabal palmetto* Leafstalk extends through leaf blade.	+	–	±	–	–	+	W	D	–	219
Dwarf Palmetto[6] *Sabal minor* Leafstalk enters leaf blade 2″ or less.	+	–	±	–	–	–	W	D	–	220
Saw-palmetto[6] *Serenoa repens* Leafstalk sawtoothed with 1/10″ spines.	–	+	+	–	+	–	W	D	–	220
Paurotis Palm *Acoelorrhaphe wrightii* Thorns 3/16″–1/4″; usually curved.	–	+	+	+	+	–	G	D	+	220
Florida Thatchpalm *Thrinax radiata* Leaves 3'–4'; yellow-green, pale beneath.	–	–	–	±	–	+	W	W	+	221
Key Thatchpalm *Thrinax morrisii* Leaves 2'–3'; pale green, silvery beneath.	–	–	–	±	–	+	W	W	+	221
Florida Silverpalm *Coccothrinax argentata* Leaves 1'–2'; dark green, silvery beneath.	–	–	–	±	–	–	W	D	+	221

[1] Trunk branched in some Saw-palmetto specimens.

[2] Trunks wrapped with sheets of woven fibers, but these may fall away on old trees, leaving the trunks ring-scarred.

[3] Split at attachment to the trunk.

[4] D = dark (blue to black), G = green, W = whitish.

[5] Species not restricted to Fla. may occur north to the Carolinas; Fla. species also range into the Caribbean.

[6] Trunks sometimes sprawling rather than upright.

VI

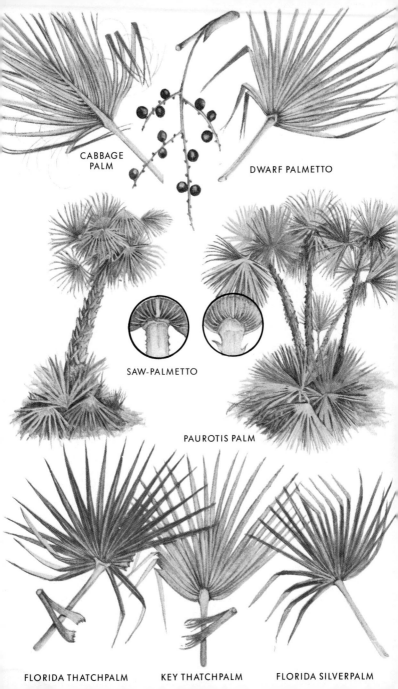

CABBAGE
PALM

DWARF PALMETTO

SAW-PALMETTO

PAUROTIS PALM

FLORIDA THATCHPALM   KEY THATCHPALM   FLORIDA SILVERPALM

PLATE 48
Feather-leaved Palms, Tree-cacti, and Yuccas

Evergreen leaves large and feather-shaped, bristly, or swordlike. Native Fla. palms with single, unbranched trunks. Those on this plate are ring-scarred and free of old leafstalk bases. These palms do not have thorny leafstalks. Cacti and yuccas distinctive.

Species and remarks

	Leaves feather-compound[1]	Crownshaft present[2]	Flat thorny pads present[3]	Leaves simple, swordlike[4]	Flower color[5]	Fruit color[5]	Occurs in s. Fla. only[6]	Text page
Florida Royalpalm *Roystonea elata* Trunk cement gray; crownshaft 5'–6'.	+	+	–	–	Y	D	+	221
Coconut Palm *Cocos nucifera* Fruits three-sided; fiber-webbed leaf bases.	+	–	–	–	Y	G/B	+	221
Buccaneer Palm *Pseudophoenix sargentii* Rare on Keys. Crownshaft 1'–3'.	+	+	–	–	G	R	+	222
Brazil Pricklypear *Opuntia brasiliensis* Cactus; some branches cylindrical.	–	0	+	–	Y	Y	+	222
(Indian-fig Pricklypear *O. ficus-indica)* Cactus; only flat pads present.	–	0	+	–	Y	R	+	222
(Key Giant-cactus *Cereus robinii)* Trunk a spiny, grooved pole. Rare; Florida Keys only.	–	0	–	–	G	R	+	223
Spanish Bayonet *Yucca aloifolia* Leaves 1'–3' long; edges fine-toothed.	–	0	–	+	W	G/D	–	223
Moundlily Yucca *Y. gloriosa* Leaves 1'–2' long; edges smooth.	–	0	–	+	W	G/D	–	223

[1] In contrast to the fan-compound leaves of palms on Pl. 48.
[2] A smooth, green cylinder of tightly rolled leaf bases topping the trunk of some palms; trunk bulges in these species. 0 = not applicable (not palms).
[3] Technically the fleshy pads are modified stems, and the leaves are evolved bristles.
[4] And spine tipped; yucca flower clusters are upright, showy.
[5] Flower/fruit clusters: B = brown, D = dark (blue to black), G = green, R = orange-red, W = white, Y = yellow.
[6] Fla. species range into the Caribbean. Yuccas may occur north to the Carolinas. Key Giant-cactus rare.

VI

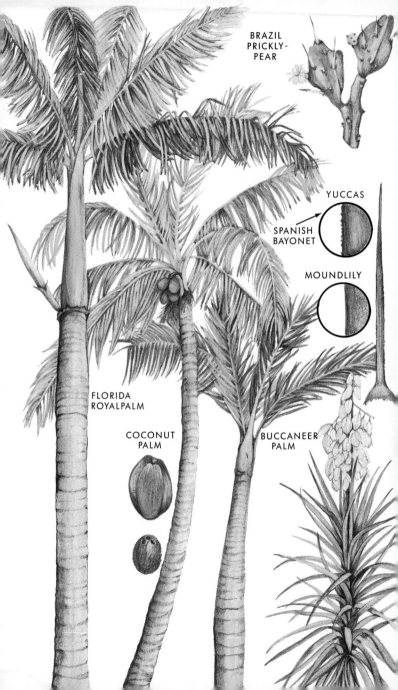

BRAZIL PRICKLY-PEAR

YUCCAS

SPANISH BAYONET

MOUNDLILY

FLORIDA ROYALPALM

COCONUT PALM

BUCCANEER PALM

Small Trees of Florida with Opposite Compound Leaves

Leaves evergreen, three-parted or feather-compound; leaflets pointed. See also Pl. 7.

Species and remarks

	Leaflets per leaf	Leaflets toothed	End leaflet present	Crushed leaves aromatic[1]	Flower color[2]	Fruit color[2]	Fla. distribution[3]
Small Torchwood *Amyris elemifera* Leaflets 1″–2″; fruits round, ¼″.	3–5	±	+	+	W	B	E/S
Balsam Torchwood *A. balsamifera*[4] Leaflets 2″–4″; fruits elliptic, ⅜″.	(3–)5	−	+	+	W	B	S
Roughbark Lignumvitae *Guaiacum sanctum* Leaflets stalkless; bark whitish. Keys only.	4–8	−	−	−	U	Y	S
Yellow-elder *Tecoma stans*[5] Flowers showy; fruits cigarlike; escapes cultivation.	5–13	+	+	−	Y	D	S

[1] Leaves with gland dots; wood also fragrant.
[2] B = black; D = dry, brownish; U = blue; W = white, Y = yellow.
[3] E = eastern coastal counties; S = s. or tropical Fla. (Collier, Dade, and Monroe counties).
[4] Probably extirpated (R. Hammer, Goulds, Fla.).
[5] Native in Fla. and possibly spreading in southern states; rarely tree size.

VII

SMALL TORCHWOOD

BALSAM TORCHWOOD

ROUGHBARK LIGNUMVITAE

YELLOW-ELDER

Trees of Lower Florida with Opposite, Evergreen Leaves, Not Toothed

Caribbean species not found north of cen. Fla.[1] Leaves somewhat leathery and sometimes in whorls. See also Pls. 13 and F-13B.

Species and remarks

	Leaf length in inches	Leaf tips blunt	Leaf tips may be notched	Leaf bases wedge-shaped	Leafstalks under ¼"	Leaves with tiny dots[2]	Leaf edges rolled under	Color of flowers[3]	Color of fruits[3]
Longleaf Blolly *Guapira discolor* Flower clusters at twig ends.	1–2	+	+	+	–	–	–	G	R
Leadwood *Krugiodendron ferreum* Flower clusters in leaf angles.	1–2	±	+	–	+	–	–	G	D
Red Stopper *Eugenia rhombea* Leaf edge yellow; menthol odor. Keys only.	1–2	–	–	±	±	+	–	W	D
Boxleaf Stopper *Eugenia foetida* No odor near plant.	1–3	+	–	+	+	+	+	W	D
White Stopper *Eugenia axillaris* Skunk odor near plant.	1–3	–	–	–	–	+	+	W	D
Surinam-cherry *Eugenia uniflora*[4] Fruits edible, to 1".	1–3	–	–	–	+	+	+	W	O
Joewood *Jacquinia keyensis* Flowers showy, fragrant.	1–3	+	+	+	±	+	+	Y	O
Twinberry Stopper *Myrcianthes fragrans* Crushed leaves aromatic.	1–3	±	+	+	±	+	±	W	R
Downy-myrtle *Rhodomyrtus tomentosa* Leaves with 3 main veins, velvety.	1–3	+	+	+	–	±	±	P	D
Guava *Psidium guajava*[4] Leaf veins parallel; twigs lined.	2–4	±	–	–	±	–	–	W	Y
Seven-year-apple *Casasia clusiifolia* Twigs ringed; leaves wide.	3–6	+	–	+	–	–	–	W	G
Scarletbush *Hamelia patens* Leaves often in 3's; twigs ridged.	2–9	–	–	±	–	–	–	R	D
Florida Fiddlewood *Citharexylum fruticosum* Twigs ridged, ringed.	3–6	±	+	+	–	–	–	W	T

VII

[1] Not reported occurring north of Citrus, Sumpter, Lake, and Volusia counties.

[2] Use lens; very fine gland dots on one or both surfaces.

[3] D = dark, G = green, O = orange-red, P = pink, R = red, W = white, Y = yellow.

[4] Escapes cultivation.

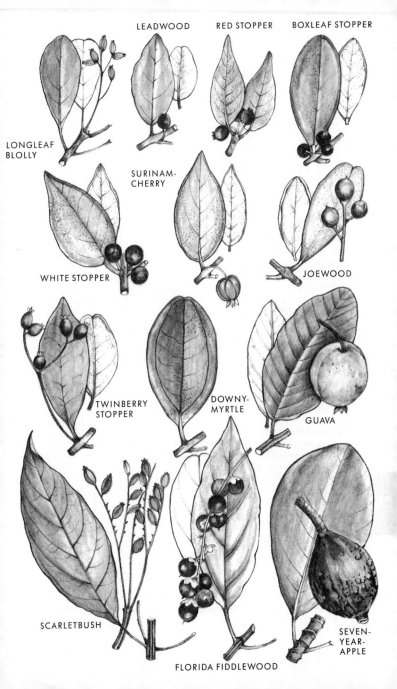

LEADWOOD   RED STOPPER   BOXLEAF STOPPER

LONGLEAF
BLOLLY

SURINAM-
CHERRY

WHITE STOPPER

JOEWOOD

TWINBERRY
STOPPER

DOWNY-
MYRTLE

GUAVA

SCARLETBUSH

FLORIDA FIDDLEWOOD

SEVEN-
YEAR-
APPLE

Trees of Southern Florida with Opposite, Evergreen Leaves, Not Toothed

Caribbean plants reported in extreme s. Fla. only from Collier, Dade, and Monroe counties. Five species occur only in the Fla. Keys.[1] Leaves mostly leathery. See also Pls. 13 and F-13A.

Species	Leaf length in inches, including stalk	Leaf tips blunt	Leaf tips may be notched	Leaf bases wedge-shaped	Leafstalks less than 1/4" long	Leaf edges rolled under	Leaves with tiny dots[2]	Color of flowers[3]	Color of ripe fruits[3]
Longstalk Stopper *Psidium longipes*	1–2	±	+	±	±	−	±	W	D
Florida Crossopetalum *Crossopetalum rhacoma*	1–2	±	+	+	+	−	−	R	R
Locustberry *Byrsonima lucida*	1–2	±	−	+	+	±	−	W/P	O
Elliptic-leaf Velvetseed *Guettarda elliptica*	1–2	±	−	−	−	−	−	W	D
Redberry Stopper *Eugenia confusa*	1–3	−	−	±	−	+	±	W	R
Myrtle-of-the-river *Calyptranthes zuzygium*	2–3	−	−	+	+	−	+	W	O
Pale Lidflower *Calyptranthes pallens*	2–3	−	−	+	−	±	±	W	R
Roughleaf Velvetseed *Guettarda scabra*	3–4	±	−	−	−	+	−	W	R
Florida Tetrazygia *Tetrazygia bicolor*	3–5	−	−	−	−	−	−	W	D
False-boxwood[1] *Gyminda latifolia*	1–2	+	+	+	+	+	−	W	D
Darling-plum[1] *Reynosia septentrionalis*	1–2	+	+	±	+	+	−	G	D
Princewood[1] *Exostema caribaeum*	1–2	−	−	±	−	−	−	W/O	D
Pisonia[1] *Pisonia rotundata*	1–3	+	+	±	−	−	−	G	−
Florida Clusia[1] *Clusia rosea*	4–7	+	+	±	−	+	−	W	G

VII

[1] Absent from mainland.
[2] Use lens; very fine gland dots on one or both surfaces of some specimens.
[3] D = dark, G = greenish, O = orange, P = pink, R = red, W = white.

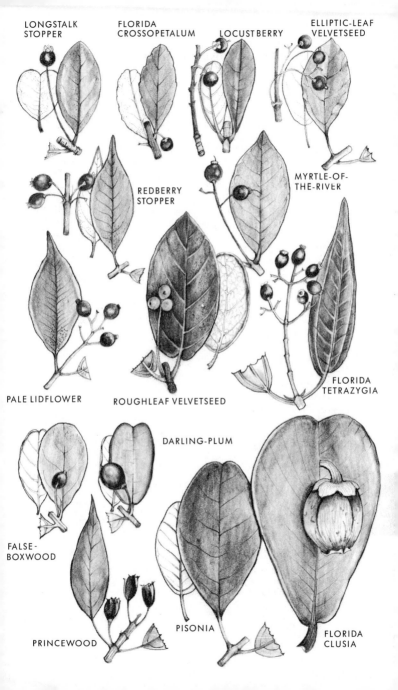

LONGSTALK STOPPER

FLORIDA CROSSOPETALUM

LOCUST BERRY

ELLIPTIC-LEAF VELVETSEED

REDBERRY STOPPER

MYRTLE-OF-THE-RIVER

PALE LIDFLOWER

ROUGHLEAF VELVETSEED

FLORIDA TETRAZYGIA

DARLING-PLUM

FALSE-BOXWOOD

PRINCEWOOD

PISONIA

FLORIDA CLUSIA

Thorny Florida Trees with Alternate Compound Leaves

Thorns mostly paired, at leafstalk bases.[1] Leaflets blunt-tipped. Species of s. Fla. with some in central counties[2] but none northward. See also Pl. 15 and Cinnecord (Pl. F-22).

Species and remarks

Species and remarks	Leaves twice-compound	Leaflets per leaf	Leaflet length (inches), including stalk	Leaflet bases V-shaped	Crushed leaves aromatic	Leaflets toothed[3]	Flower color[4]	Bean pod length (inches)	Also cen. Florida[2]
Biscayne Prickly-ash *Zanthoxylum coriaceum* Flowers/fruits at twig ends.	−	4–14	1–3	±	+	−	G	−	+
Wild-lime Prickly-ash *Z. fagara*[5] Flowers/fruits in leaf angles.	−	5–11	1–2	+	+	+	G	−	+
Catclaw Blackbead *Pithecellobium unguis-cati* Leaves thin, not leathery; pods coiled.	+	(2)4	1–2	±	−	−	P	2–6	+
Guadeloupe Blackbead *P. guadalupense*[5] Leaves leathery; pods coiled. See also Pl. F-22.	+	(2)4	1–3	−	−	−	P	2–6	+
Flowerfence Poinciana *Caesalpinia pulcherrima*[1] Rare escape from gardens.	+	120–400	1	−	−	−	R/Y	3–5	−
Huisachillo[6] *Acacia tortuosa* Major leaflets 4–8 pairs.	+	200–650	¼	−	−	−	Y	3–4	+
Longspine Acacia *Acacia macracantha* Major leaflets 10–22 pairs. Keys only.	+	400–1800	¼	−	−	−	Y	3–5	+

[1] Thorns may also be elsewhere or lacking in Flowerfence Poinciana.
[2] S. Fla. counties are Collier, Monroe, and Dade; cen. Fla. counties extend north to include Citrus, Sumpter, Lake, and Volusia.
[3] And leafstalks winged.
[4] G = green, P = pink, Y = yellow, R/Y = red/yellow.
[5] Thorns may be few or none.
[6] Pronounced weesatchEEyo.

VII

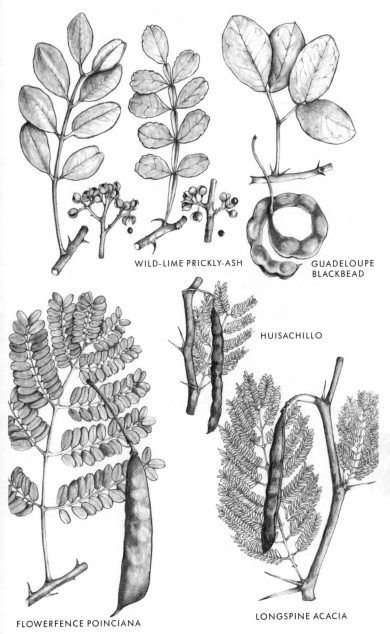

BISCAYNE PRICKLY-ASH

CATCLAW BLACKBEAD

WILD-LIME PRICKLY-ASH

GUADELOUPE BLACKBEAD

HUISACHILLO

FLOWERFENCE POINCIANA

LONGSPINE ACACIA

Thornless Florida Trees with Alternate Once-compound Leaves

Most of these trees have leathery evergreen foliage. Tropical species that occur in Collier, Dade, and Monroe counties. Some range north into cen. Fla. See also Pls. 21 and F-21B.

Species and remarks

Species and remarks	Leaflets per leaf[1]	Leaflets opposite	Leaflets blunt-tipped[2]	Leaflet bases V-shaped	Leaflet length (inches), including stalk	Flower color[3]	Fruit color[3]	North to cen. Fla.[4]
White Ironwood *Hypelate trifoliata* Leaflets not stalked.	3		+	+	1–2	G	B	–
Inkwood *Exothea paniculata* Leaflets often 2; sap dries black.	2–6	+	±	+	3–5	W	B	+
Gumbo-limbo *Bursera simaruba* Leaflet bases uneven; bark red, peels.	3–7	+	–	–	2–3	G	R	–
Florida Poisonwood *Metopium toxiferum* Avoid: see p. 15. Brown bark flakes, shows orange.	3–7	+	±	–	1–3	Y	O	+
Jamaica-dogwood *Piscidia piscipula* Shredded bark stuns fish.	5–9	+	–	±	2–4	W	Br	+
Bitterbush *Picramnia pentandra* Not on Fla. Keys. Inner bark bitter.	5–9	±	–	±	3–5	G	R	–
Brazilian Peppertree *Schinus terebinthifolius* Leafstalks red, winged; foliage aromatic.[5]	3–11	+	±	+	2–3	W	R	+

[1] Leaves with even pairs of leaflets may lack an end leaflet, but sometimes a single end leaflet occurs although the total number of leaflets is even.
[2] And sometimes notched.
[3] B = black, Br = brown, G = green, R = red, W = white, Y = yellow-green, O = orange.
[4] Including Citrus, Sumpter, Lake, and Volusia counties.
[5] Crushed leaves with turpentine odor.

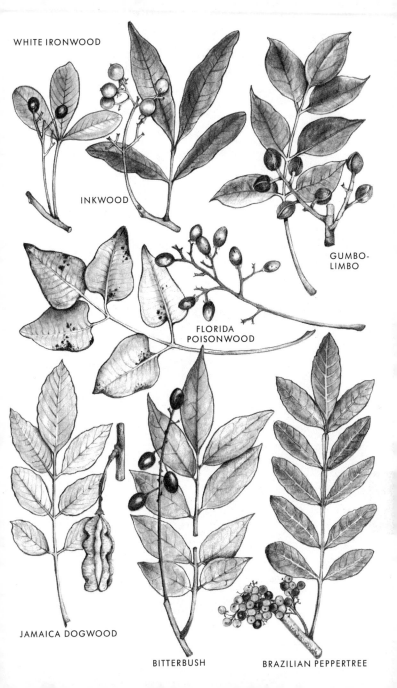

WHITE IRONWOOD

INKWOOD

GUMBO-LIMBO

FLORIDA POISONWOOD

JAMAICA DOGWOOD

BITTERBUSH

BRAZILIAN PEPPERTREE

Thornless Florida Trees with Alternate Once-compound Leaves

Thornless species, mostly with leathery evergreen foliage. Tropical species with restricted ranges in cen. and s. Fla. See also Pls. 21 and F-21A. Species and remarks	Leaflets per leaf[1]	Leaflets opposite	Leaflets blunt-tipped[2]	Leaflet bases V-shaped	Leaflet length (inches), including stalk	Flower color[3]	Fruit color[3]	Cen. Fla. and south[4]
Satinwood *Zanthoxylum flavum* Fla. Keys only; rare. Tiny gland dots (use lens).	5–11	+	±	±	1–3	P	D	–
Florida Cupania *Cupania glabra* Fla. Keys only; rare. Leaflets toothed.	6–10	–	+	±	3–4	W	D	–
West Indies Mahogany *Swietenia mahagoni*[5] Leaflet bases uneven; fruits 3″–5″.	8–16	+	–	–	1–2	G	Br	–
Paradise-tree *Simarouba glauca*[5] Leaflet bases often uneven; fruits ¾″.	8–16	±	+	±	2–4	G	R/D	+
Tamarind *Tamarindus indica*[5] Leaflets not stalked.	20–30	+	+	–	½–1	Y	Br	+
Mexican Alvaradoa *Alvaradoa amorphoides*[5] Fingerlike fruit. Rare.	21–41	–	+	±	½–1	G	D	–

VII

[1] Leaves with even pairs of leaflets may lack an end leaflet, but sometimes a single end leaflet occurs although the total number of leaflets is even.

[2] Sometimes notched.

[3] B = black, Br = brown, D = dark, G = green, P = pink, R = red, W = white, Y = yellow.

[4] Including Citrus, Sumpter, Lake, and Volusia counties.

[5] All species occur in tropical Collier, Dade, and Monroe counties.

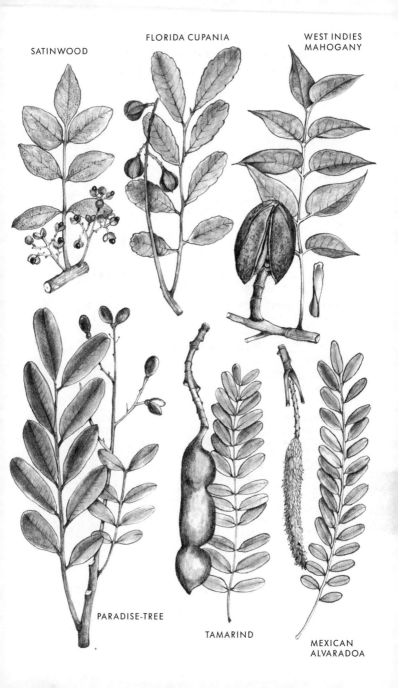

SATINWOOD

FLORIDA CUPANIA

WEST INDIES MAHOGANY

PARADISE-TREE

TAMARIND

MEXICAN ALVARADOA

Thornless Trees of Southern Florida with Twice-compound Leaves

Plants of the Florida Keys; some also occur on the maionland in s. Fla.[2] Leaves large; leaflets blunt, not toothed. Twigs hairless, leaf scars large; buds hairy; end buds false. Fruits bean pods. See also Pls. 22 and F-15.

Species and remarks	Leaflets more than 3/4" long, including stalk	Leaflets blunt-tipped	Major leaflet pairs	Flower color[1]	S. Fla. mainland[2]
Leadtree *Leucaena leucocephala* Pods 4"–6" × 3/4". Native of Mexico.	–	–	4–8	W	+
Bahama Lysiloma *Lysiloma latisiliquum* Pods 4"–8" × 1"–2".	–	±	3–5	W	–
Cinnecord *Acacia choriophylla*[3] Pods 2"–3" × 1". Rare. Occasional small thorns.	–	+	1–3	Y	–
(**Guadeloupe Blackbead** *Pithecellobium guadalupense*)[4] Pods 2"–6" × 1". See Pl. F-15.	+	+	2–4	P	+
(**Flowerfence Poinciana** *Caesalpinia pulcherrima*)[5] Pods 3"–5" × 1". See Pl. F-15.	±	+	5–10	R/Y	+

[1] P = pink, W = white, Y = yellow, R/Y = red/yellow.
[2] Collier, Dade, and Monroe counties.
[3] Tiny paired stipules at some leaf scars may be found upon careful examination (use lens). Perhaps these represent spines, but they are not usually noticed, and the species is listed here as thornless.
[4] May have weak thorns.
[5] Prickly or not.

VII

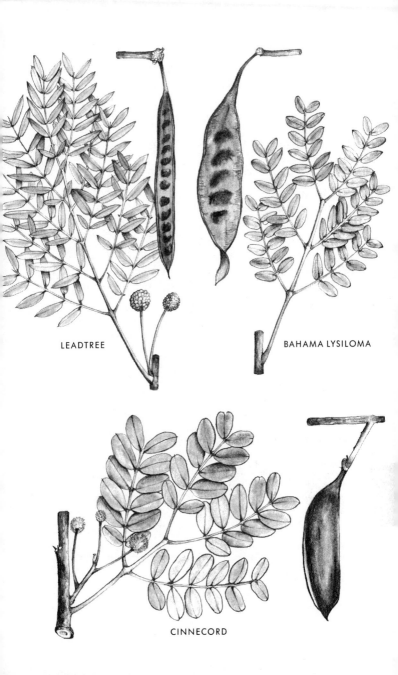

LEADTREE

BAHAMA LYSILOMA

CINNECORD

Trees of Peninsular and Southern Florida with Alternate Evergreen Leaves, Not Toothed

Plants of the semitropics and tropics, occurring north to Marion and Levy counties. Leaves mostly leathery.
See also Pls. 46 and F-46B, F-46C, and F-46D.

Species	Leaf length (inches), including stalk	Twigs ringed	Sap milky[1]	Leaves crowded at twig tips	Leafstalks essentially lacking	Leaf tips blunt[2]	Leaf bases wedge-shaped	Leaves thick, leathery	Flowers/fruits at twig tips	Flower color[3]	Fruit color[3]
Bay-cedar *Suriana maritima*	1	−	−	+	+	±	+	−	+	Y	D
Florida Mayten *Maytenus phyllanthoides*	1–2	−	−	−	−	±	+	+	−	W	R
Cocoplum *Chrysobalanus icaco*	1–3	−	−	±	±	±	+	+	±	W/D	W/D
Graytwig *Schoepfia chrysophylloides*	1–3	−	−	−	−	±	+	+	−	R	R
Myrsine *Myrsine floridana*	2–4	−	−	+	−	±	+	+	−	G	D
Buttonwood *Conocarpus erectus*	2–4	−	−	±	−	±	+	+	±	G	D
Limber Caper *Capparis flexuosa*	2–4	+	−	−	−	+	−	+	+	W	D
Bigflower Pawpaw *Asimina obovata*	2–4	−	−	−	−	+	±	−	−	G/D	G
Cajeput-tree *Melaleuca quinquenervia*	2–4	−	−	−	−	−	+	−	−	W	D
Satinleaf *Chrysophyllum oliviforme*	3–4	−	+	−	−	±	−	−	−	W	D
Yellow Anise-tree *Illicium parviflorum*[4]	3–5	−	−	+	−	±	+	+	+	Y	D
Seagrape *Coccoloba uvifera*	3–5	+	−	−	−	+	−	+	+	W	D

VII

[1] Try broken leafstalk or twig.
[2] Often notched.
[3] D = dark, G = greenish, R = red, W = white, Y = yellow.
[4] Reported by Lakela and Wunderlin (1980) as occurring north to Ga.

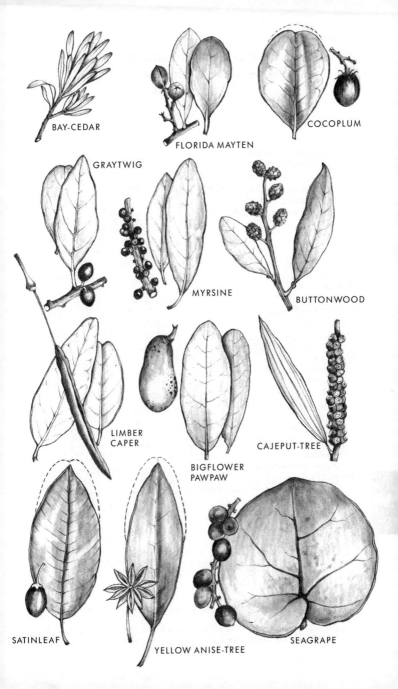

BAY-CEDAR

FLORIDA MAYTEN

COCOPLUM

GRAYTWIG

MYRSINE

BUTTONWOOD

LIMBER CAPER

BIGFLOWER PAWPAW

CAJEPUT-TREE

SATINLEAF

YELLOW ANISE-TREE

SEAGRAPE

Trees of Peninsular and Southern Florida with Alternate Evergreen Leaves, Not Toothed

Plants of the semitropics and tropics, occurring north to Marion and Levy counties. Leaves mostly leathery, with distinct stalks. See also Pls. 46, F-46A, F-46C, and F-46D.

Species	Leaf length (inches), including stalk	Twigs ringed[1]	Sap milky[1]	Leaves crowded at twig tips	Leaf tips blunt[2]	Leaf bases wedge-shaped	Leaves thick, leathery	Flowers/fruits at twig ends	Flower color[3]	Fruit color[3]
Strangler Fig *Ficus aurea*	3–5	+	+	−	−	±	−	−	−[4]	R
Shortleaf Fig *F. citrifolia*	3–5	+	+	−	−	−	−	−	−[4]	R
Varnishleaf *Dodonaea viscosa*	3–6	−	−	+	±	+	−	−	Y	G/B
Jamaica Caper *Capparis cynophallophora*	3–6	−	−	±	±	±	+	+	W	D/R
Sugar-apple *Annona squamosa*	3–6	−	−	−	±	±	−	−	W	G
Pond-apple *A. glabra*	3–6	−	−	−	±	−	−	+	W	Y
Lancewood *Nectandra coriacea*	3–6	−	−	−	±	+	−	+	W	D
Guiana-plum *Drypetes lateriflora*	3–6	−	−	−	−	±	−	−	G	R
Marlberry *Ardisia escallonioides*	3–6	−	−	−	−	+	+	+	W	D
Mastic *Mastichodendron foetidissimum*	3–7	−	+	+	±	±	−	−	Y	Y
Sapodilla *Manilkara zapota*	4–7	−	+	+	±	±	−	±	W	D
Pigeon-plum *Coccoloba diversifolia*	5–7	+	−	−	+	±	−	+	W	D
Mango *Mangifera indica*	6–11	−	−	+	−	±	−	+	Y	G/P

VII

[1] Try broken leafstalk or twig.

[2] Often notched.

[3] B = brown (dry), D = dark, G = greenish, P = pink, R = red, W = white, Y = yellow.

[4] Fig flowers hidden within developing walls of fruits; aerial roots drop from tree branches; gray-barked fig tissues envelop host trees.

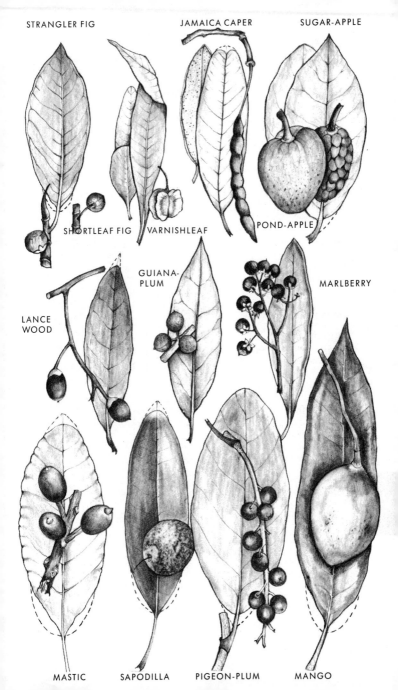

STRANGLER FIG JAMAICA CAPER SUGAR-APPLE

SHORTLEAF FIG VARNISHLEAF POND-APPLE

GUIANA-PLUM MARLBERRY

LANCE WOOD

MASTIC SAPODILLA PIGEON-PLUM MANGO

Trees of Extreme Southern Florida with Alternate Evergreen Leaves, Mostly Not Toothed

Tropical species recorded only from Collier, Dade, and Monroe counties. No species has leafstalks lacking or twigs ringed. Sour Orange (Pl. 24) may lack thorns; it has winged leafstalks half an inch wide. See also Tawnyberry Holly (Pl. 41).

Species	Leaf length (inches), including stalk	Sap milky [1]	Leaves crowded at twig tips	Leaf tips blunt [2]	Leaf bases wedge-shaped	Leaves thick, leathery	Leaf edges wavy	Flowers/fruits at twig tips	Flower color [3]	Fruit color [3]
Cinnamon-bark *Cannella winterana*	2–4	–	–	+	+	+	–	+	W/R	D
Florida Licaria *Licaria triandra* [4]	2–4	–	–	–	–	+	+	–	W	D/R
Bahama Strongbark *Bourreria ovata*	2–5	–	–	±	+	–	–	+	W	O
Wild-dilly *Manilkara bahamensis*	2–5	+	+	+	±	+	–	+	Y	D
Soldierwood *Colubrina cubensis*	3–4	–	–	+	±	–	+	–	W	D
Crabwood *Gyminanthes lucida*	3–5	–	–	±	+	±	±	–	G	D
Manchineel *Hippomane mancinella* Poisonous! [4]	3–5	+	+	–	–	±	±	–	G	Y/R
Willow Bustic *Dipholis salicifolia*	3–5	–	–	–	+	+	+	–	W	D
West Indies Cherry *Prunus myrtifolia*	3–5	–	–	–	–	+	+	–	W	D
(Governor's-plum *Flacourtia indica*)	2–4	–	–	±	±	+	+	–	Y	D

[1] Try broken leafstalks or twigs.
[2] Often notched.
[3] D = dark, G = green, O = orange, R = red, W = white, Y = yellow.
[4] Possibly extirpated (Roger Hammer, Goulds, Fla.).
[5] It is said (Morton 1971) that Manchineel smoke and even rainwater dripping from the leaves can cause skin irritations, that native Americans once used the sap as arrow poison, and that they poisoned the spring water of enemies with the leaves.

VII

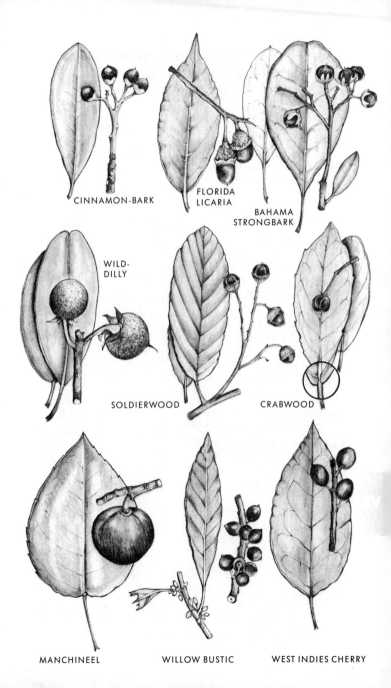

CINNAMON-BARK

FLORIDA LICARIA

BAHAMA STRONGBARK

WILD-DILLY

SOLDIERWOOD

CRABWOOD

MANCHINEEL

WILLOW BUSTIC

WEST INDIES CHERRY

Trees of Extreme Southern Florida with Alternate Evergreen Leaves, Mostly Not Toothed

Tropical species recorded only from Collier, Dade, and Monroe counties. No species has sap milky, leafstalks lacking, or twigs ringed.

Species and remarks

Species and remarks	Total length (inches)	Leaves crowded at twig tips	Leaf tips blunt[1]	Leaf bases wedge-shaped	Veins follow leaf edges	Flowers/fruits at twig tips	Flower color[2]	Fruit color[2]
Coffee Colubrina *Colubrina arborescens* New growth rusty-hairy.	3–8	−	−	−	+	−	G	D
Potato-tree *Solanum erianthum* Leaves woolly, with tar odor; stalks 1″–2″.	3–8	−	−	±	−	+	W	Y
Black-calabash *Amphitecna latifolia* Leaves shiny; flowers malodorous. Rare.	5–8	−	±	+	−	+	W	G
India-almond *Terminalia catappa* Beaches, cultivation. Edible.	4–12	±	±	+	−	±	W	D
Fla. Keys (not on mainland):[3]								
Maidenbush *Savia bahamensis* Clusters of flower buds ball-like.	1–2	−	+	±	−	−	G	D
Florida-boxwood *Schaefferia frutescens* Twigs green, lined.	1–2	±	−	+	−	−	G	R
Rough Strongbark *Bourreria radula* Leaves sandpapery.	1–3	−	±	+	−	+	W	O
Nakedwood *Colubrina elliptica* Leaves long-pointed, basal glands.[4]	3–4	−	−	−	+	−	Y	O
Milkbark *Drypetes diversifolia* Bark white; toothed leaves few.	3–5	−	±	±	−	−	G	W

[1] Sometimes notched.
[2] D = dark, G = greenish, O = orange, R = red, W = white, Y = yellow.
[3] According to Little (1979), but Long and Lakela (1971) state that the range of some includes s. Fla.
[4] Small glands present on base of leaf blades; use lens.

VII

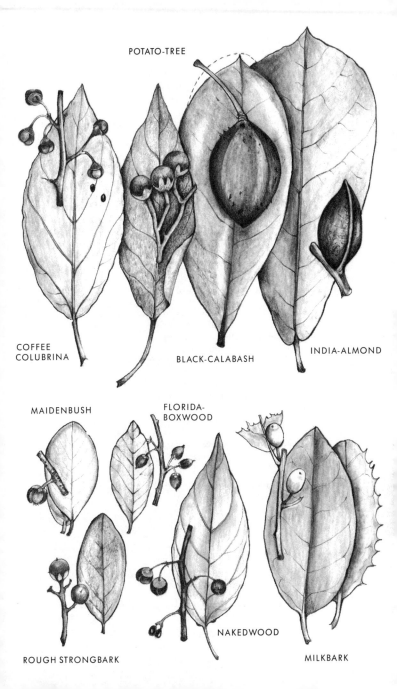

POTATO-TREE

COFFEE
COLUBRINA

BLACK-CALABASH

INDIA-ALMOND

MAIDENBUSH

FLORIDA-
BOXWOOD

ROUGH STRONGBARK

NAKEDWOOD

MILKBARK

between species. Additional foliage data appear below for each species. As an aid to winter identification, see the identification charts (pp. 136–137, before the Plates section).

Where a species is listed as having hairy twigs, the degree of hairiness is often slight. An adequate magnifying lens should be used to determine whether twigs or buds are hairy. Twigs taken for identification from unknown specimens should be carefully selected for their full, mature growth.

Acorns and their cups are often of great assistance in identifying oak species. If none is growing on the tree, look for old ones on the ground (but try to verify that they fell from the tree being examined). Acorns always grow partly enclosed in basal growths universally called "cups," but the cups are nevertheless nearly always described as saucerlike, bowl-like, goblet-shaped, or otherwise uncuplike.

Not every oak specimen can be identified with certainty by the amateur. Even professional botanists are frequently puzzled by apparent hybrids and variants. Winter identifications are often especially difficult.

Oaks provide about half the annual production of hardwood lumber in the United States. They are slow-growing, long-lived, and relatively disease- and insect-resistant. Bark of several oaks is rich in tannin used in curing leather.

By grinding the nuts and pouring hot water through the flour to leach out the tannic acid, the native Americans converted even the acorns of red oaks into staple articles of diet. In ancient England oak forests were valued highly for fattening swine, and laws provided that anyone wantonly injuring or destroying an oak should be fined according to the size of the tree and its ability to bear fruits.

Extensive browsing by livestock on early spring foliage occasionally causes poisoning. Twigs and fruits of oaks form a large

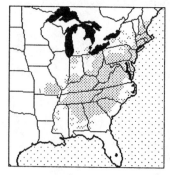
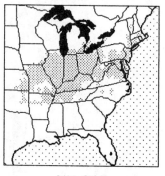

SCARLET OAK   PIN OAK

portion of the food consumed by many game birds and mammals. Acorns are eaten by nearly all herbivorous birds and mammals. The list of species eating these nuts in our area includes many songbirds as well as the ruffed and sharp-tailed grouse, prairie chicken, bobwhite, wild turkey, pheasant, mourning dove, wood duck, white-tailed deer, black bear, red fox, gray fox, raccoon, opossum, gray squirrel, and fox squirrel. Deer, cottontail, and snowshoe hare browse twigs; porcupine eats the growing layer beneath bark.

Oaks I: Leaves Feather-lobed, with Bristle Tips (Plate 28)

All species on this plate are members of the red oak group.

SCARLET OAK *Quercus coccinea* Muenchh. **Pl. 28**
A medium-sized tree of the red oak group. Leaves *deeply lobed,* shiny above and either hairless or with tufts of hair in angles of veins beneath. Twigs hairless; end buds *scraggly-hairy,* nearly ¼" long, blunt or sharp, often *whitish tipped.* Trunk dark, finely grooved. Acorn cup brownish, hairless or nearly so (use lens); more than ¼" deep, *bowl-like,* and ⅝"–⅞" in diameter. Leaves 3"–6". Height 40'–50' (80'); diameter 1'–2' (3'). Dry soils.
Similar species: (1) Northern Red Oak and (2) Black Oak leaves not so deeply lobed. This and next 4 species have similar foliage; best identified by acorn cups (see drawings below). (3) Pin Oak has drooping lower branches and occurs on moister sites.

PIN OAK *Quercus palustris* Muenchh. **acorn, Fig. 18**
Similar to Scarlet Oak, but end buds *hairless,* small, sharp. Twigs hairless. Lower branches characteristically *slope* downward; many stubby pinlike branches usually present. Acorn cup brownish and hairless but shallow and *saucerlike,* only ⅜"–⅝" in diameter, and less than ¼" high. Leaves 3"–7"; dead leaves tend to *remain* on tree in winter. Height 70'–80' (110'); diameter 2'–3' (5'). Bottomlands.
Similar species: See (1) Scarlet Oak, (2) Jack Oak occurs on dry soils and has deeper, more tapered acorn cups.

Fig. 18. Pin Oak.

JACK OAK   *Quercus ellipsoidalis* E. J. Hill   **acorn, Fig. 19**
Similar to Pin Oak but growing on uplands. Acorn cup bowl-
shaped and somewhat *conical*, with sides sloping gradually. Cups
finely *gray-hairy;* mostly less than ½″ across. Buds small, red-
brown, sharp, hairless. Leaves 3″–7″. Height 60′–70′; diameter
2′–3′.
Similar species: See (1) Pin Oak. (2) Nuttall Oak and (3)
Shumard Oak also have gray-hairy acorn cups. Nuttall Oak
occupies a more southern range and acorn cups, if cone-shaped,
have a basal constriction. Shumard Oak is also more southern;
leaves and acorns generally larger.
Remarks: Also known as Northern Pin and as Hill's Oak.

Fig. 19. Jack Oak.   **Fig. 20. Nuttall Oak.**

NUTTALL OAK   *Quercus nuttallii* Palmer.   **acorn, Fig. 20**
Similar to the more northern Jack Oak but with acorn cup usually
constricted to form a definitely *distinct* basal portion. Acorn cup
varies from cone- to bowl-shaped, is ⅝″–¾″ across, with a con-
tracted scaly basal portion 1/16″–¼″ long. End buds less than ¼″
long, pointed, not angled, and with *hairy* scales. Leaves 4″–8″.
Height to 120′; diameter to 3′. Lowlands, s. Mississippi Valley.

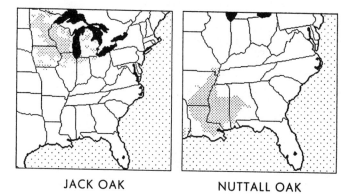

JACK OAK   NUTTALL OAK

SHUMARD OAK   *Quercus shumardii* Buckl.   **acorn, Fig. 21**
Resembles Scarlet Oak, but mature leaves mostly more than 6″
long. End buds clay- or straw-colored, more than ¼″ long, pointed,
hairless, and angled. Twigs hairless. Acorn cup *gray,* shallow,
saucerlike, ¾″–1¼″ in diameter. Leaves 6″–8″. Height 70′–100′
(120′); diameter 2′–3′ (6′). Bottomlands, mostly Coastal Plain.
Similar species: (1) Scarlet, (2) Pin, (3) Jack, and (4) Nuttall oaks
have smaller leaves. Also see winter identification chart, p. 136.

Fig. 21. Shumard Oak.

NORTHERN RED OAK   *Quercus rubra* L.   **Pl. 28**
A large tree. Leaves *moderately lobed,* hairless, thin, *dull above.*
Twigs hairless; end buds ³⁄₁₆″–⁵⁄₁₆″, sharp or blunt, *hairless, not
angled.* Acorn cup flat and *saucerlike,* ¾″–1¼″. Trunk dark,
furrowed, often laced with *broad, shiny strips.* Leaves 4″–10″.
Height 70′–80′ (150′); diameter 3′–4′ (5′). Woods.
Similar species: Best separation point between this and Black
Oak is the buds, which are hairless and smaller in Northern Red
Oak. Mature buds usually not available between May and Aug.,
during which period leaf textures (and possibly acorn cups) are
helpful.

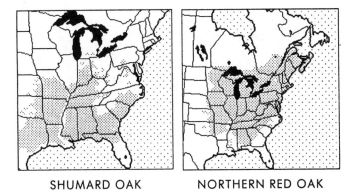

SHUMARD OAK   NORTHERN RED OAK

BLACK OAK *Quercus velutina* Lam. **Pl. 28**

Similar to Northern Red Oak but with leaves somewhat *thickened*, generally *glossy* above and mostly hairless beneath. Twigs angled, hairless; end buds ¼″–½″, pointed, densely *gray-hairy* and *sharply angled*. Trunk dark, blocky, usually but not always *without* shiny ridges. Orange inner bark, often relied upon as an identification mark of Black Oak, frequently seems to be similar to that of Northern Red Oak. Acorn cup *bowl-shaped* and finely gray-hairy; edge rough with fringelike scales. Leaves 4″–10″. Height 70′–80′ (100′); diameter 3′–4′ (5′). Dry soils.
Similar species: (1) Shumard Oak has leaves more deeply lobed and acorn cups shallow, not fringed. (2) See Northern Red Oak.

SOUTHERN RED (SPANISH) OAK **Pl. 28**
Quercus falcata Michx.

A moderate-sized to tall tree; leaves *variable*, usually with *3 main lobes* toward tip. Leaf bases *rounded*. Leaf undersides and twigs gray-hairy. End buds ³⁄₁₆″–⁵⁄₁₆″, *hairy*, sharp-pointed but not angled. Acorn cup flat, gray-hairy, saucerlike. Bark dark, somewhat furrowed. Leaves 4″–12″. Height 70′–80′ (100′); diameter 2′–3′ (5′). Sandy uplands.
Similar species: Three-lobed leaves are distinctive. (1) Cherry-bark Oak has wider, 7–11 lobed, angled-base leaves (Fig. 22). (2) Turkey Oak has more prominent basal leaf lobes, forming a "turkey track" shape (Fig. 24). (3) A form of Water Oak (Pl. 31) has deeply three-parted leaf tips, but they are not as sharp-pointed and are nearly hairless beneath.

CHERRYBARK OAK **leaf, Fig. 22**
Quercus falcata var. *pagodaefolia* Ell.

Though classified only as a variety of Southern Red Oak, this oak has distinctively different foliage. The leaves are wider, resembling those of Northern Red Oak, but with *7–11* lobes that are

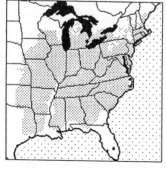

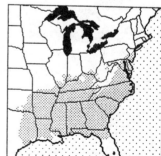

BLACK OAK   SOUTHERN RED OAK

often *single-pointed.* If the leafstalk is pointed skyward, the angled lobes of the upside-down leaf are reminiscent of the several overlapping roofs of an oriental pagoda.

TURKEY OAK   acorn, Fig. 23; leaf, Fig. 24
Quercus laevis Walt.
Leaves and buds of this small *southern* tree most closely resemble Southern Red Oak. Lower lobes of leaves *longer* than upper ones. Leaves leathery, hairless, often three-lobed, with central and lower lobes all narrow, resembling turkey tracks in outline. Twigs hairless; end buds *slender, pointed,* ¼″–½″, somewhat fine-hairy. Trunk *blue-gray,* furrowed. Acorn cups about ¾″ in diameter, deeply *bowl-shaped,* gray-hairy. Leaves 4″–10″. Height 15′–20′ (60′); diameter 1′–2′. Sandy Coastal Plain soils.
Similar species: Southern Red Oak has smaller buds, hairy twigs, and shallow acorn cups.

Fig. 22. Cherrybark Oak.   **Fig. 23. Turkey Oak.**

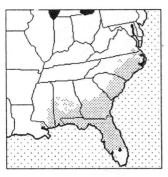

TURKEY OAK

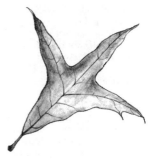

Fig. 24. Turkey Oak.

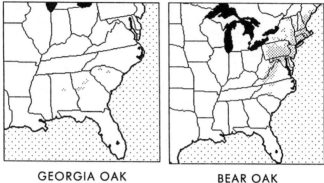

GEORGIA OAK

BEAR OAK

GEORGIA OAK
Quercus georgiana M.A. Curtis
acorn, Fig. 25

A small tree of rocky soils in northern *Georgia* and nearby portions of South Carolina. Leaves and buds resemble those of Bear Oak but leaves somewhat *glossy* above and *hairless* beneath. Twigs *hairless*. Bark light brown. Acorn cup *shallow,* saucerlike, ½″. Leaves 2″–5″. Height to 25′.

Fig. 25. Georgia Oak.

BEAR (SCRUB) OAK
Quercus ilicifolia Wangenh.
Pl. 28

A thicket-forming shrub or small tree with leaves also *small* and *white-hairy* beneath. Twigs *hairy:* end buds small, blunt, hairless, not angled. Acorn less than ⅜″ long and cup *bowl-shaped.* Bark dark. Leaves 2″–5″. Height 3′–9′ (18′). Northeastern.
Similar species: See Georgia Oak.

BLACKJACK OAK
Quercus marilandica Muenchh.
Pl. 28

A low to medium-sized tree. Leaves thick, *leathery, shallow-lobed, brownish-scaly* or hairy beneath. Twigs angled, *hairy;* end buds *large, hairy, sharp-pointed, angled.* Dark trunk bark broken into *squarish blocks.* Acorn cup somewhat hairy, *deep,* with a narrowed base, somewhat goblet-shaped. Cup scales appear loosely

attached. Leaves 4″–8″. Height 40′–50′ (70′); diameter 1′–2′ (4′).
Similar species: (1) Post Oak (Pl. 29) also has leathery foliage;
(1) often grows with Blackjack, but leaves more deeply lobed and
not bristle-tipped. (2) Black Oak may have leathery leaves, but
the sinuses are deeper; foliage and twigs are hairless.

Oaks II: Leaves Feather-lobed, without Bristle-tips (Plate 29)

The species on this plate are all members of the white oak group.

WHITE OAK   *Quercus alba* L.   **Pl. 29**
A tall tree with rather *evenly lobed, hairless* leaves that may be
somewhat whitened beneath. Lobes *7–11*. Twigs hairless; end
buds red-brown, small, blunt, hairless, and not angled. Bark light
gray, slightly furrowed to scaly. Acorn cup bowl-shaped, covering
⅓ or less of acorn. Leaves 3″–9″. Height 60′–80′ (150′); diameter
2′–3′ (5′). Dry to moist woods.
Similar species: (1) Overcup and (2) Bur Oak leaves usually
have deeper divisions; their acorn cups are unique. In winter, the
end-bud stipules of Bur Oak help to differentiate that species. (3)
Swamp Oak (Pl. 30) has 1″–3″ acorn stalks, and leaves may have
shallow lobes.

POST OAK   *Quercus stellata* Wangenh.   **Pl. 29**
A small tree with *often leathery* leaves and 3–5 lobes usually
arranged so that they resemble a *cross*. Leaves typically shiny
above and gray or *brown-hairy beneath*. Twigs somewhat gray-
hairy; end buds less than ¼″ long, blunt and rather hairy. Bark
brownish, broken by long shallow cracks and often divided into

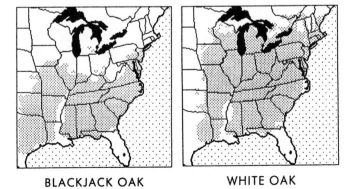

BLACKJACK OAK   WHITE OAK

rectangular blocks. Bowl-shaped acorn cups cover ⅓–½ of acorn. Leaves 3″–8″. Height 50′–60′ (100′); diameter 1′–2′ (3′). Dry soils. **Similar species:** See Blackjack Oak (Pl. 28). In winter, the unique acorns, terminal stipules, and often-winged branchlets of Bur Oak will distinguish that species.

OVERCUP OAK *Quercus lyrata* Walt. Pl. 29

A moderate-sized tree, mainly of Coastal Plain bottomlands. Leaves vary (may even resemble White Oak somewhat) but generally have *deep indentations* near base and narrow basal lobes; *fine-hairy* and often whitened beneath. Twigs and end buds as in White Oak except that buds are chestnut brown. Bark light, broken by shallow cracks. Rough acorn cup is unique, *enclosing nearly all of globular nut;* only very tip visible. Leaves 3″–10″. Height 50′–80′ (100′); diameter 2′–3′ (4′). Swamp forests.

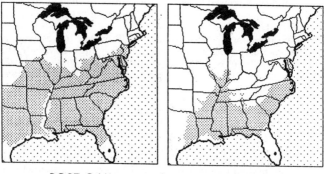

POST OAK

OVERCUP OAK

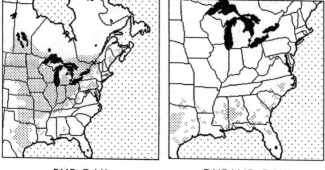

BUR OAK

DURAND OAK

Similar species: (1) Bur Oak leaves have deep sinuses more centrally located. Acorn cups of both species distinctive. (2) White Oak has shallower leaf sinuses with wider basal lobes; its acorn cup is bowllike.

BUR (MOSSYCUP) OAK   *Quercus macrocarpa* Michx.   **Pl. 29**
A tall tree with variable foliage, usually marked by at least *1 deep pair* of indentations that divide leaves *into 2* or more portions. Leaves often leathery and shiny above, usually somewhat *hairy and whitish beneath*. Twigs yellow-brown, variably hairless to rather hairy; end buds hairy, blunt, not angled. Slender *stipules* commonly present. Branchlets sometimes have *corky wings* like those of Sweetgum (Pl. 25). Acorn cups bowl-shaped, with a peculiar "bur" or "mossy" *fringe* of elongate scales. Bark light gray, shallowly grooved. Leaves 4″–10″. Height 70′–80′ (170′); diameter 2′–3′ (7′).
Similar species: See (1) White and (2) Overcup oaks.

ENGLISH OAK   *Quercus robur* L.   **Pl. 29**
A handsome imported tree. Leaves *small,* hairless, with 7–11 lobes. Twigs mostly hairless; end buds *more than* ¼″ long, blunt, hairless, often somewhat angled. Acorns on *1″–3″ stalks,* cups deep. Leaves 3″–5″. Height to 150′ in Britain. Spreading from upland plantings in a few northern localities.
Similar species: (1) White Oak usually has fewer leaf lobes and is much more widespread. (2) Only Swamp Oak (Pl. 30) also has 1″–3″ acorn stalks. (3) Live Oak (Pl. 31) has acorn stalks to 1″.

Oaks III: Leaves Wavy-edged or Toothed
(Plate 30)

The species of this plate are all members of the white oak group.

DURAND OAK   *Quercus durandii* Buckl.   **Pl. 30**
A rare, medium-sized tree that grows on fertile soils of the southeastern Coastal Plain. Foliage even on a single tree often *varies widely,* sometimes resembling the lobed leaves of White Oak (Pl. 29); sometimes being merely wavy-edged. Leaves leathery and glossy above, hairless and whitened beneath. Twigs somewhat hairy and buds small, nearly *globular,* with red-brown hairs. Bark light gray. Acorns ½″–¾″ long, in a *saucerlike* cup. Leaves 3″–8″. Height 60′–90′; diameter 2′–3′. Damp to dry sites.

CHAPMAN OAK   *Quercus chapmanii* Sarg.   **Pl. 30**
A shrub or small tree of sandy Coastal Plain soils from S. Carolina to s. Florida (see map, p. 148). Leaves *wavy-edged,* hairless, mostly leathery, often *notched* at the tip. The nearly evergreen

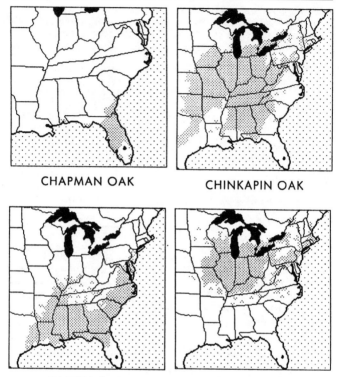

CHAPMAN OAK

CHINKAPIN OAK

BASKET OAK

SWAMP OAK

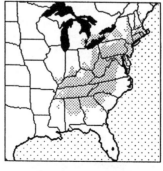

CHESTNUT OAK

leaves may be held late in the year. Twigs variably hairy. Buds small, *blunt,* hairless. Bark light gray. Acorns ½"–1" long, cup bowl-shaped. Leaves 2"–5". Height to 25'. Dry soils.

CHINKAPIN OAK *Quercus muehlenbergii* Engelm. **Pl. 30**
A medium-sized *upland* tree whose leaves have 8–13 pairs of *sharp* teeth. Leaf undersides fine-hairy. Twigs hairless. End buds narrow, *sharp,* hairless, not angled, and mostly about ³/₁₆" long. Bark *light gray* and often flaky, not ridged. Acorn cup bowl-shaped, less than 1" across, with tight scales free only at the tips. Leaves 4"–9". Height 20'–50' (160'); diameter 6"–24" (4').
Similar species: (1) Chestnut Oak has dark, ridged bark. (2) A shrub, Dwarf Oak (Dwarf Chinkapin Oak—*Q. prinoides* Willd.) also has sharp leaf teeth, but leaves are smaller and teeth are fewer. (3) Live Oak (Pl. 31) may have some leaves with sharp teeth, but foliage is leathery and evergreen.
Remarks: Also spelled Chinquapin.

BASKET OAK *Quercus michauxii* Nutt. **Pl. 30**
Leaves with *7–16* pairs of *rounded* teeth. Typically more deeply and sometimes more sharply toothed than Swamp Oak and also often *white-hairy* beneath. Twigs hairless. Buds *more than* ¼" long, hairless, and pointed. Trunk bark *light gray,* rough, and flaky like Chinkapin Oak. Acorn cup similar to that of Chestnut Oak but *broader* (1"–1¼" in diameter) and bowl-shaped, with scales attached *only at base.* Leaves 4"–8". Height to 100'; diameter to 4'. Coastal Plain *bottomlands.*
Remarks: Also known as Swamp Chestnut Oak.

SWAMP OAK *Quercus bicolor* Willd. **Pl. 30**
Leaves wedge-based, with only *4–6* pairs of *large, rounded teeth* (occasionally sharp-toothed and sometimes forming shallow lobes). Foliage shiny above, hairless and often whitened beneath. Twigs hairless. Chestnut brown end buds *small, blunt,* hairless. Acorn cup bowl-shaped, with *stalks 1"–3".* Bark *light gray,* ridged or flaky. Leaves 4"–9". Height 60'–70' (100'); diameter 2'–3' (8'). Wet woods.
Similar species: (1) Only English Oak (Pl. 29) also has acorn stalks 1"–3". (2) Live Oak (Pl. 31) has 1" acorn stalks. (3) White Oak leaves much more deeply lobed.
Remarks: Also known as Swamp White Oak. The lumber not distinguished from that of White Oak.

CHESTNUT OAK *Quercus prinus* L. **Pl. 30**
An *upland* tree whose leaves have *7–16* pairs of *rounded teeth* (sometimes sharp). Foliage somewhat leathery, glossy above and slightly hairy beneath. Twigs and buds resemble those of Basket Oak, but trunk bark *dark, deeply ridged,* quite distinctive. Acorn cups deeply bowl-shaped, less than 1" across, with tight scales free

only at the tips. Leaves 4″–9″. Height 60′–70′ (100′); diameter 3′–4′ (7′). Dry woods.

Similar species: (1) Basket Oak has light-colored bark, more scaly and wider, but less deep, acorn cups. (2) Chinkapin Oak has sharp leaf teeth and smaller acorns. (3) Swamp Oak has small, blunt buds. (4) Chestnut (Pl. 32) lacks clustered end buds and has sharp leaf teeth.

Oaks IV: Leaves Typically Smooth-edged (Plate 31)

Though these oaks usually lack leaf lobes, teeth, or wavy edges, some specimens of several species may have such leaf edges. Oglethorpe Oak and Virginia Live Oak are "white oaks"; all others on this plate are in the red oak group.

ARKANSAS OAK   *Quercus arkansana* Sarg.   **Pl. 31**
Resembling Blackjack Oak (Pl. 28) but with *smaller* and less leathery leaves, *saucerlike* acorn cups and a more restricted and scattered *southern* range. The leaves are without teeth and *wide,* with several of the bristle points typical of the red oak group. Foliage *hairless,* sometimes slightly three-lobed. Twigs hairy; end buds small, sharp, hairless, and not angled. Acorns small, ¼″–⁷⁄₁₆″ long, with shallow cups. Trunk bark dark, thick, furrowed. Leaves 2″–4″. Height to 80′. Sandy soils.

WATER OAK   *Quercus nigra* L.   **Pl. 31**
A *southern* tree with wedge-shaped hairless leaves that are *broadest near tip.* Leaves bristle-tipped. Leaf tips sometimes three-parted. Twigs hairless; end buds narrow, sharp, quite *hairy* and *angled,* often white-tipped. Acorn cup flat, saucer-shaped, ³⁄₈″–⁵⁄₈″ across. Trunk dark and rather smooth. Leaves 2″–5″. Height 50′–60′ (80′; diameter 2′–3′ (4′). Lowlands.

Similar species: (1) See Shingle Oak. (2) If leaves are deeply three-lobed at tips, see Southern Red Oak (Pl. 28).

SHINGLE OAK   *Quercus imbricaria* Michx.   **Pl. 31**
A mainly *midwestern* tree whose leaves *lack* either teeth or lobes but whose single bristle tip shows it to belong to red oak group. Foliage *shiny* above and densely *hairy beneath.* Twigs hairless; end buds small, more or less *silky,* sharp, and angular; bud-scale edges hairy. Acorn cup *bowl-shaped,* covering ⅓–½ of acorn and ⁹⁄₁₆″–¹³⁄₁₆″ across. Trunk dark, irregularly grooved. Leaves *4″–10″*. Height 50′–60′ (100′); diameter 2′–3′ (4′). Fertile forests.

Similar species: Shingle Oak leaves average wider than those of the other non-evergreen oaks in this group. Water Oak, however, has leaves that are wider near the tips.

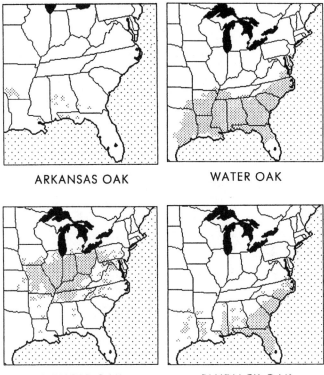

ARKANSAS OAK   WATER OAK

SHINGLE OAK   BLUEJACK OAK

BLUEJACK (SAND) OAK *Quercus incana* Bartr.   **Pl. 31**
A small tree or shrub of the *southeastern* states with somewhat *leathery but not evergreen* leaves, shaped like those of Shingle Oak but narrower and occasionally wavy-edged. Foliage shiny and bristle-tipped and with *fine, whitish woolliness* beneath. Twigs densely woolly to nearly hairless; buds (³⁄₁₆″–⁵⁄₁₆″) *longer* than those of others in this group, sharp, hairy, and not angled. Acorn cup saucer-shaped, ³⁄₈″–⁵⁄₈″ across. Trunk black or gray, bark divided into squarish blocks. Leaves 2″–5″. Height to 35′. Dry Coastal Plain soils.
Similar species: Shingle Oak has larger and thinner leaves, hairless twigs, and bowl-shaped acorn cups.

OGLETHORPE OAK   *Quercus oglethorpensis* Duncan   **Pl. 31**
A rare tree of the *white oak* group. Known *only* from bottomlands in extreme w. South Carolina and adjacent ne. Georgia. Leaves thin, narrow, *blunt-tipped* and pale *yellow-hairy* beneath. Twigs and buds hairless, the buds pointed or not and not angled. Acorns small, ⅜″, in a *bowl-shaped* cup. Trunk bark gray and flaky. Leaves 3″–5″. Height to 45′. Named for Oglethorpe County, Georgia, and General James Oglethorpe, founder of Georgia.

WILLOW OAK   *Quercus phellos* L.   **Pl. 31**
A tall tree with thin, *narrow, bristle-tipped* leaves that are shiny and hairless, or, infrequently, gray-hairy beneath. Twigs hairless; end buds narrow, sharp, hairless, somewhat angular, mostly less than ⅛″ long. Acorns to ½″ long, cups very *shallow* and saucerlike, ⅜″–½″ across. Trunk dark and shallowly grooved. Leaves 2″–5″. Height 70′–80′ (100′); diameter 2′–3′ (4′). Lowlands.
Similar species: (1) Shingle Oak has wider leaves and deeper acorn cups; (2) Bluejack Oak has leaf undersides and twigs woolly. (3) Laurel Oak leaves are somewhat shiny beneath, mostly thicker, nearly evergreen.
Remarks: Not related to willows. Widely used in street and park plantings in the South.

LAUREL (DARLINGTON) OAK   **Pl. 31**
Quercus laurifolia Michx. (*Q. hemisphaerica* Bartr.)
A large, *nearly evergreen* tree whose leaves may be leathery or not. It is intermediate in shape between Shingle and Willow oaks, somewhat *shiny* and *hairless* except for tufts in angles of veins beneath. Twigs hairless or slightly hairy. End buds sharp, hairless, angled, ⅛″–³⁄₁₆″ long. Acorns nearly globular, to 1″ long; cups saucer-shaped, ⅝″–⅞″ across. Trunk *gray,* scaly. Leaves 3″–6″. Height to 80′. Coastal Plain swamps.
Similar species: See Willow Oak.
Remarks: Laurel and Darlington Oaks, once viewed as distinct, have been combined as one species.

MYRTLE OAK   *Quercus myrtifolia* Willd.   **Pl. 31**
An *evergreen* shrub or small tree of Coastal Plain soils in Florida and nearby states. Leaves *leathery,* shiny and quite veiny above, but nearly *hairless* beneath. The edges are rolled under. Some may lack a bristle tip. Twigs usually *hairy;* end buds *pointed,* hairless and not angled. Trunk light gray, rather smooth. Leaves 1″–2″. Height to 40′. Acorns to ½″, nearly globular, stalks *short,* cups *saucerlike.* Dry soils.

VIRGINIA LIVE OAK   *Quercus virginiana* Mill.   **Pl. 31**
A spreading southern *evergreen* tree of the *white oak* group, with *leathery* leaves. Leaves usually have rolled edges, shiny above

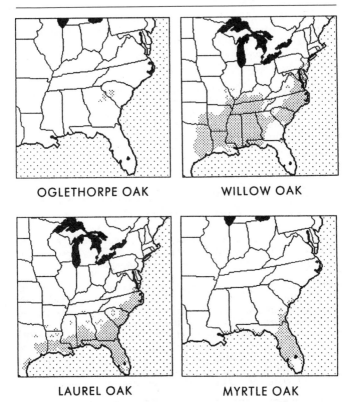

OGLETHORPE OAK

WILLOW OAK

LAUREL OAK

MYRTLE OAK

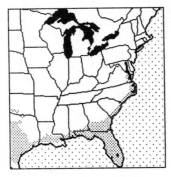

VIRGINIA LIVE OAK

and mostly gray- or white-hairy beneath. Some may be sharply toothed in part. Leaves *not bristle-tipped.* Twigs hairless, rarely gray-hairy; end buds small, hairless, *blunt;* not angled. Acorns are on ¾"–1" *stalks,* and cup is *bowl-shaped.* Trunk dark, bark somewhat broken into squares. Leaves 1"–4". Height to 60'; diameter to 8'.

Similar species: Any evergreen oak species may be called a live oak. There are many kinds, especially in the West. In our area, no other oak with leathery, smooth-edged leaves has long acorn-stalks or small blunt buds. Toothed leaves do occur on Virginia Live Oak, but they are shaped unlike leaves on any of the oaks on Pl. 30.

Trees with Alternate, Coarse-edged Leaves (Plate 32)

These species have coarse-toothed or conspicuously scalloped foliage. All have 3 bundle scars per leaf scar. They also *lack* the end clusters of leaves and buds present in oaks.

CHESTNUT *Castanea dentata* (Marsh.) Borkh. **Pl. 32**
Originally a large tree, but now there are only occasional new plantings plus a few survivors sprouting from old stumps. Leaves *large but narrow,* hairless; undersides somewhat paler, *coarse-toothed.* Buds blunt, few-scaled; twigs brownish, hairless. End buds false. Bundle scars 3, occasionally more. Mature bark dark, with numerous wide-topped shiny ridges. Leaves 5"–8". Height 60'–80' (100'), now mostly less than 25' high; diameter 2'–4' (17'). Flowers June–Aug., male blossoms small, in long catkins.

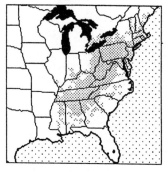

CHESTNUT

OZARK CHINKAPIN

Fruits nuts, *several* to each *spiny* husk, each nut *flattened* on 1 or more sides, edible. Sept.–Oct.

Similar species: Species name should not be confused with that of the compound-leaved Horsechestnut (Pl. 6). (1) Chestnut Oak (Pl. 30) has leaves and buds clustered at twig tips: buds have more scales. (2) Beech has shorter leaves and long, slender buds. See (3) Ozark, (4) Eastern, and (5) Florida chinkapins. In winter, basswoods (Pl. 26) also have only 2–3 bud scales. Their branchlets, however, have tough inner bark and the twigs are mostly red or green.

Remarks: The Chestnut not very long ago was a dominant tree in dry forests throughout much of our region. Soon after 1900, however, a fungus bark disease believed to be of Asiatic origin became epidemic and in less than a human generation completely eliminated the Chestnut as an important forest tree. Sprouts may continue from some old stumps, and these may flower and produce fruits. As soon as these shoots attain a moderate size, however, the bark-shattering blight usually girdles them near their bases. Blight-resistant strains are being developed, and planted specimens may be encountered.

Chestnut lumber was quite valuable. It was used for furniture, musical instruments, interiors, caskets, and fences. Tannin was derived from the bark, and the nuts were marketed. Bobwhite, wild turkey, squirrels, and whitetailed deer are among the many forms of wildlife that once fed on the nuts.

OZARK CHINKAPIN *Castanea ozarkensis* Ashe   **Pl. 32**
Similar to Chestnut but smaller and with leaves *white-downy* beneath. Leaf teeth coarse. Twigs and buds fine-hairy. The edible nuts *occur singly*. Nuts *not flattened*. Leaves 5"–8". Height to 65'. The next species has more woolly leaves and twigs. Dry woods in the Ozarks region.

ALLEGHENY (EASTERN) CHINKAPIN   **Pl. 32**
Castanea pumila Mill.
Similar to Ozark Chinkapin but with smaller leaves and *white-woolly* leaf undersides. Twigs *woolly*. Leaves 3"–5". Height to 40'. Flowers June. Dry woods of Appalachia (see map, p. 156).

FLORIDA CHINKAPIN *Castanea alnifolia* Nutt.   **Pl. 32**
A shrub or small tree of the southeastern Coastal Plain. Leaves *small*, resembling those of Beech. Leaves and twigs hairless; buds *short*, hairless or somewhat hairy. Leaves 2"–4". Height to 20'. Nuts single in a husk that is spiny but less so than that of other Chinkapins. Dry soils. See map, p. 156.

BEECH *Fagus grandifolia* Ehrh.   **Pl. 32**
A tall tree with distinctive *smooth gray bark and long, slender,*

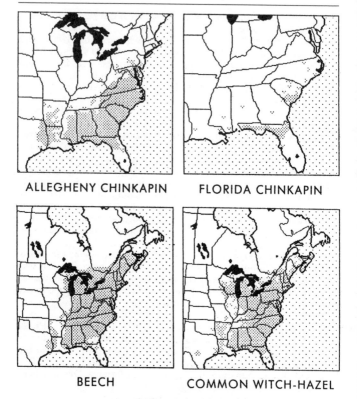

ALLEGHENY CHINKAPIN   FLORIDA CHINKAPIN

BEECH   COMMON WITCH-HAZEL

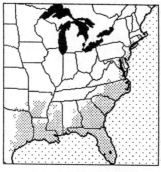

GROUNDSEL-TREE

many-scaled buds. Leaves are elliptic or egg-shaped and *coarse-toothed.* Twigs hairless or somewhat long-hairy, *encircled* or almost encircled by stipule scars at each leaf scar. End buds true. Leaves 3″–6″. Height 60′–80′ (120′); diameter 2′–3′ (4′). Flowers April–May. Fruits small, *triangular nuts,* Sept.–Oct., edible. Fertile woods.

Similar species: Combination of bark, twig, bud, and leaf characteristics is unique. (1) Yellowwood (Pl. 21) has similar bark but compound leaves; not common. (2) See Chestnut and (3) Florida Chinkapin.

Remarks: An important timber species. Quality of wood only fair but used for cheap furniture, tool handles, veneer, shoe lasts, and fuel. Beeches are planted widely for ornament. Fruits eaten by ruffed grouse, wild turkey, bobwhite, pheasant, black bear, raccoon, red and gray foxes, white-tailed deer, cottontail rabbit, gray, red, and flying squirrels, porcupine, and opossum.

COMMON WITCH-HAZEL *Hamamelis virginiana* L.   **Pl. 32**

A shrub or small tree with *wavy-toothed, uneven-based* leaves. Leaves and twigs typically hairless but rarely hairy and leathery. Buds are *without scales, hairy,* and somewhat stalked at the base. End buds true. Some pairs or tight groups of stubby, four-parted seedpods can usually be found at any time of year. Bark smooth or rough in patches, often with some cross-stripes. Leaves 3″–6″. Height 10′–25′ (30′); diameter 2″–10″ (14″). Flowers yellow, Sept.–Nov. Fruits Aug.–Oct.

Similar species: The only other species with naked buds and 3 bundle scars are the buckthorns (Pl. 43). They have more egg-shaped leaves and buds without narrowed bases.

Remarks: Colloquial names Winter-bloom and Snapping-alder indicate peculiarities of this plant. In late autumn, after the leaves drop and the old fruit pods pop their seeds up to 20′ away — and sometimes even after snow is on the ground — the straggly blossoms appear. An extract of the bark has long been used for medicinal purposes. Branches are used as "divining rods" in locating underground water. Witch-hazel seeds, buds, or twigs are dietary items of pheasant, bobwhite, ruffed grouse, white-tailed deer, cottontail rabbit, and beaver. A shrubby relative, Springtime Witch-hazel (*H. vernalis* Sarg.), occurs in the lower Mississippi Valley and flowers January–April.

GROUNDSEL-TREE *Baccharis halimifolia* L.   **Pl. 32**

A shrub or small tree with *green, ridged* twigs. Wedge-shaped leaves of lower portions of plant have large and often deep teeth; those of upper portions often lack teeth. Buds two- to three-scaled; end buds false. Leaves 1″–3″. Height to 15′. Flowers Aug.–Sept. Fruits small, dry, white, silky, Sept.–Dec. Coastal regions and nearby inland areas.

Similar species: No other tree with 3 bundle scars has green, ridged twigs.

STRAWBERRY-TREE   *Muntingia calabura* L.   **Pl. 32**
A fast-growing *evergreen* Caribbean species occurring also in cen. and s. Florida. Leaves are narrow, toothed, pointed, and hairy beneath and have *3 main veins* meeting at the very *uneven* base. Twigs and buds *hairy;* end bud false. Leaves 2″–4″. Height to 25′. Flowers white. Fruits reddish or yellowish, fleshy. The bark is fibrous and is used in making rope and baskets. Moist soils and pine woods. See Pl. 26 for other fan-veined trees.

Elms and Water-elm (Plate 33)

Elms have double-toothed (except Siberian Elm and Water-elm), feather-veined leaves, with uneven or often somewhat heart-shaped bases. Buds are many-scaled, with scales in 2 vertical rows; end buds are false. Leaf scars are unusually smooth; the 3 bundle scars are sunken. Trunk bark grayish, with vertical, often cross-thatched ridges. Flowers are inconspicuous and give rise to small, flat, papery-winged, oval to circular fruits. Birches (Pl. 34) have even-based leaves, buds with only 2–3 scales, and trunks with many narrow cross-stripes. The several double-toothed plants illustrated on Pl. 35 can be separated from elms by their distinctive buds and other characteristics.

Water-elm, or Planer-tree, is included as a close relative of the true elms, although it is in a different genus. It differs in having fruits that are small, wingless, soft-spiny nuts. Leaves are single-toothed.

Most elms are ornamental. Inner bark, particularly of roots, is generally tough and fibrous and can be twisted into improvised rope, fishline, nets, or snares. The wood is difficult to split. Fruits are eaten by many game and songbirds and by squirrels. Twigs and foliage are consumed by rabbits, deer, and muskrats.

AMERICAN ELM   *Ulmus americana* L.   **Pl. 33**
Full-sized wild trees are becoming rare as a result of disease. When growing in the open as a large tree, however, trunk divides near the ground into large limbs, giving a *unique vase-shaped form*. Leaves variable, smooth or sandpapery above, hairless or hairy beneath. Twigs hairless or barely hairy; branchlets *without* corky "wings." Buds more than ¼″ long, with light brown but *dark-edged* scales. Leaves 4″–6″. Height 80′–100′ (125′); diameter 2′–5′ (10′). Flowers March–May. Fruits ⅜″–½″, hairless except for hairy margin, deeply notched, long-stemmed, April–May. Principally bottomlands.

Similar species: Other elms have small leaves and/or distinctive buds. See Rock Elm.

Remarks: Seeds eaten by bobwhite, European partridge, ruffed grouse, prairie chicken, gray and fox squirrels, and opossum. Cottontail rabbit, snowshoe hare, and white-tailed deer browse twigs. Like the Chestnut (p. 154) in an earlier generation, this beloved species has been decimated by disease. Stands of dead trees occupy lowland sites in many places. "Dutch" elm disease is a fungus spread by a beetle.

SLIPPERY ELM   *Ulmus rubra* Muhl.   **Pl. 33**

A medium-sized tree with either single or divided trunk. Leaves *short-stalked,* very *rough* and sandpapery above and hairy beneath. Twigs *rough-hairy;* buds prominently *red-hairy* and more than ⅛" long. Leaves 4"–8". Height 40'–60' (70'); diameter 1'–2' (3'). Flowers March–May. Fruits ½", nearly circular, hairless except for centers of each side, slightly notched, short-stemmed, and tightly bunched, May–June. Fertile uplands.

Similar species: No other elm has rough-hairy twigs and red-hairy buds.

Remarks: The common name of this coarse-textured tree refers to the slimy inner bark, once well known as a scurvy preventive. It was ground into flour or chewed piecemeal. Cottontail rabbits and deer eat the twigs. Porcupines may eat the growing layer beneath bark.

WINGED ELM   *Ulmus alata* Michx.   **Pl. 33**

A small, single- or divided-trunk tree, usually bearing some branchlets with *wide corky "wings."* Leaves *small,* hairy beneath, *smooth* above. Leafstalks *short,* less than ¼" long, often nearly lacking. Twigs and buds hairless or nearly so; buds less than ³⁄₁₆"

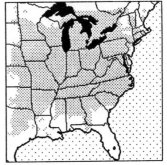

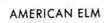

AMERICAN ELM   SLIPPERY ELM

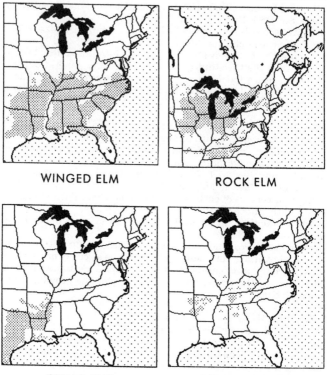

WINGED ELM

ROCK ELM

CEDAR ELM

SEPTEMBER ELM

long; bud scales with dark borders. Leaves 1″–2″. Height 40′–50′ (60′); diameter 1′–2′. Flowers March. Fruits ¼″–⅜″ long, deeply notched, hairy or not, with fringed edges and pointed tips, long-stemmed, March–April. Bottomlands.

Similar species: (1) Rock Elm has drooping lower branches, larger leaves, longer leafstalks, hairy twigs, and larger fruits. (2) Cedar Elm has sandpapery leaves, narrow wings, hairless twigs, and fruits in autumn. (3) September Elm has hairless twigs, bud scales without dark edges, and flowers in fall. (4) Sweetgum (Pl. 25) and (5) Bur Oak (Pl. 29) are the only alternate-leaved woody plants besides elms that regularly possess corky "wings." Sweetgum has star-shaped leaves and true end buds; Bur Oak has feather-lobed leaves and clustered end buds.

ROCK ELM *Ulmus thomasii* Sarg. **Pl. 33**
A single-trunked tree, usually with *corky "wings"* on some branchlets and often with strongly *drooping* lower branches. Leaves hairless, with leafstalks ¼" long. Twigs and buds somewhat *hairy*. Buds more than ¼" long; brown, with *dark* scale edges. Leaves 2"–4". Height 60'–80' (100'); diameter 2'–3' (4'). Flowers April–May. Fruits ⅜"–⅝" long, with a *moderate* notch, fringed margins, long-stemmed, May. Upland sites.
Similar species: (1) When corky wings are present, see Winged Elm. (2) When wings are lacking, hairy twigs and buds, columnar trunk, and upland habitat distinguish it from American Elm. (3) Slippery Elm buds are red-hairy.

CEDAR ELM *Ulmus crassifolia* Nutt. **Pl. 33**
A *small-leaved, fall-flowering* tree of the lower Mississippi Valley with *sandpaper-surfaced* foliage. *Narrow* corky wings may occur on the branchlets. Twigs and buds hairless; buds ⅛"–³⁄₁₆"; bud scales *without* dark borders. Leaves 1"–2". Height to 70'; diameter 1'–2'. Flowers Aug.–Oct. Fruits ³⁄₁₆"–½", deeply notched and white-hairy, Sept.–Oct. Bottomlands.
Similar species: See Winged and September elms.

SEPTEMBER ELM *Ulmus serotina* Sarg. Not illus.
A rare, mostly southern-midwestern species which, like Cedar Elm, may have corky branchlet wings and flowers and fruits in the *fall* of the year. Its leaves are *larger* and *not* sandpapery. Twigs and buds hairless; buds ³⁄₁₆"–⁵⁄₁₆" and scales *not* dark-edged. Leaves 2"–4". Height to 65'. Flowers Sept. Fruits ½" long, deeply notched, edges hairy, Oct.–Nov. Floodplains.

SIBERIAN ELM *Ulmus pumila* L. Not illus.
A hardy shrub or small tree introduced from Asia and established from Minnesota to Kansas and westward. The 1"–3" leaves are mostly narrow and only *single-toothed*. Twigs and buds nearly hairless; twigs without wings and buds small, *dark*, and *blunt*. Fruits hairless, nearly circular, ⅜"–⅝" long and deeply notched.
Similar species: Water-elm (below) occurs eastward.
Remarks: Also known as the Chinese Elm.

WATER-ELM *Planera aquatica* (Walt.) J. F. Gmel. **Pl. 33**
A small *southern* tree with egg-shaped, *single-toothed*, somewhat rough-surfaced but nearly hairless leaves. Twigs not winged; twigs and buds *hairless,* the latter mostly less than ⅛" long and *pointed*. Trunk bark more scaly than in true elms. Leaves 2"–4". Height 40'–50'; diameter 18"–20". Flowers April. Fruits *wingless nuts* covered with irregular protuberances, April–May. Coastal Plain swamps. See map, p. 162.
Similar species: In this group, only Siberian Elm also has

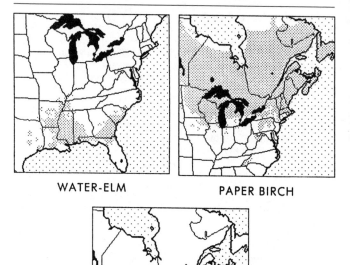

WATER-ELM

PAPER BIRCH

GRAY BIRCH

single-toothed leaves. Ranges, fruit, and bud shapes, however, are dissimilar.

Remarks: Fruits eaten by mallard, black, and ring-necked ducks and by squirrels.

Birches (Plate 34)

Birches are trees and shrubs of mostly northern distribution. The leaves are double-toothed, more or less egg-shaped or triangular, and with blunt bases. Bark of most species tends to separate into papery sheets and is marked by numerous cross-streaks. Buds are two- or three-scaled; bundle scars 3. Short spur branches of densely clustered leaves and leaf scars are usually present. End buds are false except on spurs.

Native birches that possess dark bark might be confused with some cherries (Pl. 36). Birches differ in that (1) bud scales are fewer, (2) leafstalks do not have glands, (3) broken twigs may have a strong wintergreen odor rather than the sour scent of cherry twigs, (4) bark of many birches can be separated into papery sheets, and (5) the leaves of all species are double-toothed and usually do not taper at base. Though the blossoms and fleshy fruits of a few cherries occur in lengthened clusters, the flowers of birches are always in caterpillarlike catkins that become lengthened clusters of small dry fruits.

Birch lumber is of value in cabinetmaking and interior finishing. It is also used in the manufacture of agricultural implements, spools, clothespins, etc. The bark of some species was once used in making canoes. In several birches the curling older bark is highly flammable, providing excellent tinder even when damp. The fermented sap of some birches has been used in beverages. Seeds and buds are eaten by numerous song and game birds. Several mammals consume the twigs and bark.

PAPER (AMERICAN WHITE) BIRCH   Pl. 34
Betula papyrifera Marsh.

White birches grow from small saplings with brownish bark to be small to medium-sized trees with white trunks. This is our only tree with *clear white peeling bark* that readily separates into layers and is marked by narrow *horizontal stripes*. Dark, chevron-shaped trunk markings are few. Twigs slightly rough-warty, if at all, and without wintergreen odor. Buds blunt, hairless. Some local varieties have brown bark in maturity, drooping twigs, or heart-shaped leaves. Leaf blades 1"–4". Height 70'–80' (120'); diameter 1'–3' (4'). Flowers spring. Fruiting catkins drooping, *slender,* ¼" × ½", Aug.–Sept. Open woods and cutover areas.

Similar species: Gray Birch has more triangular and distinctly long-pointed leaves. Its white trunk is non-peeling and marked by large black chevrons at the bases of most branches. Its twigs, too, are conspicuously rough-warty, and the fruiting catkins are less slender and more blunt at the ends.

Remarks: Bark layers have been used for canoe and wigwam coverings (tied in place with spruce rootlets), boxes, cups, makeshift shoes, and emergency snow goggles. Leaves have been used for tea but are not as good as those of Sweet and Yellow birches. Paper birch lumber used for woodenware, pulp, and fuel. Seeds and buds eaten by ruffed and sharp-tailed grouse. Twigs are cropped by moose, deer, and snowshoe hare.

GRAY BIRCH   *Betula populifolia* Marsh.   Pl. 34
A one- to many-stemmed small tree of New England and the Maritime Provinces with *chalky white* bark and *triangular, long-tapering* leaves. Twigs are rough-warty and without wintergreen odor. Trunks are marked by *many dark chevrons* (shallow, in-

verted Vs) at bases of branches as well as by narrow horizontal marks characteristic of all birches (and most cherries). Bark does *not* peel or readily separate into layers. Leaf blades 1″–4″. Height 20′–30′ (40′); diameter 10″–18″. Flowers April–May. Fruiting catkins drooping, *sturdy*, ⅜″ × ¾″, Sept. Mixed woods.

Similar species: Long-pointed leaves; hairless, rough-warty twigs; and chalky white (not creamy) non-peeling bark distinctive.

Remarks: Gray Birch used mainly for fuel and charcoal but may be made into small woodenware. Seeds and buds eaten by ruffed grouse and several songbirds. Twigs browsed by white-tailed deer.

SWEET (BLACK) BIRCH   *Betula lenta* L.   Pl. 34

A tall, straight, brown- or *black-barked* tree, mainly of Appalachian forests. Young trunk bark tight, marked by thin horizontal stripes. Leaves short-pointed. Main side veins may be *branched*. Broken twigs have delightful spicy *wintergreen* odor. Buds and twigs *hairless*, or lower bud scale alone is fringed with sparse hairs. Leaves 1″–6″. Height 50′–70′ (80′); diameter 2′–3′ (5′). Flowers April–May. Fruiting catkins erect, fruits Aug.–Oct. Moist forests.

Similar species: (1) A mature Yellow Birch normally has distinctive yellow- to silver-gray bark, but small specimens look and smell like Sweet Birch and may grow side by side with it. Sometimes branched leaf veins and hairless twigs and buds help identify this species. (2) See Virginia Birch.

Remarks: Sweet Birch wood is hard and heavy and is frequently made into furniture. Rare "curly" and "wavy" grain woods are especially valuable. Oil of wintergreen is obtainable from sap and leaves. Fermented sap may be an ingredient of birch beer. Buds and seeds eaten by ruffed and sharp-tailed grouse; twigs browsed by white-tailed deer, moose, and cottontail rabbit. Also known as Cherry Birch.

YELLOW BIRCH   *Betula alleghaniensis* Britton   Pl. 34

A tall tree, often growing with Sweet Birch and Hemlock. Bark *shiny yellow to silver-gray* with narrow horizontal lines and *peeling* in small thin curls. Broken twigs give off *wintergreen* odor like, but a bit weaker than, that of Sweet Birch. Leaves short-pointed, with main side veins *unbranched*. Twigs and buds (at least scale edges) somewhat *hairy*. Leaves 1″–5″. Height 70′–80′ (100′); diameter 2′–3′ (4′). Flowers spring. Fruits Aug.–Oct.; fruiting catkins more or less upright. Moist northern and mountain forests.

Similar species: Mature Yellow Birch is usually distinctive, but see Sweet Birch.

Remarks: Oil of wintergreen occurs in sap and leaves. Wood

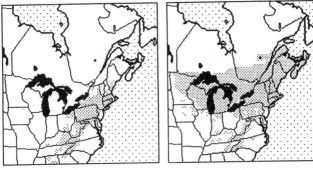

SWEET BIRCH　　　　　　YELLOW BIRCH

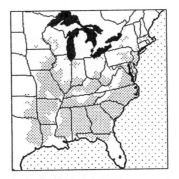

RIVER BIRCH

important in commerce; often stained for cherry or mahogany finishes. Ruffed and sharp-tailed grouse, prairie chicken, white-tailed deer, moose, cottontail rabbit, and red squirrel use the plant for food.

RIVER BIRCH *Betula nigra* L.　　　　　　　　　**Pl. 34**
A *shaggy-barked* tree of streambanks; most *southern* of our birches. Bark varies from smooth and *red-brown* on youngest branches to *orange* and *peeling* and rough, near-black plates on trunk. Undersides of leaves whitish and sometimes velvety. Leafstalks, twigs, and buds hairy. Twigs sometimes rough-warty. Buds narrowed at base. Leaves 1″–5″. Height 60′–80′ (90′); diameter 2′–3′ (5′). Flowers April–May. Fruiting catkins erect, fruits mature over winter, June–Sept.

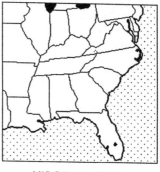

VIRGINIA BIRCH

Similar species: The only other streamside tree birches have white bark.
Remarks: Ruffed grouse and wild turkey sometimes eat the seeds.

VIRGINIA BIRCH   *Betula uber* (Ashe) Fern.   Not illus.
A small birch with dark bark, hairless twigs and foliage, and nearly circular, 1″-long, toothed leaves. Broken twigs have a wintergreen odor. Growing to 30′ tall, it is classified as an endangered species. Found in the mountains of Smyth County, sw. Virginia, it is little known and may be only a variety of Sweet Birch.

Other Trees with Mostly Double-toothed Leaves and/or Small, Woody Cones (Plate 35)

These species and the birches (Pl. 34) make up a group that is related to the willows, poplars, oaks, and other plants whose flowers and fruits also occur in catkins. Catkins are usually evident as caterpillarlike dangling strands of small flowers; in a few instances they may be short, inconspicuous clusters. The mature female catkins of alders are usually present and resemble tiny pinecones.

Plants of this plate (except Seaside Alder and occasionally Speckled Alder) have double-toothed leaves. All have 3 bundle scars per leaf scar. While elms and birches also have double-toothed leaves, elms have uneven-based leaves and bud scales in 2 rows, while birches have even-based leaves and only 2–3 bud scales per bud.

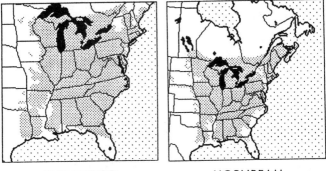

IRONWOOD   HORNBEAM

IRONWOOD *Carpinus caroliniana* Walt.   **Pl. 35**
A small tree whose smooth gray trunk has a distinctly *muscular*
appearance. The trunk has a deeply rippled and sinewy look.
Leaves egg-shaped, double-toothed, and sometimes long-pointed,
with U-shaped bases. Side veins tend to be parallel and *not forked*.
Twigs variably hairy or not. Buds brown, *somewhat square* in
cross section, with numerous scales in 4 rows; end buds false.
Leaves 1"–5". Height 20'–40'; diameter 10"–24". Flowers April,
male catkins not present in winter. Fruits tiny nuts attached to
three-pointed leafy bracts, Aug.–Oct. Bottomlands and rich soils.
Similar species: Trunk and bark are unique. Angled buds and
non-forked parallel veins help separate small specimens from
those of Hornbeam.
Remarks: Nearly all botany books published during the past
generation name this plant Blue Beech and the next one Ironwood. Yet *Carpinus* (which is not in the same family as the true
Beech) is still commonly called Ironwood in many areas because
of the strong muscular appearance of the trunk. Conversely,
Ostrya appears no stronger than most small trees. The result is a
confusion of 2 "ironwoods," further complicated by the alternate
names "American Hornbeam" and "Hop Hornbeam," which are
applied to these 2 species, respectively.
  Wood of this tree is heavy and tough, but, surprisingly, decays
rapidly upon contact with the ground. Charcoal made from Ironwood was reportedly once used in manufacture of gunpowder. The
fruits are eaten by many birds, including ruffed grouse, bobwhite,
pheasant, and wild turkey, and by gray squirrels. Cottontail
rabbit and white-tailed deer nip the shoots.

HORNBEAM *Ostrya virginiana* (Mill.) K. Koch   **Pl. 35**
A small tree with foliage and twigs much like those of Ironwood
but trunk bark brownish, grooved, and *shreddy*. Some of the

parallel side veins of the leaves are usually *forked*. Buds greenish, *round* in cross section; end buds false. Bud scales 6–8, finely *grooved* (use lens), and not arranged in rows. Leaves 1″–5″. Height 20′–30′ (40′); diameter 6″–12″ (24″). Flowers April–May, male catkins usually present in winter. Fruits small, bladder-enclosed nuts, Aug.–Oct. Fertile woods.

Similar species: Ironwood has a gray, *muscular* trunk, squarish buds, and parallel leaf veins that are not forked. See note under Ironwood concerning confusion over the common name.

Remarks: Related European trees were originally used in yoking oxen and were known as Yoke-elms, or Hornbeams. Seeds eaten by ruffed and sharp-tailed grouse, bobwhite, pheasant, and ptarmigan. Deer and cottontail rabbit browse twigs.

ALDERS   Pl. 35

These trees and shrubs grow mostly on streamside and other moist sites. Our species have unique 2–3 scaled buds that are smooth, reddish, and *stalked* (narrow-based). End buds are true. Alders also usually have woody female catkins which, when mature, resemble 1″ pinecones. The dark trunk generally has short horizontal barlike markings, usually white.

SMOOTH ALDER *Alnus serrulata* (Ait.) Willd.   Pl. 35

A shrub or small tree forming thickets along watercourses. Leaves variably hairless or velvety beneath, bases *wedge-shaped* or only slightly rounded. Leaf edges *finely* single- or double-toothed and somewhat wavy. Dark trunk usually *lacks* speckles or may have some of the white barlike markings of Speckled Alder, but these are shorter and fewer. Leaves 2″–5″. Height 6′–12′ (25′); diameter 1″–2″ (4″). Flowers Feb.–May; only slender

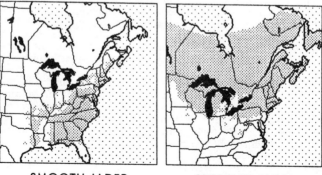

SMOOTH ALDER   SPECKLED ALDER

male catkins droop. Fruits (woody "cones"—usually present) do *not* droop.

Similar species: Wedge-shaped leaf bases, non-drooping "cones," fine-toothed leaf edges, and relatively unspeckled bark distinguish this species from (1) Speckled Alder. (2) Seaside Alder has single-toothed, sharply pointed leaves and separated bud scales.

Remarks: Deer eat twigs, but they are not a favorite food.

SPECKLED ALDER *Alnus rugosa* (Du Roi) Spreng. **Pl. 35**

Similar to Smooth Alder but more northern. Leaves egg-shaped, sometimes leathery, edges *coarsely* double-toothed and not wavy. Leaf bases *rounded* to somewhat heart-shaped. Leaf undersurfaces typically green and hairless. Dark bark plentifully *speckled* with transverse white warty lenticels. Fruit "cones" *droop*. Leaves 2"–5". Height 6'–12' (25'); diameter 1"–2" (4").

Similar species: See Smooth Alder.

Remarks: Ptarmigan and sharp-tailed grouse feed on buds; muskrats, cottontail rabbits, deer, and moose browse twigs. Sometimes called Black Alder, not to be confused with the next species or with Common Winterberry Holly (Pl. 40), both also sometimes given that name.

EUROPEAN (BLACK) ALDER **Pl. 35**

Alnus glutinosa (L.) Gaertn.

An upright tree with *wide, blunt-tipped,* sometimes notched, and usually double-toothed leaves. Leaf bases *rounded.* Twigs and young leaves *gummy.* Buds, as in most alders, smooth, few-scaled, reddish, narrow-based. Bark of stout trunk *dark,* with numerous short warty stripes. Leaves 2"–5". Height 20'–50' (70'); diameter 1'–2'. Flowers March–May. Fruit "cones" on *long* slender stalks, usually present. Introduced and established in the northern states and e. Canada.

Similar species: This and (1) Speckled Alder have U-shaped leaf bases. This species is larger, the leaves are blunt, and the cones are long-stalked. Flowers appear in spring, and the range is more northern. (2) Seaside Alder has single-toothed, pointed leaves and separated bud scales. (3) The unrelated Common Winterberry Holly (Pl. 40) is often called Black Alder.

SEASIDE ALDER *Alnus maritima* Muhl. ex Nutt. **Pl. 35**

A shrub or tree of restricted distribution. Leaves egg-shaped to elliptic, with tips *sharp,* bases mostly *wedge-shaped,* and upper surface *glossy.* Bud scales narrow and *distinct,* the edges not joining. Stem bark smooth. Leaves 2"–5". Height to 30'; diameter to 6". Flowers in *late summer,* Aug.–Sept. Fruits require 2 years to mature. See Smooth Alder. Pond and streambanks; coastal districts of Maryland and Delaware; also reported from the Red River, Oklahoma.

Cherries and Peach (Plate 36)

The cherries, plums, and peach are all members of the genus *Prunus,* in the rose family. Only some of the first 2 groups are native to the U.S. Those illustrated on this plate are thornless species, with true end buds and fine-toothed leaves.

All 3 groups are alike in having the trunk marked with numerous cross-streaks; leaves *mostly single-toothed,* narrow-based (except Mahaleb Cherry), and frequently with long-pointed tips; buds with more than 3 scales; fruits fleshy; and twigs that when broken emit a peculiar odor. The "almond" or "sour" scent of the broken twigs is difficult to describe but, once learned (by testing a known plant), is a reliable aid to the identification of many group members, especially cherries. Flowers and fruits are borne on short spur branches when these are present. (Pl. 36). Remnants of the calyx, the circle of sepals located just beneath the flower petals, persist above the fruits of some species.

The leaves of most *Prunus* species are toothed, and their leafstalks bear small but evident glands near the leaf base. The leathery leaves of Carolina Laurelcherry (Pl. 43) and West Indies Cherry (Pl. F-46C), however, lack teeth. These evergreen species also lack leafstalk glands, as may 2 plums (Pl. 37).

Despite the edible fruits of most cherries, the leaves, twigs, and seeds frequently contain hydrocyanic acid, believed to lend the characteristic odor to their broken twigs. Depending, apparently, upon the reaction of the stomach juices, the kind of feed previously consumed, and the condition of the plant when eaten, horses and cattle may die, become ill, or remain unaffected after browsing the potentially dangerous foliage of cherries. No plums have been listed as dangerous to livestock.

Wood of the larger cherries is of commercial value. Fruits of all species are eaten by a large number of birds and mammals. Cherries and plums are among the most widely eaten of all wildlife food plants.

CHOKECHERRY *Prunus virginiana* L. **Pl. 36**
A shrub or small tree with *egg-shaped, sharp-toothed* leaves with *hairless* midribs. Winter buds hairless, *more than ³⁄₁₆″ long;* bud scales *rounded* at tips. Bark gray-brown and *smooth.* Only this cherry and the next 2 have blossoms and fruits in *long clusters* and have spur branches *lacking.* Leaves 2″–5″. Height 6′–20′ (30′); diameter 2″–6″ (8″). Flowers white, April–July. Fruits purplish, *lacking* calyx lobes, July–Oct. Young woods and thickets.
Similar species: See (1) Black Cherry and (2) European Bird Cherry. (3) Sweet, (4) Sour, and (5) Mahaleb cherries have spur branches and short-clustered fruits. Common names are similar,

but chokeberries are shrubs of a different genus (*Pyrus*, or *Aronia*).
Remarks: The tart fruits can be made into delicious jellies and are used for pies. A great number of songbirds, the ruffed grouse, sharp-tailed grouse, prairie chicken, bobwhite, pheasant, raccoon, black bear, red fox, white-tailed deer, cottontail rabbit, and gray squirrel regularly consume the fruits.

BLACK CHERRY *Prunus serotina* Ehrh..   **Pl. 36**
A small to large tree whose leaves are long, *narrow, blunt-toothed,* and distinctive among cherries in having the midrib *prominently fringed beneath* with brown to whitish hairs. Buds *less than ³⁄₁₆″* long, hairless; bud scales *pointed;* spur branches *lacking.* Mature trunk has a *rough dark* outer bark marked with short horizontal lines and often exposing red-brown underbark where cracked. Reddish bark is characteristic of smaller branches. Leaves 2″–6″. Height 60′–80′ (100′); diameter 2′–3′ (5′). Flowers white, in slender clusters, May–June. Fruits blackish, usually retaining calyx lobes; June–Oct. Woods and thickets.
Similar species: (1) Only other tree cherry with regularly narrow leaves is Fire Cherry; it, however, has non-hairy leaves, spur branches, short flower clusters, and buds clustered at twig tips. (2) Chokecherry leaves are wider, hairless, and sharp-toothed; buds are somewhat longer, with rounded scale tips; remnants of calyx lobes are not retained on fruits.
Remarks: One of the largest cherries, this species is of value for lumber and as food for humans and wildlife. The bitter fruits are often used for jelly. Bark has been used as flavoring. Fruits and twigs eaten by much the same animals as listed for Chokecherry. Wood hard and close-grained; used for furniture and interior furnishing.

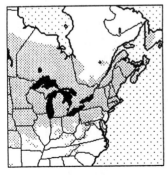

CHOKECHERRY

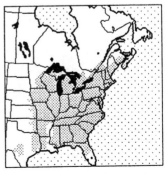

BLACK CHERRY

EUROPEAN BIRD CHERRY   *Prunus padus* L.   Not illus.
Similar to, and with elongate flower clusters like, the preceding 2
cherries. Bud scales are pointed, seeds *irregularly grooved,* and
blossoms larger. Fruits without persistent calyx. Se. Canada and
ne. U.S. Ornamental; rarely escapes to wild.

PEACH   *Prunus persica* Batsch   **Pl. 36**
Occasionally the cultivated peach, a native of Asia, escapes to
thickets. Very long, *narrow,* sharp-toothed leaves. Twigs hairless;
spur branches present; buds more than ¼″ long, hairy, blunt-
scaled, and *not* clustered at twig tips. Flowers single or paired,
pink; fruits yellow and *velvet-hairy,* seeds *pitted.*

FIRE (PIN) CHERRY   *Prunus pensylvanica* L. f..   **Pl. 36**
Growing either as a shrub or small tree, this cherry has *narrow,*
sharp-toothed, hairless leaves and clusters of nearly hairless buds
at or *near ends* of red twig tips (as well as on spur branches). Buds
are short, with *pointed* scales. Short white flower clusters are
umbrellalike, as in all remaining species of cherries and plums.
Bark red-brown and smooth. Trunk marked with crossbars; spur
branches present. Leaves 2″–5″. Height 10′–30′ (40′); diameter
2″–10″ (12″). Flowers white, March–July. Fruits red, ¼″ across,
July–Sept. Thickets and young forests, especially after burns or
land clearing.
Similar species: (1) The only other native cherry with narrow
leaves is Black Cherry, but that species has leaves with hairy
midribs beneath and lacks clustered end buds, spur branches, and
red fruits. (2) Peach does not have clustered end buds. See also (3)
Sweet and (4) Sour cherries.
Remarks: Known also as Bird Cherry. Sour fruits eaten raw or
used in jellies and cough mixtures. Consumed by bobwhite, ruffed
and sharp-tailed grouse, ptarmigan, prairie chicken. Deer, moose,

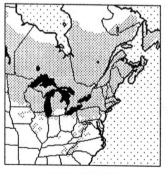

FIRE CHERRY

cottontail rabbit, beaver, and chipmunk browse the twigs.

SWEET CHERRY *Prunus avium* (L.) L.   **Pl. 36**
A rather tall tree with *single* main trunk and *red-brown smooth* bark prominently marked with horizontal stripes and often peeling. Leaves egg-shaped; rather sharply *double-toothed; 10–14 pairs* of veins; and hairless. Buds slender, light brown, more than ¼" long. Flowers or fruits may be clustered on *leafless* spur branches. Leaves 2"–6". Height 30'–50' (75'); diameter 1'–2' (3'). Flowers white, April–May. Fruits red to black, sweet, with *persistent* calyx, June–July. Cultivated, occasionally escapes to wild.
Similar species: (1) Sour Cherry is the only other of this group with double-toothed leaves and a persistent calyx (see identification chart facing Pl. 36). Sour and (2) Mahaleb cherries both have egg-shaped leaves and spur branches. Sour Cherry usually lacks a central trunk and has 6–8 pairs of leaf veins, rougher bark, and leafy fruiting spurs. Mahaleb Cherry has hairy twigs. (3) Chokecherry has long flower clusters and lacks spur branches. (4) Fire Cherry has much narrower leaves.
Remarks: Imported from Europe, this species, known also as Mazzard Cherry, is the parent of many of the sweeter garden cherries. A few ornamental varieties possess variegated foliage. Fruits attractive to many songbirds and to squirrels.

SOUR CHERRY *Prunus cerasus* L.   **Pl. 36**
A tree usually *lacking* a central trunk. *Grayish* bark, at least of older trunks, *much cracked* and broken, sometimes scaly. Leaves like Sweet Cherry but with *6–8 pairs* of veins. Buds stout, dark brown, and more than ¼" long. White flowers and fruits clustered on *leafy* spur branches. Leaves 2"–5". Height 20'–30'; diameter 10"–12". Flowers May–June. Fruits red, sour, with *persistent* calyx. May escape from cultivation.
Similar species: See Sweet Cherry.
Remarks: Believed to have originated in western Asia. Many cultivated varieties, principally those with tart flavor, are derived from this stock.

MAHALEB CHERRY *Prunus mahaleb* L.   Not illus.
Similar to Sour Cherry but with *hairy* twigs and small but wide, *almost circular, hairless* leaves, which may be heart-shaped at base. Twigs *velvety.* Flowers white, in short clusters; fruits *without* persistent calyx. Established locally; New England and s. Ontario southward to Delaware, Indiana, and Kansas.
Remarks: The Mahaleb, or Perfumed, Cherry was imported from Europe and the Caucasus for grafting stock. The fruits are inedible but yield a violet dye. Oil from seeds is used to fix perfumes. Aromatic wood is fashioned into pipes and walking sticks.

Thornless Plums (Plate 37)

Though also members of the genus *Prunus,* the plums differ from several cherries in having flowers and fruits in rounded or flat-topped clusters and from all cherries in that the end bud is false. Leaves are mostly single-toothed (except in Mexican Plum). Spur branches are present except in Hortulan Plum. Leafstalk or leaf-base glands may be present (though they are sometimes absent from Allegheny and Flatwoods plums). Bundle scars 3. Fruits are fleshy and marked with lengthwise ridges. A single large and usually flattened stone contains the seed. As in cherries, the bark is usually marked with horizontal lines.

Broken twigs may have the "almond" odor characteristic of cherries, but whether this character is consistent for all plums is not certain. Occasionally, these species bear some thorns. See Pl. 23 and p. 116 for plums that are regularly thorny.

ALLEGHENY PLUM *Prunus alleghaniensis* Porter **Pl. 37**
An eastern shrub or small tree with *hairy* twigs and narrow to egg-shaped, *sharp-toothed,* gradually *long-pointed* leaves, often somewhat hairy beneath. Leafstalk glands usually present. Occasionally twig tips are spiny. Leaves 2″–5″ long, ¾″–1¼″ wide. Height to 17′; diameter to 8″. Flowers *as* leaves appear, April–May. Fruits *purple,* about ⁷⁄₁₆″ in diameter, stones pointed at both ends, Aug.–Sept. Mountain thickets.
Remarks: The tart fruits are used for jelly and pies. They are eaten by bears, songbirds, and other wildlife.

FLATWOODS PLUM *Prunus umbellata* Ell. **Pl. 37**
Like the Allegheny Plum, this small tree or shrub has *sharp* leaf teeth, *hairy* twigs, and leafstalk glands that may be *absent.* The leaves, though, are *short*-pointed. Leaves 1″–3″ long, 1″–1½″ wide. Height to 20′; diameter 6″. Flowers early spring, *before* leaves appear. Fruits *black,* about ⅝″ in diameter, Aug.–Sept., stones pointed at both ends. Southeast Coastal Plain thickets.

MEXICAN PLUM *Prunus mexicana* Wats. **Pl. 37**
Like the previous 2 species a *sharp-toothed* plum, but with wider (to 2″), *double-toothed* leaves, and twigs that are *not* hairy. Leafstalk glands are usually *present.* Leaves are mostly short-pointed. Twigs hairless. Leaves 2″–4″. Height to 25′; diameter to 10″. Flowers March. Fruits red to purple; stone nearly spherical, *not* pointed. Midwestern thickets and bottomlands.
Remarks: Despite the name, this species occupies a wide range in the Mississippi Valley and again in northern Mexico.

HORTULAN (GOOSE) PLUM Pl. 37

Prunus hortulana Bailey
A shrub or small tree with narrow to egg-shaped, *blunt-toothed* leaves that are hairless or nearly so. Leafstalk glands *present*. The only thornless plum *lacking* spur branches; flowers and fruits are borne on the twigs instead. Twigs hairless. Leaves 3″–6″. Height 10′–20′ (30′); diameter 4″–10″ (12″). Flowers March–May. Fruits yellow or red, stones pointed at both ends. Aug.–Oct. Fertile soils.
Similar species: Wildgoose Plum has spur branches and stones not pointed at both ends.
Remarks: Grown by horticulturists, this native species has given rise to numerous cultivated varieties.

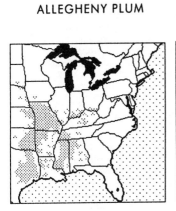

ALLEGHENY PLUM

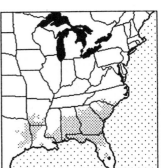

FLATWOODS PLUM

MEXICAN PLUM

HORTULAN PLUM

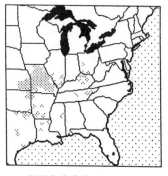

WILDGOOSE PLUM

WILDGOOSE (MUNSON) PLUM   Pl. 37
Prunus munsoniana Wight and Hedr.
A close relative of the Hortulan Plum. Has longer, quite narrow,
long-pointed and blunt-toothed leaves that may appear to be
sharp because of tiny reddish glands. Leafstalk glands also
present. Twigs hairless. Fruiting spurs *usually* present. Stones of
fruits pointed *at one end*. A native parent of horticultural varieties. Thickets.

GARDEN PLUM   *Prunus domestica* L.   Pl. 37
A small cultivated tree that has escaped to the wild in some
localities in the ne. U.S., nw. U.S., and se. Canada. Leaves
somewhat hairy beneath, with leaf teeth *rounded*. Leafstalk
glands usually present. Twigs hairless. Leaves 2″–4″. Height to
25′. Flowers spring. Fruits purple, to 1½″ diameter.
Remarks: Marketed fresh and as prunes. Originally native in e.
Europe and w. Asia. Bullace Plum (p. 117) is sometimes considered a thorny variety of this species.

Willows I–II (Plates 38 and 39)

Many willows, but not all, are easily recognized as such by the
slender leaves. The single scale of the willow bud, however, forms
a hoodlike complete covering and, although not obvious except on
close examination, is distinctive among plants with 3 bundle
scars. Many willows are only shrubs, some far northern and
high-altitude species being only a few inches tall.
    The tree willows are divided here into those (Pl. 38) with leaves
narrow (8–15 times longer than wide) or of medium width (5–7

times longer than wide) and those (Pl. 39) with wide leaves (only 2–4 times longer than wide). On the vigorous shoots of some species there are also small, somewhat leaflike stipules on the twigs at the bases of leafstalks. The stipules are useful in identification but may drop early. When stated to be large, they are reasonably leafy; when reported to be small, they are not evident except upon close examination.

Mature buds are listed as small when they are less than ⅛" long, large if they are more than ¼", and medium-long if they are in between. Twigs are said to be brittle at the base if they are easily detached, as Gordon (1960) says, "with a flick of the finger or by high winds." Frequently galls that resemble pinecones grow on the twigs. End buds are false in willows. The bark of tree willows is mostly yellow-ridged. Flowers and fruits are small and dry and occur in catkins.

Identifying willows is often a difficult task even for the professional botanist. Individual variation, minute identification marks, and hybridization are complicating factors. Winter characteristics are incompletely known. Those that seem most suitable, however, have been assembled in the winter identification chart on p. 183. For identifications of leafless, *non-shrubby* willows, see that chart. Since final identification of willows frequently depends on examination of the tiny flowers and fruits, some uncertain specimens may have to be identified professionally or accepted merely as willows. Though Willow Oak (Pl. 31) has narrow and willowlike leaves, it has clustered, scaly end buds and bears acorns.

As pioneer species invading moist soils, willows are valuable in controlling streambank and mountainside erosion. Stakes of green branches will often sprout if they are merely driven into damp ground. Several willows provide long twigs used in basketmaking. A great many are valued as ornamental plants. The wood of tree species is of some commercial value but is generally used only for fuel, charcoal, and posts. Willow bark provides tannin and a medicinal substance, salicin.

Willow leaves, twigs, and buds are of importance as browse for livestock. The many birds and mammals eating willow twigs, buds, leaves, or fruits include ruffed and sharp-tailed grouse, willow and rock ptarmigan, elk, white-tailed deer, moose, beaver, muskrat, snowshoe hare, and porcupine.

Russian-olive (*Elaeagnus angustifolia* L.), also known as Oleaster, has been introduced from Eurasia and planted widely as a windbreak on the western plains and for ornamental landscaping in the East. The leaves are narrow (occasionally egg-shaped) and willowlike. Though dark green above, the foliage of Russian-olive, unlike that of willows, is covered beneath with silvery scales. The twigs, too, are silvery, sometimes with thorns. Branchlets are brown. The buds differ from willows in having 2–4 silvery scales. Fruits silvery-red, juicy. Bundle scars 1.

Willows in Winter

Only willows have buds with a single caplike bud scale combined with leaf scars containing 3 bundle scars. Twigs mostly slender; end buds false. All species bear catkins and grow on moist, sunny sites. Winter characteristics need further investigation.

Species and remarks	Twigs hairy	Twigs brittle-based[1]	Twigs yellowish[2]	Bud size[3]	Major distribution[4]	Text page
Weeping Willow[5] Twigs long, hang limp.	–	+	–	±	N/S	181
Basket Willow[5] Buds nearly opposite.	–	–	–	±	N	185
Florida Willow Local; sw. Ga.–cen. Fla. only.	–	+	–		S	185
Coastal Plain Willow Se. U.S., local in Midwest.	+	+	–	–	S/N	181
Osier Willow Twigs long, slender, limber.	+	–	–	+	N	181
Bebb Willow Twigs gray-woolly.	+	–	–	±	N	184
Silky Willow	±	+	–	+	N/S	182
Sandbar Willow Dead leaves short-stalked (⅛").	±	–	±	±	N/S	180
Pussy Willow Opening catkins furry.	±	–	–	+	N	184
White Willow[5] Twigs hairless to silky.	±	–	–	±	N/S	182
Crack Willow[5] Buds sticky.	–	+	–	+	N	182
Shining Willow Twigs glossy.	–	+	–	±	N	183
Black Willow Trunks clustered.	–	+	–	–	N/S	179
Peachleaf Willow Twigs shiny, orange-brown.	–	–	+	–	N	183

Species and remarks	Twigs hairy	Twigs brittle-based[1]	Twigs yellowish[2]	Bud size[3]	Major distribution[4]	Text page
Broadleaf Willow Twigs white-powdered.	–	–	–	+	N	184
Ontario (Satiny) Willow Twigs white-coated.	–	–	–	±	N	183
Balsam Willow Twigs and buds reddish.	–	–	–	±	N	185

[1] Twigs easily detached at the base "with a flick of the finger or by high winds" (Gordon 1960).
[2] Twigs yellowish rather than brown or reddish.
[3] Bud sizes: large (+) = over ¼″; small (−) = ⅛″ or less; medium (±) = ⅛″–¼″.
[4] Distribution: N = n. U.S. and (often) adjacent Canada; S = s. U.S.
[5] Old World species, introduced and established in the wild.

Willows I: Leaves Very Narrow to Medium in Width (Plate 38)

BLACK WILLOW   *Salix nigra* Marsh.   **Pl. 38**
    A shrub or tree with narrow, *long-pointed* leaves that are *green* on both sides and have wedge-shaped or rounded bases. Foliage

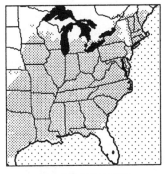

BLACK WILLOW

fine-toothed and hairless. Leafstalks *short* (less than ⁵⁄₁₆″ long) and without glands. The hairless twigs are *brittle* at the base and have small buds. Stipules usually conspicuous. Trunks often clustered. Leaves 3″–6″. Height 10′–40′ (120′); diameter 2″–24″ (96″). Flowers April–June.

Similar species: Meadow Willow has longer leafstalks, leaves whitened beneath, and no stipules.

MEADOW WILLOW   Pl. 38

Salix petiolaris J. E. Smith (*S. gracilis* Anderss.)

Leaves narrow, *long-pointed,* toothed, shiny green above, *whitish* and hairless beneath. Leafstalks ¼″–½″ long. Young leaves become *black* on drying. Twigs dark, hairless, and *not* brittle at base. Typically twigs are clustered at the branchlet ends. Buds of medium length. Stipules *absent* or very small. Leaves 2″–4″. Height to 25′. Flowers May–June.

Similar species: (1) Black Willow has leaves with green undersides, shorter leafstalks, and stipules present. (2) Sandbar Willow has very short leafstalks and leaves that often lack teeth.

SANDBAR WILLOW   Pl. 38

Salix exigua Nutt. (*S. interior* Rowlee)

A species with leaves variably toothed and/or hairy beneath. Distinguished, however, by *short-stalked* (about ⅛″), *narrow, long-pointed* foliage that either lacks teeth or has *widely spaced,* tiny, sharp teeth. Leaves are variably whitened or green beneath. Stipules are minute or lacking. Twigs yellowish to brownish, hairy or not, and not brittle-based. Buds of medium length. Leaves 2″–6″. Height to 20′. Flowers May–June.

Similar species: When the narrow leaves are without teeth, (1) Osier Willow has longer leaves, and (2) Ontario (Satiny) Willow

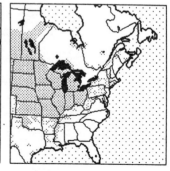

MEADOW WILLOW   SANDBAR WILLOW

has wider, short-pointed leaves. (3) Bebb and (4) Basket willows (Pl. 39) have wide leaves that sometimes lack teeth.

OSIER WILLOW *Salix viminalis* L.   **Pl. 38**
Similar to Sandbar Willow but leaves *very* long, narrow, long-pointed, *toothless,* and *silvery-hairy* beneath. Twigs *very long* and flexible, not brittle at the base; buds *large*. Stipules small or lacking. Leaves 6″–10″. Height to 25′. Flowers April–June. A European import escaped from cultivation. Ne. U.S. and se. Canada.
Remarks: The long twigs (osiers) are employed in making baskets and wickerware. Also called Basket Willow; see *S. purpurea* (p. 185).

WEEPING WILLOW *Salix babylonica* L.   **Pl. 38**
An Old World tree with *extremely long,* brittle-based twigs and branchlets that *hang vertically,* often sweeping the ground or overhanging a lake or stream. Leaves moderately narrow, hairless or silky, fine-toothed, long-pointed, whitened beneath. Small leafstalk glands may be present. Twigs *dark,* buds of medium length. Stipules small or lacking. Leaves 1″–5″. Height 30′–50′ (60′); diameter 1′–3′ (5′). Flowers April–May. Se. Canada to Georgia and Missouri.
Similar species: Brownish twigs and extreme weeping characteristics distinguish this willow from other (yellow-twigged) cultivated species with weeping growth habits.

COASTAL PLAIN (WARD) WILLOW   **Pl. 38**
Salix caroliniana Michx.
A southern tree. Leaves toothed, moderately narrow, long-pointed, *hairless,* and whitened beneath. The leafbase is

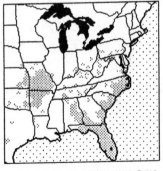

COASTAL PLAIN WILLOW

U-*shaped* and the stalks are *without glands*. Twigs somewhat hairy, reddish, and *brittle* at base. They do *not* droop. Buds are small. Leafy stipules *conspicuous* if present. Leaves 2″–7″. Height to 35′. Flowers May–June.

CRACK WILLOW　　*Salix fragilis* L.　　　　　　　　　**Pl. 38**
This European tree has hairless, *long-pointed, medium-width* leaves. Leafstalks bear *glands*. Buds large and somewhat *sticky;* twigs hairless, very *brittle* at base. Stipules small or lacking. Leaves 1″–7″. Height 50′–70′ (80′); diameter 2′–3′ (4′). Flowers April–June. Established from Newfoundland and S. Dakota to Virginia and Kansas.

WHITE WILLOW　　*Salix alba* L.　　　　　　　　　　**Pl. 38**
This naturalized European tree is our only willow with leaves that are often white-hairy *above and below*. Leafstalk glands may be present. Twigs olive-brown, nearly hairless to silky, not brittle at base; buds of medium length. Stipules mostly lacking. Leaves 2″–6″. Height to 80′. Flowers April–May. Se. Canada and S. Dakota to Georgia and Missouri.

SILKY WILLOW　　*Salix sericea* Marsh.　　　　　　　**Pl. 38**
A tree or shrub with *short-pointed,* medium-width, fine-toothed leaves, *dark green* above, *very* white-silky beneath, and lacking leafstalk glands. Young leaves become *black* on drying. Twigs brown, hairless or nearly so, and *brittle* at base; buds large. Stipules usually drop early but are sometimes obvious on vigorous shoots. Leaves 2″–5″. Height to 15′ (24′). Flowers March–May. **Similar species:** This species and the next have medium-width leaves that are *not* long-pointed. Ontario (Satiny) Willow has leaves not toothed.

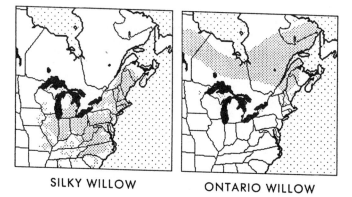

SILKY WILLOW　　　　　　　ONTARIO WILLOW

ONTARIO (SATINY) WILLOW   **Pl. 38**
Salix pellita Anderss. ex Schneid.
A large shrub to small tree with leaves *not* toothed, thick, of
medium width. Foliage *short-pointed, whitened, and silky-hairy
beneath.* Leaf undersides and twigs covered with *white powder.*
Twigs hairless; buds of medium size. Stipules small or lacking.
Leaves 2″–5″. Height to 30′. Flowers May–June.
Similar species: The only tree willow with medium-width, short-
pointed leaves that are not toothed. (1) Osier and (2) Sandbar
willows have narrow, long-pointed foliage. See (3) Bebb and (4)
Basket willows (Pl. 39).

Willows II: Leaves Relatively Wide (Plate 39)

This group of willows has relatively wide leaves, only 2–4 times
as long as broad. Most have U-shaped leaf bases.

SHINING WILLOW   *Salix lucida* Muhl.   **Pl. 39**
The somewhat wide, *long-pointed* leaves are *shiny,* hairless,
fine-toothed, green beneath, and often rather leathery. Leafstalks
have heavy *glands* near or at leaf bases. Twigs *dark,* hairless,
brittle-based; buds of medium size. Stipules usually large. Leaves
2″–7″. Height 10′–15′ (25′); diameter 1″–6″ (12″). Flowers April–
June.
Similar species: Peachleaf Willow also has long-pointed leaves
but they are dull above and lack leafstalk glands and stipules.
Also, its leaf undersides are whitened.

PEACHLEAF WILLOW   *Salix amygdaloides* Anderss.   **Pl. 39**
A shrub or small tree with leaves *long-pointed, not shiny,* fine-

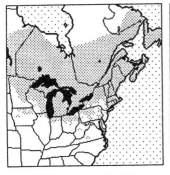

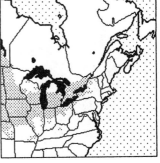

SHINING WILLOW   PEACHLEAF WILLOW

toothed, hairless, somewhat leathery, *whitened* beneath. The *shiny,* hairless, *red-brown or orange,* flexible twigs droop moderately. Stipules *small or lacking.* Leaves 3"–7". Height to 40'. Flowers April–June.
Similar species: See Shining Willow.

PUSSY WILLOW   *Salix discolor* Muhl.   **Pl. 39**
A shrub or tree. Leaves elliptic, whitened beneath, hairless, short-pointed, *wedge-based,* and toothed mainly above the middle. Leafstalks more than ½" long. Twigs generally hairless; buds medium-long. Stipules often large. Leaves 2"–5". Height to 30'. Flowers Feb.–May, opening catkin buds very *furry.*
Similar species: Basket Willow also has leaves toothed mainly above the middle, but its leaves and buds are mainly opposite, and the leaf bases are U-shaped.

BROADLEAF WILLOW   *Salix glaucophylloides* Fern.   **Pl. 39**
A shrub or small tree of ne. U.S. and e. Canada. Leaves hairless, semileathery, fine-toothed to the base, shiny dark green above, whitened beneath; bases *broad,* sometimes heart-shaped. Young leaves become *black* on drying. Twigs dark, hairless, and white-powdered. Stipules usually present and conspicuous. Leaves 1"–6". Height to 17'. Flowers May–June.

BEBB WILLOW   *Salix bebbiana* Sarg.   **Pl. 39**
A variable shrub or small tree with leaves wide and *coarse-toothed,* less commonly nearly without teeth. Foliage *tapered* at both ends, dull above, *grayish woolly* and veiny beneath. Leafstalks short, less than ⅜" long. Twigs *gray-woolly;* buds medium-long. Stipules small or lacking. Leaves 2"–5". Height to 25'; diameter to 8". Flowers April–June.

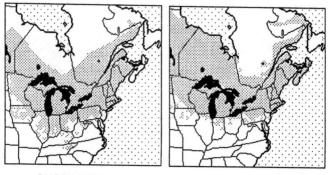

PUSSY WILLOW   BEBB WILLOW

Similar species: The only tree willow with wide, coarse-toothed, and gray-hairy leaves with wedge-shaped tips and bases. When both lack teeth, (1) Bebb and (2) Basket willows have different leaf-base shapes.

BASKET WILLOW *Salix purpurea* L.   **Pl. 39**
A tall shrub or small tree with narrow leaves that have small teeth *only near tips* or not at all. Leaves usually opposite or *nearly opposite* each other, hairless, whitened beneath, and with *rounded* bases. Twigs *purplish* and hairless; buds nearly opposite and of medium length. Leaves 1″–5″. Height to 20′. Flowers April–May. Northern states and se. Canada. Introduced.
Similar species: Leaf type and nearly opposite leaves and buds are distinctive. See (1) Sandbar (Pl. 38) and (2) Bebb willows.
Remarks: Osier Willow (p. 181) is also called Basket Willow.

BALSAM WILLOW *Salix pyrifolia* Anderss.   **Pl. 39**
A shrub or small tree with fine-toothed, mostly hairless, broad, thin leaves on long slender stalks. Foliage is dark green above and *whitened* beneath, with a pleasant, *firlike aroma* when crushed. Twigs and buds *reddish* and hairless. Bud length is intermediate. Stipules small or lacking. Leaves 1″–5″. Height to 20′. Flowers May–Aug.

FLORIDA WILLOW *Salix floridana* Chapm.   **Pl. 39**
Found scattered locally from s. Georgia to cen. Florida, this is a rather rare species. It grows only to small-tree size, mainly on *limestone* soils. The short-pointed leaves are up to 2″ across, dark green, and hairless above and *white-hairy* beneath. Leaf teeth are small, and leaf bases are broadly rounded. Twigs brittle-based. Leaves 5″–6″. Height to 20′. Flowers spring.

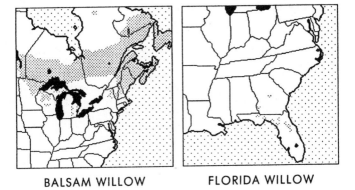

BALSAM WILLOW   FLORIDA WILLOW

Hollies (Plates 40 and 41)

Hollies as a group are difficult to identify. No readily apparent characteristic occurs throughout. Non-evergreen species are particularly nondescript. Minute black, pointed *stipules* are reported to be characteristic of hollies. These flank the leaf scars or, more often, are evident at the twig bases. They are difficult to see, however, and may drop off with age.

Hollies frequently develop short, stubby spur branches crowded with leaf scars or terminating in a whorl of leaves. Leaf blades of most hollies are toothed and wedge-shaped at the bottom. Buds are commonly more numerous near tips of the twigs; often they are clustered there. There may be more than 1 bud above each leaf scar. Hollies usually have 2 paired bud scales, but sometimes 4–6 are present. Bundle scars are single and end buds true. Holly bark is usually smooth. The small white or greenish male and female flowers may occur on different plants, being produced in the leaf angles or along the twigs. The small nutlets in the fleshy red or dark fruits are either smooth or grooved on the outside surface, varying with the species.

The hollies are divided here into those with thin, deciduous (non-evergreen) leaves (Pl. 40) and those with thicker evergreen foliage (Pl. 41).

Deciduous Hollies (Plate 40)

Deciduous trees drop their leaves seasonally. These hollies have rather thin, toothed, and mostly pointed leaves that are alternate on fast-grown twigs and clustered on spur branches. Twigs are hairless; fruits are red or orange.

POSSUMHAW (DECIDUOUS) HOLLY   Pl. 40
Ilex decidua Walt.
Shrubby or growing to small-tree size, this non-evergreen holly has variable narrow to egg-shaped leaves, generally thin but sometimes somewhat thickened. Leaf bases *narrow*, tips *blunt*, edges *wavy-toothed*. Twigs *stiff*; buds somewhat *pointed*. Leaves 2″–3″. Height 10′–20′ (30′); diameter 2″–6″ (10″). Flowers short-stalked, April–May. Fruits shiny red, nutlets grooved. Sept.–March. Wet sites.
Similar species: Yaupon (Pl. 41) leaves are smaller and evergreen.
Remarks: Fruits eaten by several birds, including bobwhite. Sometimes called Possumhaw, but see p. 76.

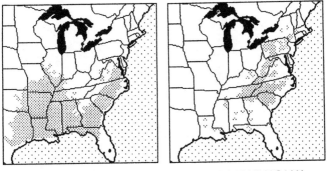

POSSUMHAW HOLLY   LARGELEAF HOLLY

LARGELEAF HOLLY *Ilex montana* Torr. & Gray **Pl. 40**
 A tall shrub or tree with *large* leaves for a holly. Leaves narrow
to elliptic, long-pointed, sharply *fine-toothed,* with bases mostly
narrow. Side twigs not especially stiff. Twigs green to reddish;
buds somewhat *pointed;* nutlets grooved. Leaves 4″–6″. Height
6′–20′ (40′); diameter 2″–10″ (12″). Flowers June. Fruits short-
stalked (under ½″), red, Oct.–Nov. Fertile soils.
 Similar species: (1) Smooth Winterberry Holly and (2) Juneberry Holly also have fine teeth. Smooth Winterberry Holly has
smaller and shinier leaves, blunt buds, seeds not ridged. Juneberry Holly has smaller leaves that are not long-pointed and has
long-stalked fruits. These species, too, grow on wet sites.
 Remarks: An alternate name, Mountain Holly, should not cause
this species to be confused with the shrubby, non-toothed
Mountain-holly, *Nemopanthus mucronata* (L.) Trel.

COMMON WINTERBERRY HOLLY **Pl. 40**
 Ilex verticillata (L.) Gray
 A shrub or small tree whose leaves are usually wide but vary from
narrow to nearly circular. Leaves *dull* above, with distinct *coarse*
teeth; may be thin or thickish, somewhat *hairy* beneath, with leaf
bases V-*shaped.* Buds *blunt* with broadly pointed scales. Leaves
2″–4″. Height to 25′. Flowers June–Aug. Fruits short-stalked,
red, rarely yellow, nutlets *smooth,* Sept.–Oct. or later. Wet sites.
 Similar species: Dull upper leaf surfaces, coarse leaf teeth, and
hairy leaf undersides separate this species from the next. Largeleaf Holly has long-pointed leaves and grooved nutlets.
 Remarks: Sometimes called Black Alder (see *Alnus,* Pl. 35).

SMOOTH WINTERBERRY HOLLY **Pl. 40**
 Ilex laevigata (Pursh) Gray
 Similar to but less variable than the preceding; foliage may

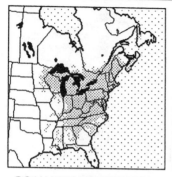

COMMON WINTERBERRY
HOLLY

SMOOTH WINTERBERRY
HOLLY

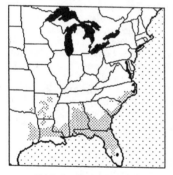

CAROLINA HOLLY

JUNEBERRY HOLLY

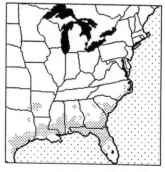

YAUPON HOLLY

nevertheless be narrow to elliptic. Leaves *shiny* above, *hairless* or nearly so beneath, and *fine-toothed*. Buds blunt but with *sharp-pointed* scales. Leaves ½″–4″. Height to 20′. Flowers May–July. Fruits red, rarely yellow, nutlets ridged, Sept.–Jan. Wet sites.

CAROLINA HOLLY   *Ilex ambigua* (Michx.) Torr.   **Pl. 40**
Leaves *fine-toothed,* usually somewhat hairy beneath; bases usually V-shaped. Twigs hairy or not. Buds pointed. Leaves 2″–3″. Height to 20′. Flowers April–June. Fruits red with grooved seeds, Aug.–Sept. Upland woods.

GEORGIA HOLLY   *Ilex longipes* Chapm. ex Trel.   **Pl. 40**
A large shrub or small tree with leaves similar to those of Carolina Holly but sometimes rather leathery. Leaf bases *not* narrowly V-shaped. Buds *blunt.* Fruit stalks slender, *up to 1″ long.* Leaves ½″–4″. Height to 20′. Flowers May–June. Fruits red, nutlets grooved, Oct. Southeastern states; streamsides and wooded slopes.
Similar species: All other deciduous hollies have short-stalked fruits except Juneberry Holly, which has wedge-shaped leaves and pointed buds.

JUNEBERRY HOLLY   Not illus.
Ilex amelanchier M. A. Curtis
A rare small tree of southern swamps with foliage resembling that of some juneberries (Pl. 42). Leaves *fine-toothed,* somewhat oblong, leathery and veiny, and slightly hairy beneath. Buds pointed. Nutlets grooved. Fruits dull red and on stalks ⅜″–⅞″ long. Leaves 1″–3″. Height to 7′.
Similar species: (1) Largeleaf Holly and (2) Smooth Wintergreen Holly, also fine-toothed, have larger leaves and blunt buds, respectively. See (3) Georgia Holly. (4) Juneberries (p. 192) have 3 (not 1) bundle scars per leaf scar.

Evergreen Hollies (Plate 41)

While Juneberry Holly of Pl. 40 may have leaves that are somewhat leathery, its foliage is fine-toothed, unlike that of the truly evergreen hollies of this plate. These hollies have leathery leaves with the edges smooth and rolled under or with only a limited number of pointed teeth. One species, Yaupon Holly, has wavy-edged leaves.

YAUPON HOLLY   *Ilex vomitoria* Ait.   **Pl. 41**
A distinctive plant whose red-fruited branches are often gathered for decorative purposes. Evergreen leaves *small,* blunt-tipped, and *wavy-edged.* A strong medicinal "black drink" once brewed by Indians is believed to have been made from Yaupon leaves. The

caffeine-containing dried leaves reportedly make a desirable tea. Leaves ½″–1½″. Height 5′–15′ (30′); diameter 2″–4″ (12″). Flowers May–June. Fruits red, berrylike, nutlets grooved, Sept.–Oct. Sandy Coastal Plain.

Similar species: Possumhaw Holly (Pl. 40) has wavy-edged leaves, but these are thin and non-evergreen.

MYRTLE HOLLY *Ilex myrtifolia* Walt. **Pl. 41**
Sometimes regarded as a variety of the next species, this southern shrub or small tree has *small* but pointed leaves only ½″–1½″ long. Side twigs stiff. The foliage is narrow-based and either *smooth-edged* or few-toothed above the middle. Height to 25′. Flowers spring. Fruits red with ridged nutlets, late fall. Wet soils.
Similar species: (1) Yaupon Holly has small, wavy-edged leaves. (2) Dahoon Holly has larger leaves.

DAHOON HOLLY *Ilex cassine* L. **Pl. 41**
Similar to the Myrtle Holly but with leaves 2″–4″. Twigs may be *hairy*. Flowers May–June. Fruits red, seeds grooved. Oct.–Nov. or longer. Bottomlands.

TALL GALLBERRY HOLLY **Pl. 41**
Ilex coriacea (Pursh) Chapm.
A southern shrub or tree whose leaves may have sharp teeth near the pointed tips or may lack teeth. Leaves with *narrow* bases and often marked with fine black dots beneath (use lens). Twigs hairless or sticky. Leaves 2″–3″. Height to 20′. Flowers May.

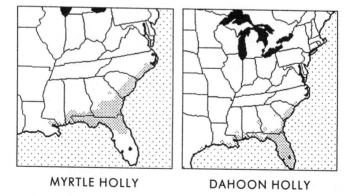

MYRTLE HOLLY   DAHOON HOLLY

Fruits *black,* nutlets *smooth,* Sept.–Oct. Swamps and sandy soils.
Remarks: Called "tall" in contrast to its shrubby relative, the
Low Gallberry Holly (*Ilex glabra*), which has blunt leaf tips.

AMERICAN HOLLY   *Ilex opaca* Ait.   **Pl. 41**
One of the most universally recognized eastern trees. The *prickly*
evergreen leaves are distinctive. Buds minute. Leaves 2″–4″.
Height 10′–40′ (100′); diameter 6″–24″ (48″). Flowers May–June.
Fruits *red,* rarely yellow, Aug.–June, nutlets grooved. Bottomlands.
Remarks: This is the Christmas holly. The collection of foliage
sprays has become a sizable business, and because of overhar-
vesting, this decorative plant is less common than formerly in
some areas. Holly lumber, peculiarly ivory white, is in demand for
special products such as piano keys, ship models, and inlays.
Though reported to be toxic to some animals, the fruits are eaten
by numerous songbirds, bobwhite, and wild turkey.

TAWNYBERRY HOLLY   *Ilex krugiana* Loes.   **Pl. 41**
A Caribbean holly found in this country *only* near Miami, Florida.
Young plants may have toothed leaves; foliage of older ones *lacks*
teeth but has *wavy* edges. Dropped leaves turn black. Leaves
3″–5″. Fruits *black.*
Similar species: (1) Guiana-plum (Pl. F-46B) has reddish fruits
and lacks tiny black stipules. (2) The crushed leaves of West
Indies Cherry (Pl. F-46C) have the distinctive "almond" odor of
cherries.

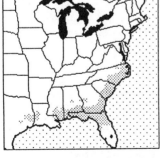

TALL GALLBERRY HOLLY

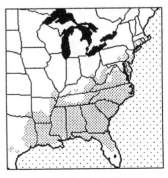

AMERICAN HOLLY

Miscellaneous Trees with Alternate, Toothed Leaves (Plate 42)

All except Sourwood, of the following miscellaneous species, have true end buds.

JUNEBERRIES   Pl. 42

These are shrubs or small trees with the leaves toothed and often blunt-tipped. The buds are pink to reddish, slender, with scales dark-tipped and usually somewhat twisted. Bundle scars are 3 per leaf scar. The trunk bark is usually tight and rather dark, with low, vertical, twisting ridges.

Known variously as serviceberries, shadbushes, shadblows, and sarvis, the amelanchiers make up one of the "difficult" groups within the rose family. Whether there are few or many species depends upon the botanist consulted. The species are quite variable, and some apparently hybridize. Marks of identification in winter have not been determined for all species. Fine-toothed species have 14–30 leaf teeth per inch, while coarse-toothed plants possess only 6–12 teeth per inch.

Though the group is composed mostly of shrubs, small-tree juneberries are often prominent in the forest understory. In the early spring, before the leaves develop, the terminal drooping white flower clusters are quite attractive. In the eastern states, near tidal rivers, the name Shadbush alludes to the appearance of the flowers as the shad ascend coastal streams to spawn.

The small, applelike fruits of the juneberries are eaten by some people. Heavy crops are rare because numerous birds and mammals are quick to take advantage of any fruits that mature. When available, they are delicious in jams, jellies, and pies. They are eaten by many songbirds, wild turkey, ruffed and sharp-tailed grouse, bobwhite, mourning dove, striped skunk, red fox, raccoon, black bear, red and gray squirrels, and chipmunks. Cottontail rabbit, beaver, white-tailed deer, and moose browse the twigs. Juneberry Holly (p. 189) has only 1 bundle scar per leaf scar.

DOWNY JUNEBERRY   Pl. 42

Amelanchier arborea (Michx. f.) Fern

One of the juneberries that often grows to tree height. Leaves fine-toothed, usually *heart-shaped* at base, *somewhat long-pointed,* white-hairy beneath, at least along veins and leafstalk. Leaves 3″–5″, with stalks, slender, more than ¼″ long. Height 20′–40′ (50′); diameter 8″–16″ (24″). Flowers March–June. Fruits reddish purple, *dryish, not tasty,* June–Aug. Woods.

Similar species: (1) Bartram Juneberry is also fine-toothed but has short-pointed and short-stalked leaves and blossom clusters with few flowers. (2) Oblongleaf Juneberry has blunt-tipped foliage.

Remarks: Wood heavy, hard, close-grained. Sometimes used for tool handles.

BARTRAM JUNEBERRY   Not illus.
Amelanchier bartramiana (Tausch) M. J. Roem.

Rather than having long clusters of flowers, this species is alone among juneberries in having small *groups of 1–4* flowers scattered in angles of leaves. Fine-toothed leaves are *short-pointed* and unlike those of all other juneberries in that they have *short stout* stalks (less than ¼″ long) and leaf blades that tend to be pointed *at both ends.* Leaves 2″–3″. Height to 9′; mostly shrubby. Flowers May–Aug. Fruits blackish, July–Sept. Northern woods.

Similar species: See Downy Juneberry.

OBLONGLEAF JUNEBERRY   Not illus.
Amelanchier canadensis (L.) Medic.

An upright tall shrub or small tree growing in clumps. Leaves *oblong, fine-toothed,* mostly *rounded* at tips, and toothed nearly to base. Although white-woolly when they are growing, leaves soon become nearly hairless. Leaves 1″–3″. Height to 25′. Flowers March–June. Fruits blackish, June–July. Coastal Plain thickets, se. Quebec to se. U.S.

Similar species: Downy Juneberry has larger leaves, mostly heart-shaped at the base and with pointed tips.

ROUNDLEAF JUNEBERRY   Pl. 42
Amelanchier sanguinea (Pursh) DC.

Leaves *coarse-toothed* and at least somewhat *pointed,* toothed to the base or nearly so, hairy beneath when young but soon hairless

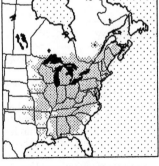

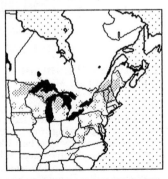

DOWNY JUNEBERRY   **ROUNDLEAF JUNEBERRY**

except for leafstalk; shape somewhat oblong to nearly circular.
Clumped or not, *rarely* spreading by underground stems. Twigs
reddish. Leaves 1″–3″. Height to 9′ (23′). Flowers May–June.
Fruits purple, July–Aug. Woods.
Similar species: Also coarse-toothed, Alderleaf Juneberry is
very similar but mainly western, though reported to occur locally
in s. Ontario and se. Quebec. Its leaves are blunt- to square-tipped
and it regularly spreads by underground runners.

SASKATOON (ALDERLEAF) JUNEBERRY Not illus.
Amelanchier alnifolia (Nutt.) Nutt.
A clumped upright shrub or small tree principally ranging from
w. Minn. to n. Calif. and Alaska. Leaves *coarse-toothed,* often
square-tipped, yellow-hairy when young but nearly hairless when
mature; *nearly circular,* heart-shaped at base, and toothed mainly
above the middle. This species normally spreads by *underground
runners.* Leaves 1″–3″. Height to 22′. Flowers May. Fruits June–
Aug. Thickets.
Similar species: See Roundleaf Juneberry.
Remarks: Also known as the Saskatoon Juneberry.

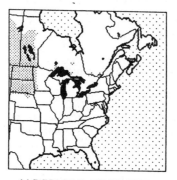

ALDERLEAF JUNEBERRY

MOUNTAIN PEPPERBUSH Pl. 42
Clethra acuminata Michx.
A shrub or tree of southern mountains, with usually *hairy* twigs,
large true end buds with loose or shedding hairy outer scales, and
long-pointed, fine-toothed leaves. Bundle scars 1. Outer bark
red-brown, separating into loose strips. Leaves 3″–6″. Height to
18′. Flowers small, white, bell-like, at twig ends in dense, slender
spikes that are *not* one-sided, July–Aug. Fruits small, dry, *three-
parted* capsules. Mountain woods.
Similar species: Pepperbushes are the only plants with 1 bundle

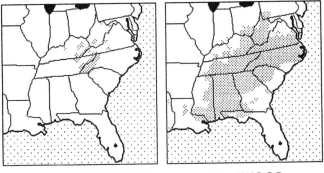

MOUNTAIN PEPPERBUSH   SOURWOOD

scar that have large end buds (much bigger than side buds) whose outer scales are as long as the buds. They are the only upright non-evergreen, heathlike plants with dry fruits and true end buds that also have hairy twigs. Leaves of this species larger and more long-pointed than those of the shrubby Coast Pepperbush (*C. alnifolia* L.).

SOURWOOD *Oxydendrum arboreum* (L.) DC.   **Pl. 42**
The only full-sized tree with long, slender, dry fruit clusters. Leaves *narrow* to egg-shaped, with a sour taste and sometimes somewhat leathery texture. Twigs hairless. Buds small; end buds *false*. Bark dark and furrowed. Leaves 4″–8″. Height 20′–50′ (70′); diameter 18″–20″. Flowers small, white, bell-like, in slim *one-sided clusters* at twig ends, June–July. Fruits small, dry capsules, *five-parted*. Rich woods.
Similar species: The only tall non-evergreen tree with 1 bundle scar and toothed simple leaves. Sourgum (Pl. 44), with a similar common name, has chambered pith and leaves without teeth.
Remarks: Highly ornamental at all seasons but especially so when in flower or in crimson autumn color. Deer eat twigs.

CAROLINA SILVERBELL *Halesia carolina* L.   **Pl. 42**
A southeastern shrub or small tree with somewhat white-striped bark. Leaves toothed, egg-shaped, somewhat hairy beneath. Twigs hairless to hairy. Buds reddish and *sharp;* pith *chambered*. Leaves 2″–7″. Height 10′–20′ (90′); diameter 6″–12″ (3′). Flowers produced along the twigs; *showy, white,* bell-shaped, with 4 *shallowly notched* petals, each ½″–1″ long. May. Fruits dry, *broadly four-winged,* 1″–2″. Hilly woods. See map, p. 196.
Similar species: (1) Sweetleaf (Pl. 43) and (2) Persimmon (Pl. 44)

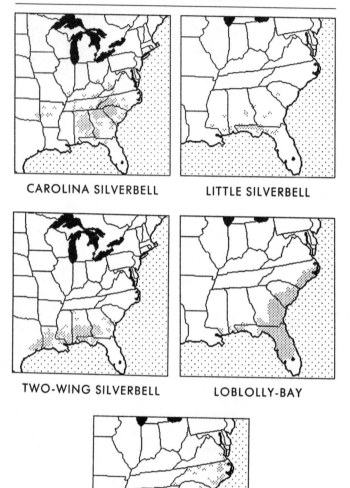

CAROLINA SILVERBELL   LITTLE SILVERBELL

TWO-WING SILVERBELL   LOBLOLLY-BAY

VIRGINIA STEWARTIA

also have chambered pith and single bundle scars, but they have dark buds. Sweetleaf has few teeth, and Persimmon has none. See Little Silverbell.

LITTLE SILVERBELL   *Halesia parviflora* Michx.   Not illus.
Similar to the Carolina Silverbell but with leaves 2″–4″, buds *blunt*, pith less definitely chambered, flower petals *shorter* (¼″–½″ long), and fruits *narrowly* four-winged. Height to 30′. Coastal Plain woods.
Similar species: See (1) Carolina and (2) Two-wing silverbells.

TWO-WING SILVERBELL   *Halesia diptera* Ellis   **Pl. 42**
Like the other silverbells, but leaves 3″–5″, flower petals *deeply lobed*, and fruits with only 2 wings. Wet woods.

LOBLOLLY-BAY   *Gordonia lasianthus* (L.) Ellis   **Pl. 42**
A small *evergreen* tree of the southeastern Coastal plain with large, dark, shiny, *leathery, wedge-based* leaves and large *showy* blossoms. Leafstalks may be winged near the leaf base. Buds are broad-based and *hairy;* bundle scar single. Leaves 3″–6″. Height to 65′. Flowers white, fragrant, 2″–3″ across, with stalks 1″–3″ long, at the leaf junctions, July–Sept. Fruits dry, hairy, five-parted capsules. Sept.–Oct. Wet woods.
Similar species: Over most of its range, the large, toothed, leathery leaves of this species are distinctive. Franklinia, apparently surviving only in gardens, has thin deciduous leaves and shorter flower stalks. In extreme s. Florida, see also Pl. F-46C.
Remarks: Like Franklinia and the stewartias, Loblolly-bay is a member of the tea family. About a dozen other members of the genus *Gordonia* occur in se. Asia. It is presumed that this species became isolated from its relatives in earlier geologic times.

FRANKLINIA   Not illus.
Franklinia alatamaha Bartr. ex Marsh.
Evidently extinct in the wild. Similar to Loblolly-bay but with leaves that are *thin,* neither leathery nor evergreen, and with flower stalks *less than* ¾″ long. Flowers white, in leaf angles, 3″–3¾″ in diameter, summer.
Remarks: Found along the Altamaha River in coastal se. Georgia in 1765, the plant has not been seen in the wild since 1790 (Elias 1980; Little 1980). Thought by some to have been exterminated when the original plants were transplanted, the species still survives in cultivation. Perhaps wild specimens will be rediscovered.

VIRGINIA STEWARTIA (SILKY CAMELLIA)   **Pl. 42**
Stewartia malachodendron L.
A shrub or tree with thin, elliptic leaves, soft-hairy beneath, with U-*shaped* bases and somewhat winged leafstalks. Buds slender,

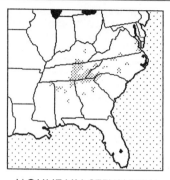

MOUNTAIN STEWARTIA

less than ⅛" long, *hairless* to slightly hairy; end buds true. Twigs may be fine-hairy. Trunk bark *much mottled.* Leaves 2"–4". Height to 15'. Flowers white, 2"–3" across, at junctions of the leaves, June. Fruits dry, five- to ten-seeded, round and *short-pointed.* Moist forests. See map, p. 196.

Similar species: Only a few trees have toothed leaves, showy blossoms, and winged leafstalks. (1) Loblolly-bay leaves are thick and leathery. (2) Mountain Stewartia has non-mottled trunk bark, larger leaves, and buds that are more hairy and more hidden by enfolding leafstalk wings.

Remarks: Closely related to cultivated camellias.

MOUNTAIN STEWARTIA   **Pl. 42**
(MOUNTAIN CAMELLIA)
Stewartia ovata (Cav.) Weath.
Similar to Virginia Stewartia, but leaves 5"–6" long; buds *hairy,* more than ⅛" long; trunk bark *smooth;* and fruits *long-pointed.* Flowers May–Aug. Bottomland forests.

Miscellaneous Trees with Alternate Leaves, Sometimes Toothed (Plate 43)

BAYBERRIES   **Pl. 43**
Of the several plants of this group, the first four are related species of the bayberry or waxmyrtle family. These species are among the few outside the pea (legume) family that enrich the soil through nitrogen-fixing bacteria contained in root nodules. The crushed foliage has a pleasant aroma. The short-stalked leaves and usually the twigs are marked with tiny yellow resin dots. The

dots, ordinarily not visible except when magnified, are good identification marks. End buds are true; bundle scars 3. The flowers and fruits are small and clustered in short, stout catkins. (Odorless Bayberry of Pl. 46 lacks resin dots and is not aromatic.)

SOUTHERN BAYBERRY *Myrica cerifera* L.   Pl. 43

An *evergreen southern* shrub or tree. Leaves *narrow,* leathery, *wedge-based,* toothed or not toward tip, hairless, with resin dots on *both* surfaces. Twigs sparsely hairy or hairless. Buds yellowish and globular. Leaves 2″–3″ long, to ½″ wide. Height 10′–30′ (40′); diameter 3″–10″ (12″). Flowers April–June. Fruits ⅛″, wax-covered nuts, Aug.–Oct. Wet sandy soils.

Similar species: (1) Evergreen and (2) Northern bayberries have resin dots numerous only on the leaf undersides.

Remarks: The wax is collected for making scented candles. A pound of nutlets immersed in hot water yields 4 ounces of wax. Fruits are eaten by many birds, including bobwhite and wild turkey. Also known as Common Waxmyrtle.

EVERGREEN (BLACK) BAYBERRY   Pl. 43

Myrica heterophylla Raf.

Similar to Southern Bayberry but leaves dull, *1″–2″* wide, somewhat leathery with edges rolled under, and resin dots almost entirely on leaf *undersides.* Twigs *black-hairy.* Leaves 2″–5″. Height to 15′. Flowers April–June. Fruits hairless, waxy, ⅛″–³⁄₁₆″. Aug.–Oct. Coastal Plain wet soils.

NORTHERN BAYBERRY   Pl. 43

Myrica pensylvanica Loisel.

Non-evergreen, with egg-shaped, shiny, *thin* leaves *to 1″* wide. Resin dots few or lacking on the often somewhat hairy upper surface. Twigs *gray-hairy;* buds whitish. Leaves 1″–5″. Height to

SOUTHERN BAYBERRY   EVERGREEN BAYBERRY

NORTHERN BAYBERRY

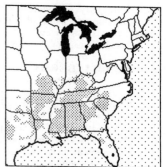

CAROLINA BUCKTHORN

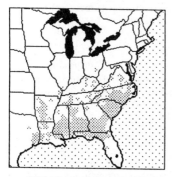

BIGLEAF SNOWBELL

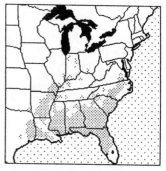

AMERICAN SNOWBELL

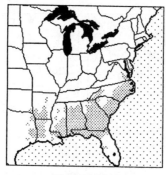

SWEETLEAF

35'; diameter to 6". Flowers May–July. Fruits hairy, becoming wax-covered, more than 3/16" across. June–April. Damp sandy soils.
Similar species: (1) Southern and (2) Evergreen blueberries have more leathery, evergreen leaves. The former has resin dots on both leaf surfaces.
Remarks: Many songbirds (notably myrtle warbler) and also ruffed grouse, bobwhite, and pheasant eat the fruits.

CAROLINA BUCKTHORN   Pl. 43
Rhamnus caroliniana Walt.
This tree and the next species are our only plants with alternate simple leaves and 3 bundle scars which also have *long naked buds that are not stalked.* This species taller. Leaves either few-toothed or with rounded teeth and either hairless or hairy beneath. End buds false. Twigs *fine-hairy.* Leaves 2"–6". Height to 40'. Flowers on *branched* stalks at the leaf angles, tiny, greenish, May–June. Fruits black, fleshy, *three-seeded,* Aug.–Oct. Open fertile sites.
Similar species: (1) Snowbells, also without bud scales, have only 1 bundle scar. (2) Common Buckthorn (Pl. 12) has opposite leaves and scaly buds. See (3) European Buckthorn and (4) Witch-hazel (Pl. 32).

EUROPEAN BUCKTHORN   *Rhamnus frangula* L.   Not illus.
Escaped from cultivation. Similar to Carolina Buckthorn but not as tall and leaves *rarely toothed* and hairy beneath. Twigs hairy. Each individual flower/fruit has its *own* long stalk. Leaves 2"–6". Height to 40'. Leaves 1"–3". Height to 20'. Flowers pale yellow, May–July. Fruits black, *two-seeded.* Fencerows. Ne. U.S. and se. Canada.

BIGLEAF SNOWBELL   *Styrax grandifolius* Ait.   Pl. 43
A shrub or small tree with few-toothed, egg-shaped leaves, *white-hairy* beneath. Buds with *no scales,* blunt and brown-hairy, often one above the other; end buds false. Bundle scar *single,* sometimes somewhat broken. Twigs very *hairy* or scaly. Leaves 2"–8". Height to 40'. Flowers white, showy, in 2"–6" elongate clusters at twig ends. Fruits dry, one-seeded, Sept.–Oct. Rich woods.
Similar species: No trees other than the Snowbells have naked buds and single bundle scars. See American Snowbell.

AMERICAN SNOWBELL   *Styrax americanus* Lam.   Not illus.
Similar to the Bigleaf Snowbell but shorter and with *smaller* leaves that are nearly *hairless.* Twigs also *hairless* or nearly so. Leaves 1"–4". Height to 15'. Flowers in 2"–5" clusters.

SWEETLEAF   *Symplocos tinctoria* (L.) L'Her.   Pl. 43
A large shrub or small tree of the Coastal Plain. Leaves narrow to egg-shaped, with yellowish midribs, usually at least partially

toothed and semileathery, often remaining until spring; *sweet* to
the taste. Buds dark with several scales. Pith *chambered*. Bark
grayish smooth, often with shallow vertical cracks. Leaves 3″–7″.
Height to 40′; diameter to 10″. Flowers yellow, April–May. Fruits
fleshy but becoming dry, reddish, single-seeded, about ⅜″, clustered in leaf angles, Aug.–Sept. Damp places.
Similar species: Of species with chambered pith and single
bundle scars, (1) the silverbells (Pl. 42) have reddish buds, while
(2) the dark buds of Persimmon (Pl. 44) have only 2 scales.

WATER TUPELO   *Nyssa aquatica* L.   Pl. 43
Leaves *pointed,* frequently with 1–3 or more large teeth, sometimes somewhat hairy beneath; rarely heart-shaped at base.
Twigs *hairless* or nearly so. Pith tends to be *chambered,* with
cross-plates at intervals. Buds broad and pressed against twigs;
end buds true. Bundle scars 3. In swamps, the trunk base is often
swollen. Leaves 4″–13″. Height to 100′; diameter to 4′. Flowers
greenish, April–May. Fruits single, near the twig ends, more than
¾″, dark *purple* with a single stone. Coastal Plain swamps.
Similar species: (1) Ogeechee Tupelo has blunt leaves, velvety
twigs, and red fruits. (2) Sourgum (Black Tupelo) has leaves not
toothed, twigs not hairy, buds not pressed against the twigs, and
fruits in 2's and 3's (see Pl. 44).

OGEECHEE TUPELO   Not illus.
Nyssa ogeche Bartr. ex Marsh.
Like Water Tupelo but with leaf tips *blunt,* twigs *velvety-hairy,*
and fruits *red.* Leaves 3″–6″. Height to 60′. Flowers January–
May. Coastal Plain swamps.

DOMESTIC APPLE   Pl. 43
Malus (Pyrus) sylvestris (L.) Mill.
The apple and pear are the only species on this plate that usually
have short *spur branches* of crowded leaves and leaf scars. Apple
is a *round-topped* small tree. Leaves egg-shaped, more or less
round-toothed, usually somewhat white- or *gray-hairy* beneath;
may be heart-shaped at base. Twigs short, stiff, sometimes with
thorny tips; usually somewhat *hairy.* Leaf scars somewhat raised;
short lines leading downward at sides. Buds usually blunt and
woolly; end buds true. Bundle scars 3. Bark scaly and brownish.
Leaves 1″–4″. Height 20′–30′ (50′); diameter 6″–18″. Flowers
white or pinkish, clustered on spur branches, April–June. Fruits
more than 1″ across, Sept.–Nov. Hedgerows and old farms, south
to Georgia and Missouri.
Similar species: (1) The 3 crabapples (Pl. 23) are almost always
thorny and have sharp buds. The Domestic Apple, unlike other
apples, has blunt leaf teeth. (2) The Domestic Pear is mostly
hairless, more often thorny, and usually has long, not round,

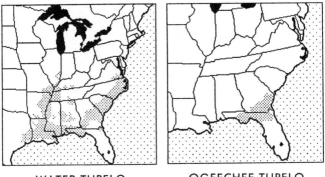

WATER TUPELO   OGEECHEE TUPELO

fruits, which contain grit cells. A pear tree has 1 or several strong upright branches, giving the tree a pointed silhouette rather than the round-topped crown shape of the apple. In winter, the apple has hairier twigs, blunter buds, and more raised leaf scars than the pear.

Remarks: The exact origin of the apple is lost in antiquity, but the etymology of the name indicates that it originated in the w. Himalayas and traveled westward by way of n. Persia, Asia Minor, the Caucasus, and the Mediterranean countries. The apple of the Bible is believed to have been not our northern fruit but the apricot, still common in the Holy Land. The Domestic Apple persisting in old orchards or locally gone wild is an important food of deer, pheasant, mourning dove, gray fox, and many other animals.

DOMESTIC PEAR *Pyrus communis* L.   **Pl. 43**

Similar to Domestic Apple but nearly *hairless,* more often thorny, with *elongate fleshy fruits* containing *grit* cells, and usually with several strong upright branches, making a *narrow-topped* tree. Leaves 1"–3". Height 20'–35' (60'); diameter 6"–15". Flowers white, early spring. Fruits green, autumn. Hedgerows and abandoned farms throughout our area.

CAROLINA LAURELCHERRY   **Pl. 43**

Prunus caroliniana (Mill.) Ait.

A southern evergreen cherry whose shiny, *leathery* leaves sometimes bear a few sharp teeth. Foliage and twigs *hairless.* Buds reddish brown, sharp-pointed, and *hairless;* bundle scars 3. Leaves 2"–5". Height to 40'. Flowers white, March–April. Fruits ½" across, nearly spherical, dry, *black,* inedible, clustered in leaf

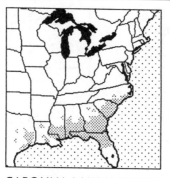

CAROLINA LAURELCHERRY

angles with a single stone, usually remaining all winter. Moist lowlands.

Similar species: (1) When leaf teeth are present, this leathery-leaved species can be separated from similar hollies (Pl. 41) by the 3 bundle scars (rather than 1) and the single-seeded fruit. Otherwise, it may resemble (2) plants of Pl. 46. Those of the same leaf length differ in flowers and fruits and have only a single bundle scar. (3) Cyrilla and (4) Odorless Bayberry also have leaves widest toward the tip; (5) crushed Redbay foliage is spicy.

Remarks: Sometimes used in hedges and other landscape plantings. Partially wilted foliage, like that of other cherries, contains hydrocyanic acid and may poison livestock.

GEIGER-TREE *Cordia sebestena* L.　　　　　Not illus.
A shrub or small tree of peninsular Florida. Leaves evergreen, *broad* (2″–4″), more or less heart-shaped, *sandpaper-rough* above and usually hairy beneath. Twigs *hairy.* Leaves 4″–6″. Height to 30′; diameter to 6″. Flowers *orange-red,* clustered at twig ends, tubular, to 1½″ across, all year. Fruits 1″–2″ long, white, somewhat pointed, with a large seed. Poor soils, seashores.

Remarks: Reportedly named after John Geiger, an early ship captain in the Florida Keys. Sometimes planted as an ornamental.

Trees with Leaves Neither Toothed nor Evergreen (Plate 44)

The foliage of Persimmon and Sourgum may occasionally be

somewhat leathery but not to the extent seen in the evergreen species of Pl. 46. Except on Persimmon, end buds are true.

COMMON (TALL) PAWPAW   Pl. 44
Asimina triloba (L.) Dunal
A shrub or small tree with *large, toothless* leaves and long, *naked, deep brown-hairy* or reddish-hairy end buds. Side buds shorter, also hairy. Twigs and young leaves often hairy, like buds. Bundle scars 5–7. Pith usually, but not always, partitioned by transverse woody diaphragms. Bark dark, smooth or somewhat broken. Leaves 6″–12″. Height 6′–20′ (40′). Flowers on the previous year's growth, purplish, more than 1″ across, April–May. Fruits large, fleshy, green, *somewhat bananalike,* seeds flattened, Aug.–Oct. Bottomlands.
Similar species: (1) Magnolias (Pl. 45) have similar leaves, but twigs are encircled by stipule scars at each leaf scar. Dark naked end buds and (usually) chambered pith are unique among plants with more than 3 bundle scars. (2) See next species.
Remarks: A northern representative of the tropical custard-apple family. Fully ripened fruits difficult to find, since they are eaten by opposum, squirrels, raccoon, foxes, etc. They can be eaten raw or made into desserts.

SMALLFLOWER (DWARF) PAWPAW   Not illus.
Asimina parviflora (Michx.) Dunal
Similar to Common Pawpaw but with leaves less than 7″ long, flowers less than 1″ across, seeds plump. Dry woods, southeastern states.

AMERICAN SMOKETREE   *Cotinus obovatus* Raf.   Pl. 44
One of the rarest American trees, this relative of the sumacs is found in only a few areas (see range map). Leaves wide, usually

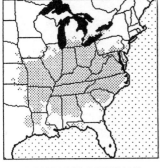

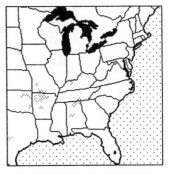

COMMON PAWPAW   AMERICAN SMOKETREE

blunt-tipped; side buds small, with 2–4 scales, and long-pointed. Wood *yellow* and odorous. Bundle scars 3. Name alludes to *foot-long* hazy end sprays of small feathery fruits that resemble puffs of smoke. Foliage becomes a brilliant red in autumn. A European relative (*C. coggygria* Scop.) is used in landscaping. Leaves 3″–6″. Height 6′–25′ (35′); diameter 1″–12″ (14″). Flowers April–May. Fruits June–Sept. Mountain slopes.

ALTERNATE-LEAF DOGWOOD   Pl. 44
Cornus alternifolia L. f.

Among the dogwoods (see Pl. 14), this small tree or shrub is the only species that does not have opposite leaves. Leaf veins tend to *follow leaf edges.* Leaves sometimes crowded (some may be opposite or whorled) toward tips of *greenish* twigs. Side twigs clustered near ends of central stem. Pith white. Buds have only 2 scales. Leaf scars narrow and raised; bundle scars 3. Leaves 2″–5″. Height to 25′. Flowers May–July. Fruits clustered at twig ends, blue-black with red stems, July–Sept. Streambanks and pondsides. **Remarks:** Fruits eaten by many birds, including ruffed grouse. Twigs browsed by deer and rabbits.

CORKWOOD   *Leitneria floridana* Chapm.   Pl. 44

A shrub or small tree related to poplars and other catkin-bearing plants but peculiar enough to be classified in a family by itself. Leaves narrow to elliptic, gray-hairy beneath. Twigs *hairy.* End buds *clustered;* much larger than some side ones. Bark smooth and, as on many other swamp trees, trunk swollen at base. Wood more buoyant than cork; local fishermen are said to use Corkwood blocks for net floats. Leaves 3″–6″. Height to 25′. Flowers March. Fruits leathery, ½″–1″, produced on the previous year's growth, May.

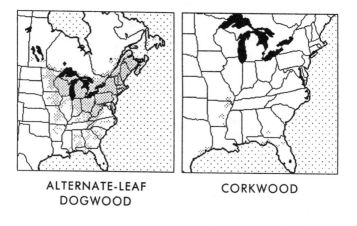

ALTERNATE-LEAF
DOGWOOD

CORKWOOD

Similar species: Its *swamp* habitat and *3* bundle scars separate this species from the oaks, which also have clustered buds at twig tips.

COMMON PERSIMMON *Diospyros virginiana* L.   **Pl. 44**
A tree with distinctive *dark thick* bark, typically broken into *small, squarish blocks*. Leaves somewhat thickened, egg-shaped, and *not toothed*. Twigs typically hairless. Buds *very dark with 2 overlapping scales*. End buds *false*. Pith solid or sometimes divided into chambers by *weak* partitions. Bundle scars 1. Leaves 2″–5″. Height 30′–50′ (130′); diameter 10″–12″ (7′). Flowers yellowish, in the leaf angles, May–June. Fruits slightly larger than cultivated cherries, orange-colored, edible when ripe, Aug.–Oct. or later. Uplands.
Similar species: No other tree has the combination of toothless leaves, dark buds, and regularly cracked bark. Bark of (1) blackhaw viburnums (Pl. 12) and Flowering Dogwood (Pl. 14) is similar, but those plants have opposite leaves. (2) Sweetleaf (Pl. 43) has chambered pith and dark bark, but there are more than 2 bud scales, and some leaves may bear teeth. (3) See Sourgum, below.
Remarks: The green fruit causes the mouth to "pucker up" for some time after being tasted. Cool, ripe persimmons that are soft and fully colored, however, are delicious. They are eaten by nearly all birds and mammals, from songbirds to turkeys and from dogs to deer. The Common Persimmon, a member of the ebony family, has strong, heavy, close-grained wood that has occasionally been used for shoe lasts and shuttles.

SOURGUM *Nyssa sylvatica* Marsh.   **Pl. 44**
A tree with dark, deeply *checkered* bark. Leaves shiny, hairless or nearly so, egg-shaped to elliptic (less commonly roundish), often somewhat leathery; scarlet in autumn. Pith *distinctly chambered.*

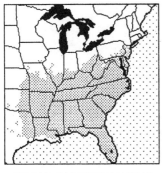

COMMON PERSIMMON

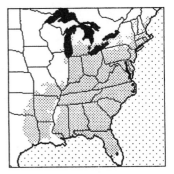

SOURGUM

Brown buds stand out from twigs; bud scales 4. Bundle scars 3. In southern swamps, trunks growing in water are swollen at base. Leaves 3″–6″. Height 40′–60′ (125′); diameter 1′–2′ (5′). Flowers greenish, April–June. Fruits in 2's and 3's along the twigs, less than ¾″, bluish, berrylike, Aug.–Oct.

Similar species: (1) Plain foliage and checkered bark are most like Persimmon, but chambered pith rather than the usually solid pith, triple rather than single bud scars, and lowland rather than upland habitat characterize this species. (2) Water Tupelo has leaves toothed, twigs hairy, buds pressed against the twigs, and fruits single (see Pl. 43). Sourwood (Pl. 42) should not be confused because of the similarity of names. It has toothed leaves and solid pith. (3) Also see Persimmon (above).

Remarks: Lumber of Sourgum, also called Black Gum or Black Tupelo, is useful for furniture, boxes, crates, veneer, and paper pulp. Fleshy bitter fruits are relished by black bear and by over 30 species of birds, including ruffed grouse, prairie chicken, pheasant, and wild turkey.

CRAPEMYRTLE *Lagerstroemia indica* L. **Pl. 44**
An Asiatic plant possibly not spreading to grow wild but commonly planted in southern towns and found around abandoned homesites. Leaves and buds are in both alternate and opposite patterns, with the alternate arrangement predominant on the upper branches. Leaves pointed or somewhat rounded. Twigs *four-lined* or four-winged; buds with 2 scales; bundle scars 1. Bark flakes to leave smooth greenish surface; trunk has vertical fluted ridges. Leaves 1″–3″. Height to 35′. Flowers *showy,* pink or white, in terminal clusters. Fruits dry, ½″ capsules.

ELLIOTTIA *Elliottia racemosa* Muhl. ex Ell. **Pl. 44**
Very *rare* in e. Georgia (and formerly in adjacent S. Carolina), this member of the heath (rhododendron) family also has elliptical

ELLIOTTIA

SOUTHERN MAGNOLIA

leaves. Buds with 2–3 scales; bundle scars 1. Leaves 2″–6″. Height to 30′. Flowers in end clusters, white, August. Fruits small, dry, nearly spherical capsules. Coastal Plain dry ridges.
Remarks: Reported to be so scarce that cross-pollination between plants is unlikely. Plant patches may spread only through rootstock growth.

Magnolias (Plate 45)

The magnolias are distinctively marked plants of tropical appearance and with southern and Appalachian affinities. The ranges of a number extend into the northern states, however, especially in the mountains. The leaves are smooth-edged and often large; twigs are ringed by stipule scars, buds are covered by a single scale; true end buds are especially large, and bundle scars are many. The leaf scars are crescent-shaped (but U-shaped in Cucumber Magnolia). Magnolias are frequently cultivated for their large leaves and terminal showy white flowers. Their large, brownish, conelike fruit clusters are frequently ornamental when ripe. They release bright red seeds on silklike threads from many slitlike openings.

Among deciduous (non-evergreen) trees, only the magnolias, Sycamore, and Tuliptree have ringed twigs and more than 3 bundle scars per leaf scar. Sycamore (Pl. 25) has peculiar mottled bark and buds surrounded by the leaf scars; Tuliptree (Pl. 25) has notched leaves, buds spicy when crushed, and chambered pith; it is a member of the magnolia family. Beech (Pl. 32) has ringed twigs, but the leaves are toothed and bundle scars are only 3. Common Pawpaw and other plants (Pl. 44) have similar foliage but lack stipular rings. In peninsular and s. Florida, see also Pl. F-46A to F-46D.

SOUTHERN MAGNOLIA *Magnolia grandiflora* L. **Pl. 45**
A *leathery-leaved* evergreen tree whose foliage is shiny above and *rusty-hairy* beneath. Leaves are *rounded* at the base and not crowded at the twig tips. Twigs and buds *rusty-hairy;* end buds less than 1″ long. Pith *chambered.* Leaves 6″–8″. Height 60′–80′; diameter 2′–3′. Flowers 6″–8″ across, white, fragrant, May–June. Cones 3″–4″, egg-shaped, Sept.–Oct. Moist forests.
Similar species: See Sweetbay Magnolia.
Remarks: Frequently planted in parks and gardens.

SWEETBAY MAGNOLIA *Magnolia virginiana* L. **Pl. 45**
A large shrub or small tree with thick, *somewhat leathery,* elliptic leaves that may be evergreen in the South. Leaf bases mostly V-shaped. Foliage *spicy* when crushed, *hairless and white beneath.* Buds green, *hairy,* and less than 1″ long; twigs often

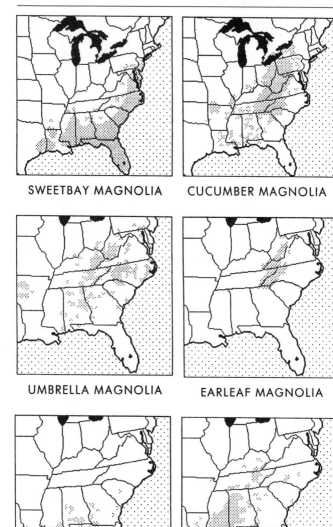

SWEETBAY MAGNOLIA   CUCUMBER MAGNOLIA

UMBRELLA MAGNOLIA   EARLEAF MAGNOLIA

PYRAMID MAGNOLIA   BIGLEAF MAGNOLIA

hairless. Pith *chambered.* Leaves 4″–6″. Height to 50′ (rarely 70′); diameter to 2′ (rarely 3′). Flowers 2″–2½″, white, fragrant, May–July. Cones 1″–2″, egg-shaped, Sept.–Oct. Wet soils.
Similar species: Only Southern Magnolia also has both leathery leaves and chambered pith. Its leaf undersides are brown, however, and the crushed foliage is not spicy-scented.

CUCUMBER MAGNOLIA *Magnolia acuminata* L. Pl. 45

A hardy magnolia of tree size with large, *thin,* egg-shaped leaves that are *green, pale,* slightly hairy beneath, U-*shaped* at base, and not crowded at the twig tips. Twigs brown, hairless; pith *not* chambered. Buds *hairy;* leaf scars U-*shaped;* end buds whitish and up to ¾″ long. Trunk bark dark and furrowed, much like that of ashes (Pls. 7 and 8). Leaves 4″–10″. Height 40′–70′ (90′); diameter 1′–2′ (3′). Flowers green or green and yellow, with unpleasant odor at close range, May–June. Cones dark red, and cucumberlike when young, 2″–3″, Aug.–Oct. Moist soils.
Similar species: Among non-evergreen magnolias, (1) Bigleaf and (2) Ashe Magnolia also have hairy buds, but leaves and end buds are larger, and leaves are crowded at the twig tips.
Remarks: Wood is of some commercial value for interiors, cabinetmaking, and woodenware. Twigs eaten by deer.

UMBRELLA MAGNOLIA *Magnolia tripetala* L. Pl. 45

Similar to Cucumber Magnolia but with leaves larger and crowded at twig tips. Leaf bases V-*shaped.* End buds hairless, purplish, *more than* 1⅛″ long. Twigs *stout;* pith not chambered. Trunk bark *brown* and smooth. Leaves 10″–24″. Height 20′–30′ (40′); diameter 10″–12″ (18″). Flowers 7″–10″, white, odor not pleasant, May. Fruits candle-shaped, 3″–4″, Sept.–Oct. Moist mountain forests.

EARLEAF MAGNOLIA *Magnolia fraseri* Walt. Pl. 45

The only magnolia with leaf bases *deeply* "ear-lobed." Leaves usually large and crowded near twig tips. Leafstalks *more than* 3″ long. Buds and slender twigs hairless. Purplish end buds *less than* 1⅛″ long. Pith often *faintly* chambered. Trunk bark smooth, *gray.* Leaves 8″–12″. Height 20′–30′ (40′); diameter 10″–12″ (18″). Flowers 8″–10″ across, white, May. Fruits cylindrical, 3″–4″, Sept.–Oct. Moist mountain forests.

PYRAMID MAGNOLIA *Magnolia pyramidata* Bartr. Not illus.

Similar to Earleaf Magnolia but leaves smaller, less deeply "ear-lobed," and leafstalks *less than* 3″ long. Leaves 5″–9″. Height 30′–40′; diameter 1′. Flowers 4″, white, spring. Fruits 1½″–2½″, fall. Moist Coastal Plain soils.

BIGLEAF MAGNOLIA *Magnolia macrophylla* Michx. Pl. 45

A small southern tree with the *largest* simple leaves of any tree

north of the tropics. Leaves often clustered near twig tips; *white and hairy* beneath, bases often shallowly "ear-lobed." Twigs and buds greenish, *hairy;* end buds 1″–2″; pith not chambered. Trunk bark smooth, grayish. Leaves *20″–30″*. Height 20′–30′ (50′); diameter 12″–18″ (24″). Flowers white with purple spots, often 12″ across, fragrant, May–June. Fruits *egg-shaped,* reddish, 2″–3″, Sept.–Oct. Moist forested slopes.
Similar species: See Ashe Magnolia.

ASHE MAGNOLIA   *Magnolia ashei* Weatherby   Not illus.
Sometimes regarded only as a variety of Bigleaf Magnolia. Foliage and blossoms smaller. Rare and local in nw. Florida. Leaves *14″–22″*. Height to 30′, often shrubby. Fruiting cones 2″–3″, *candle-shaped*. Upland slopes.

Trees with Leathery Evergreen Leaves, Mostly Not Toothed (Plate 46)

Mainly southern plants—only Mountain Laurel and the rhododendrons extend their ranges along the Appalachians into the North. Myrtle and Virginia Live oaks (Pl. 31) and Tawnyberry Holly (Pl. 41) plus several trees on Pls. 43 and 45 may also have evergreen leaves not toothed. Within Florida many tropical and semitropical trees have foliage of this type; see Pls. F-46A to F-46D.

SPARKLEBERRY (FARKLEBERRY)   **Pl. 46**
Vaccinium arboreum Marsh.
Shrubby or a small crooked tree, a member of the blueberry genus. Leaves elliptic, *1″–2″* long, *short-stalked,* sometimes fine-toothed, hairless, and with a slender *tip.* Twigs hairy or not. End buds false. Height to 30′. Flowers white, bell-shaped, in drooping clusters, April–June. Fruits fleshy, edible but not tasty, black, Sept.–Oct.

TREE LYONIA (STAGGERBUSH)   **Pl. 46**
Lyonia ferruginea (Walt.) Nutt.
A straggling shrub or small tree. Leaves *small,* edges often finely wavy and rolled under, tips mostly pointed, stalks normal. Twigs and leaf undersides *rusty-hairy.* End buds false. Bundle scar 1. Leaves 1″–3″. Height to 20′. Flowers white, bell-shaped, in open clusters in leaf angles, May–June. Fruits dry, urn-shaped, five-parted capsules, Sept.–Oct. or later.

BUCKWHEAT-TREE   **Pl. 46**
Cliftonia monophylla (Lam.) Britton ex Sarg.
Leaves *crowded* near the twig tips; the *small* leaves are mostly

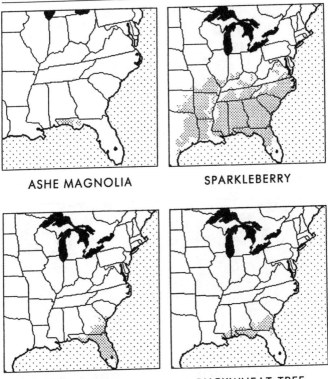

ASHE MAGNOLIA

SPARKLEBERRY

TREE LYONIA

BUCKWHEAT-TREE

wedge-based, short-stalked, and with rolled edges and *rather pointed* tips. Twigs hairless; end bud true. Leaves 1″–2″. Flowers white, often erect, in *elongate* clusters at twig *tips*. Fruits small, *four-winged,* buckwheatlike.

Remarks: Also called Titi (see Cyrilla). A source of honey.

CYRILLA (TITI)   *Cyrilla racemiflora* L.   **Pl. 46**

Leaves shiny, short-stalked, wedge-based, with rolled edges and *somewhat-rounded* tips. Twigs hairless; end bud true. Leaves 2″–4″. Height to 35′. Flowers white, in 3″–8″ long clusters at twig *bases,* June–July. Fruits small, dry capsules, Aug.–Sept. Bottomlands and damp places. See map, p. 214.

Remarks: Related to Buckwheat-tree. Colorful in autumn. Despite its natural occurrence only in the South, it is reported (Elias

CYRILLA

ODORLESS BAYBERRY

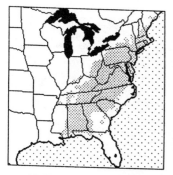

MOUNTAIN LAUREL

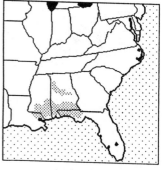

FLORIDA ANISE-TREE

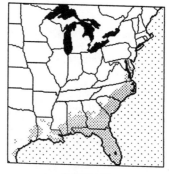

REDBAY

1980) that the species can tolerate temperatures as low as $-10°F$. A useful honey plant.

ODORLESS BAYBERRY *Myrica inodora* Bartr. **Pl. 46**
The only bayberry to lack resin dots and a fragrant scent (see Pl. 43), this small tree ranges only in a narrow coastal belt from sw. Georgia to se. Louisiana. It differs from its relatives also in its leathery leaf texture (but see Evergreen Bayberry, p. 199) and in its lack of leaf teeth. Leaves shiny, wedge-based, with rolled edges and short, stout leafstalks, and *not* crowded near the twig tip. Twigs hairless. Bark whitish. Leaves 2″–4″. Height to 25′. Flowers are *inch-long* catkins in *leaf angles*, the sexes on separate plants. Fruits whitish, wax-covered, in short clusters. Wet places.

MOUNTAIN LAUREL *Kalmia latifolia* L. **Pl. 46**
A gnarled shrub or small tree. Leaves pointed or blunt, light green beneath, hairless, edges *not* rolled, and often crowded near the twig ends (sometimes a few are opposite). Twigs hairless. Large flower buds of rhododendron type lacking; side buds minute, silky. Leaves 2″–5″. Height to 10′, rarely to 35′. Flowers showy, medium-sized, white to purple, clustered, with (pollen-bearing) stamens tucked into *pockets* in the fused petals, May–July. Fruits rounded dry capsules. Mainly mountain and hill slopes.
Similar species: (1) See Great Rhododendron. (2) Devilwood has leaves that are regularly opposite.
Remarks: When a bee lights on the flower, one or more stamens spring out of their pockets and slap the insect. Pollen is then carried to other blossoms. Leaves poisonous to cattle, sheep, and deer and eaten only when better foods are lacking.

FLORIDA ANISE-TREE *Illicium floridanum* Ellis. **Pl. 46**
Leaves slender, pointed at both ends, and crowded toward the twig tips. Twigs hairless. Flowers and bruised foliage have an unusual but generally unpleasant *odor*. Leaves 3″–6″. Height to 25′. Flowers showy, star-shaped, dark red, at twig *tips*, March. Fruits dry, *star-shaped*, summer. Wet areas. Gulf Coast from nw. Florida to e. Louisiana.

REDBAY *Persea borbonia* (L.) Spreng. **Pl. 46**
A Coastal Plain tree. Leaves narrow, elliptic, shiny above, pale beneath, edges rolled under, and tips pointed or somewhat blunt. Crushed foliage with a *spicy* odor. Twigs greenish, hairy, and *angled*. Bark dark reddish, deeply grooved. Leaves 3″–8″. Height to 50′ or 70′; diameter to 3′. Flowers May–July. Fruits blue or black, single-seeded, in red-stemmed clusters, *along* the twigs, Aug.–Sept.

CATAWBA RHODODENDRON   Pl. 46
Rhododendron catawbiense Michx.
A dense thicket-forming shrub or small tree, mostly of the mountains. Leaves *large, rounded* at base and broadly pointed at tip, edges *rolled,* lighter green beneath. Twigs hairy. Large flower buds smooth, *lacking* slender bracts. Leaves 3″–8″. Height to 30′ or 40′; diameter to 10′ or 12′. Flowers large, pink to purple, in large clusters, May–June. Fruits elongate capsules, *rusty-hairy.*
Similar species: The 2 rhododendrons plus Mountain Laurel form almost impenetrable tangles on many mountain slopes. (1) Great Rhododendron has narrow leaf bases. (2) Mountain Laurel has smaller leaves without rolled edges.
Remarks: When in full bloom, a rhododendron-covered slope is beautiful. Frequently cultivated for ornament. The hard wood may be used for tool handles, decorative objects, and fuel. Leaves sometimes poisonous to cattle and deer but usually avoided by them.

GREAT RHODODENDRON   Pl. 46
Rhododendron maximum L.
Like the preceding but more northern and with *wider, hairless leaves.* Leaf bases and tips *pointed.* Leaves usually somewhat *hairy and whitish* beneath. Flower buds have long, thin bracts. Leaves 3″–8″. Height to 20′. Flowers large, rose-purple, clustered, June–July. Fruits elongate capsules, *not* rusty-hairy. Damp slopes and streamsides.

CAMPHOR-TREE   Pl. 46
Cinnamomum camphora (L.) J. S. Presl.
Escaped from cultivation in a few southern areas. Some leaves may be opposite, but all leaves are short- or long-pointed and have

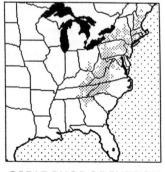

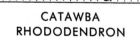

CATAWBA   GREAT RHODODENDRON
RHODODENDRON

a *camphor odor* when crushed. *Glands* occur in the vein angles on leaf undersides. There are 3 main veins from the leaf base. Leaf edges sometimes curled and wavy. Twigs *green*. Leaves 2″–6″. Height to 40′; diameter to 2′. Flowers small, yellow, 1″–3″ clusters, spring. Fruits blue-black, one-seeded, in a greenish cup.

Remarks: A native of the Orient. Distillation of the leaves and wood produces the oil used in medicine and industry. Often planted in the South for shade.

VI

Palms, Cacti, and Yuccas
(Plates 47–48)

The palms, yuccas, and cacti are distinctive and recognizably different from other woody plants. The first 2 groups have evergreen, parallel-veined leaves. In the palms, these are long-stalked and clustered at the ends of the stems.

Palms from all over the world have been imported and planted over much of Florida. Only the species native to the U.S. are considered here. Most have single unbranched trunks, but the leafy fronds of palms are of 2 types. They are either fan-shaped, with segments radiating from the end of a central leafstalk or a quite short "partial midrib" (Pl. 47), or long and featherlike with a central midrib (Pl. 48). The fan-leaved species range north to the Carolinas and west to the Mississippi Valley; the feather-leaved palms grow wild only in Florida.

Yuccas have long, sword-shaped, and usually sharp-pointed leaves whose bases clasp the stem in dense abundance. They

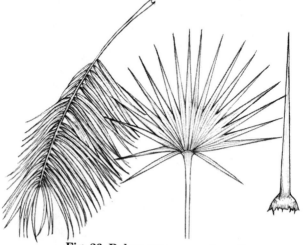

Fig. 26. Palms, yuccas, and cacti.

range widely in coastal districts of the Southeast. A tree-sized pricklypear and giant cactus are included in this group for convenience. Their unique succulent and spiny stems are like those of no other trees. They occur only in s. Florida.

Fan-leaved Palms (Plate 47)

Fan-leaved palms are southern trees which, like the feather-leaved palms on Pl. 48, have large evergreen leaves whose segments show parallel veins. The leaf blades of the fan-leaved palms, however, are nearly circular. For most species, the leaf-stalk ends at the base or barely enters the leafy portion of the frond. Cabbage Palm differs in having the leafstalk extend almost through the leaf (especially evident as viewed from the leaf underside), essentially forming a midrib. Dwarf Palmetto leaf-stalks also penetrate the leaf blade but only slightly. The other fan-leaved palms have leafstalks merely attached strongly to the edge of the leaf blade. Also unusual is the occasional branching of the Saw-palmetto. This is the only native palm that may have a branched trunk. The Cabbage Palm and palmettos are distributed more widely than the other palms.

CABBAGE PALM   Pl. 47
Sabal palmetto (Walt.) Lodd. ex J. A. & J. H. Schult.
The 2 *Sabal* species have leafstalks that continue into the leaf blade. In this palm, it extends almost *completely* through the frond. At the trunk end, the leafstalk base is *forked*. The leafstalk bases often remain *attached,* especially on the upper portions of the trunk, after the leaves die and drop off. Leaves 4'–6' plus

CABBAGE PALM

leafstalk 6'–7'. Height 40'–50' (90'); diameter 2' (3'). Flowers yellowish white, in *loose* clusters to 6' long, June. Fruits ½", spherical, becoming black.

Similar species: (1) The leafstalk of Dwarf Palmetto barely penetrates the leaf blade. (2) Saw-palmetto has saw-edged leafstalks.

DWARF PALMETTO *Sabal minor* (Jacq.) Pers.   **Pl. 47**
Like the Cabbage Palm but with leafstalks extending into the leaf blade for *only 2"* or so and bases *not* split. Usually shrubby in the eastern portions of its range but often developing a trunk westward. Leaves 3'–5' plus leafstalks of equal length. Height 5'–15'; diameter to 12". Flower clusters *narrow, to 3' long.*

SAW-PALMETTO *Serenoa repens* (Bartr.) Small   **Pl. 47**
Often creeping and thicket-forming with underground stems but sometimes one or *several* trunks upright and occasionally *branched.* The leaves are up to 3' across, with segments radiating from the ends of the leafstalks. The leafstalk does *not* extend into the leaf blade and is *saw-edged* with tiny (¹⁄₁₀") spines. Old leaf bases cover the trunk. Height to 20'. Flowers small, white; clusters as long as the leaves. Fruits fleshy, ¾" in diameter, blue-black.

PAUROTIS PALM *Acoelorrhaphe wrightii*   **Pl. 47**
(Griseb. & H. Wendl.) H. Wendl. ex Becc.
Known also as Everglades Palm, this s. Florida plant grows in clumps. *Several* trunks, each covered with *fibrous* matting and slender leafstalk bases. Leafstalks 2' long, not penetrating the blade, and edged with stout orange curved *thorns* ¼" long. Leaves 2'–3' in diameter. Height to 25'; diameter to 6". Flowers greenish, in 2'–3' clusters. Swamps.

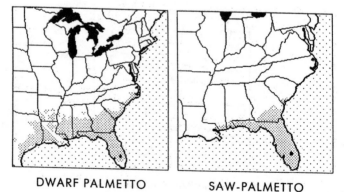

DWARF PALMETTO   SAW-PALMETTO

FLORIDA THATCHPALM   Pl. 47
Thrinax radiata Lodd. ex J. A. & J. H. Schult.
The Thatchpalms are slender trees. This species has leaves 3'–4'
in diameter and pale *yellow-green* beneath. The 2'–3' leafstalks
do not penetrate the leaf blade and bases are *forked* or split where
they attach to the trunk. Height to 35'. Flowers white on short
stems and in *3'–4'* clusters. Fruits *white,* spherical, dry. Coasts, s.
Florida.

KEY THATCHPALM   *Thrinax morrisii* H. Wendl.   Pl. 47
Like the preceding species but with leaves 2'–3' in diameter,
silvery-white beneath, and flowers *stemless,* in clusters *4'–7'* long.
Coasts, s. Florida north to Broward County.

FLORIDA SILVERPALM   Pl. 47
Coccothrinax argentata (Jacq.) Bailey
A small tree of limestone soils that is similar to the Thatchpalms
but has leaves *1'–2'* in diameter, with very thin segments that are
dark green above and quite *silvery* beneath. Leafstalks 2'–3' and
not forked at the base. Trunks *covered* with fibrous matting.
Flowers white, in *8'–9'* clusters. Fruits purple to *black,* fleshy
spheres to ¾". Florida Keys north to Palm Beach County.

Feather-leaved Palms, Tree-cacti, and Yuccas (Plate 48)

These feather-leaved palms are native in s. Florida and have
ring-scarred trunks free of old leafstalk bases. Their leafstalks
are not thorny. The only tree cacti in the eastern U.S. occur in s.
Florida. The yuccas range more widely.

FLORIDA ROYALPALM   Pl. 48
Roystonea elata (Bartr.) F. Harper
The smooth, cement-colored and *bulging* lower trunk topped by a
smooth *bright-green crownshaft* cylinder is distinctive. Ring scars
faint. The fronds are *featherlike* and 15' or longer. Height to 125'.
Flowers greenish white, developing from a spearlike green spathe
at the *base* of the *5'–6'* long crownshaft. Fruits blue to purple,
leathery. Rich soils, hammocks (swamp islands).

COCONUT PALM   *Cocos nucifera* L.   Pl. 48
Ranging along tropical coastlines throughout the world, the wild
form of this palm characteristically has a brownish *leaning* trunk
with *prominent* ring scars and usually a swollen base. The
feather-shaped leaves may be over 15' long; there is *no* crownshaft. A clothlike fiber *matting* occurs at the bases of the leaf-

stalks. Height to 65'. Flowers in sheathed clusters up to 5' long, in leafstalk angles. Fruits to 1', more or less *three-sided,* heavy, green maturing to brown, clustered.

Remarks: One of the most useful trees worldwide. The seeds (coconuts) are nearly globular, 5"–10" in diameter, and hollow, with a nutritious liquid center and a lining of tasty white copra "meat." In tropical communities, the thick husk surrounding the coconut is removed by pounding the hand-held fruit against a sharpened stake. The brownish material of the husk is sold as a commercial fiber. Dried copra (white coconut "meat") is exported widely for use in candies, cakes, cookies, etc. Because it is more soft, slippery, and easier to swallow in quantity, however, the "green" or soft copra is usually eaten by residents in the tropics. There are many cultivated varieties of coconuts, including the dwarf Malaysian strain with gold-colored fruits. This variety is reported to be resistant to the increasingly serious lethal yellowing disease of coconuts.

BUCCANEER PALM   Pl. 48
Pseudophoenix sargentii H. Wendl. ex Sarg.

Rare in the U.S., growing naturally only on the upper Florida Keys and largely destroyed there by real estate development. The grayish trunk is topped by a *1'–3'* crownshaft leading to feather-like leaves 8'–9' long. Height to 25'. Flowers yellow-green, at the *top* of the crownshaft. Fruits 1"–2" in diameter, orange-red.

Remarks: An endangered species requiring strict protection. Also called Florida Cherrypalm or Sargent's Cherrypalm. *Phoenix* is the generic name of the date palm; the Buccaneer Palm with similar foliage is a "false date" named after Charles Sprague Sargent, an eminent botanist of the late 1800s and early 1900s.

BRAZIL PRICKLYPEAR   Pl. 48
Opuntia brasiliensis (Willd.) Haw.

An introduced upright succulent and prickly cactus of s. Florida. The cylindrical trunk gives rise to *rounded* branches with *flattened* joints. Stem and flat pads armed with sharp, slender, white, brown-tipped spines up to ¾" long as well as with numerous tiny, sharp bristles. Leaves not readily evident as such. Height to 15'. Flowers yellow, 2" long. Fruits 1"–1½", nearly spherical, *yellow,* fleshy, edible. Dry disturbed sites.

INDIAN-FIG PRICKLYPEAR   Not illus.
Opuntia ficus-indica (L.) Mill.

Like the Brazil Pricklypear, this cactus may become treelike. It has only flattened joints, which may bear only short bristles or none. Ranging widely throughout the world tropics, this importation has become established locally in s. Florida. Height to 13'. Flowers yellow, *3"–4"* long. Fruits 2"–4", *red,* edible.

KEY GIANT-CACTUS   Not illus.

Cereus robinii (Lem.) L. Benson
Either polelike or branched and with a *vertically grooved* succulent stem, this relative of the western giant cactus is now rare on the Florida Keys. Trunk and branches *9–13 ribbed,* leafless, gray- or blue-green and covered with clusters of short spines. Leaves absent. Height to 30'. Flowers single, 1"–2" long, *greenish.* Fruits fleshy, *reddish.*

SPANISH BAYONET (ALOE YUCCA)   Pl. 48

Yucca aloifolia L.
A unique shrub or small tree covered with live green (and usually over lower portions of the tree, with dead brown), *sword-shaped,* and pointed leaves, each *1'–3'* long. Leaves with numerous tiny marginal *teeth* and sharp, brown tips. Height to 16'. Flowers showy, white, 1"–2" long, in prominent end clusters 1'–3' tall. Fruits 3"–4" long, green to black, somewhat leathery. Coastal areas, N. Carolina to Alabama and the Florida Keys.
Similar species: Moundlily Yucca is a somewhat similar plant with smooth-edged leaves.
Remarks: Yuccas are woody members of the lily family often planted for ornament. The specific name refers to the aloes of s. Africa, which have similarly thickened leaves.

MOUNDLILY YUCCA   *Yucca gloriosa* L.   Pl. 48
Like the Spanish Bayonet but with shorter, *smooth-edged* leaves and fruits with 6 prominent ridges. Height to 12' or so. Occurs only along the Atlantic Coast from N. Carolina to n. Florida.

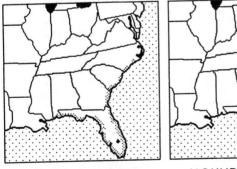

SPANISH BAYONET   **MOUNDLILY YUCCA**

VII

Trees Found
Only in Florida

Florida is home to nearly half as many native and naturalized tree species as occur in all other eastern states and provinces together. Including 5 species (Sand Pine, Wingleaf Soapberry, Florida Torreya, Florida Willow, and Florida Yew) that scarcely cross the Florida border to enter Alabama and/or Georgia, 133 native trees occur naturally only in Florida. The complex genus of hawthorns (*Crataegus*) is omitted in this tally (see p. 114). Three other species that attain tree size only in Florida but occur as shrubs in other states are also not counted here. Species like Florida Chinkapin, Florida Forestiera, and Florida Maple, which also occur well outside Florida, are excluded from this count despite their names.

Persons attempting to identify a tree in the states and provinces north and west of Florida could be confused if all of Florida's species were discussed and illustrated along with the more northern plants. In consequence, it seemed wise to separate most of those plants which are found only in the Sunshine State. Only readers *in* Florida need consider the many Caribbean species that occur there, often only in certain parts of the state.

Thirty-six Florida-only trees receive more or less full treatment in the main body of the text. Mostly these are illustrated on the color plates or by drawings in the text. Ninety-six Florida-only trees, however, are identified in the final plate section preceding p. 138.

To identify a tree found growing in Florida, first use the main plates (numbers 1–48) and text to see whether it is one of the many species that occur *both* in Florida and elsewhere in the eastern U.S. and Canada. Plants of n. or n.-cen. Florida are especially likely to be distributed also in other states and provinces. If the identity of the unknown tree is still uncertain, then review the plants on the black-and-white plates preceding p. 138. These plates show the tropical and subtropical trees of s. and cen. Florida that have not been illustrated earlier in the Plates section. Many of them will have thickened, leathery, evergreen leaves. A nice collection of labeled specimens of these trees can be seen growing just outside the visitor center at Everglades National Park.

As a guide to Florida-only species found throughout the book, the following key will serve as an index:

1. Leaves needlelike, conifers and coniferlike species:
  2. Needles long, slender:
    3. Needles bound in clusters of 2.   **Sand Pine, Pl. 2.**
    3. "Needles" of jointed, fine-grooved segments.
      Casuarinas (Australian-pine, Brazilian Beefwood), p. 43.
  2. Needles flat. **Florida Yew and Florida Torreya, Pl. 4.**
1. Leaves with broad blades (broad-leaved trees):
  4. Leaves opposite.
    5. Leaves compound.   **See Pl. F-7.**
    5. Leaves simple:
      6. Seashore trees.
        Mangroves, Pl. 13.
      6. Mainly upland tropical trees.
        See Pls. F-13A, F-13B.
  4. Leaves alternate:
    7. Leaves compound:
      8. Plants thorny, aromatic.
        Tropical Prickly-ashes, Pl. F-15.
      8. Plants not thorny:
        9. Leaves once-compound:
          10. Midribs not winged:
            11. Leaflets triangular, with black spots.   **Florida Poisonwood! p. 106, Pls. 20, F-21A.**
            11. Leaflets otherwise; not poisonous.
              Scrub Hickory, etc., Pls. 19, F-21A, and F-21B.
          10. Midribs winged:
            12. Leaflets 3"–5", not aromatic.
              Wingleaf Soapberry, Pl. 21.
            12. Leaflets 1"–3", turpentine-scented:
            Brazilian Peppertree, Pl. F-21A.
        9. Leaves twice-compound:
          13. Leaflets more than ¾" long.
            Lebbek, Pl. 22.
          13. Leaflets less than ¾" long.
            Leadtree, etc., Pl. F-22.
    7. Leaves simple:
      14. Plants thorny.   **Saffron-plum Bumelia, Tallowwood, *Citrus* species, Pl. 24 and p. 121.**
      14. Plants not thorny:
        15. Leaves fan-lobed.   **Papaya* and Castorbean,* p. 126.**

---

* Growing to tree size only in Florida but occurring elsewhere as shrubs.

15. Leaves not lobed:
  16. Leaves fan-veined:
    17. Leaves triangular or heart-shaped.
                **Tremas, Sea Hibiscus,
                Portiatree, Pl. 26 and
                pp. 126, 128.**
    17. Leaves narrow. **Strawberry-tree,
                Pl. 32.**
  16. Leaves feather-veined:
      18. Leaves sandpapery above.
                Geiger-tree, p. 204.
      18. Leaves smooth, not sand-
          papery:
        19. Leaves toothed, fruits dry, in cat-
            kins. N. and cen. Fla.
                Florida Willow, Pl. 39.
        19. Leaves toothed or not, fruits fleshy.
            Miami area. **Tawnyberry Holly,
                Pl. 41.**
        19. Leaves not toothed:
          20. Trees of nw. Fla.
                Ashe Magnolia, p. 212.
          20. Trees of cen. and s. Fla.
                See Pls. F-46A, F-46B.
          20. Trees of tropical Fla.
                See Pls. F-46C, F-46D.
1. Palms and tree-cacti.
                Pls. 47–48.

Complete Scientific Names of Trees Found Only in Florida

Because of lack of space, the identification charts facing the plates of Florida-only species do not name the authorities (authors) who assigned the Latin names. Complete scientific names, including the species authors, appear here for these 96 Florida-only trees, followed by the corresponding plate number. The 36 additional Florida-only species (see p. 224) described in the main text are not repeated here.

Scientific Name	Common Name and Plate
Acacia choriophylla Benth.	Cinnecord, Pl. F-22
Acacia macracantha Humb.& Bonpl. ex. Willd.	Longspine Acacia, Pl. F-15
Acacia tortuosa (L.) Willd.	Huisachillo, Pl. F-15

Scientific Name	Common Name and Plate
Alvaradoa amorphoides Liebm.	Mexican Alvaradoa, Pl. F-21B
Amphitecna latifolia (Mill.)	Black-calabash, Pl. F-46D
Amyris balsamifera L.	Balsam Torchwood, Pl. F-7
Amyris elemifera L.	Small Torchwood, Pl. F-7
Annona glabra L.	Pond-apple, Pl. F-46B
Annona squamosa L.	Sugar-apple, Pl. F-46B
Ardisia escallonioides Schiede & Deppe ex Schlecht. & Cham.	Marlberry, Pl. F-46B
Asimina obovata (Willd.) Nash	Bigflower Pawpaw, Pl. F-46A
Bourreria ovata Miers	Bahama Strongbark, Pl. F-46C
Bourreria radula (Poir.) G. Don	Rough Strongbark, Pl. F-46D
Bursera simaruba (L.) Sarg.	Gumbo-limbo, Pl. F-21A
Byrsonima lucida DC.	Locustberry, Pl. F-13B
Caesalpinia pulcherrima (L.) Sw.	Flowerfence Poinciana, Pl. F-15
Calyptranthes pallens Griseb.	Pale Lidflower, Pl. F-13B
Calyptranthes zuzygium (L.) Sw.	Myrtle-of-the-river, Pl. F-13B
Canella winterana (L.) Gaertn.	Cinnamon-bark, Pl. F-46C
Capparis cynophallophora L.	Jamaica Caper, Pl. F-46B
Capparis flexuosa (L.) L.	Limber Caper, Pl. F-46A
*Casasia clusiifolia (Jacq.) Urban	Seven-year-apple, Pl. F-13A
Chrysobalanus icaco L.	Cocoplum, Pl. F-46A
Chrysophyllum oliviforme L.	Satinleaf, Pl. F-46A
Citharexylum fruticosum L.	Florida Fiddlewood, Pl. F-13A
Clusia rosea Jacq.	Florida Clusia, Pl. F-13B
Coccoloba diversifolia Jacq.	Pigeon-plum, Pl. F-46B
Coccoloba uvifera (L.) L.	Seagrape, Pl. F-46A
Colubrina arborescens (Mill.) Sarg.	Coffee Colubrina, Pl. F-46D
Colubrina cubensis (Jacq.) Brongn.	Soldierwood, Pl. F-46C
Colubrina elliptica (Sw.) Briz. & Stern	Nakedwood, Pl. F-46D
Conocarpus erectus L.	Buttonwood, Pl. F-46A

* Two names do not follow Little (1979) but have been accepted for a forthcoming five-volume *Flora of Florida.*

Scientific Name	Common Name and Plate
Crossopetalum rhacoma Crantz	Florida Crossopetalum, Pl. F-13B
Cupania glabra Sw.	Florida Cupania, Pl. F-21B
Dipholis salicifolia (L.) A. DC.	Willow Bustic, PL. F-46C
Dodonaea viscosa Jacq.	Varnishleaf, Pl. F-46B
Drypetes diversifolia Krug & Urban	Guiana-plum, Pl. F-46B
Drypetes laterifloria (Sw.) Krug & Urban	Milkbark, Pl. F-46D
Eugenia axillaris (Sw.) Willd.	White Stopper, Pl. F-13A
Eugenia confusa D.C.	Redberry Stopper, Pl. F-13B
Eugenia foetida Pers.	Boxleaf Stopper, Pl. F-13A
Eugenia rhombea (Berg) Krug & Urban	Red Stopper, Pl. F-13A
Eugenia uniflora L.	Surinam-cherry, Pl. F-13A
Exostema caribaeum (Jacq.) Roem. & Schult.	Princewood, Pl. F-13B
Exothea paniculata (Juss.) Radlk.	Inkwood, Pl. F-21A
Ficus aurea Nutt.	Strangler Fig, Pl. F-46B
Ficus citrifolia Mill.	Shortleaf Fig, (Pl. F-46B)
Flacourtia indica (Burm. f. Merr.)	Governor's-plum (not shown)
Guaiacum sanctum L.	Roughbark Lignumvitae, Pl. F-7
Guapira discolor (Spreng.) Little	Longleaf Blolly, Pl. F-13A
Guettarda elliptica Sw.	Elliptic-leaf Velvetseed, Pl. F-13B
Guettarda scabra (L.) Vent.	Roughleaf Velvetseed, Pl. F-13B
Gyminda latifolia (Sw.) Urban	False-boxwood, Pl. F-13B
Gymnanthes lucida Sw.	Crabwood, Pl. F-46C
Hamelia patens Jacq.	Scarletbush, Pl. F-13A
Hippomane mancinella L.	Manchineel, Pl. F-46C
Hypelate trifoliata Sw.	White Ironwood, Pl. F-21A
Illicium parviflorum Michx. ex Vent.	Yellow Anise-tree, Pl. F-46A
Jacquinia keyensis Mez	Joewood, Pl. F-13A
Krugiodendron ferreum (Vahl) Urban	Leadwood, Pl. F-13A

Scientific Name	Common Name and Plate
Leucaena leucocephala (Lam.) de Wit	Leadtree, Pl. F-22
Licaria triandra (Sw.) Kosterm.	Florida Licaria, Pl. F-46C
Lysiloma latisiliquum (L.) Benth.	Bahama Lysiloma, Pl. F-22
Mangifera indica L.	Mango, Pl. F-46B
Manilkara bahamensis (Baker) Lam & Meeuse	Wild-dilly, Pl. F-46C
Manilkara zapota (L.) v. Royen	Sapodilla, Pl. F-46B
Masticodendron foetidissimum (Jacq.) H. J. Lam	Mastic, Pl. F-46B
Maytenus phyllanthoides Benth.	Florida Mayten, Pl. F-46A
Melaleuca quinquenervia (Cav.) S. T. Blake	Cajeput-tree, Pl. F-46A
Myrcianthes fragrans (Sw.) Mc-Vaugh	Twinberry Stopper, Pl. F-13A
*Myrsine floridana A. DC.	Myrsine, Pl. F-46A
Nectandra coriacea (Sw.) Griseb.	Lancewood, Pl. F-46B
Picramnia pentandra Sw.	Bitterbush, Pl. F-21A
Piscidia piscipula (L.) Sarg.	Jamaica-dogwood, Pl. F-21A
Pisonia rotundata Griseb.	Pisonia, Pl. F-13B
Pithecellobium guadalupense (Pers.) Chapm.	Guadeloupe Blackbead, Pl. F-15
Pithecellobium unguis-cati (L.) Benth.	Catclaw Blackbead, Pl. F-15
Prunus myrtifolia (L.) Urban	West Indies Cherry, Pl. F-46C
Psidium guajava L.	Guava, Pl. F-13A
Psidium longipes (Berg) Mc-Vaugh	Longstalk Stopper, Pl. F-13B
Reynosia septendrionalis Urban	Darling-plum, Pl. F-13B
Rhodomyrtus tomentosa (Ait.) Hassk.	Downy-myrtle, Pl. F-13A
Savia bahamensis Britton	Maidenbush, Pl. F-46D
Schaefferia frutescens Jacq.	Florida-boxwood, Pl. F-46D
Schinus terebinthifolia Raddi.	Brazilian Peppertree, Pl. F-21A

* Two names do not follow Little (1979) but have been accepted for a forthcoming five-volume *Flora of Florida*.

Scientific Name	Common Name and Plate
Schoepfia chrysophylloides (A. Rich.) Planch.	Graytwig, Pl. F-46A
Simarouba glauca DC.	Paradise-tree, Pl. F-21B
Solanum erianthum D. Don	Potato-tree, Pl. F-46D
Suriana maritima L.	Bay-cedar, Pl. F-46A
Swietenia mahagoni Jacq.	West Indies Mahogany, Pl. F-21B
Tamarindus indica L.	Tamarind, Pl. F-21B
Tecoma stans (L.) H.B.K.	Yellow-elder, Pl. F-7
Terminalia catappa L.	India-almond, Pl. F-46D
Tetrazygia bicolor (Mill.) Cogn.	Florida Tetrazygia, Pl. F-13B
Zanthoxylum coriaceum A. Rich.	Biscayne Prickly-ash, Pl. F-15
Zanthoxylum fagara (L.) Sarg.	Wild-lime Prickly-ash, Pl. F-15
Zanthoxylum flavum Vahl.	Satinwood, Pl. F-21B

Appendixes
Glossary
References and Supplemental Reading
Index

APPENDIX A

Winter Key to Non-evergreen Trees

See drawings (Fig. 4, p. 17) and learn the characteristics of our few poisonous plants before handling unknown specimens.

1. Coniferous trees whose needles fall in winter. Fruits dry cones. Swamps and wet soils:
    2. Stubby spur branches numerous on branchlets. Northern. **Larches, Pl. 1.**
    2. Small "leaf scars" (actually twig scars) but no spurs present. Southern. **Baldcypresses, Pl. 4.**
1. Broad-leaved trees; fruits of some (alders, magnolias) called "cones," but not coniferlike. Sites various:
    3. Leaf scars opposite (Sections II and III of text).
        4. Twigs with thorns:
            5. Twigs silver-scaly. Inner bark not yellow. **Silver Buffaloberry, Pl. 14.**
            5. Twigs not silvery. Inner bark yellow. **Common Buckthorn, Pl. 12.**
        4. Twigs thornless:
            6. Twigs four-angled or four-lined; bundle scar 1:
                7. Broken twigs spicy-scented, gray-hairy. **Chastetree, Pl. 6.**
                7. Broken twigs not spicy; twigs green or red. **Burningbush, Pl. 12.**
            6. Twigs otherwise; bundle scars 1 or more:
                8. Twigs stout, inflexible; end buds mostly more than ½″ long, sometimes gummy. **Buckeyes, Pl. 6.**
                8. Twigs slender to moderately stout; end buds less than ⅜″ long, not gummy:
                    9. Central end bud missing; a single pair of buds present at the twig tip; bundle scars 4 or more:
                        10. Leaf scars four-sided to crescent shaped. **Bladdernut, etc., Pl. 7.**

    10. Leaf scars circular or nearly so.
                        Princess-tree, etc., Pl. 10.

  9. One or 3 buds present at twig tip; bundle scars variable:
      11. Buds with a single caplike scale.
                      Basket Willow, Pl. 39.

      11. Buds with 2 or more scales:
          12. Twigs only moderately slender, rather stiff:
             13. Twigs green or purplish; leaf scars meeting in raised points; bundle scars 3.
                    Ashleaf Maple, Pl. 9.

             13. Twigs mostly grayish; leaf scars not meeting in raised points; bundle scars 4 or more.   **Ashes, Pls. 8, 9.**

          12. Twigs slender, flexible:
             14. Bundle scar single:
                15. Buds short, somewhat ball shaped.
                    Forestieras, Pls. 12, 13.

                15. Buds longer than broad.
                    Fringetree, etc., Pl. 14.

             14. Bundle scars 3:
                16. Buds with only a pair of scales:
                  17. Leaf scars much raised:
                    Dogwoods, Pl. 14.

                  17. Leaf scars not much raised:
                    18. Fruits dry, winged; twigs hairy, or trunk white-striped.
                      Maples, Pl. 11.

                    18. Fruits fleshy; twigs and trunk otherwise.
                      Viburnums, Pls. 12, 13.

                16. Bud scales 4 or more.
                  Maples, Pl. 11.

  3. Leaf scars alternate (Sections IV and V of text):
      19. Twigs silvery; branchlets brown; sometimes thorny.
                      Russian-olive, p. 177.

      19. Twigs not silvery, branchlets variable:
          20. Trees thorny or bristly:
             21. Thorns paired:
                22. Twigs hairy, usually green. In South.
                    Jujube, Pl. 23.

       22. Twigs otherwise. Some in North.
                                      Locusts, etc., Pl. 15.

21. Thorns not paired:
       23. Sap milky. **Bumelias, Osage-orange, Pl. 24.**
       23. Sap not milky:
           24. Thorns on short, bud-bearing branches.
                           Crabapples, Plums, Pl. 23.
           24. Thorns without buds:
               25. Trunk and twigs with many prickles;
                   twigs stout. Leaf scars large: bundle
                   scars 20 or more.
                            Hercules-club, Pl. 15.
               25. Tree otherwise:
                   26. Buds ball-shaped; fruits like small
                       apples.   **Hawthorns, Pl. 23.**
                   26. Buds various; fruits are pea pods
                     or small oranges.
                         Mesquite, etc. Fig. 14.

20. Trees thornless:
   27. Buds encircled, or nearly so, by 0-, U-, or V-shaped leaf
      scars:
       28. Leaf scars with numerous bundle scars:
           29. Buds not woolly, with only 1 caplike bud
               scale.   **Eastern Sycamore, Pl. 25.**
           29. Buds often woolly, with several scales. Bundle
               scars sometimes in 3 groups.
                               Sumacs, Pl. 20.
       28. Leaf scars with 3–5 bundle scars.
                         Hoptree, Yellowwood,
                         Texas Sophora, Pl. 21.

   27. Buds located above leaf scars:
           30. Leaf scars large, triangular or shield-
               shaped; twigs stout, relatively inflexible;
               bundle scars 4 or more, sometimes in 3
               groups:
               31. Buds with a single caplike bud
                   scale; twigs encircled by narrow
                   lines (stipule scars).
                           Magnolias, Pl. 45.
               31. Buds with more than 1 bud scale;
                 twigs not ringed:
                  32. Fruits small, white, dry clus-
                     ters; twigs hairless. Wet or
                     damp sites.
                         Poison-sumac, Pl. 20.
                  32. Fruits otherwise; twigs vari-
                     ous. Upland sites:
                    33. Buds woolly:

34. Pith chambered; end buds true.   **Walnuts, Pl. 16.**
34. Pith continuous; end buds false:
   35. Buds often several at each leaf scar, above one another:
      36. Buds embedded in bark; twigs whitish; pith pink.   **Coffeetree, Pl. 22.**
      36. Buds raised; twigs not whitish; pith whitish.   **Soapberries, Pl. 21.**
   35. Buds single, 1 per leaf scar:
      37. Leaf scars three-lobed, bundle scars in 3 groups.   **Chinaberry, Pl. 22.**
      37. Leaf scars deeply triangular; bundle scars scattered.   **Tree-of-heaven, Pl. 16.**
33. Buds sometimes silky or hairy, not woolly; end buds often larger; pith continuous.   **Hickories, Pls. 17–19.**
30. Leaf scars narrow; twigs mostly slender; bundle scars various:
   38. Twigs nearly or completely encircled by narrow lines (stipule scars) beneath buds:
      39. Buds with only 1 caplike bud scale.
         Magnolias, Pl. 45.
      39. Buds with more than 1 bud scale:
         40. Buds blunt, two-scaled, spicy when crushed; pith chambered.   **Tuliptree, Pl. 25.**
         40. Buds long-pointed, many-scaled, not aromatic; pith continuous.   **Beech, Pl. 32.**
   38. Twigs without encircling stipule scars:
      41. Buds clustered at twig tips:
         42. Bundle scars numerous.
            Oaks, Pls. 28–31.
         42. Bundle scars 3:
            43. End buds much larger than side buds. Southern states.
               Corkwood, Pl. 44.
            43. End buds about same size as side buds. Northern states and Canada.   **Fire Cherry, Pl. 36.**
      41. Buds not clustered at twig tips:
         44. Pith chambered or at least partitioned at leaf scars:
            45. Trunk bark divided into small squares; dark:
               46. Bundle scar 1; buds dark, two-scaled.
                  Persimmon, Pl. 44.
               46. Bundle scars 3; buds brown, four-scaled.
                  Sourgum, Pl. 44.

45. Trunk bark not checkered:
 47. Bundle scar 1; end buds true. Southern trees:
  48. Buds dark. **Sweetleaf, Pl. 43.**
  48. Buds reddish. **Silverbell, Pl. 42.**
 47. Bundle scars 3–5; end buds false:
   49. Growing on periodically flooded sites
   in South. Trunk bases often swollen;
   bundle scars 3. **Tupelos, Pl. 43.**
   49. Growing on upland sites; widespread:
    50. Bundle scars 3; twigs hairless.
    Hackberries, Pl. 26.
    50. Bundle scars 5; twigs rough-hairy.
    Paper-mulberry, Pl. 25.

44. Pith continuous:
 51. Buds without scales:
  52. End buds much larger than side buds; bundle
  scars 5–7. **Pawpaws, Pl. 44.**
  52. End buds about the same size as side buds;
  bundle scars 1–3:
   53. Buds narrowed at the base (stalked);
   bundle scars 3. **Witch-hazel, Pl. 32.**
   53. Buds not stalked; bundle scar 1.
   Snowbells, Buckthorns, Pl. 43.
 51. Buds with scales:
  54. Bud scale single. **Willows, Pls. 38, 39.**
  54. Bud scales more than 1:
   55. Twigs green:
    56. Twigs ridged or lined
    lengthwise:
     57. Twigs with many fine
     ridges.
     Groundsel-tree, Pl. 32.
     57. Twigs four-lined or four-
     angled.
     Crape-myrtle, Pl. 44.
    56. Twigs without lengthwise
    ridges or lines:
     58. Broken twigs spicy
     scented, twigs forked;
     bundle scars 1.
     Sassafras, Pl. 25.
     58. Broken twigs not spicy
     scented:
      59. Bundle scar single or
      indistinct; buds
      brown-hairy. **Chinese**
      Parasoltree, p. 123.

59. Bundle scars 3; buds not hairy, two-scaled.
   Alternate-leaf Dogwood, Pl. 44.
55. Twigs not green:
   60. Sap milky in broken twigs (if weather not too cold):
      61. Buds tiny (1/16"); fruits dry, white, at twig ends.
         Tallowtree, p. 132.
      61. Buds larger (1/4"); fruits fleshy, along twigs.
         Mulberries, Pl. 25.
   60. Sap not milky:
      62. Inner bark of branches peels in fibrous strips:
         63. Buds red or green, with 2–3 scales.
            Basswoods, Pl. 26.
         63. Buds brown, many scales in 2 rows.
            Elms, Pl. 33.
      62. Inner bark not especially fibrous:
         64. Bundle scar 1:
            65. Spur branches usually present; fruits
               fleshy, berrylike; tiny black stipules
               may flank leaf scars (use lens).
                  Hollies, Pl. 40.
            65. Spur branches lacking; fruits and
               stipules various:
               66. Buds blackish, with 2 scales;
                  fruits fleshy.
                     Persimmon, Pl. 44.
               66. Buds otherwise; fruits dry:
                  67. Buds more than 1/4" long;
                     end buds true.
                        Mountain Pepperbush,
                        Stewartias, Pl. 42.
                  67. Buds less than 1/8" long; twigs
                     hairless; fruits small, dry
                     capsules at twig ends; end
                     buds false:
                     68. Fruits in one-sided
                        clusters; widespread in
                        South.
                           Sourwood, Pl. 42.
                     68. Fruits in rounded clusters;
                        rare—only in Georgia.
                           Elliottia, Pl. 44.
         64. Bundle scars more than 1:
            69. Bundle scars 4 or more:
               70. Leaf scars narrow; bundle scars
                  in a curved line.
                     Mountain-ashes, Pl. 16.
               70. Leaf scars oval or triangular;
                  bundle scars not in a line.
                     Chestnuts, Pl. 32.

69. Bundle scars 3:
  71. Buds blunt, with a narrow base (stalked), reddish; woody, conelike catkins usually present.
        Alders, Pl. 35.
  71. Buds without constricted base:
    72. Twigs with small yellow resin dots (use lens).
        Bayberries, Pl. 43.
    72. Twigs without resin dots (use lens):
      73. Buds with the lowermost scale centered directly above leaf scar; bark often smooth and greenish on young trunks and branches.
        Poplars, Pl. 27.
      73. Buds with lowermost scale not centered directly above leaf scar:
        74. Buds quite long and slender:
          75. Buds brownish, with 2–4 paired scales.   **Smoketree, Pl. 44.**
          75. Buds reddish; but scales not paired, often twisted and with black notched tips; second bud scale usually less than half length of bud.
            Juneberries, Pl. 42.
        74. Buds relatively short and stout, blunt to sharp but not long-pointed:
          76. Older bark usually with narrow cross-stripes; spur branches often present:
            77. Buds with 2–3 scales; broken twigs with or without a peppermint odor.   **Birches, Pl. 34.**
            77. Buds with 4–6 scales; broken twigs usually with almond or sour odor:
              78. End buds true; fruit with a rounded stone.
                Cherries, Pl. 36.
              78. End buds false; fruit with a usually flattened stone.
                Thornless plums, Pl. 37.
          76. Older bark without cross-stripes; buds with 4 or more scales:
            79. Spur branches present.
              Apple, Pear, Pl. 43.
            79. Spur branches absent:
              80. Branchlets usually with corky "wings"; bud scales hairy-fringed (use lens); end buds true.
                Sweetgum, Pl. 25.

80. Branchlets and buds otherwise; end bud false:

    81. Leaf scars raised, with 2 obvious lines leading down, upper edge often hairy-fringed; some buds narrow at base (stalked); a third line sometimes leads from centers of leaf-scar bases.

           Redbud, Pl. 26.

    81. Leaf scars not raised or at least without obvious lines leading from them:

        82. Twigs somewhat zigzag and often angled; beanpod fruits often present.

           Silktree, Lebbek, Pl. 22.

        82. Twigs and fruits otherwise:

           83. Buds four-angled, scales in 4 rows; trunk smooth, gray, "sinewy."   **Ironwood, Pl. 35.**

           83. Buds not angled, rounded, scales finely grooved (use lens) and not in regular rows.

           Hornbeam, Pl. 35.

APPENDIX B

Plant Relationships

Field identification does not require a knowledge of major classification groups or even of family or scientific names. Yet it is often
desirable to know the general relationships of the various plant
species. The following list indicates the family relationships of the
genera of trees within our area. This classification is mainly that
of Arthur Cronquist (1981); Cronquist is senior scientist at the
New York Botanical Garden. All major and many minor botanical
subdivisions are based on flower and fruit structures. Family
names tend to be standardized by the ending *-aceae,* orders by
-ales, subclasses by *-idae,* classes by *-opsida,* and divisions by
-ophyta.

Kingdom Plantae
Subkingdom Embryobionta
Division Pinophyta
Class Pinatae
Subclass Pinidae

Order Taxales
Family Taxaceae: *Taxus, Torreya*
Family Taxodiaceae: *Taxodium*
Family Cupressaceae: *Chamaecyparis, Juniperus, Thuja*

Order Pinales
Family Pinaceae: *Abies, Cedrus, Larix, Picea, Pinus, Tsuga*

Division Magnoliophyta
Class Magnoliopsida
Subclass Magnoliidae
Order Magnoliales
Family Magnoliaceae: *Liriodendron, Magnolia*
Family Annonaceae: *Annona, Asimina*
Family Canellaceae: *Canella*

Order Laurales
Family Lauraceae: *Cinnamomum, Licaria, Nectandra, Persea, Sassafras*

Order Illiciales
Family Illiciaceae: *Illicium*

Subclass Hamamelidae
Order Hamamelidales
Family Platanaceae: *Platanus*
Family Hamamelidaceae: *Hamamelis, Liquidambar*

Order Urticales
Family Ulmaceae: *Celtis, Planera, Trema, Ulmus*
Family Moraceae: *Broussonetia, Ficus, Maclura, Morus*

Order Leitneriales
Family Leitneriaceae: *Leitneria*

Order Juglandales
Family Juglandaceae: *Carya, Juglans*

Order Myricales
Family Myricaceae: *Myrica*

Order Fagales
Family Fagaceae: *Castanea, Fagus, Quercus*
Family Betulaceae: *Alnus, Betula, Carpinus, Ostrya*

Order Casuarinales
Family Casuarinaceae: *Casuarina*

Subclass Caryophyllidae
Order Caryophyllales
Family Nyctaginaceae: *Guapira, Pisonia*
Family Cactaceae: *Cereus, Opuntia*

Order Polygonales
Family Polygonaceae: *Coccoloba*

Subclass Dilleniidae
Order Theales
Family Theaceae: *Franklinia, Gordonia, Stewartia*
Family Clusiaceae: *Clusia*

Order Malvales
Family Tiliaceae: *Tilia*
Family Sterculiaceae: *Firmiana*
Family Malvaceae: *Hibiscus, Thespasia*

Order Violales
Family Flacourtiaceae: *Flacourtia, Muntingia*
Family Tamaricaceae: *Tamarix*
Family Caricaceae: *Carica*

Order Salicales
Family Salicaceae: *Populus, Salix*

Order Capparales
Family Capparaceae: *Capparis*

Order Ericales
Family Cyrillaceae: *Cliftonia, Cyrilla*
Family Clethraceae: *Clethra*
Family Ericaceae: *Elliottia, Kalmia, Lyonia, Oxydendrum, Rhododendron, Vaccinium*

Order Ebenales
Family Sapotaceae: *Bumelia, Chrysophyllum, Dipholis, Manilkara, Mastichodendron*
Family Ebenaceae: *Diospyros*
Family Styracaceae: *Halesia, Styrax*
Family Symplocaceae: *Symplocos*

Order Primulales
Family Theophrastaceae: *Jacquinia*
Family Myrsinaceae: *Ardisia, Myrsine*

Subclass Rosidae
Order Rosales
Family Rosaceae: *Amelanchier, Crataegus, Malus, Prunus, Pyrus, Sorbus*
Family Chrysobalanaceae: *Chrysobalanus*
Family Surianaceae: *Suriana*

Order Fabales
Family Mimosaceae: *Acacia, Albizia, Leucaena, Lysiloma, Prosopis, Pithecellobium*
Family Caesalpiniaceae: *Caesalpinia, Cercis, Gleditsia, Gymnocladus, Parkinsonia, Tamarindus*
Family Fabaceae: *Cladrastis, Erythrina, Piscidea, Robinia, Sophora*

Order Proteales
Family Eleagnaceae: *Eleagnus, Shepherdia*

Order Myrtales
Family Lythraceae: *Lagerstroemia*
Family Myrtaceae: *Calyptranthes, Eugenia, Melaleuca, Myrcianthes, Psidium, Rhodomyrtus*

Family Melastomataceae: *Tetrazygia*
Family Combretaceae: *Conocarpus, Laguncularia, Terminalia*

Order Rhizophorales
Family Rhizophoraceae: *Rhizophora*

Order Cornales
Family Nyssaceae: *Nyssa*
Family Cornaceae: *Cornus*

Order Santalales
Family Olacaceae: *Schoepfia, Ximenia*

Order Celastrales
Family Celastraceae: *Crossopetalum, Euonymus, Gyminda, Maytenus, Schaefferia*
Family Aquifoliaceae: *Ilex, Nemopanthus*

Order Euphorbiales
Family Euphorbiaceae: *Drypetes, Gymnanthes, Hippomane, Ricinus, Sapium, Savia*

Order Rhamnales
Family Rhamnaceae: *Colubrina, Krugiodendron, Reynosia, Rhamnus, Ziziphus*

Order Polygales
Family Malpighiaceae: *Byrsonima*

Order Sapindales
Family Staphyleaceae: *Staphylea*
Family Sapindaceae: *Cupania, Dodonaea, Exothea, Hypelate, Sapindus*
Family Hippocastanaceae: *Aesculus*
Family Aceraceae: *Acer*
Family Burseraceae: *Bursera*
Family Anacardiaceae: *Cotinus, Mangifera, Metopium, Rhus, Schinus, Toxicodendron*
Family Simaroubaceae: *Ailanthus, Alvaradoa, Picramnia, Simarouba*
Family Meliaceae: *Melia, Swietenia*
Family Rutaceae: *Amyris, Citrus, Poncirus, Ptelea, Zanthoxylum*
Family Zygophyllaceae: *Guaiacum*

Order Apiales
Family Araliaceae: *Aralia*

Subclass Asteridae
Order Solanales
Family Solanaceae: *Solanum*

Order Lamiales
Family Boraginaceae: *Bourreria, Cordia*
Family Verbenaceae: *Avicennia, Citharexylum, Vitex*

Order Scrophulariales
Family Oleaceae: *Chionanthus, Forestiera, Fraxinus, Ligustrum, Osmanthus*
Family Bignoniaceae: *Amphitecna, Catalpa, Paulownia, Tecoma*

Order Rubiales
Family Rubiaceae: *Casasia, Cephalanthus, Exostema, Guettarda, Hamelia, Pinckneya*

Order Dipsacales
Family Caprifoliaceae: *Sambucus, Viburnum*

Order Asterales
Family Asteraceae: *Baccharis*

Class Liliopsida
Subclass Arecidae
Order Arecales
Family Arecaceae: *Acoelorraphe, Coccothrinax, Cocos, Pseudophoenix, Roystonia, Sabal, Seronoa, Thrinax*

Subclass Liliidae
Order Liliales
Family Agavaceae: *Yucca*

Glossary

See also diagrams and text (pp. xvi–xviii and 1–15) in "How to Use This Book."

Aerial rootlet (vine). Small, rootlike organs along stems of some climbing vines. See Poison-ivy, p. 17.

Alternate (leaves, buds). Not opposite but arranged singly at intervals along twigs.

Angled (twig, bud). With evident ridges; not smoothly rounded.

Aromatic. Having a distinctive odor, at least when crushed.

Base (leaf). The lower portion, toward the leafstalk.

Berry (fruit). Strictly speaking, a fleshy fruit that contains small seeds (such as a grape). "Berry" or berrylike fruits are mentioned, indicating fleshy fruits that are not true berries.

Blade (leaf). The broad, expanded portion.

Bloom (twig, leaf, fruit, etc.). A whitish powdery coating.

Bract. A somewhat leaflike, petal-like, or woody structure occurring beneath a flower or fruit or their clusters.

Branchlet. Except for the twig, the youngest and smallest division of a branch. See **Twig.**

Bristle. A stiff hair, sometimes pricklelike.

Bundle scars. Tiny dots or lines within the leaf scar, caused by the breaking of bundles of ducts leading into the leafstalk. Sometimes elongate or curved.

Capsule. A dry fruit that splits partly open at maturity.

Catkin. A cluster of tiny flowers or fruits, usually fuzzy and caterpillar-shaped, often drooping. It occurs in willows and relatives. Where there are flowers of only 1 sex, male catkins usually are larger.

Chambered (pith). Pith divided crosswise by numerous plates or membranes. Term is here used broadly to include all types of segmented and transversely divided pith (diaphragmed, partitioned). When the twig is cut lengthwise, such a pith looks ladderlike. See **Partitioned.**

Coarse-toothed (leaf edge). With large teeth; dentate, serrate.

Compound (leaf). Divided into leaflets, each of which usually has the general appearance of a leaf. See pp. xvii and 3.

Continuous (pith). Smoothly pithy, the twig center neither chambered nor hollow.

Deciduous (leaf, stipule, bud scale, etc.). Falls off seasonally, usually in autumn.

Double-toothed (leaf edge). Each tooth bearing smaller teeth.

Egg-shaped (leaf). Broader near the base than at the tip, the base broadly rounded (but leaf tip is sharper than apex of an egg); ovate.

Elliptic (leaf). Widest in the middle and tapering evenly to both ends like the cross section of a football.

End bud (twig). True end bud or sometimes several, clustered, located at the precise end of the twig. False end bud occurs in some species when the end bud is shed and a nearby side bud acts as end bud. A scar marks the site of the shed bud and lies beside the false end bud. See drawing, p. 6.

Fan-compound (leaf). A compound leaf with leaflets radiating from a point; palmate-compound.

Fan-lobed (leaf). Major lobes radiating from a point; palmate-lobed.

Fan-veined (leaf). Main veins radiating from a point; palmate-veined.

Feather-compound (leaf). Midribs of main leaflets branching from a central main midrib at several points in a featherlike pattern; pinnate-compound.

Feather-lobed (leaf). The main lobes more or less at right angles to the midrib, not radiating from a central point; pinnate-lobed.

Feather-veined (leaf). The main veins more or less at right angles to a main midrib; pinnate-veined.

Fine-toothed (leaf edge). With small teeth; denticulate or serrulate.

Form. Used in this volume to include all populations of plants of the same species which vary slightly from the typical, whether such variation is limited geographically (see **Variety**) or not; forma.

Four-lined (twig). With 4 more or less equidistant lines running lengthwise along the twig.

Four-sided (twig; bud). Approximately square in cross section.

Fruit. The seed-bearing portion of a plant with its associated structures. The term does not imply that it is either fleshy or edible.

Genus. A group of species sufficiently closely related to be given the same generic name.

Gland. Strictly speaking, a surface or protuberance that secretes a substance, but generally any small knob or wart that is a normal part of the plant and has no other known function.

Glandular-toothed (leaf). Having teeth that bear glands. See Tree-of-heaven, Pl. 16.

Hairy. Covered with hairs; pubescent, hirsute, etc.

Heart-shaped (leaf). The shape of the valentine heart; cordate.

Hollow (pith). Twig actually without pith but with the space present.

Hybrid. The offspring of a cross between 2 species.

Involucre. A circle or cluster of bracts beneath flowers or fruits.

Lateral (bud). To the side rather than at the end of twig or branchlet.

Leaf scar. The mark left on the twig at the point of attachment of a leafstalk when the leaf falls.

Leaflet. A leaflike subdivision of a compound leaf.

Leafstalk. The stalk supporting a leaf; petiole.

Leathery (leaf). Of a smoothly tough texture; coriaceous.

Legume. A plant of the pea family or the one- to many-seeded podlike fruit of a pea-family plant.

Lenticel. A corky spot on the bark originating as a breathing pore and either circular or somewhat stripelike (see Cherries).

Lobed (leaf, flower petal, sepal). Divided into rounded, incompletely separated sections.

Long-pointed (leaf). The tip gradually tapering to a point; acuminate.

Midrib (leaf, leaflet). The central rib or main vein.

Naked (bud). Without bud scales.

Narrow (leaves). Shaped like the top view of a canoe; slender and pointed at each end. Often slightly wider near the base; lanceolate.

Net-veined (leaf). With a network of veins.

Node. The place, sometimes swollen, on a stem or twig where a leaf is attached or a leaf scar occurs.

Oblong (leaf). Longer than broad, with the longer sides somewhat parallel.

Once-compound (leaf). A compound leaf with a single set of undivided leaflets (see **Twice compound**).

Opposite (leaves, leaf scars, buds). Two at a node; in opposing pairs.

Ovary. The ovule-bearing (egg-bearing) portion of the flower.

Ovule. See **Ovary.**

Palmate. See various **Fan** prefixes.

Parasitic (plant). Growing on another plant and deriving food from it.

Partitioned (pith). The pith divided crosswise by woody plates, usually near the leaf scars.

Pendent: Hanging from a stem.

Persistent (scales, fruits, leaves). Remaining attached.

Petal (flower). One of a circle of modified leaves immediately outside the reproductive organs; usually brightly colored.

Petiole. See **Leafstalk.**

Pinnate. See various **Feather** prefixes.

Pith. The spongy or hollow center of twig or some stems. See **Chambered** and **Continuous.**

Pod. The dryish fruit of some plants, especially legumes, containing one to many seeds and usually flattened, splitting down 1 or both sides; see **Legume.**

Prickle. A small, sharp outgrowth involving only the outer epidermal layer; generally more slender than a thorn. But in this book no stress is placed on the technical distinctions between prickles and thorns. See also **Bristle.**

Prostrate. Flat on the ground.

Reclining (stem). The lower portion somewhat flattened along the ground but the upper parts curving upward.

Resin-dot. Tiny circular or globular yellow spots, usually not obvious except under magnification.

Ridged (twig). Angular, with lengthwise lines.

Ringed (twig). With narrow encircling stipule scars at leaf scars.

Rolled (leaf edge). Curled under; revolute.

Scale (bud, leaf, twig). (1) A thin, membranelike covering of the bud or twig base, or (2) a fine, grainlike surface material.

Seed. That portion of the ripened fruit which contains the embryo and its closely associated essential coats.

Sepal (flower). One of the outermost circle of modified leaves surrounding the reproductive organs; usually green.

Sheath (conifer needle). Thin tissues present at needle bases and binding the needle bundles.

Short-pointed (leaf tip). Abruptly constricted and sharply pointed; not gradually tapering.

Shreddy (bark). Dividing into fragile, thin, narrow sheets.

Shrub. A woody plant usually growing with several equally strong stems and less than about 15 feet maximum height.

Side (buds). In a lateral, not end, position.

Simple (leaf). Composed of only a single blade, though frequently lobed.

Single-toothed (leaf edge). Bearing only a single set of teeth. See also **Double-toothed.**

Sinus (leaf). The space between 2 leaf lobes.

Solid (pith). See **Continuous.**

Species. For practical purposes here: populations whose individuals freely breed with one another and vary only slightly from one another.

Spicy-scented. Aromatic, with a spicy odor.

Spike (flowers, fruits). A cluster with a narrow, fingerlike shape, the individual flowers or fruits without separate stalks or with only very short ones.

Spine. See **Thorn.**

Spur branch. A stubby branchlet with densely crowded leaves and leaf scars. See drawing, p. 6.

Stalked (buds). Having a narrow necklike base.

Sterile (flower). Infertile, unproductive.

Stipule. A growth at the base of the leafstalk, usually small and in pairs, leaving scars on the twig when they drop. See also **Ringed.**

Straggling. Semi-upright.

Thorn (twig, branchlet, branch, stem). A stout, sharp, woody outgrowth of the stem. Technically, prickles and spines are of different origin, but this book does not require a distinction to be made.

Thrice-compound (leaf). Divided into leaflets that in turn are divided into leaflets, which are further subdivided into subleaflets; an uncommon type.

Tip (leaf). The apex.

Tree. A woody plant with a single main stem at least 3 inches in diameter at breast height (4½ feet) and growing more than 13 feet tall.

Trunk. The main stem of a tree.

Tubular (flower). With the basal portion hollow and tubelike.

Tundra. Vegetation type of very cold climates, especially in Far North, overlying permafrost and consisting of lichens, sedges, mosses, grasses, and low woody plants.

Twice-compound (leaf). With the leaflets again divided into leaflets.

Twig. The end subdivision of a branch; the current year's growth.

Variety. That portion of a species which in a certain geographic area differs slightly from the remainder of the species elsewhere.

Wavy-edged (leaf edge). With shallow, rounded undulations.

Wavy-toothed (leaf edge). Wavy-edged but with more toothlike projections; crenate.

Wedge-shaped (leaves, leaf bases, leaf tips). With narrow, tapering bases or, less often, tips (cuneate, acute).

Whorled (leaves, leaf scars). Arranged in circles around the twigs.

Winged (leafstalk, twig). With projecting thin flat membranes or corky outgrowths.

Woody plant. With the stems and limbs containing lignin (wood).

References and
Supplemental Reading

Barnes, Burton V., and Warren H. Wagner. 1981. *Michigan Trees*. Univ. Mich. Press, Ann Arbor, Mich.

Blackburn, Benjamin. 1952. *Trees and Shrubs in Eastern North America*. Oxford Univ. Press, New York.

Blackwell, Will H., Jr. 1976. *Guide to the Woody Plants of the Tri-state Area*. Kendall Hunt, Dubuque, Iowa.

Brown, Clair A. 1945. *Louisiana Trees and Shrubs*. La. For. Comm. Bull. No. 1. Baton Rouge, La.

Clark, G. Thomas. 1981. *Winter Twigs of Arkansas*. Rose, Little Rock, Ark.

Core, Earl L., and Nelle P. Ammons. 1958. *Woody Plants in Winter*. Boxwood Press, Pittsburgh.

Cronquist, Arthur. 1981. *An Integrated System of Classification of Flowering Plants*. Columbia Univ. Press, New York.

Davis, Donald E., and Norman D. Davis. 1975. *Guide and Key to Alabama Trees*. Kendall Hunt, Dubuque, Iowa.

Elias, Thomas S. 1980. *The Complete Trees of North America*. Van Nostrand Reinhold, New York.

Fernald, M. L. 1950. *Gray's Manual of Botany,* 8th ed. Amer. Book, New York.

Gordon, Robert B. 1960. *A Winter Field Key to Willows of Pennsylvania*. Proc. Penn. Acad. Sci. 34:10–14.

Gupton, Oscar W., and Fred C. Swope. 1981. *Trees and Shrubs of Virginia*. Univ. Press of Virginia, Charlottesville, Va.

Harrar, Ellwood S., and J. George Harrar. 1962. *Guide to Southern Trees,* 2nd ed. Dover, New York.

Hicks, Ray R., Jr., and George K. Stephenson. 1978. *Woody Plants of the Western Gulf Region*. Kendall Hunt, Dubuque, Iowa.

Hosie, R. C. 1969. *Native Trees of Canada*. Canadian Forestry Service, Ottawa.

Hough, Romeyn Beck. 1947. *Handbook of the Trees of the Northern States and Canada*. Macmillan, New York.

Kurz, Herman and Robert F. Godfrey. 1962. *Trees of Northern Florida*. Univ. Florida Press, Gainesville.

Lakela, Olga and Richard P. Wunderlin. 1980. *Trees of Central Florida*. Banyan Books, Miami, Florida.

Little, Elbert L., Jr. 1971. *Atlas of United States Trees*. Vol. 1:

Conifers and Important Hardwoods. U.S. Dept. Agric. Misc. Publ. 1146.

———. 1977. *Atlas of United States Trees*. Vol. 4: Minor Eastern Hardwoods. U.S. Dept. Agric. Misc. Publ. 1342.

———. 1978. *Atlas of United States Trees*. Vol. 5: Florida. U.S. Dept. Agric. Misc. Publ. 1361.

———. 1979. *Checklist of United States Trees (Native and Naturalized)*. Agric. Handbook 541, Forest Service, U.S. Dept. Agric., Washington, D.C.

Long, Robert W., and Olga Lakela. 1971. *A Flora of Tropical Florida*. Univ. Miami Press, Coral Gables, Florida.

Miller, Howard A., and H. E. Jaques. 1972. *How to Know the Trees*. Wm. C. Brown, Dubuque, Iowa.

Morton, Julia F. 1971. *Plants Poisonous to People in Florida and Other Warm Areas*. Hurricane House, Miami, Florida.

Muenscher, W. C. 1950. *Keys to Woody Plants*. Comstock, Ithaca, New York.

Oosting, H. J. 1956. *The Study of Plant Communities*. Freeman, San Francisco.

Petrides, George A. 1972. *A Field Guide to Trees and Shrubs*, 2nd ed. Houghton Mifflin, Boston.

Radford, Albert E., Harry E. Ahles, and C. Ritchie Bell. 1968. *Manual of the Vascular Flora of the Carolinas*. Univ. North Carolina Press, Chapel Hill.

Sargent, Charles Sprague. 1965. *Manual of the Trees of North America*. Dover, New York.

Small, John Kunkel. 1933. *Manual of the Southeastern Flora*. Published by author, New York.

Stevenson, George B. 1969. *Trees of Everglades National Park and the Florida Keys*. Everglades Natural History Assoc.

Symonds, George W. D. 1958. *The Tree Identification Book*. William Morrow, New York.

———. 1963. *The Shrub Identification Book*. William Morrow, New York.

Tomlinson, P. B. 1980. *The Biology of Trees Native to Tropical Florida*. Harvard Univ., Allston, Mass.

Trelease, William. 1931. *Winter Botany*. Dover, New York.

Van Dersal, William R. 1938. *Native Woody Plants of the United States: Their Erosion Control and Wildlife Values*. Misc. Publ. 303, U.S. Dept. Agric., Washington, D.C.

Vines, Robert A. 1977. *Trees of East Texas*. Univ. Texas Press, Austin, Texas.

Wagner, W. H., Jr. 1974. Dwarf Hackberry (Ulmaceae: *Celtis tenuifolia*) in the Great Lakes Region. *Mich. Botanist* 13:73–99.

Wharton, Mary E., and Roger W. Barbour. 1975. *Trees and Shrubs of Kentucky*. Univ. Press of Kentucky, Lexington.

Index

Page references in italics refer to illustrations in the text. Entries in boldface type refer to the color and black-and-white plates at the center of the book.

LEAF SHAPES

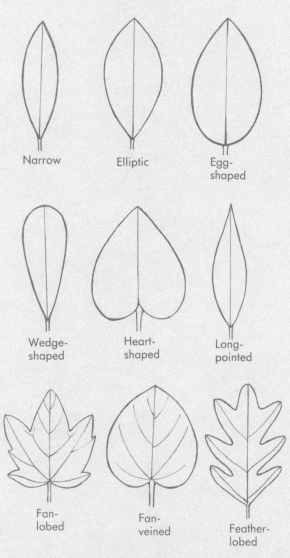

Narrow

Elliptic

Egg-shaped

Wedge-shaped

Heart-shaped

Long-pointed

Fan-lobed

Fan-veined

Feather-lobed

LEAF AND TWIG TERMINOLOGY

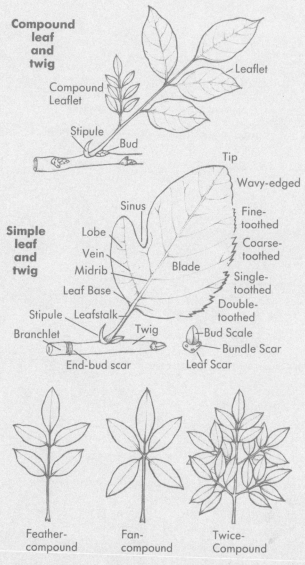

Compound leaf and twig

Compound Leaflet
Leaflet
Stipule
Bud

Simple leaf and twig

Tip
Wavy-edged
Sinus
Fine-toothed
Lobe
Coarse-toothed
Vein
Midrib
Blade
Single-toothed
Leaf Base
Double-toothed
Stipule
Leafstalk
Twig
Bud Scale
Branchlet
Bundle Scar
End-bud scar
Leaf Scar

Feather-compound
Fan-compound
Twice-Compound